The Timber Press
Encyclopedia of Flowering Shrubs

THE TIMBER PRESS
Encyclopedia of Flowering Shrubs

Jim Gardiner

Timber Press
Portland · London

Title page photo *Hibiscus syriacus* 'Aphrodite'
Frontispiece *Chaenomeles speciosa* 'Nivalis'

Published in 2011 by Timber Press, Inc.

The Haseltine Building
133 S.W. Second Avenue, Suite 450
Portland, Oregon 97204-3527
timberpress.com

2 The Quadrant
135 Salusbury Road
London NW6 6RJ
timberpress.co.uk

Printed in China

Library of Congress Cataloging-in-Publication Data

Gardiner, James M. (James Milton), 1946–
The Timber Press encyclopedia of flowering shrubs / Jim Gardiner. — 1st ed.
p. cm.
Includes bibliographical references and index.
ISBN 978-0-88192-823-5
1. Flowering shrubs—Encyclopedias. 2. Flowering shrubs—Pictorial works. I. Title.
SB435.G378 2011
635.9'76—dc23

2011020264

A Catalogue record for this book is also available from the British Library.

Contents

Acknowledgements 7

Introduction 9

Flowering Shrubs A to Z 17

Table of Selected Shrubs by Key Design and Cultural Characteristics 407

Glossary 429

Collectors' References 430

Further Reading 431

Index of Common Names and Synonyms 433

Acknowledgements

I would like to thank Chris Sanders who has let me use quality images of shrubs for this book. Chris has been taking slides of plants for as long as I have, enabling this unique assemblage of slides covering the A to Z of shrubs to be brought together for many to appreciate.

Thanks are also due the Royal Horticultural Society for their support; Diana Miller and Simon Akeroyd for their help with the text; and Anna Mumford and the staff at Timber Press for enabling this encyclopedia to proceed.

I also thank my wife, Allison, for her patience and understanding while I burned the midnight oil.

Opposite: *Iochroma australe*

Introduction

A recurring theme throughout my horticultural career has been the delight of discovering new plants in gardens, nurseries, and occasionally in the wild. Few experiences can touch the excitement of finding any new plant, but flowering shrubs present a particularly diverse and rewarding group for gardeners.

As a teenager, my first encounter with a flowering shrub—and at the time I regarded it as pretty exotic—was receiving a consignment of plants from Hillier Nurseries which included *Paeonia ludlowii*. It was a bare-rooted rather leggy specimen which went on to produce beautiful clear yellow flowers to complement its magnificent foliage. However it wasn't until I became a student at the Savill Garden and the gardens of Windsor Great Park that I realized what plant diversity was all about. Here, the collection of woody plants, in particular, was stunning and it was during the course of discussing these plants and their performance with Sir Eric Savill, Hope Findlay, or John Bond (mentors to me then as an impressionable trainee) that I really became hooked on flowering shrubs.

Working within the famous plant collections of the University of Cambridge Botanic Garden, the Royal Botanic Garden Edinburgh, the City of Liverpool Botanic Garden, the Sir Harold Hillier Gardens and Arboretum, and the four gardens of the Royal Horticultural Society (primarily Wisley) has brought home to me the enormous wealth of plants that may be successfully grown in the British Isles and indeed comparable climates the world over.

It has also been a privilege for me to see many of these plants growing in the wild or in cultivation in the United States, northern Europe, Japan, Korea, New Zealand, and most recently in southeastern China, and a testament to

Opposite: *Berberis* ×*lologensis* 'Boughton Red'

The heather garden at the Royal Horticultural Society's Garden Wisley.

both the diversity of plants and the resourcefulness of gardeners. When I was president of the Magnolia Society International, I met many keen gardeners primarily throughout the eastern and western United States, and visited their gardens including many that are open to the public. This resulted in seeing many magnolias as well as a huge number of shrubs. Also being on the Plant Masterplanning group at the New York Botanical Garden enabled me to see first hand the wealth of woody plants in collections there and how they performed.

It is interesting to look at the forces that have shaped the plants we grow in our gardens over the centuries. In the United Kingdom, climate has been a key factor. It is thought that the dominant force in determining the climate here is the Gulf Stream. Originating in the Gulf of Mexico, it causes the greatest temperature anomaly in the world with up to 20 degrees Celsius (68 degrees Fahrenheit) average temperature difference with similar latitudes around the world. The Gulf Stream, together with undercurrents from the North Atlantic Drift or Conveyor, has "set" our climate since the last Ice Age. However it is also considered it may be due to air movement influenced by the Rocky Mountains and the continental versus maritime climates. The climate now, however, is comparatively warm with most of the British Isles falling into Zones 8 and 9 of the USDA system.

Three hundred years ago plants were being introduced to England in quantity primarily from North America, the Cape of Good Hope, Japan, and China. Taking an active role were the leading botanical institutions of Kew, Edinburgh, and the Horticultural Society (later the Royal Horticultural Society). Later, towards the end of the nineteenth and early twentieth century, often regarded as the Golden Age of plant exploration, American institutions such as the Arnold Arboretum were extremely active in making expeditions to China in particular.

Private investors financed in whole or in part major plant collecting trips at this time, too. For example, nurseryman James Harry Veitch, Liverpool cotton broker Arthur Bulley, and land owner J. C. Williams of Caerhays in Cornwall all independently financed at considerable expense either E. H. "Chinese" Wilson and/or George Forrest on their expeditions to China. In the United States, Longwood

Dwarf *Rhododendron* species, including *R. calostrotum*, *R. pemakoense*, and *R. sanguineum*, growing in their natural habitat on the Showa La in southeastern Tibet.

Gardens in Pennsylvania also funded expeditions to China including those of Frank Kingdon Ward in the 1950s.

Since China reopened its doors to exploration after 1980, the second Golden Age of plant collecting has taken place, not only to China but to most of the four corners by scientific institutions, private collectors, and bursaries such as those funded by the Royal Horticultural Society that enable students to travel in search of plants. One of the first was the Sino American Expedition to western Hubei in 1980 funded by the Botanical Society of America, the National Geographic Society, and the American Association of Botanic Gardens and Arboreta.

But the wealth of plants introduced to gardens is not purely the result of species collected in the wild. Thumbing through the pages of the Royal Horticultural Society's *Plant Finder* or the *List of Names of Woody Plants* published by the European Plant Association, you will see thousands of cultivated plants that have been introduced through hybridizers, nurseries, gardens, and institutions throughout the world. The *List of Names of Woody Plants* published in 2005 contains more than 30,000 woody plant names alone!

Publications covering woody plants are many with a large number providing a great depth of information on a single genus. In addition there are many other works that deal comprehensively with woody plants including W. J. Bean's *Trees and Shrubs Hardy in the British Isles* and Michael Dirr's *Hardy Trees and Shrubs*.

One of the most accessible for use in gardens however is *The Hillier Manual of Trees and Shrubs*, first published in 1971 and the text most recently updated and revised in 2007. It contains the descriptions of more than 10,500 plants covering 650 genera. To many this is still regarded as the bible of woody plants, but to the majority of keen gardeners, the distinction between one cultivar and another is lost without the addition of a photographic reference. This, for me, has long been a challenge—to create a Hillier-like manual with photographs highlighting all the best plants and selecting where possible AGM winners as well as showing the diversity within each genus.

To this end, and for over forty years, I have been taking colour slides of flowering shrubs that I have found through experience to be rewarding garden plants. My aim has been to make the pleasant task of choosing between different species or cultivars that much easier by means of a photograph for each plant along with a description of essential data. By storing slides in suspension files in filing cabinets and initially using Kodachrome 25, Ektachrome 64, then Kodachrome 100 or 64, and most recently Fujichrome Sensia 100, I have ensured that all slide colours have remained as true as the day they were taken. This marathon task has enabled me to illustrate more than 1700 flowering shrubs whether in flower, foliage, fruit, bark, or habit and make them accessible to gardeners.

My hope is that this book will take you on a journey of discovery, no less exciting than those of the early plant hunters, as you uncover a wealth of outstanding flowering shrubs for different parts of your garden.

What Are Shrubs?

Shrubs are woody-stemmed plants that are generally branched from ground level, although many can equally be grown on a single stem. They are either deciduous or evergreen, and there are some that are intermediate depending on the severity of the winter.

There are also shrubs that die back each winter, regenerating from the base in the spring with last year's growth being cut back. A further group of plants are woody at the base and are regarded as subshrubs.

Shrubs vary in size from prostrate ground-covering plants to treelike plants. Their spread depends on whether they have an erect or spreading habit. Some can become as wide as they are high, but the majority can be controlled in size by pruning at the appropriate time of year.

Garden Uses

Shrubs often form the framework for the garden providing height and structure. They are often used to divide the space into separate areas. No other garden plants offer the size that shrubs do while providing the added bonuses of flowers, fruits, attractive bark, stem colour, and an amazing array of foliage colour.

There is a fragrant flowering shrub for every season, and many of these emit a fragrance which can fill the entire garden especially when humidity is high or at the beginning and the end of the day. Foliage too can emit distinctive aromas.

With careful selection shrubs will provide interest during every month of the year, and they associate well with all other plant groups such as alpines, annuals, half hardy plants, vegetables and fruit, bulbs, perennials, grasses and bamboos, ferns, palms and cycads, climbers and trees. They can be pruned to form topiary or hedges and screens and can be grown in containers.

Practical Points

Soil

It is important to assess your soil to determine whether it is acid or alkaline. The majority of shrubs are tolerant of both acid and alkaline, and it will be the texture of the soil that will be more likely to need attention. In most instances

Cornus sanguinea Winter Flame 'Anny' (left) and *C. sanguinea* 'Magic Flame' (right) grown in nursery rows in the Netherlands.

▶ *Cornus sanguinea* 'Midwinter Fire' (left), Winter Flame 'Anny' (centre), and 'Magic Flame' (right) grown in nursery rows in the Netherlands.

▼ *Salix alba* cultivars and *S.* 'Erythroflexuosa' produce elegant yellow stems in winter which contrast nicely with the red stems of *Cornus sanguinea* and *C. sericea* cultivars. These coloured stems are especially effective when reflected by water, as here at the Royal Horticultural Society's Garden Wisley.

soils will be clay-, sand-, or silt-based with a small minority being fertile well-drained loam. Therefore in most cases soil amelioration using grit or organic matter will be necessary.

Planting Advice

The vast majority of shrubs will be bought as container-grown plants. Deep planting causes more deaths than any other factor. The depth of the hole needs to be only as deep as the pot; however, when planting in grass or into soil that has not been cultivated for sometime, always prepare a generously wide planting pit.

Do not add organic matter under the root ball but light organic matter such as leaf mold can be added during backfill. Add 6 mm sharp grit when planting in clay soils. When planting add mycorrhizal fungi which helps establishment. It may be necessary to remove excess compost from the top to expose the "root flare" (the place where the stem meets the root system), and to tease out the root system. It may be beneficial to mound plants on clay soils.

Mulch with a layer of well-rotted garden compost or grit with clay soils but keep this away from the stem. Water after planting and irrigate thoroughly when necessary during the first two growing seasons. To continue getting the best out of your shrub, mulch with garden compost or grit on a regular basis from year to year.

Pruning

The majority of shrubs will not need pruning apart from formative pruning that eliminates dead and diseased wood and maintains the overall shape of the plant. Shrubs should be pruned to maintain their scale and prevent them from getting too large for the garden. However if you are growing a shrub primarily for its flowering effect, then prune it immediately after flowering if its flower buds were produced on last season's wood or in early spring if the flowers are carried on the current year's growth. This will increase flower production for the next season.

Hardiness

Some shrubs are hardier than others. This is based on how well the wild species tolerate winter weather in their native habitats or, in the case of hybrids, how well the parents do. Most plants in this book are reliably hardy to USDA hardiness zones 7 and 8.

Each plant description in this volume includes a hardiness zone rating; the lower the number, the hardier the plant. This is a valuable, though not foolproof piece of information. The hardiness of a plant depends on a wide range of factors including the physiological condition of the plant, site aspect, soil type, summer heat, rainfall, and whether winter temperatures fluctuated. In addition, microclimate and protection within a garden also need to be taken into consideration.

How to Use the Encyclopedia

The plants in this encyclopedia are listed alphabetically by genus name. Each entry describes the special attributes of the plant and advice on how to grow it. A photograph accompanies each description. A glance at the photographs reveals the astonishing variety of flowering shrubs and the extraordinary diversity of habit, flower, foliage, fruit, and stem seen across over more than 300 genera.

Plant Names

The Royal Horticultural Society's *Plant Finder* has been used to ensure the correct, up-to-date plant name has been used on every occasion. Each plant has a Latin-based botanical name that is unique to it and by which it can be known unambiguously worldwide. These names are governed by either the *International Code of Botanical Nomenclature* or the *International Code for the Nomenclature of Cultivated Plants*. Some cultivars have been given an additional selling, or trade, name for commercial purposes, in which case that information is included in the description for reference. In all instances, the names are as described in the RHS *Plant Finder 2010–2011*.

Also included are a number of wild-collected plants containing the collectors' reference number. These represent distinct forms of a species with unique characteristics. For example, *Rhododendron augustinii* subsp. *hardyi* Rock 195 refers to a particular collection (no. 195) of *R. augustinii* subsp. *hardyi* made by Joseph Rock at a particular place and time. Unless you have access to the named form, your plant, which may have the same Latin name, may be from a different collection and thus not match the given description.

Description

A general description of the plant provides information about its habit, principal attributes, and reasons for growing it.

Size

The size a shrub reaches at maturity will depend on its physiological condition, site aspect (including location within the garden), soil type, local weather conditions, and how often it is pruned. The five sizes used may be broadly defined as follows:

PROSTRATE: ground covering
COMPACT: up to 1 m (3 ft.)
SMALL: up to 1.5 m (5 ft.)

MEDIUM: up to 3 m (10 ft.)
LARGE: over 3 m (10 ft.)

Position

Position refers to the site aspect best suited for a shrub. Three positions are given in the descriptions:

SUN
PARTIAL SHADE
SHADE

These provide broad guidelines, and gardeners will be aware of the numerous subcategories within the groups. For example, a sunny sheltered site offers very different conditions to a sunny windy site. Furthermore, many of the plants will tolerate and even thrive in more than one of these positions.

Flowering Period

Seasons have been used to indicate the primary period of flowering of each shrub. These are based on many years of careful observation, but are of course variable depending on local conditions. Monthly equivalents for gardeners living in the Northern Hemisphere are given below.

MID WINTER = January
LATE WINTER = February
EARLY SPRING = March
MID SPRING = April
LATE SPRING = May
EARLY SUMMER = June
MID SUMMER = July
LATE SUMMER = August
EARLY AUTUMN = September
MID AUTUMN = October
LATE AUTUMN = November
EARLY WINTER = December

Soil Type

Shrubs are generally adaptable to most garden soils; however, it is important to know whether you have a strongly acid or alkaline soil. Nearly all garden centres sell pH testing kits which are easy to use and will provide sufficient information for gardeners. The plant descriptions indicate where a shrub requires a specifically acid or alkaline soil. If you do want to grow a plant that needs acid conditions and you have alkaline soil, think about growing it in a container filled with a proprietary compost bought from your local garden centre.

Most shrubs prefer a moisture-retentive soil but never waterlogged soils. The plant descriptions note the exceptions where a shrub needs a particularly well-drained soil.

The majority of soils are sufficiently fertile for shrub growth; however, free-draining sandy soils will quickly become depleted of nutrients so will need to be top-dressed with organic matter or fertilizer added sparingly a year or so after planting, during early to late winter, depending on location. Clay soils are generally nutrient-rich. In all instances, be sure to follow the suggestions given above in "Planting Advice."

Cultivation Notes

Shrubs are generally easy to grow, so unless there is a specific growing requirement, none will be given in most plant descriptions in this volume. Following are examples of specific instructions that will be included in the descriptions:

- where variegation can revert, then guidelines on cutting out reverted shoots are made
- where a plant has an alternative use, for example, as a hedging plant
- where the shrub performs better in a particular location, for example, when planted against a wall
- where the shrub can be grown in a specific situation, for example, exposed coastal locations or as a conservatory plant
- where the shrub has specific pruning needs

Award of Garden Merit

The Award of Garden Merit (AGM), a plant award of the Royal Horticultural Society, is intended to be of practical value to anyone who wants to buy a plant and needs guidance on which one to grow. Plants are awarded the AGM after a period of assessment by the Society's Plant committees which are made up of volunteers who have expert knowledge of particular plants and their performance. An AGM plant must satisfy the following criteria:

- must be available in the trade at some level
- must be excellent for ordinary use in appropriate conditions
- must be of good constitution
- must be reasonably resistant to pests and diseases
- must be essentially stable in form and colour

Hardiness Zone

The system of hardiness zones was developed in the 1960s by the United States Department of Agriculture and divides the continent into 12 hardiness zones. This very well-researched and comprehensive system has since been adapted for use in most countries of the world. As the information about and movement of plants becomes commonplace, a uniform system is increasingly valuable though difficult to precisely align. The USDA system is based on the lowest average winter temperature that plants will tolerate. Once you know the lowest average winter temperature in your area, you can work out which hardiness zone your garden falls into and plant accordingly. For example, *Abelia chinensis* has a hardiness rating of Zone 7 so can be grown in Zones 7 and above.

ZONE	TEMPERATURE (°F)	TEMPERATURE (°C)
1	Below –50	Below –45.6
2	–40 to –50	–40 to –46
3	–30 to –40	–34 to –40
4	–20 to –30	–29 to –34
5	–10 to –20	–23 to –29
6	0 to –10	–18 to –23
7	10 to 0	–12 to –18
8	20 to 10	–7 to –12
9	30 to 20	–1 to –7
10	40 to 30	4 to –1
11	50 to 40	10 to 4
12	60 to 50	16 to 10

To see the U.S. Department of Agriculture Hardiness Zone Map, go to the U.S. National Arboretum site at http://www.usna.usda.gov/Hardzone/ushzmap.html.

Flowering Shrubs A to Z

Abelia chinensis ▲▼

A semievergreen or deciduous shrub with long-lasting masses of small, pale pink flowers and persistent calyces long after the flowers have dropped.

Medium; full sun; flowers mid summer to mid autumn; fertile, well-drained soil

Grow in a sheltered location. Prune out dead wood in early spring. Zone 7

Abelia 'Edward Goucher' ▼

A graceful semievergreen shrub with bronze young growth and long-lasting masses of rich pink flowers.

Small; full sun; flowers mid summer to mid autumn; fertile, well-drained soil

Grow in a sheltered location. Prune out dead wood in early spring. Zone 7

Abelia floribunda ▲

An evergreen shrub that bears beautiful tubular bright pink flowers. **AGM**

Small to medium; full sun; flowers late spring to early summer; fertile, well-drained soil

Best when trained on a south- or west-facing wall but can be grown as a free-standing shrub in mild locations. Formative pruning after flowering. Zone 9

Opposite: *Lavatera* ×*clementii* 'Blushing Bride'

Abelia ×grandiflora ◄

A semievergreen shrub producing glossy, dark green leaves and arching flowering shoots with long-lasting pale pink flowers followed by persistent dull pink calyces. **AGM**

Medium; full sun; flowers early summer to mid autumn; fertile, well-drained soil

Grow in a sheltered position. Prune out dead wood in early spring. Zone 7

Abelia ×grandiflora 'Francis Mason' ▼

A semievergreen shrub with bright yellow, variegated leaves and pale lilac-pink flowers over a long period.

Small to medium; full sun; flowers mid summer to mid autumn; fertile, well-drained soil

Grow in a sheltered position. To maintain variegation, remove all-green shoots during the growing season as they appear. Prune dead wood in early spring. Zone 7

Abelia ×grandiflora 'Hopleys' ▼

A semievergreen shrub with pale yellow leaves variegated along the margins and dark green at the centres. The pale pink flowers are long-lasting.

Small; full sun; flowers mid summer to mid autumn; fertile, well-drained soil

Grow in a sheltered position. To maintain variegation, remove all-green shoots during the growing season as they appear. Prune dead wood in early spring. Zone 7

Abelia ×grandiflora 'Kaleidoscope' ►

A semievergreen shrub with pale yellow variegated leaves which are a pale pink on unfurling and with long-lasting pale pink flowers.

Small; full sun; flowers mid summer to mid autumn; fertile, well-drained soil

Grow in a sheltered position. To maintain variegation, remove all-green shoots during the growing season as they appear. Prune dead wood in early spring. Zone 8

Abelia ×grandiflora 'Sunrise' ▲

A semievergreen shrub with long-lasting rich pink flowers followed by pink calyces with a very thin band of golden variegation.

Medium; full sun; flowers mid summer to mid autumn; fertile, well-drained soil

Grow in a sheltered position. Prune dead wood in spring. Zone 7

Abelia mosanensis ▶

A deciduous shrub with masses of fragrant pale pink flowers.

Medium to large; full sun or partial shade; flowers late spring to early summer; fertile, well-drained soil

Prune selected shoots after flowering to shape the bush. Zone 6

Abelia parvifolia ◀

A deciduous shrub that produces long-lasting, showy pink flowers with a pale orange blotch in the centre. **AGM**

Small; full sun; flowers late spring to late autumn; fertile, well-drained soil

Grow in a sheltered position. Prune dead wood in early spring. Zone 7

Abelia spathulata ▲
A graceful, deciduous shrub bearing pale pink flowers with pale orange centres.

Small; full sun and partial shade; flowers late spring to mid summer; fertile, well-drained soil

Grow in a sheltered position. Prune out dead wood in early spring. Zone 8

Abelia triflora ▲
A deciduous shrub with rich pink floral buds opening to pale pink, scented flowers.

Large; full sun or partial shade; flowers early summer; fertile, well-drained soil

Prune selected shoots after flowering to restrict size. Zone 7

Abeliophyllum distichum ▲▶
A twiggy deciduous shrub bearing small white flowers set against dark calyces. The leaves can turn purple in mid to late autumn.

Small to medium; full sun; flowers mid winter to early spring; fertile soil

To achieve good flowering, grow on a south- or west-facing wall. Cut out dead wood after flowering. Zone 4

Abeliophyllum distichum Roseum Group ◄

A twiggy deciduous shrub with small, pale pink flowers set against dark calyces. The leaves can turn purple in mid to late autumn.

Small to medium; full sun; flowers mid winter to early spring; fertile soil

To achieve good flowering, train on a south- or west-facing wall. Cut out dead wood after flowering. Zone 4

Abutilon 'Golden Fleece' ►

A tender evergreen shrub with pendant yellow flowers and bold green leaves.

Medium; sun or partial shade; flowers mid summer to mid autumn; fertile, well-drained soil

Grow in a conservatory in cool climates. Needs winter protection when grown as a containerized plant for the patio. Prune in mid spring. Raise new plants from cuttings in early autumn. Zone 10

Abutilon megapotamicum ◄

A tender (semi)evergreen shrub of which there are two forms, one pendant and sprawling and the other more upright and vigorous. Both forms produce bell-shaped flowers with contrasting yellow petals and a rich red calyx. **AGM**

Prostrate or small when trained against a wall, otherwise medium; sun or partial shade; flowers late spring to early autumn; fertile, well-drained soil

The vigorous form is hardier (to zone 8), but both forms are best suited to a sheltered south- or west-facing wall. Prune during early to mid spring or raise new plants in early autumn. Zone 9

Abutilon 'Nabob' ◄

A tender evergreen shrub with pendant, deep red, lantern-shaped flowers and bold green leaves. **AGM**

Medium; sun or partial shade; flowers mid summer to mid autumn; fertile, well-drained soil

Grow in a conservatory in cool climates. Needs winter protection when grown as a containerized plant for the patio. Prune in mid spring. Raise new plants from cuttings in early autumn. Zone 10

Abutilon ×suntense 'Jermyns' ◀ ▶

A deciduous, fast-growing, short-lived, free-flowering shrub with dark mauve flowers and green leaves. **AGM**

Medium to large; full sun; flowers late spring to early summer; fertile, well-drained soil

Grow in a sheltered site. Prune young wood immediately after flowering during the first or second growing season; thereafter leave alone, only removing dead wood in early spring. Zone 8

Abutilon vitifolium 'Tennant's White' ▼ ▶

A deciduous, fast growing, short-lived, free-flowering shrub with white flowers and grey-felted leaves. **AGM**

Medium to large; full sun; flowers late spring to mid summer; fertile, well-drained soil

Grow in a sheltered position. Prune young wood immediately after flowering during the first or second growing season; thereafter leave alone, except to remove dead wood in early spring. Zone 8

Abutilon vitifolium 'Veronica Tennant' ◀

A deciduous, fast growing, short-lived, free-flowering shrub with mauve flowers. **AGM**

Medium to large; full sun; flowers late spring to mid summer; fertile, well-drained soil

Grow in a sheltered position. Prune young wood immediately after flowering during the first or second growing season; thereafter leave alone, except to remove dead wood in early spring. Zone 8

Acca selloana ◄

The pineapple guava is an evergreen shrub with distinctive, edible flowers that display a prominent boss of red stamens and fleshy white and red petals. The leaves are grey-green.

Medium to large; full sun; flowers mid summer to early autumn; fertile, well-drained soil

Can be used as a hedging plant in mild localities where pruning during early spring is necessary to restrict size and thickness. Zone 7

Acradenia frankliniae ►

An evergreen shrub with glossy, dark green aromatic leaves and masses of small starry white flowers.

Medium to large; partial shade but can grow in both sun and shade; flowers mid and late spring; fertile soil

This Tasmanian plant is proving hardier than originally thought and requires no pruning unless restricting its size, done immediately after flowering. Zone 7

Adenocarpus decorticans ▲

An evergreen shrub with hairy silvery leaves and bright golden yellow flowers.

Medium; full sun; flowers mid to late spring; fertile, well-drained soil

Often seen against a wall. No pruning needed unless restricting its size, done immediately after flowering. Zone 8

Agapetes incurvata ▲

A tender evergreen shrub with long arching branches and pendant, tubular pink flowers with distinctive markings.

Compact; partial shade; flowers early to late spring; fertile, well-drained, acid soil

Can be grown as an epiphyte, or scrambling over rocks, or as a conservatory plant in a hanging basket. No pruning necessary. Zone 10

Agapetes serpens ▲

A tender evergreen shrub with long, arching branches and pendant rich orange-red tubular flowers along the stems. AGM

Prostrate to compact; partial shade; flowers early to late spring; fertile, well-drained, acid soil

Can be grown as an epiphyte, or scrambling over rocks, or as a conservatory plant in a hanging basket. No pruning necessary. Zone 10

Alangium chinense ▲

A deciduous shrub or small tree producing delicate, white, faintly scented flowers with recurved petals and bold maple-like foliage.

Medium to large; full sun and partial shade; flowers early to mid summer; fertile soil

Grow as a multistemmed shrub or a single-stemmed small tree. No pruning necessary. Zone 7

Aloysia citrodora ▶

A short-lived deciduous shrub with small panicles of white flowers. It is grown for its aromatic foliage which at the end of the season can be dried and used for a herbal tea. Synonym: *Aloysia triphylla*. AGM

Small to medium; full sun; flowers mid summer to mid autumn; fertile, well-drained soil

Can be grown outside in mild localities, in which case it needs to be pruned back to a framework in early to mid spring. Can also be grown in a conservatory. Zone 10

Amelanchier alnifolia ◀

The alder-leaved serviceberry is a deciduous multistemmed upright to fastigiate shrub with white flowers and yellowish brown autumn foliage.

Medium to large; full sun; flowers mid to late spring; fertile soil

Requires little pruning. Zone 4

Amelanchier laevis 'R. J. Hilton' ▶

This Allegheny serviceberry is a deciduous shrub or tree grown for its masses of white flowers which on opening are pink, especially on the outside of the petals. Autumn foliage is orange-red.

Large; full sun; flowers mid to late spring; fertile soil

Can be grown as a multistemmed shrub or single-stemmed small tree. Zone 4

Amelanchier laevis 'Snowflakes' ▲▶

This Allegheny serviceberry is a deciduous shrub or tree grown for its masses of pure white flowers and its orange-red autumn foliage.

Large; full sun; flowers mid to late spring; fertile soil

Can be grown as a multistemmed shrub or single-stemmed small tree. Zone 4

Amelanchier lamarckii ◀▲

A deciduous shrub or tree grown for its masses of white flowers and its orange-red autumn foliage. **AGM**

Large; full sun; flowers mid to late spring; fertile soil

Can be grown as a multistemmed shrub or small tree and is the most widely cultivated of the snowy mespilus (*Amelanchier* species). Zone 4

Amelanchier 'La Paloma' ◀◀

A deciduous shrub grown for its masses of clear starry white flowers and its orange-red autumn colour.

Medium; full sun; flowers mid to late spring; fertile soil

Grown as a multistemmed shrub. Possibly the most beautiful *Amelanchier* cultivar. Zone 4

***Amelanchier ovalis* 'Edelweiss'** ▶
A deciduous upright shrub or tree grown for its masses of white flowers, which are larger than other amelanchiers, and for its orange, yellow, and red autumn foliage.

Large; full sun; flowers mid to late spring; fertile soil

Can be grown as a multistemmed shrub or small tree. Zone 4

Amomyrtus luma ◀
The caucho is a large evergreen shrub or small tree grown for its masses of starry, white, scented flowers, aromatic copper-red new foliage, and flaking bark.

Large; partial shade but can be grown in full sun in protected sites in sheltered maritime climates; flowers mid and late spring; fertile soil

Clean up the lower limbs to reveal the attractive bark. Especially good when grown as a multistemmed shrub, but is a tree in its native habitat. Zone 7

Amomyrtus meli ICE 127 ▶
A recent introduction from Chile grown for its creamy white flowers and richly scented foliage which is a beautiful bronze-red when young.

Medium to large; partial shade but can be grown in full sun in protected sites in sheltered maritime climates; flowers late summer; fertile soil

Grown as a multistemmed shrub but is a tree in its native habitat. Zone 8

Amorpha fruticosa ▼
A deciduous shrub with dull bluish purple flowers.

Medium; partial shade to full sun; flowers mid to late summer; fertile, well-drained soil

Grown as a multistemmed shrub with the last season's growth pruned back to two or three buds during early spring. Zone 5

Andrachne colchica ▼
A deciduous shrub with yellowish green flowers.

Compact; full sun; flowers mid to late summer; well-drained soil

Prune out dead wood in early spring. Zone 6

Andromeda polifolia 'Blue Ice' ▶

This bog rosemary is an evergreen shrub grown for its outstanding blue foliage best seen in winter, and for its pink bell-shaped flowers.

Compact; partial shade to full sun; flowers mid spring to early summer; fertile, acid soil

Trim lightly with shears immediately after flowering. Zone 4

Andromeda polifolia 'Macrophylla' ▼

This bog rosemary is an evergreen shrub grown for its deep pink bell-shaped flowers. AGM

Compact; partial shade to full sun; flowers mid spring to early summer; fertile, acid soil

Trim lightly with shears immediately after flowering. Zone 4

Anopterus glandulosus ▶

The Tasmanian laurel is an evergreen shrub grown for its pure white cup-shaped flowers and leathery glossy green leaves with bronze-red new growth.

Medium but can grow large in its native habitat; partial shade; flowers mid to late spring; fertile soil

Prune after flowering only to maintain shape and restrict size. Zone 8

Aralia cachemirica ◀

A deciduous shrub with large compound leaves and long arching panicles of tiny white flowers followed by small purplish black fruits.

Medium; partial shade; flowers mid to late summer; fertile soil but can grow in heavy wet and light sandy soils

Can sucker when grown in moist sites. If necessary, remove suckers at ground level in early spring. Zone 7

Aralia elata ▼

The Japanese angelica tree is a deciduous shrub with large compound leaves and large rufflike sprays of white flowers followed by small black fruits on red stems. AGM

Medium to large; partial shade; flowers late summer to early autumn; fertile soil but can grow in heavy wet and light sandy soils

Can sucker when grown in moist sites. If necessary, remove suckers at ground level in early spring. Zone 5

Aralia elata 'Aureovariegata' ◀

A deciduous shrub with beautiful large compound golden variegated leaves and sprays of white flowers not so frequently seen as in the green-leaved form. The foliage becomes pale towards the end of the growing season looking more like the silver-variegated form.

Medium; partial shade; flowers late summer to early autumn; fertile soil

Sold as a grafted plant; if it sends up suckers from the rootstock, cut them off at ground level as soon as seen. Zone 6

Arbutus andrachne ▶

An evergreen shrub with clusters of lily-of-the-valley-shaped white flowers and glossy green leaves followed by persistent orange-red fruits. Large plants have a beautiful reddish brown bark.

Medium to large; partial shade but will tolerate full sun; flowers early to mid spring; fertile soil and, unlike most ericaceous plants, will grow in alkaline soil

The least common *Arbutus* species in cultivation. Comparatively slow to grow. Dislikes transplanting. Zone 7

Arbutus ×andrachnoides ◀▲

An evergreen shrub with clusters of lily-of-the-valley-shaped white flowers and glossy green leaves followed by persistent orange-red fruits. Large plants have a beautiful reddish brown bark. **AGM**

Medium to large; partial shade but will tolerate full sun; flowers mid autumn to early spring; fertile soil and, unlike most ericaceous plants, will grow in alkaline soil

Comparatively slow growing. Dislikes transplanting. Zone 7

Arbutus menziesii ►▼▼

An evergreen shrub with large clusters of lily-of-the-valley-shaped white flowers and glossy green leaves followed by masses of orange-red fruits. Large plants have a beautiful cinnamon brown bark which peels during autumn to reveal smooth pale, greenish brown new bark. **AGM**

Large; partial shade; flowers late spring; fertile, acid soil

Slow to establish but grows quickly thereafter. Dislikes transplanting. Zone 7

Arbutus unedo ►►

The strawberry tree is an evergreen shrub with clusters of lily-of-the-valley-shaped white flowers tinged with pink. The flowers appear at the same time as the yellow fruits from the previous year's flowers. The fruits turn orange-red when ripe. **AGM**

Medium to large; partial shade but will tolerate full sun; flowers early to late autumn; fertile soil and, unlike most ericaceous plants, will grow in alkaline soil

Slow growing apart from protected mild maritime climates where it is seen as a small round-headed tree. Zone 7

Arbutus unedo 'Rubra' ◄

This strawberry tree is an evergreen shrub with clusters of lily-of-the-valley-shaped rich pink flowers which appear at the same time as the abundant yellow fruits from the previous year's flowers. Ripe fruits are an orange-red. **AGM**

Medium; partial shade but will tolerate full sun; flowers early to late autumn; fertile soil and, unlike most ericaceous plants, will grow in alkaline soil

Slow growing. Zone 7

▶ *Arctostaphylos manzanita* at The Cedars, California.

Arctostaphylos manzanita ▼

An evergreen shrub (or small tree in the wild) with pink or white urn-shaped flowers followed by reddish brown fruit in the autumn. The attractive smooth dark reddish brown bark can be hidden by strips of older bark.

Medium; full sun, but will tolerate partial shade; flowers mid to late spring; well-drained, acid soil

Drought tolerant. Slow growing. Dislikes transplanting. Zone 8

Arctostaphylos pajaroensis ▶

An evergreen shrub (or small tree in the wild) with pink flowers and beautiful mahogany-red bark on old plants.

Medium; full sun, but will tolerate partial shade; flowers early to mid spring; well-drained, acid soil

Drought tolerant. Slow growing. Dislikes transplanting. Zone 8

Ardisia japonica ▲

A creeping, rhizomatous ground cover shrub with evergreen leaves and small white flowers followed by red fruits.

Compact; partial shade to shade; flowers early autumn; fertile soil

Provides a good fruiting display in mild locations. Zone 9

Arctostaphylos uva-ursi 'Vancouver Jade' ▶

A vigorous evergreen ground cover shrub with small pink flowers followed by red fruits. The leaves are bright green, with the occasional leaf turning bright red in autumn.

Prostrate; full sun; flowers early to mid spring; well-drained, acid soil

Drought tolerant. Disease resistant. Pruning necessary only if spread is to be restricted. Zone 4

Aristotelia chilensis ▶

An evergreen shrub or small tree with glossy green foliage and greenish white flowers followed by purple fruits that mature black.

Large; full sun and partial shade; flowers early to mid summer; fertile, well-drained soil

Fast growing. For mild, sheltered maritime localities. A variegated foliage form is better known. Zone 9

Aronia arbutifolia ▲

The red chokeberry is a deciduous shrub with white flowers followed by persistent bright red fruits and rich red autumn foliage.

Medium; full sun; flowers mid spring; fertile soil, not tolerant of thin dry chalky soils

Flowering, fruiting, and foliage qualities are best in full sun. A seed-raised cultivar, 'Brilliant', delivers the best autumn colour. Zone 4

Aronia melanocarpa ◀

The black chokeberry is a spreading deciduous shrub with white flowers followed by glossy black fruits.

Small to medium; full sun; flowers mid spring; fertile soil, not tolerant of thin chalky soils

Easily grown. Best flowering and fruiting in full sun. Zone 5

Aronia melanocarpa 'Autumn Magic' ▲

A spreading to upright deciduous shrub with white flowers followed by purple black fruits and red-purple autumn foliage.

Small to medium; full sun; flowers mid spring; fertile soil, not tolerant of thin chalky soils

Best flowering and fruiting in full sun. Zone 4

Artemisia arborescens ▶

An evergreen shrub grown for its silvery grey foliage and small yellowish flowers. AGM

Small; full sun; flowers mid to late summer; well-drained soil

Short-lived. Requires a light prune in early spring. 'Faith Raven' is a hardier selection. Zone 8

Asimina triloba ◄

A deciduous shrub with purple to maroon flowers followed by edible green fruits which ripen to a yellow-brown colour. The distinctive foliage has yellow autumn colour.

Large; full sun; flowers mid spring; fertile, well-drained soil

The edible fruits only ripen during hot summers. Pruning only necessary to restrict size. Zone 5

Astelia chathamica 'Silver Spear' ►

A clump-forming evergreen perennial grown for its bold silver foliage. Flowers are tiny. **AGM**

Small; full sun; flowers early summer; fertile, well-drained soil.

Zone 10

Atherosperma moschatum ◄◄

An upright evergreen shrub with white flowers and greyish green leaves. The bark has a peppery nutmeg fragrance.

Large; partial shade to full sun; flowers early to mid spring; fertile soil

Needs a sheltered location. Zone 8

Aucuba japonica 'Crotonifolia' ▼

An evergreen shrub grown for its bold evergreen variegated foliage, green star-shaped flowers, and rich red fruits. **AGM** female

Medium to large; partial shade and dense shade; flowers mid spring; fertile soil

Tolerates many adverse growing conditions. Can be pruned hard in early spring to restrict size. Prune out reverted foliage. Zone 7

Aucuba japonica 'Hillieri' ◄

An evergreen shrub grown for its bold evergreen foliage and large pointed rich red fruits.

Medium to large; partial shade and dense shade; flowers mid spring; fertile soil

Tolerates many adverse growing conditions. Can be pruned hard in early spring once it becomes too large for the site. Zone 7

Aucuba japonica 'Shunka Benten' ▶

An evergreen shrub grown for its bold foliage with splashes of yellow variegation.

Medium to large; partial shade and dense shade; flowers mid spring; fertile soil

Tolerates many adverse growing conditions. Prune out reverted foliage. Zone 7

Aucuba japonica 'Yellow Delight' ▼

An evergreen shrub grown for its bold foliage with bright yellow variegation around the leaf margins.

Medium to large; partial shade and dense shade; flowers mid spring; fertile soil

Tolerates many adverse growing conditions. Prune out reverted foliage. Zone 7

Azara integrifolia ▼

An evergreen shrub grown for its golden yellow fragrant flowers and glossy, dark green foliage.

Large; full sun and partial shade; flowers late spring and early summer; fertile soil

Needs a sheltered location. Often grown against a south- or west-facing wall. Zone 8

Aucuba omeiensis ▲

An evergreen shrub grown for its bold evergreen foliage and large red fruits.

Large; partial shade and dense shade; flowers mid spring; fertile soil

Tolerates many adverse growing conditions. Can be pruned hard in early spring once it becomes too large for the site. Zone 8

Azara lanceolata ▼

An evergreen shrub grown for its golden yellow scented flowers.

Large; full sun and partial shade; flowers late spring and early summer; fertile soil

Needs a sheltered location. Often grown against a south- or west-facing wall. Zone 7

▼ *Aucuba omeiensis* male flowers

Azara microphylla ▼▶

An evergreen shrub or small tree grown for its clusters of tiny strongly scented flowers accompanying fine dark green foliage. **AGM**

Large; full sun and partial shade; flowers early to mid spring; fertile soil

Needs a sheltered location. Often grown against a south- or west-facing wall. Zone 7

Azara serrata ▼

An evergreen shrub with golden yellow scented flowers. **AGM**

Medium to large; full sun and partial shade; flowers late spring and early summer; fertile soil

Needs a sheltered location. 'Andes Gold' is the clone often grown. Zone 8

Ballota acetabulosa ▲

An evergreen subshrub grown for its aromatic silvery grey foliage and mauve flowers with purple markings nestling in prominent tubular calyces. **AGM**

Small; full sun; flowers mid to late summer; well-drained soil

Needs sun to intensify the silvery foliage colour in a sheltered location. Requires a light prune in early to mid spring. Zone 8

Baccharis patagonica ▼

A dense evergreen shrub with pale yellow flowers that contrast against the dark green leaves.

Small to medium; full sun; flowers mid to late summer; well-drained soil

Tolerates salt spray in mild localities. Zone 8

Azara microphylla 'Variegata' ▼

An evergreen shrub grown for its clusters of tiny strongly scented flowers with fine variegated foliage.

Large; full sun and partial shade; flowers early to mid spring; fertile soil

Needs a sheltered location. Often grown against a south- or west-facing wall. Prune out reverted shoots. Zone

Ballota pseudodictamnus ▲

A mound-forming evergreen subshrub grown for its green aromatic foliage with rather small inconspicuous pale purple flowers and attractive tubular calyces. AGM

Compact; full sun; flowers mid summer to mid autumn; well-drained soil

Requires a sheltered location. Prune lightly in early to mid spring. Zone 8

Banksia integrifolia ▶▶

The coast banksia is an evergreen shrub or small tree with long-lasting pale yellow cylindrical flowers and green leaves with a greyish green underside. Both flowers and foliage are variable. AGM

Medium to large; full sun; flowers late summer to early spring; well-drained, acid soil

Tolerates coastal sheltered conditions. Zone 9

Berberis amurensis var. *latifolia* ▲

A deciduous shrub grown for its pendulous racemes of yellow flowers, bright red fruits, and red autumn foliage.

Medium to large; sun and partial shade; flowers mid to late spring; fertile soil

Requires pruning after flowering once size has been achieved. Zone 5

Berberis ×antoniana ▶

An evergreen shrub with glossy, dark green leaves and golden yellow flowers on red stems followed by blue-black fruits in autumn.

Small; full sun to partial shade; flowers early to mid spring; fertile soil

Needs occasional pruning to tidy up the habit. Zone 6

Berberis buxifolia ▶

An evergreen shrub grown for its bright yellow flowers and leathery glossy, dark green leaves.

Small to medium; sun and partial shade; flowers mid spring; fertile soil

Zone 5

Berberis calliantha ▼

An evergreen shrub grown for its glossy, dark green hollylike leaves, white-grey beneath, and for its large pale yellow flowers followed by purple fruits.

Compact; sun; flowers mid to late spring; fertile soil

Zone 4

Berberis darwinii ▼

An evergreen shrub grown for its glossy, dark green leaves and pendulous racemes of bright orange flowers, tinged red on opening, followed by blue-black fruits. **AGM**

Medium; full sun and partial shade; flowers early to mid spring; fertile soil

Requires pruning after flowering once size has been exceeded in mid spring but will tolerate severe pruning in early spring. Zone 7

Berberis empetrifolia ▼

An evergreen shrub grown for its golden yellow flowers and blue-black fruits. Has long spines on arching stems.

Compact to small; sun and partial shade; flowers mid to late spring; fertile soil

Zone 7

Berberis 'Georgei' ◀

A deciduous shrub with yellow flowers on arching stems followed by large pendulous clusters of red fruit in abundance. Autumn foliage is orange-red. **AGM**

Medium to large; full sun and partial shade; flowers mid to late spring; fertile soil

Produces flowers and fruits more prolifically in full sun. Zone 4

Berberis 'Goldilocks' ▲

An evergreen shrub grown for its pendulous racemes of rich golden yellow flowers and its glossy, dark green spiny foliage.

Large; sun and partial shade; flowers mid spring; fertile soil

Requires pruning after flowering once size has been reached, but will tolerate severe pruning in early spring. Zone 7

Berberis linearifolia 'Jewel' ▼

An erect evergreen shrub grown for its large clusters of bright orange flowers that are red in bud.

Medium; full sun; flowers mid spring; fertile soil

Not the most elegant of shrubs in growth but makes up for it by its floristic display. Requires pruning after flowering to maintain habit. Zone 6

Berberis ×lologensis 'Mystery Fire' ▼

An evergreen shrub with dark green leaves and abundant clusters of rich orange flowers.

Medium; full sun to partial shade; flowers mid spring; fertile soil

Better flowering in full sun. Occasionally prune old stems to promote new basal growth. Generally this cultivar is raised from cuttings. Zone 7

Berberis ×lologensis 'Boughton Red' ▲

An evergreen shrub with dark green leaves and clusters of rich orange-red flowers.

Medium; full sun to partial shade; flowers mid spring; fertile soil

Better flowering in full sun. Occasionally prune old stems to promote new basal growth. Remove suckers from grafted plants. Zone 7

Berberis manipurana ▼

A spiny evergreen shrub grown for its handsome glossy green foliage, yellow flowers, and blue-black fruits.

Medium; full sun and partial shade; flowers mid to late spring; fertile soil

Can be used as an informal hedge, which can be pruned in late spring after flowering when required. Zone 7

Berberis montana ▲

A stiffly upright deciduous shrub grown for its bright greenish yellow flowers and greyish blue fruits.

Medium; full sun; flowers mid to late spring; fertile soil

Requires periodic pruning after flowering to maintain habit. Zone 6

Berberis pruinosa ▲

An evergreen shrub with short spines on the toothed margins of the leaves, green above and often greyish green beneath. Canary yellow flowers are followed by black fruits covered in a grey bloom.

Medium; full sun and partial shade; flowers mid to late spring; fertile soil

Little or no pruning. Zone 6

Berberis sieboldii ▲

A suckering deciduous shrub with yellow flowers grown for its bright green foliage that turns a brilliant scarlet in autumn and is followed by red fruits.

Small; full sun; flowers mid to late spring; fertile soil.

The only thorny berberis not to scratch you. Zone 5

Berberis ×*stenophylla* 'Pink Pearl' ►

An evergreen shrub with arching slender stems. Dark green leaves can show variegation. Flowers are pink, orange-yellow, and ivory on the same plant.

Medium; full sun to partial shade; flowers mid spring; fertile soil.

Zone 5

Berberis temolaica ▲◄

A deciduous shrub with vigorously upright then arching stems and pale yellow flowers. Foliage and stems are quite glaucous, especially when young. Autumn foliage is orange-red. AGM

Medium; full sun and partial shade; flowers mid to late spring; fertile soil

Prune out old wood periodically in early spring to encourage young vigorous shoots. Zone 5

Berberis thunbergii f. *atropurpurea* 'Aurea' ▲

A deciduous shrub grown for its golden yellow foliage. Yellow flowers are followed by red fruits in autumn.

Small; partial shade; flowers mid spring; fertile soil

Foliage may scorch when not grown in partial shade. Zone 5

Berberis thunbergii f. *atropurpurea* 'Bagatelle' ▶

A deciduous slow-growing densely branched shrub with dull reddish purple new growth turning red to scarlet in the autumn. Flowers are yellow. AGM

Compact; full sun; flowers mid to late spring; fertile soil

Can be grown as a dwarf hedge. Plants grow twice as wide as high. Zone 5

Berberis thunbergii f. *atropurpurea* 'Dart's Red Lady' ▼

A deciduous shrub grown for its deep purple foliage that turns a rich red or scarlet in autumn. Flowers are yellow.

Compact to small; full sun; flowers mid to late spring; fertile soil

Autumn foliage colour intensifies given higher light levels. Zone 4

Berberis thunbergii Bonanza Gold 'Bogozam' ▶

A deciduous shrub grown for its bright golden yellow foliage with orange-red new growth. Yellow flowers are followed by red fruits in the autumn. AGM

Compact; full sun and partial shade; flowers mid to late spring; fertile soil

Foliage does not scorch in sun. Zone 5

Berberis valdiviana ▲▶

An upright evergreen shrub with shiny green leaves and rich yellow flowers in long pendulous racemes.

Medium to large; full sun and partial shade; flowers mid to late spring; fertile soil

Requires little or no pruning. Zone 8

Berberis wilsoniae ▶

A deciduous spreading spiny shrub grown for its green to bluish green leaves that turn orange-red in autumn. Small yellow flowers are followed by fruits in variable shades of red in autumn.

Compact to small; full sun; flowers mid to late spring; fertile soil

Leaf and fruit colour vary when plants are grown from seed. Zone 5

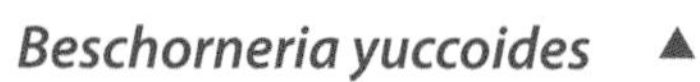

Beschorneria yuccoides ▲

A woody perennial grown for its striking glaucous swordlike foliage and exotic arching flower spikes with green flowers and large pinkish bracts.

Medium; full sun; flowers mid spring to mid summer; fertile, well-drained soil

Requires a sheltered position, space, and may need winter protection. Zone 9

Beschorneria yuccoides 'Variegata' ▶▶

A woody perennial from New Zealand grown for its striking variegated swordlike foliage and exotic arching flower spikes with green flowers and large pinkish bracts.

Medium; full sun; flowers mid spring to mid summer; fertile, well-drained soil

Grow in a sheltered position. Needs winter protection. Zone 10

Boronia heterophylla ▲

The red boronia is a short-lived evergreen shrub with rich pink bell-shaped flowers and mildly aromatic foliage.

Small to medium; full sun; flowers early spring to early summer; well-drained soil with no added fertilizer

Grow in a sheltered position. Prune lightly immediately after flowering. Can be grown in a conservatory. Zone 10

Bouvardia ternifolia ▲

An evergreen shrub grown for its bright red tubular flowers.

Compact; partial shade; flowers mid to late summer; fertile, well-drained soil

Grow in a sheltered position at the base of a wall, and prune lightly at the start of the growing season. Can also be grown in a conservatory. Zone 10

Brachyglottis grayi ▼

An evergreen shrub grown for its bright yellow daisylike flowers and foliage that is silvery grey below.

Small; full sun; flowers mid to late summer; fertile, well-drained soil

Requires a light prune at the start of the growing season. Can be grown as a low informal hedge. Zone 8

Brachyglottis hectoris ▲

An evergreen shrub grown for its large clusters of white flowers and large green leaves that are greyish white beneath.

Medium to large; full sun to partial shade; flowers mid to late summer; fertile, well-drained soil

Prune lightly at the start of the growing season. Zone 8

Brachyglottis 'Otari Cloud' ◄

An evergreen shrub grown for its butter yellow daisylike flowers and silvery grey new growth. Leaves retain the silvery grey colour on the underside.

Compact to small; full sun; flowers mid to late summer; well-drained soil

Prune lightly at the start of the growing season. Zone 8

Brachyglottis repanda ▼

An evergreen shrub grown for its large panicles of small white flowers and large wavy-edged green leaves that are silvery white beneath.

Large; full sun to partial shade; flowers mid to late spring; fertile, well-drained soil

Suitable for a sheltered location. Prune after flowering. Zone 10

Brachyglottis rotundifolia ▲▲

An evergreen shrub grown for its thick leathery green leaves, felted beneath. Flowers are yellowish green. Synonym: *Senecio reinholdii*.

Medium to large; full sun and partial shade; flowers mid to late summer; fertile, well-drained soil

Tolerates exposed coastal locations. Can be used as a wind break in mild localities. Zone 9

Brachyglottis 'Sunshine' ▶

An evergreen shrub grown for its bright yellow daisylike flowers and foliage that is silvery grey on the underside. AGM

Compact to small; full sun; flowers mid to late summer; fertile, well-drained soil

Requires light pruning at the start of the growing season. Can be grown as a low informal hedge. Zone 8

Buddleja alternifolia ▲▶

A deciduous shrub grown for its dense clusters of fragrant lilac flowers along the stem. AGM

Medium to large; full sun; flowers late spring to early summer; well-drained soil

Prune immediately after flowering. Zone 5

Buddleja colvilei 'Kewensis' ▼

A deciduous shrub grown for its rich magenta-red clusters of flowers.

Medium to large; full sun to partial shade; flowers late spring to early summer; fertile, well-drained soil

Prune immediately after flowering. Zone 7

Buddleja crispa ►

A deciduous shrub grown for its young leaves and stems, which are covered with a silvery white pubescence that ages to grey-green, and for its pinkish lilac cylindrical panicles of delicately fragrant flowers. AGM

Medium to large; full sun; flowers mid to late summer; fertile, well-drained soil

Prune during late winter or early spring. Zone 7

Buddleja davidii 'Black Knight' ▲►

This butterfly bush is a deciduous shrub grown for its long panicles of deep royal purple flowers. AGM

Medium; full sun; flowers mid to late summer; well-drained soil

Prune by up to 50 percent during late winter or early spring. Zone 6

Buddleja davidii NANHO PURPLE 'Monum' ▼

This butterfly bush is a deciduous broad-spreading shrub grown for its slender panicles of purple flowers. AGM

Small to medium; full sun; flowers mid to late summer; well-drained soil

Prune by up to 50 percent during late winter or early spring. Zone 6

Buddleja davidii 'Royal Red' ▼

This butterfly bush is a deciduous shrub grown for its long panicles of rich red flowers. AGM

Medium; full sun; flowers mid to late summer; wel-drained soil

Prune by up to 50 percent during late winter or early spring. Zone 6

Buddleja fallowiana 'Alba' ▶

A deciduous shrub grown for its fragrant large panicles of white flowers with an orange eye. The grey-green leaves have a white felt covering when young. **AGM**

Medium to large; full sun; flowers mid to late summer; well-drained soil

Prune by up to 50 percent during late winter or early spring. Zone 8

Buddleja globosa ▲

The orange ball tree is a semievergreen shrub grown for its ball-shaped clusters of pale orange-yellow flowers. The veined green leaves are yellowish grey-green on the underside. **AGM**

Medium to large; full sun; flowers early to mid summer; well-drained soil

Prune immediately after flowering in mid to late summer. Zone 7

Buddleja lindleyana ▼

A semievergreen shrub grown for its slender arching panicles of purple-violet flowers.

Medium; sun and partial shade; flowers mid summer to early autumn; well-drained soil

Lightly prune during late winter or early spring. Zone 7

Buddleja 'Lochinch' ◀▲

A deciduous shrub grown for its dense conical panicles of lilac-blue scented flowers with an orange eye. The leaves are grey-green above and grey-felted beneath. **AGM**

Medium; full sun; flowers mid to late summer; well-drained soil

Prune during late winter and early spring. Zone 8

Buddleja madagascariensis ◀

An evergreen shrub grown for its profuse large pale orange-yellow panicles of flowers with green leaves that are woolly greenish white beneath. **AGM**

Medium to large; full sun; flowers late winter to early spring; fertile, well-drained soil

Generally grown in a conservatory where it is pruned by up to 50 percent immediately after flowering in mid spring. Zone 10

Buddleja officinalis ▶

An evergreen or semievergreen shrub grown for its fragrant short pyramidal panicles of lilac-mauve flowers and pale green leaves that are a woolly grey-green beneath. **AGM**

Medium; full sun; flowers late winter to early spring; fertile, well-drained soil

Generally grown in a conservatory and pruned immediately after flowering in mid spring. Zone 10

Buddleja ×*weyeriana* 'Sungold' ▼

A deciduous shrub grown for its long slender panicles made up of ball-shaped heads of bright orange-yellow flowers. **AGM**

Medium to large; full sun; flowers mid summer to early autumn; well-drained soil

Prune during late winter or early spring. Zone 6

Buddleja 'Pink Delight' ▼

A deciduous shrub grown for its large panicles of bright pink flowers. **AGM**

Medium; full sun; flowers mid to late summer; well-drained soil

Prune by up to 50 percent during late winter or early spring. Zone 7

Buddleja salviifolia ▼

The South African sage wood is a deciduous or semievergreen shrub grown for its short panicles of lilac to mauve flowers and its felted sagelike grey-green leaves.

Medium to large; full sun; flowers mid summer to early autumn; fertile, well-drained soil

Prune in mid spring. Will flower in early summer onwards if not pruned. Zone 8

Bupleurum fruticosum ▼

An evergreen shrub grown for its yellowish green flowers and its shiny sea green leaves.

Small to medium; full sun; flowers mid summer to early autumn; fertile, well-drained soil

Tolerates exposed coastal locations. Zone 7

Buxus balearica ▶

The Balearic boxwood is an evergreen shrub grown for its large bright green leathery leaves with clusters of yellow flowers in the leaf axils. **AGM**

Medium to large; partial shade, shade and full sun; flowers early to mid spring; fertile, well-drained soil

Generally requires no pruning, but can be used for hedging where appropriate pruning is necessary. Zone 8

Buxus microphylla var. *japonica* 'Morris Dwarf' ▲

This Japanese box is an evergreen shrub grown for its bright green foliage, tight growth, and compact habit.

Compact; partial shade, shade, and full sun; flowers early to mid spring; fertile, well-drained soil

Slow growing and not generally needing clipping. Zone 6

Buxus sempervirens 'Elegantissima' ▶

This common box is an evergreen shrub grown for its creamy white variegated foliage. It is the best variegated boxwood clone. **AGM**

Small to medium; partial shade; flowers early to mid spring; fertile, well-drained soil

Tolerates clipping but is generally grown as a slow-growing specimen shrub. Zone 6

Buxus sempervirens 'Rotundifolia' ◀

This common box is an evergreen shrub grown for its round dark green leaves.

Small to medium; partial shade, shade, and full sun; flowers early to mid spring; fertile, well-drained soil

Useful as a specimen because of its slow rate of growth. Zone 6

Caesalpinia decapetala var. *japonica* ▶

A scrambling deciduous shrub grown for its bright yellow flowers in racemes with spiny stems.

Large; sun; flowers early summer; fertile, well-drained soil

Best grown against a south-facing wall. Prune in early spring. Zone 9

Caesalpinia gilliesii ▶

The bird of paradise is a deciduous shrub (but can be evergreen in mild climates) grown for its bright pale yellow flowers with prominent bright red stamen with dainty fern-like foliage.

Large; sun; flowers mid to late summer; fertile, well-drained soil

Best grown against a south-facing wall. Prune in early spring. Zone 8

Calceolaria integrifolia ▼

An evergreen subshrub grown for its panicles of bright yellow flowers. **AGM**

Small; sun; flowers late summer; fertile, well-drained soil

Can be grown in a conservatory. Zone 9

Callicarpa bodinieri var. *giraldii* ▲

A deciduous shrub grown for its masses of small mauve-lilac fruits preceded by mauve-lilac flowers followed by dull purple-red ultimately yellow autumn foliage. Differs from *C. bodinieri* by its glabrous foliage.

Medium to large; sun or partial shade; flowers late summer; fertile, well-drained soil

Prune in early to mid spring to maintain size. Zone 6

Callicarpa bodinieri ◀

A deciduous shrub grown for its masses of small mauve-lilac fruits preceded by mauve-lilac flowers, followed by dull purple-red ultimately yellow autumn foliage.

Medium; sun or partial shade; flowers late summer; fertile, well-drained soil

Prune in early to mid spring to maintain size. Zone 6

Callicarpa dichotoma ◀

A deciduous shrub grown for its masses of violet-purple fruits preceded by pink flowers followed by yellow autumn foliage.

Compact to small; sun or partial shade; flowers mid to late summer; fertile, well-drained soil

Prune in early to mid spring to maintain size. Zone 6

Callistemon citrinus 'Splendens' ▶

This scarlet bottlebrush is an evergreen shrub grown for its masses of cylindrical spikes of large brilliant red flowers with persistent woody seed capsules along the stem. **AGM**

Small to medium; sun; flowers mid to late summer; fertile, well-drained, preferably acid soil.

Zone 8

Callistemon pallidus ▶

The lemon bottlebrush is an evergreen shrub grown for its masses of cylindrical spikes of pale, lemon yellow flowers with persistent woody seed capsules along the stem. Foliage is a silky silvery pink on opening.

Medium; sun; flowers mid to late summer; fertile, well-drained, preferably acid soil.

Zone 8

Calluna vulgaris 'Anette' ▼

An evergreen shrub grown for its clear pink buds opening to long-lasting rose pink flowers. **AGM**

Compact; sun; flowers late summer to early autumn; fertile, acid soil

Trim back last year's growth in early spring with shears. Zone 4

▲ *Calluna vulgaris* covers tracts of moorland particularly in Scotland (seen here in Dumfriesshire) and the north of England. Sections of moorland are control-burned to maintain plant vigour.

Calluna vulgaris 'Arran Gold' ▼

An evergreen shrub with rich gold and orange foliage and sparse pink flowers.

Compact; sun; flowers late summer to early autumn; fertile, acid soil

Trim back last year's growth in early spring with shears. Zone 4

Calluna vulgaris

Ling, or heather, is an evergreen shrub with single to double, white to pink to purple flowers and with green to grey to gold foliage, depending on the cultivar.

Compact; sun; flowers late summer to early autumn; fertile, acid soil

Trim back last year's growth in early spring with shears. Zone 4

Calluna vulgaris 'Elsie Purnell' ▶

An evergreen shrub with long silvery pink double flower spikes. AGM

Compact; sun; flowers late summer to mid autumn; fertile, acid soil
Trim back last year's growth in early spring with shears. Zone 4

Calluna vulgaris 'Fritz Kircher' and *C. vulgaris* 'Violet Bamford' ▼

Evergreen shrubs grown for their masses of rose pink flowers and compact growth with yellowish green foliage.

Compact; sun; flowers late summer to mid autumn; fertile, acid soil
Trim back last year's growth in early spring with shears. Zone 4

Calluna vulgaris 'Jimmy Dyce' ▼

An evergreen shrub with long pink double flower spikes and compact growth.

Compact; sun; flowers late summer to mid autumn; fertile, acid soil
Trim back last year's growth in early spring with shears. Zone 4

Calluna vulgaris 'Kinlochruel' ▼

An evergreen shrub grown for its pure white double flower spikes and green foliage that turns a dark bronze in winter. AGM

Compact; sun; flowers late summer to early autumn; fertile, acid soil
Trim back last year's growth in early spring with shears. Zone 4

Calluna vulgaris 'Mick Jamieson' ▼

An evergreen shrub with long rich rose pink double flower spikes.

Compact; sun; flowers late summer to early autumn; fertile, acid soil
Trim back last year's growth in early spring with shears. Zone 4

Calluna vulgaris 'Parsons' Grey Selected' ▲

An evergreen shrub grown for its silvery grey foliage and single pink flowers.

Compact; sun; flowers late summer to early autumn; fertile, acid soil

Trim back last year's growth in early spring with shears. Zone 4

Calluna vulgaris 'Peter Sparkes' ▲

An evergreen shrub with deep pink double flower spikes. AGM

Compact; sun; flowers late summer to early autumn; fertile, acid soil

Trim back last year's growth in early spring with shears. Zone 4

Calycanthus floridus 'Athens' ◄

This Carolina allspice is a deciduous shrub grown for its fragrant yellowish green flowers and camphor-scented glossy green foliage, felted beneath.

Medium; sun to partial shade; flowers early to late summer; fertile soil

Zone 5

Calycanthus floridus 'Michael Lindsey' ◄

A deciduous shrub grown for its fragrant brownish red flowers and camphor-scented glossy green foliage, felted beneath.

Medium; sun to partial shade; flowers early to late summer; fetile soil

Zone 5

Calycanthus occidentalis ▲

The California allspice is a deciduous shrub grown for its fragrant reddish flowers that fade to yellowish white with age. Both the bark and foliage are aromatic.

Medium; sun to partial shade; flowers early to late summer; fertile soil

Zone 7

Camellia 'Bravo' ▲

An evergreen shrub grown for its large semidouble rose-coloured flowers and bronze new growth.

Large; partial shade; flowers late winter to early spring; fertile, neutral to acid soil

Formative pruning after flowering. Zone 9

Camellia 'Doctor Clifford Parks' ▲▼

An evergreen shrub grown for its very large semidouble rich red flowers. **AGM**

Large; partial shade; flowers early to late spring; fertile, neutral to acid soil

Formative pruning after flowering. Zone 8

Camellia 'Freedom Bell' ▼

An evergreen shrub grown for its semidouble bell-shaped pale red flowers. **AGM**

Large; partial shade; flowers early to late spring; fertile, neutral to acid soil

Formative pruning after flowering. Zone 8

Camellia hiemalis 'Sparkling Burgundy' ▲

An evergreen shrub with peony-form ruby rose flowers. Synonym: *Camellia sasanqua* 'Sparkling Burgundy'.

Medium to large; partial shade; flowers late autumn to mid winter; fertile, neutral to acid soil

Formative pruning during early to mid spring. Zone 8

Camellia 'Inspiration' ▲◀

An evergreen shrub grown for its large semidouble rich pink flowers. **AGM**

Large; partial shade; flowers early to late spring; fertile, neutral to acid soil

Formative pruning after flowering. Zone 8

▲ *Camellia japonica* cultivars at Harthill, Liverpool.

Camellia japonica

The common or bush camellia is an evergreen shrub with more than 2000 named cultivars displaying differences in flower forms, colours, petal markings, and size as well as habit. **AGM**

Variable sizes; partial shade; flowers early to late spring; fertile, neutral to acid soil

Formative pruning after flowering. Zone 7

Camellia japonica 'Bob Hope' ▼

An evergreen shrub grown for its large semidouble dark red flowers. **AGM**

Large; partial shade; flowers early to late spring; fertile, neutral to acid soil.

Zone 7

Camellia japonica 'Bob's Tinsie' ▲

An evergreen shrub grown for its small anemone-form brilliant red flowers. **AGM**

Medium to large; partial shade; flowers early to late spring; fertile, neutral to acid soil

Formative pruning after flowering. Zone 7

Camellia japonica 'Gigantea' ▼

An evergreen shrub grown for its large semidouble red flowers with conspicuous irregularly shaped variegations on the petals.

Large; partial shade; flowers early to late spring; fertile, neutral to acid soil

Formative pruning after flowering. Zone 7

Camellia japonica 'Mars' ▼

An evergreen shrub with large semidouble crimson flowers. **AGM**

Large; partial shade; flowers early to late spring; fertile, neutral to acid soil

Formative pruning after flowering. Zone 7

Camellia japonica 'Mikuni-no-homare' ▲

One of the Higo Group camellias, this evergreen shrub has single pink flowers with prominent flared stamens. **AGM**

Large; partial shade; flowers early to late spring; fertile, neutral to acid soil

Formative pruning after flowering. Zone 8

Camellia japonica 'Nobilissima' ▼

An evergreen shrub grown for its peony-form white flowers with yellow shading on the reverse of the petals.

Large; partial shade; flowers late winter to mid spring; fertile, neutral to acid soil

Formative pruning after flowering. Zone 7

Camellia japonica 'Sylvia' ▲

An evergreen shrub grown for its saucer-shaped single scarlet flowers with prominent stamens. **AGM**

Large; partial shade; flowers early to late spring; fertile, neutral to acid soil

Formative pruning after flowering. Zone 7

Camellia japonica 'Tama-no-ura' ▶

An evergreen shrub grown for its cup-shaped single red flowers with a heavy white border and prominent stamens.

Large; partial shade; flowers early to late spring; fertile, neutral to acid soil

Formative pruning after flowering. Zone 7

Camellia japonica 'Tricolor' ▼

An evergreen shrub grown for its cup-shaped single white flowers with pink veins, broad carmine streaks, and prominent stamens. **AGM**

Large; partial shade; flowers early to late spring; fertile, neutral to acid soil

Formative pruning after flowering. Zone 7

Camellia japonica 'Rubescens Major' ▼

An evergreen shrub with large formal double rose-red flowers. **AGM**

Medium to large; partial shade; flowers early to late spring; fertile, neutral to acid soil

Formative pruning after flowering. Zone 7

Camellia japonica 'White Nun' ▶

An evergreen shrub with very large semidouble white flowers.

Large; partial shade; flowers early to late spring; fertile, neutral to acid soil

Formative pruning after flowering. Zone 7

Camellia 'Knight Rider' ▼

An evergreen shrub grown for its semidouble waxy very dark red flowers. **AGM**

Medium to large; partial shade; flowers early to late spring; fertile, neutral to acid soil

Formative pruning after flowering. Zone 7

Camellia 'Leonard Messel' ▼

An evergreen shrub with large semidouble rose pink flowers. A hybrid between *C. saluenensis* and *C. ×williamsii* 'Mary Christian'. **AGM**

Large; partial shade; flowers early to late spring; fertile, neutral to acid soil

Formative pruning after flowering. Zone 7

Camellia oleifera ▼

An evergreen shrub grown for its fragrant single white flowers with prominent flared stamens.

Medium to large; partial shade; flowers mid to late autumn; fertile, neutral to acid soil

Formative pruning after flowering. Zone 8

Camellia 'Purple Gown' ▲

Also called 'Zipao', this evergreen shrub is grown for its large peony-form dark purple-red flowers with occasional wine-red pinstripes in the petals. **AGM**

Large; partial shade; flowers late winter to early spring; fertile, neutral to acid soil

Formative pruning after flowering. Zone 7

Camellia reticulata

An evergreen shrub with more than 400 named cultivars and hybrids exhibiting some of the largest flowers of the genus. Flower form, colour, and petal markings vary with the cultivar.

Large; partial shade; flowers late winter to early spring; fertile, neutral to acid soil

Formative pruning after flowering. Zone 9

▼ *Camellia reticulata* cultivars

Camellia reticulata 'Ruby Queen' ▲

An evergreen shrub grown for its very large semidouble rich red flowers.

Large; partial shade; flowers late winter to early spring; fertile, neutral to acid soil

Formative pruning after flowering. Zone 9

Camellia reticulata 'Valentine Day' ◄

An evergreen shrub grown for its very large formal double salmon-pink flowers.

Large; partial shade; flowers mid winter to mid spring; fertile, neutral to acid soil

Formative pruning after flowering. Zone 7

Camellia saluenensis ▼

An evergreen shrub with single white to deep rose pink flowers. **AGM**

Medium to large; partial shade; flowers early to mid spring; fertile, neutral to acid soil

Formative pruning after flowering. Zone 8

Camellia reticulata 'Captain Rawes' ▲

An evergreen shrub with very large semidouble carmine to rose pink flowers.

Large; partial shade; flowers late winter to early spring; fertile, neutral to acid soil

Formative pruning after flowering. Zone 9

Camellia reticulata 'Houye Diechi' ▼

An evergreen shrub grown for its very large semidouble rose pink flowers.

Large; partial shade; flowers late winter to early spring; fertile, neutral to acid soil

Formative pruning after flowering. Zone 9

▶ *Camellia sasanqua* at the Imperial Palace in Tokyo.

Camellia sasanqua

An evergreen shrub with more than 300 named cultivars all with fragrant flowers and glossy green leaves. Flower form and colour, as well as plant habit, are variable, depending on the cultivar.

Medium to large; partial shade; flowers late autumn to mid winter; fertile, neutral to acid soil

Formative pruning during early to mid spring. Zone 8

Camellia sasanqua 'Autumn Sun' ▲

An evergreen shrub grown for its large fragrant single rose pink flowers.

Medium to large; partial shade; flowers late autumn to mid winter; fertile, neutral to acid soil

Pruning during early to mid spring. Zone 8

Camellia sasanqua 'Crimson King' ▼

An evergreen shrub with fragrant single rich red flowers. **AGM**

Medium to large; partial shade; flowers late autumn to mid winter; fertile, neutral to acid soil

Formative pruning during early to mid spring. Zone 8

Camellia sasanqua 'Narumigata' ◀

An evergreen shrub grown for its fragrant single white flowers that are shaded pink at the margins and on the outside of the petals.

Medium to large; partial shade; flowers late autumn to mid winter; fertile, neutral to acid soil

Formative pruning during early to mid spring. Zone 8

Camellia sasanqua 'Variegata' ▼

An evergreen shrub grown for its white variegated foliage and fragrant single white flowers.

Medium; partial shade; flowers late autumn to mid winter; fertile, neutral to acid soil

Formative pruning during early to mid spring. Zone 8

Camellia transarisanensis ▲

An evergreen shrub with small single white flowers.

Medium; partial shade; flowers early to mid spring; fertile, neutral to acid soil

Little pruning needed. Zone 8

Camellia ×vernalis 'Yuletide' ▲

An evergreen shrub with fragrant single rich red flowers.

Medium to large; partial shade; flowers late autumn to mid winter; fertile, neutral to acid soil

Formative pruning during early to mid spring. Zone 8

▶ *Camellia ×williamsii* at the Royal Horticultural Society's Garden Wisley.

Camellia ×williamsii

An evergreen shrub with about 300 named cultivars, all of which are free-flowering and have glossy, dark green leaves. Depending on the cultivar, habits differ as well as the form and colour of individual flowers.

Large; partial shade; flowers mid winter to mid spring; fertile, neutral to acid soil

Formative pruning after flowering. Zone 7

Camellia ×williamsii 'Anticipation' ▶

An evergreen shrub grown for its large peony-form deep rose flowers. **AGM**

Large; partial shade; flowers early to late spring; fertile, neutral to acid soil

Formative pruning after flowering. Zone 7

Camellia ×williamsii 'Brian' ▼

An evergreen shrub with semidouble silvery pink flowers.

Large; partial shade; flowers mid winter to mid spring; fertile, neutral to acid soil

Formative pruning after flowering. Zone 7

Camellia ×williamsii 'Brigadoon' ▲

An evergreen shrub with semidouble rose pink flowers. AGM

Large; partial shade; flowers mid winter to mid spring; fertile, neutral to acid soil

Formative pruning after flowering. Zone 7

Camellia ×williamsii 'Brushfield Yellow' ▼

An evergreen shrub with peony-form pale yellow flowers.

Medium; partial shade; flowers mid winter to mid spring; fertile, neutral to acid soil

Formative pruning after flowering. Zone 7

Camellia ×williamsii 'China Clay' ►

An evergreen shrub with semidouble pure white flowers. AGM

Medium to large; partial shade; flowers mid winter to mid spring; fertile, neutral to acid soil

Formative pruning after flowering. Zone 7

Camellia ×williamsii 'Daintiness' ▲

An evergreen shrub with large semi-double salmon-pink flowers. AGM

Large; partial shade; flowers mid winter to mid spring; fertile, neutral to acid soil

Formative pruning after flowering. Zone 7

Camellia ×williamsii 'Debbie' ▼

An evergreen shrub with large peony-form clear pink flowers. AGM

Large; partial shade; flowers mid winter to mid spring; fertile, neutral to acid soil

Formative pruning after flowering. Zone 7

Camellia ×williamsii 'Donation' ▼

An evergreen shrub with large semi-double orchid pink flowers. AGM

Large; partial shade; flowers mid winter to mid spring; fertile, neutral to acid soil

Formative pruning after flowering. Zone 7

Camellia ×williamsii 'Dream Boat' ▶

An evergreen shrub with large formal double bright pink flowers. AGM

Large; partial shade; flowers mid winter to mid spring; fertile, neutral to acid soil

Formative pruning after flowering. Zone 7

Camellia ×williamsii 'Glenn's Orbit' ▲

An evergreen shrub with large semi-double clear orchid pink flowers. AGM

Large; partial shade; flowers mid winter to mid spring; fertile, neutral to acid soil

Formative pruning after flowering. Zone 7

Camellia ×williamsii 'Leonora' ▲

An evergreen shrub with large semi-double rose pink flowers.

Large; partial shade; flowers mid winter to mid spring; fertile, neutral to acid soil

Formative pruning after flowering. Zone 7

Camellia ×williamsii 'Les Jury' ▶

An evergreen shrub grown for its double pillar box red flowers and bronze new growth. **AGM**

Large; partial shade; flowers mid winter to mid spring; fertile, neutral to acid soil

Formative pruning after flowering. Zone 7

Camellia ×williamsii 'Muskoka' ▼

An evergreen shrub with large semi-double rich pink flowers. **AGM**

Large; partial shade; flowers mid winter to mid spring; fertile, neutral to acid soil

Formative pruning after flowering. Zone 7

Camellia ×williamsii 'Water Lily' ▼

An evergreen shrub with formal double bright pink flowers. **AGM**

Large; partial shade; flowers mid winter to mid spring; fertile, neutral to acid soil

Formative pruning after flowering. Zone 7

Camellia ×williamsii 'Saint Ewe' ▼

An evergreen shrub with single cup-shaped rich rose pink flowers. **AGM**

Large; partial shade; flowers mid winter to mid spring; fertile, neutral to acid soil

Formative pruning after flowering. Zone 7

Camellia yuhsienensis ▲

An evergreen shrub with fragrant single white flowers.

Medium; partial shade; flowers mid to late winter; fertile, neutral to acid soil

An important landscape plant in China with some clones very scented. Zone 8

Campylotropis macrocarpa ▲

A deciduous shrub grown for its racemes of rose-purple flowers.

Small; sun; flowers late summer to early autumn; well-drained soil

Prune out dead wood in early to mid spring. Zone 7

Cantua bicolor ▲

An evergreen shrub grown for its pendulous clusters of bicoloured rich yellow and white tubular flowers.

Small to medium; sun; flowers mid spring; fertile, well-drained soil

Prune after flowering. Zone 9

Cantua buxifolia ◀ ▼

The sacred flower of the Incas is an evergreen shrub grown for its pendulous clusters of generally deep pink to purple flowers. When raised from seed, the flowers can be pink and white or yellow and white. **AGM**

Small to medium; sun; flowers mid to late spring; fertile, well-drained soil

Prune after flowering. Zone 9

Caragana microphylla ▼

A deciduous shrub grown for its small bright yellow flowers.

Medium; sun; flowers late spring to early summer; well-drained soil

Prune one-year-old wood to maintain plant shape. Zone 3

Caragana sinica ▲

A deciduous shrub with pale yellow flowers that flush bronze-red with age and with small glossy green leaves.

Medium; sun; flowers late spring to early summer; well-drained soil

Prune one-year-old wood to maintain plant shape. Zone 6

Carmichaelia australis ▲▼

A leafless shrub grown for its graceful arching green stems bearing racemes of white flowers flushed purple.

Medium; sun; flowers mid summer; fertile, well-drained soil

Fertile soil encourages flowering. Zone 8

Carmichaelia stevensonii ◄▲

A leafless shrub grown for its graceful arching habit and clusters of rich lavender-pink flowers.

Medium; sun; flowers mid summer; fertile, well-drained soil

Fertile soil encourages flowering. Zone 8

Carpenteria californica ▲▼

The tree anemone is an evergreen shrub grown for its delicately fragrant large pure white flowers with rich yellow stamens and glossy green leaves. **AGM**

Medium; sun; flowers early to mid summer; well-drained soil

Formative pruning after flowering. Zone 8

Caryopteris ×clandonensis 'Longwood Blue' ▲

A deciduous shrub with deep sky blue flower spikes and grey-green leaves.

Compact; sun; flowers late summer to early autumn; well-drained soil

Prune last season's growth during early spring. Zone 7

Caryopteris ×clandonensis 'Dark Knight' ▲

A deciduous shrub with dark purple-blue flower spikes and silvery grey-green leaves.

Compact; sun; flowers late summer to early autumn; well-drained soil

Prune last season's growth during early spring. Zone 7

Caryopteris ×clandonensis 'Ferndown' ▼

A deciduous shrub grown for its rich violet-purple flower spikes. Paired with yellow-leaved *Choisya ternata* SUNDANCE 'Lich' in the photo.

Compact; sun; flowers late summer to early autumn; well-drained soil

Prune last season's growth during early spring. Zone 7

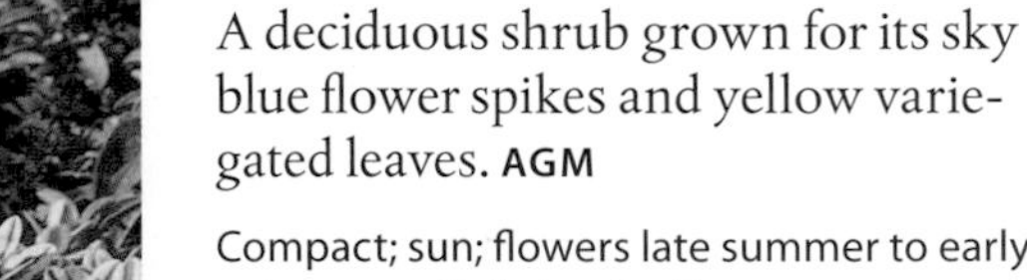

Caryopteris ×clandonensis 'Summer Sorbet' ▲▼

A deciduous shrub grown for its sky blue flower spikes and yellow variegated leaves. **AGM**

Compact; sun; flowers late summer to early autumn; well-drained soil

Prune last season's growth during early spring. Zone 7

Caryopteris ×clandonensis 'Worcester Gold' ▲

A deciduous shrub grown for its blue flower spikes and pale yellow-green leaves, golden yellow on opening. **AGM**

Compact; sun; flowers late summer to early autumn; well-drained soil

Prune last season's growth during early spring. Zone 7

Cassiope lycopodioides ▼

An evergreen dwarf shrub grown for its nodding bell-shaped white flowers and dark green leaves wrapped around whipcordlike stems. **AGM**

Prostrate; partial shade; flowers late spring to early summer; fertile, acid soil

Requires cool, moisture-retentive conditions in a rock garden. Zone 3

Cassiope 'Randle Cooke' ▲

An evergreen dwarf shrub grown for its large nodding bell-shaped white flowers and dark green leaves wrapped around whipcordlike stems. **AGM**

Prostrate; partial shade; flowers late spring to early summer; fertile, acid soil

Requires cool, moisture-retentive conditions in a rock garden. Zone 3

Cassiope 'George Taylor' ▼

A rare hybrid of *C. wardii*, this evergreen dwarf shrub is grown for its nodding urn-shaped white flowers and green leaves covered in fine white hairs.

Prostrate; partial shade; flowers late spring to early summer; fertile, acid soil

Requires cool, moisture-retentive conditions in a rock garden. Zone 4

Cassiope wardii ◄

An evergreen dwarf shrub grown for its nodding urn-shaped white flowers and green leaves covered in fine white hairs.

Prostrate; partial shade; flowers late spring to early summer; fertile, acid soil

Requires cool, moisture-retentive conditions in a rock garden. Zone 4

Ceanothus arboreus 'Trewithen Blue' ►

A spreading evergreen shrub grown for its large panicles of slightly fragrant deep powder blue flowers and large green leaves. **AGM**

Large; sun; flowers late spring; fertile, well-drained soil

Often trained against a wall. Prune immediately after flowering. Zone 8

Ceanothus 'Blue Buttons' ▲

A mound-forming evergreen shrub grown for its masses of powder blue flowers and small green leaves.

Medium; sun; flowers late spring to early summer; well-drained soil

Prune after flowering. Zone 8

Ceanothus 'Blue Cushion' ▼

A compact mound-forming evergreen shrub grown for masses of buttonlike clusters of bright blue flowers and small green leaves.

Small; sun; flowers late spring to early summer; well-drained soil

Prune after flowering. Zone 8

Ceanothus 'Blue Jeans' ▼

A mound-forming evergreen shrub grown for its clusters of pale violet flowers lining stiff arching stems and for its small green leaves.

Small; sun; flowers late spring; well-drained soil

Prune after flowering. Zone 8

Ceanothus 'Burkwoodii' ▼

A mound-forming evergreen shrub grown for its panicles of rich blue flowers and glossy green leaves. **AGM**

Medium; sun; flowers late spring to late summer; fertile, well-drained soil

Prune immediately after first flush of flowering. Zone 8

Ceanothus 'Concha' ▲

A mound-forming evergreen shrub grown for its massed clusters of vibrant dark blue flowers on arching stems and dark green leaves. **AGM**

Medium; sun; flowers late spring to early summer; well-drained soil

Prune after flowering. Zone 8

Ceanothus 'Cynthia Postan' ▼

A mound-forming evergreen shrub grown for its clusters of violet-blue flowers on arching stems and glossy green leaves.

Medium; sun; flowers late spring to early summer; well-drained soil

Prune after flowering. Zone 8

Ceanothus 'Dark Star' ◄

A mound-forming evergreen shrub grown for its clusters of cobalt blue flowers, burgundy coloured in bud, on arching stems with small dark green leaves. **AGM**

Medium; sun; flowers mid spring to late spring; well-drained soil

Prune after flowering. Zone 8

Ceanothus ×delileanus 'Basil Fox' ▼

This French hybrid ceanothus is a deciduous open-branched shrub grown for its short violet-blue flower spikes, slate blue in bud.

Medium; sun; flowers mid summer to late summer; fertile, well-drained soil

Prune in early spring. Zone 8

Ceanothus ×delileanus 'Gloire de Versailles' ▼

This French hybrid ceanothus is a deciduous shrub grown for its large powder blue flower spikes. **AGM**

Small to medium; sun; flowers mid summer to early autumn; fertile, well-drained soil

Prune back last year's growth in early spring. Zone 7

Ceanothus impressus ▶

The Santa Barbara ceanothus is a mound-forming evergreen shrub grown for its panicles of bright blue flowers and small glossy green leaves

Small to medium; sun; flowers late spring; well-drained soil

Prune immediately after flowering. Zone 7

Ceanothus 'Italian Skies' ▲▶

A mound-forming evergreen shrub grown for its panicles of luminous blue flowers on arching stems and dark glossy green leaves.

Small to medium; sun; flowers mid to late summer; fertile, well-drained soil

Prune after first flush of flowering. Zone 8

Ceanothus ×*pallidus* 'Ceres' ▼

A deciduous shrub grown for its panicles of lilac-pink flowers.

Small to medium; sun; flowers mid summer; fertile, well-drained soil

Prune back last season's growth in early spring. Zone 7

Ceanothus ×*pallidus* 'Marie Simon' ▲

A deciduous shrub grown for its large panicles of pink flowers, deep rose in bud.

Medium; sun; flowers mid summer to late summer; fertile, well-drained soil

Prune in early spring. Zone 7

Ceanothus 'Pin Cushion' ▼

A low-growing evergreen shrub grown for its clusters of light blue flowers and green leaves.

Compact; sun; flowers late spring to early summer; well-drained soil

Prune after flowering. Zone 8

Cephalanthus occidentalis ▼

The button bush is a deciduous shrub grown for its starlike fragrant creamy white flowers and glossy green leaves.

Medium; sun or partial shade; flowers late summer; fertile, neutral to acid soil

Prune last season's growth in early spring. Zone 6

Ceanothus 'Puget Blue' ▲

A mound-forming evergreen shrub grown for its panicles of lavender-blue flowers and small green leaves. **AGM**

Medium; sun; flowers mid to late spring; well-drained soil

Prune after flowering. Zone 8

Ceanothus thyrsiflorus 'Skylark' ▶

This blue brush is a mound-forming evergreen shrub grown for its late flowering clusters of light blue flowers and glossy green leaves. **AGM**

Medium; sun; flowers late spring to early summer; well-drained soil

Prune after flowering. Zone 8

Ceanothus thyrsiflorus 'Millerton Point' ▲

This blue brush is a mound-forming evergreen shrub grown for its large clusters of white flowers and glossy green leaves.

Medium; sun; flowers late spring to early summer; well-drained soil

Prune after flowering. Zone 8

Ceratostigma willmottianum ▼

The Chinese plumbago is a deciduous shrub grown for its bright blue flowers and bronze-red autumn foliage. **AGM**

Compact; sun; flowers mid summer to early autumn; well-drained soil

Prune back last season's growth in spring. Zone 7

Cercis canadensis f. *alba* 'Royal White' ▶

This eastern redbud is a deciduous shrub grown for its profuse clusters of large pure white flowers and its bronze-yellow autumn foliage.

Large; sun; flowers late spring to early summer; fertile, well-drained soil

Prune occasionally to maintain habit. Zone 4

Cercis canadensis 'Flame' ▲

This eastern redbud is an upright deciduous shrub or small tree grown for its large double bright pink flowers and bronze-yellow autumn foliage.

Large; sun; flowers late spring to early summer; fertile, well-drained soil

Prune occasionally to maintain habit. Zone 4

Cercis canadensis 'Forest Pansy' ▼▼

This eastern redbud is a broad-spreading deciduous shrub or small tree grown for its rich purple spring foliage, sometimes turning green in hot summers, followed by rich autumn foliage colour, as well as for its rich pink flowers. AGM

Large; sun; flowers late spring to early summer; fertile, well-drained soil

Prune occasionally to maintain habit. Zone 4

Cercis canadensis var. *texensis* 'Oklahoma' ▲

This Texas redbud is a deciduous shrub grown for its profuse rich magenta-red flowers and its glossy green leaves, pink on opening and followed by rich autumn foliage colour.

Large; sun; flowers late spring to early summer; fertile, well-drained soil

Prune occasionally to maintain habit. Zone 4

Cercis canadensis 'Wither's Pink Charm' ▲

This eastern redbud is an upright deciduous shrub with profuse clusters of rich pink flowers and bronze-yellow autumn foliage.

Large; sun; flowers late spring to early summer; fertile, well-drained soil

Prune occasionally to maintain habit. Zone 4

Cercis chinensis ▶

The Chinese redbud is a deciduous shrub grown for its profuse bright lavender-pink flowers and glossy green leaves.

Large; sun; flowers late spring; fertile, well-drained soil

Prune occasionally to maintain habit. Zone 6

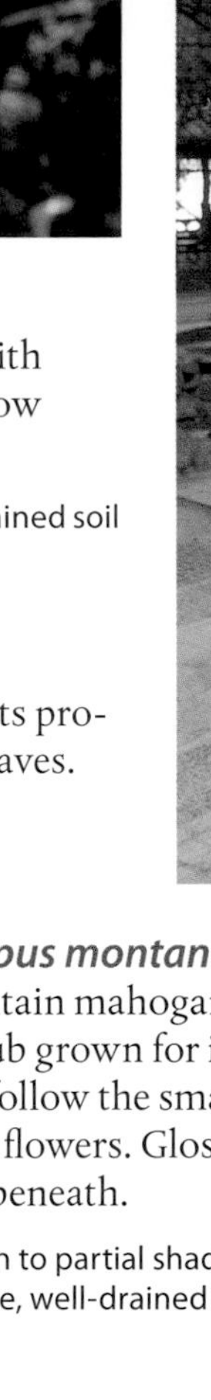

Cercis racemosa ▲

An upright deciduous shrub or small tree with pendulous racemes of pale pink flowers and with light green leaves.

Large; sun; flowers late spring; fertile, well-drained soil

Prune to maintain habit. Zone 7

Cercocarpus montanus ▼

The mountain mahogany is an evergreen shrub grown for its long plumed fruit that follow the small clusters of dull green flowers. Glossy green leaves are felted beneath.

Medium; sun to partial shade; flowers late spring; fertile, well-drained soil

Zone 4

Cestrum ×*cultum* 'Orange Essence' ▲

An upright evergreen shrub with tubular orange flowers.

Small to medium; sun or partial shade; flowers early to mid summer; fertile, well-drained soil

Can be grown in a conservatory in cold climates. Prune in early spring. Zone 9

Chaenomeles cathayensis ▶

A sparsely branched deciduous shrub with long spines grown for its white flowers, flushed with pink, and for its large green fruit that ripens to a yellow.

Large; sun or partial shade; flowers early to mid spring; fertile, well-drained soil.

Can also be trained against a wall. Prune out congested stems. Zone 6

Cestrum fasciculatum ▲

An upright evergreen shrub with clusters of carmine red flowers.

Small to medium; sun or partial shade; flowers late spring; fertile, well-drained soil

Can be grown in a conservatory in cold climates. Prune stems after flowering. Zone 9

Chaenomeles speciosa 'Geisha Girl' ▲

This flowering quince is a thicket-forming deciduous shrub with clusters of double apricot pink flowers. AGM

Medium; sun or partial shade; flowers early to mid spring; fertile, well-drained soil

Can also be trained against a wall. Prune out congested stems. Zone 5

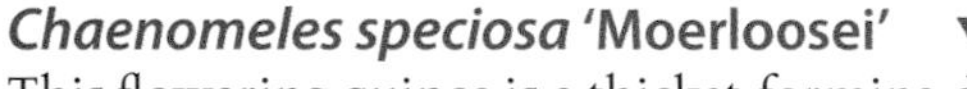

Chaenomeles speciosa 'Moerloosei' ▼

This flowering quince is a thicket-forming deciduous shrub with clusters of white flowers overlaid with pink. AGM

Medium; sun or partial shade; flowers early to mid spring; fertile, well-drained soil

Can also be trained against a wall. Prune out congested stems. Zone 5

Cestrum parqui ▲

An upright deciduous shrub with night-scented greenish yellow tubular flowers. The willowlike leaves have an unattractive smell. AGM

Small to medium; sun or partial shade; flowers early to mid summer; fertile, well-drained soil

Can be grown in a conservatory in cold climates. Prune in early spring. Zone 9

Chaenomeles speciosa 'Nivalis' ▲

This flowering quince is an upright deciduous shrub with large pure white flowers and yellowish green aromatic fruits.

Medium; sun or partial shade; flowers early to mid spring; fertile, well-drained soil

Can be grown as an informal hedge. Prune out congested stems. Zone 5

Chaenomeles speciosa 'Phyllis Moore' ▲

This flowering quince is a thicket-forming deciduous shrub grown for its clusters of double salmon pink flowers.

Medium; sun or partial shade; flowers early to mid spring; fertile, well-drained soil

Can also be trained against a wall. Prune out congested stems. Zone 5

Chaenomeles ×superba 'Coral Sea' ▲

This hybrid quince is a deciduous shrub grown for its large clusters of coral pink flowers followed by green fruit that ripens to a bright yellow.

Small to medium; sun or partial shade; flowers early to mid spring; fertile, well-drained soil

Can also be trained against a wall. Prune out congested stems. Zone 5

Chaenomeles ×superba 'Nicoline' ▶

This hybrid quince is a spreading deciduous shrub grown for its large clusters of bright scarlet red flowers followed by green fruits that ripen a bright yellow. **AGM**

Small to medium; sun or partial shade; flowers early to mid spring; fertile, well-drained soil

Can also be trained against a wall. Prune out congested stems. Zone 5

Chaenomeles ×superba 'Pink Lady' ▲

This hybrid quince is a deciduous shrub grown for its clusters of deep rich pink flowers followed by green fruits that mature a bright yellow. **AGM**

Small to medium; sun or partial shade; flowers early to mid spring; fertile, well-drained soil

Can also be trained against a wall. Prune out congested stems. Zone 5

◀ *Chaenomeles ×superba* 'Pink Lady' on a wall

Chaenomeles ×superba 'Rowallane' ▼▶

This hybrid quince is a deciduous shrub grown for its clusters of large bright red flowers with prominent yellow stamens. The green fruits mature a bright yellow. **AGM**

Medium; sun or partial shade; flowers early to mid spring; fertile, well-drained soil

Can also be trained against a wall. Prune out congested stems. Zone 5

Chimonanthus praecox 'Concolor' ▼

This wintersweet is a deciduous shrub grown for its pendent highly scented lemon yellow flowers and for its leaves that turn a pale, golden yellow in autumn. **AGM**

Medium; sun; flowers mid to late winter; fertile soil

Produces good flowers when planted in a sunny, sheltered site. Prune after flowering where needed. Zone 6

Chamaecytisus ×versicolor ▲

A deciduous shrub grown for its profuse white yellow-hued flowers that have shades of violet-pink.

Compact; sun; flowers late spring to early summer; well-drained soil

Prune immediately after flowering. Zone 6

Chiliotrichum diffusum ▶

An evergreen shrub with showy daisylike white flowers and silvery grey foliage.

Small; sun; flowers mid summer; well-drained soil

Tolerates coastal conditions. Prune in early spring. Zone 8

Chionanthus virginicus ▶▼

The fringe tree is a deciduous shrub or small tree grown for its beautiful dense yet fragile clusters of delicately scented, greenish white flowers. Small blue-black fruits follow, and autumn foliage is golden yellow.

Large; sun; flowers early to midsummer; fertile, neutral to slightly acid soil.

Zone 4

Chimonanthus praecox 'Grandiflorus' ▲

This wintersweet is a deciduous shrub grown for its pendent highly scented yellow flowers that are stained red on the inside. Its leaves turn a pale, golden yellow in autumn. **AGM**

Medium to large; sun; flowers mid to late winter; fertile soil

Produces good flowers when planted in a sunny, sheltered site. Prune after flowering where needed. Zone 6

Chionanthus retusus ▶▶▼▶

The Chinese fringe tree is a deciduous shrub or small tree grown for its beautiful panicles of delicately scented pure white flowers. Small blue-black fruits follow. Autumn foliage is yellow.

Large; sun; flowers early to mid summer; fertile, neutral to acid soil.

Zone 6

Choisya ×dewitteana 'Aztec Pearl' ▲▶

An evergreen shrub grown for its scented clusters of white flowers, pink flushed in bud, and for its aromatic glossy green narrow leaves. **AGM**

Small to medium; sun; flowers late spring, sometimes also in late summer; fertile, well-drained soil

Prune after flowering where needed. Zone 7

Choisya dumosa var. *arizonica* ▲

An evergreen shrub grown for scented clusters of white flowers and aromatic light green leaves.

Small; sun; flowers late spring; fertile, well-drained soil

Zone 8

Choisya ternata Sundance 'Lich' ▲▼

This Mexican orange blossom is an evergreen shrub grown for its aromatic golden yellow leaves and clusters of scented white flowers. **AGM**

Medium; sun; flowers late spring to mid summer; fertile, well-drained soil

Not as free-flowering as the species. Prune after flowering where needed. Zone 8

Cistus ×aguilarii ▼

A short-lived upright evergreen shrub grown for its successional display of large white flowers with a central cluster of yellow stamens, each flower lasting for a day. The large leaves have wavy margins.

Medium; sun; flowers early to mid summer; well-drained soil

Prune where necessary immediately after flowering. Zone 8

Cistus ×argenteus 'Blushing Peggy Sammons' ▲▶

A short-lived evergreen shrub grown for its successional display of large magenta pink flowers with a central white eye and cluster of yellow stamens, each flower lasting for a day.

Small to medium; sun; flowers early to mid summer; well-drained soil

Prune where necessary immediately after flowering. Zone 8

Cistus ×argenteus 'Peggy Sammons' ▲

A short-lived evergreen shrub grown for its successional display of clear pink flowers and soft grey-green leaves. Each flower lasts for a day. **AGM**

Small to medium; sun; flowers early to mid summer; well-drained soil

Prune where necessary immediately after flowering. Zone 8

Cistus ×argenteus 'Silver Pink' ▼

A short-lived evergreen shrub grown for its successional display of large silvery pink flowers and grey-green leaves. Each flower lasts for a day.

Compact; sun; flowers early to mid summer; well-drained soil

Prune where necessary immediately after flowering. Zone 7

Cistus ×canescens ◀

A short-lived evergreen shrub with bright pink flowers and greyish green leaves. Each flower lasts for a day.

Small; sun; flowers early to mid summer; well-drained soil

Zone 8

Cistus ×cyprius ▼

A short-lived evergreen shrub grown for its successional display of large white flowers with a maroon blotch on each petal, and with a central cluster of yellow stamens, each flower lasting for a day. The leaves exude a sticky resin. **AGM**

Medium; sun; flowers early to mid summer; well-drained soil

Zone 7

Cistus ×dansereaui 'Jenkyn Place' ▶

A short-lived evergreen shrub grown for its extended successional display of large white flowers with a prominent maroon blotch on each petal, and with a central cluster of yellow stamens, each flower lasting for a day. The dark green leaves are sticky.

Small; sun; flowers early to mid summer; well-drained soil
Prune where necessary immediately after flowering. Zone 7

Cistus ×dansereaui 'Little Gem' ▲

A short-lived evergreen shrub grown for its successional display of white flowers with a small magenta blotch on each petal and with a central cluster of golden yellow stamens, each flower lasting for a day.

Compact; sun; flowers early to mid summer; well-drained soil
Zone 7

Cistus ladanifer ▲

A short-lived evergreen shrub grown for its successional display of white flowers with a central cluster of golden yellow stamens, each flower lasting for a day. The narrow, dark green leaves are sticky and aromatic. **AGM**

Medium; sun; flowers early to mid summer; well-drained soil
Prune where necessary immediately after flowering. Zone 8

Cistus ladanifer 'Blanche' ▲

A short-lived evergreen shrub is grown for its successional display of white flowers with a central cluster of golden yellow stamens, each flower lasting for a day. The dark green leaves are sticky and aromatic.

Medium; sun; flowers early to mid summer; well-drained soil
Prune where necessary immediately after flowering. Zone 8

Cistus ladanifer 'Paladin' ▼

A short-lived evergreen shrub grown for its successional display of large white flowers with a prominent maroon blotch on each petal and with a central cluster of golden yellow stamens, each flower lasting for a day. The sticky, aromatic leaves are dark green.

Medium; sun; flowers early to mid summer; well-drained soil
Prune where necessary immediately after flowering. Zone 8

Cistus ladanifer var. *sulcatus* ▲

A short-lived low-growing evergreen shrub grown for its successional display of large white flowers with a central cluster of golden yellow stamens and with glossy, sticky, aromatic, dark green leaves. Each flower lasts for a day.

Compact; sun; flowers early to mid summer; well-drained soil
Prune where necessary immediately after flowering. Zone 7

Cistus ×*pulverulentus* 'Sunset' ▼

A short-lived evergreen shrub grown for its successional display of deep magenta pink flowers with a central cluster of yellow stamens and with sage green leaves. Each flower lasts for a day. AGM

Compact; sun; flowers early to mid summer; well-drained soil
Zone 8

Cistus ×*purpureus* 'Betty Taudevin' ▼

A short-lived evergreen shrub grown for its successional display of large rich pink flowers with a maroon basal blotch on each petal and a central cluster of golden yellow stamens, each flower lasting for a day.

Small; sun; flowers early to mid summer; well-drained soil
Prune immediately after flowering. Zone 7

Cistus 'Snow Fire' ▲

A short-lived evergreen shrub grown for its successional display of white flowers with a prominent maroon blotch on each petal and with a central cluster of golden yellow stamens, each flower lasting for a day. AGM

Small; sun; flowers early to mid summer; well-drained soil
Zone 7

Clerodendrum bungei ▼

The glory flower is a suckering deciduous shrub grown for its fragrant deep rosy red flowers and its dark-coloured stems with dark green leaves, sometimes purple-green above.

Medium; sun; flowers late summer to early autumn; fertile, well-drained soil
Suckers freely but may be cut back in early spring. Zone 7

Clerodendrum trichotomum var. *fargesii* ▲▶

A deciduous shrub grown for its fragrant white flowers followed by iridescent blue fruit contained within bright maroon calyces. Foliage is yellow in autumn. **AGM**

Large; sun; flowers late summer to early autumn; fertile, well-drained soil

Suckers can be removed in early spring. Zone 7

Clerodendrum trichotomum var. *fargesii* 'Carnival' ▲

A deciduous shrub grown for its variegated foliage. The heart-shaped grey-green leaves have an irregular lemon yellow margin that pales as the season progresses.

Large; sun; flowers late summer to early autumn; fertile, well-drained soil

To maintain variegation, remove any all-green shoots when they appear. Zone 7

Clethra alnifolia ▼

The sweet pepper bush or nana is a deciduous shrub grown for its racemes of fragrant white or pink flowers and bronze-yellow autumn foliage.

Medium; sun or partial shade; flowers late summer; fertile, acid soil

Zone 4

Clethra barbinervis ▲▼▼

A deciduous shrub grown for its racemes of fragrant white flowers, bronze-yellow autumn foliage, and on older plants, beautiful peeling bark. **AGM**

Medium; sun or partial shade; flowers mid to late summer; fertile, acid soil

Zone 5

Cleyera japonica ▼

The sakaki is an evergreen shrub grown for its glossy, dark green leaves that often turn red in winter and for its small white flowers that have a delicate fragrance.

Medium; sun to partial shade; flowers early to mid summer; fertile soil

Zone 8

Cleyera japonica 'Fortunei' ▼

An evergreen shrub grown for its glossy green leaves with a strong creamy yellow margin. When young, the leaves are rose flushed.

Medium; partial shade; flowers early to mid summer; fertile soil

To maintain variegation, remove any all-green shoots as they appear. Zone 8

Clianthus puniceus ▶

The parrot's beak, glory pea, or lobster claw is an evergreen scandent or sprawling shrub grown for its pendent racemes of vivid scarlet clawlike flowers. AGM

Medium; sun; flowers late spring to early summer; well-drained soil

Needs to be trained against a wall. Flowers earlier when grown as a conservatory plant. Prune after flowering. Zone 8

Clianthus puniceus 'Albus' ▼

This parrot's beak is an evergreen scandent or sprawling shrub grown for its pendent racemes of greenish white clawlike flowers. AGM

Medium; sun; flowers late spring to early summer; well-drained soil

Needs to be trained against a wall. Flowers earlier when grown as a conservatory plant. Prune after flowering. Zone 8

Coleonema album ▲▼

The confetti bush is an evergreen shrub grown for its small clusters of starlike white flowers and its aromatic foliage, bright yellow-green when young.

Small; sun; flowers late spring; fertile, well-drained, acid soil

Can be grown in a container or against a south-facing wall. Prune after flowering. Zone 9

Colletia hystrix ▼▶

A very spiny deciduous shrub grown for its dense clusters of waxy white fragrant tubular flowers.

Medium; sun to partial shade; flowers late summer to early autumn; fertile, well-drained soil

Prune out congested shoots in early spring. Zone 8

Colletia ulicina ▲

A spiny deciduous shrub grown for its clusters of delicate tubular waxy rich pink flowers.

Medium; sun to partial shade; flowers late summer to autumn; fertile, well-drained soil

Zone 8

Colquhounia coccinea ▼

A deciduous shrub grown for its clusters of tubular orange, yellow, or red flowers and for its aromatic grey-green leaves.

Medium; sun; flowers late summer to early autumn; well-drained soil

Even if cut back in cold winters, it will often grow again from the base. Prune back old stems in early spring. Zone 8

Colletia hystrix 'Rosea' ▲

A very spiny deciduous shrub grown for its dense clusters of tubular waxy white flowers, pink in bud.

Medium; sun to partial shade; flowers late summer to early autumn; fertile, well-drained soil

Prune out congested shoots in early spring. Zone 8

Colutea arborescens ▲

The bladder senna is a deciduous shrub grown for its pale green inflated seed pods that turn red and follow small yellow pealike flowers.

Large; sun; flowers early to mid summer; well-drained soil

Zone 5

Colutea ×*media* 'Copper Beauty' ▶

This bladder senna is a deciduous shrub grown for its bright orange pealike flowers followed by reddish copper inflated seed pods.

Medium; sun; flowers early to mid summer; well-drained soil

Zone 6

Convolvulus cneorum ▼▶

The silverbush is an evergreen shrub grown for its funnel-shaped white flowers with delicate shades of pink and its silky, silvery leaves. **AGM**

Compact; sun; flowers late spring to mid summer; free-draining soil

Suitable for the rock garden. Also can be grown in a container. Zone 8

Cordyline australis ◀▲

The cabbage tree is an evergreen tree generally treated as a large shrub. It has swordlike leaves and panicles of scented small white flowers. **AGM**

Large; sun or partial shade; flowers early summer; fertile, well-drained soil

Zone 8

Cordyline australis 'Albertii' ▶

A variegated evergreen shrub grown for its swordlike leaves that have creamy variegated margins and are pink tinged on emergence. **AGM**

Medium to large; sun or partial shade; flowers early summer; fertile, well-drained soil

Not as vigorous growing as the green-leaved form. Zone 9

Cordyline indivisa

The mountain cabbage tree is an evergreen shrub grown for its large broad swordlike green leaves, glaucous on the underside with a reddish central main vein.

Medium to large; sun or partial shade; flowers early summer; fertile, well-drained soil

Requires cool moist conditions to thrive. Zone 10

▼ *Cordyline indivisa* at Mount Stewart in County Down, northern Ireland.

Coriaria pteridoides ▲

A deciduous suckering subshrub grown for its fernlike foliage and shining black fruits.

Compact to small; sun to partial shade; flowers late spring to early summer; fertile, well-drained soil

Cut back old stems to ground level in early spring. Zone 8

Coriaria terminalis var. *xanthocarpa* ▼

A deciduous shrub grown for its translucent yellow fruits on arching stems. Autumn foliage is golden yellow.

Compact; sun or partial shade; flowers early to mid summer; fertile, well-drained soil

Cut back old stems to ground level in early spring. Zone 8

Cornus alba 'Aurea' ▲

A deciduous shrub grown for its foliage, soft yellow when new, turning pale green in summer and strong yellow in autumn. Young stems are dull red in winter. **AGM**

Medium; sun or partial shade; flowers early summer (if plant is not cut back in the spring); fertile soil

Prune hard in early spring to encourage the growth of coloured stems in winter and good foliage size. Zone 4

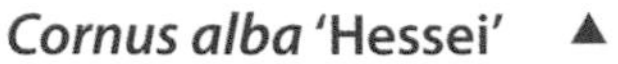

Cornus alba 'Hessei' ▲

A dwarf shrub grown for its congested deep purple shaded leaves, white flowers in dense clusters followed by bluish white fruits, and deep purple-bronze autumn foliage.

Medium; sun; flowers early summer; fertile soil

Slow-growing. Suitable for the rock garden. Zone 4

Cornus alba Ivory Halo 'Bailhalo' ▼

A compact growing deciduous shrub with creamy white variegated foliage and with red young stems in winter.

Small; sun or partial shade; flowers early summer (if stems are not cut back in the spring); fertile soil

Prune hard in early spring to encourage the growth of coloured stems in winter and good foliage size. Zone 4

Cornus alba 'Sibirica' ▲▼

A deciduous shrub grown for its bright coral red young stems during winter preceded by purple-red then bronze autumn foliage.

Medium; sun; flowers early summer (if stems are not cut back in the spring); fertile soil

Prune hard in early spring to encourage the growth of coloured stems in winter. Zone 4

Cornus alternifolia 'Argentea' ▲▶▼

A deciduous shrub grown for its creamy white variegated foliage on crowded horizontal branches with clusters of white flowers. **AGM**

Medium to large; sun or partial shade; flowers early summer; fertile soil

Zone 3

Cornus angustata ▼

An evergreen shrub grown for its creamy white bracts followed by strawberry-like red fruits. The glossy, dark green leaves take on a purplish hue during the winter.

Large; sun or partial shade; flowers mid summer; fertile, preferably acid soil

Zone 8

Cornus alternifolia 'Golden Shadows' ◀

A deciduous shrub grown for its variegated foliage with irregularly shaped golden yellow margins. New growth is pink.

Medium to large; sun or partial shade; flowers early summer; fertile soil

Zone 3

Cornus 'Ascona' ▲

A deciduous shrub grown for its large rounded white bracts on arching branches. Autumn foliage is orange and red.

Large; sun or partial shade; flowers late spring to early summer; fertile, preferably acid soil

Zone 7

Cornus bretschneideri ◄

A deciduous shrub grown for its clusters of creamy white flowers followed by blue-black fruits on pink stalks. The large leaves turn purple then bronze in autumn.

Large; sun or partial shade; flowers early summer; fertile, preferably acid soil

Zone 5

Cornus chinensis ▲▼

A deciduous shrub or small tree grown for its large conspicuously veined greyish green leaves preceded by clusters of yellow flowers.

Large; sun or partial shade; flowers late spring to early summer; fertile soil

Zone 8

▲ *Cornus capitata* at Torosay, Isle of Mull, Scotland.

Cornus capitata

Bentham's cornel is an evergreen shrub or small tree grown for its upward-facing clusters of creamy yellow bracts followed by strawberrylike red fruits. The leaves are greyish green on the underside.

Large; sun or partial shade; flowers early to mid summer; fertile, preferably acid soil

Zone 8

Cornus controversa 'Variegata' ▲◄

A slow-growing deciduous small tree grown for its architectural qualities of the branches which appear in tiers. The variegated leaves are rich creamy yellow on first opening becoming cream coloured then silvery as the season progresses. Clusters of cream-coloured flowers are held above the leaves. **AGM**

Large; sun or partial shade; flowers late spring to early summer; fertile soil

The main growing shoot needs staking to encourage a leader. Zone 5

Cornus 'Eddie's White Wonder' ▲▼

A large deciduous shrub grown for its large white bracts on spreading branches followed by red and orange foliage. AGM

Large; sun or partial shade; flowers late spring to early summer; fertile, preferably acid soil

Zone 5

Cornus florida 'Cherokee Chief' ▲◀

This flowering dogwood is a deciduous shrub or small tree grown for its deep rose pink bracts followed by red autumn foliage. AGM

Large; sun or partial shade; flowers late spring to early summer; fertile, preferably acid soil

Locate where there is good air circulation.
Zone 5

Cornus florida ▲▼▶

The flowering dogwood is a deciduous shrub or small tree grown for its white bracts followed by rich orange and red autumn foliage.

Large; sun or partial shade; flowers late spring to early summer; fertile, preferably acid soil

Locate where there is good air circulation.
Zone 5

Cornus florida 'Daybreak' ▲

This flowering dogwood is a deciduous shrub or small tree grown for its variegated foliage, edged with white but turning pink as the season progresses, together with its white bracts.

Medium to large; sun or partial shade; flowers late spring to early summer; fertile, preferably acid soil

Locate where there is good air circulation. Zone 5

Cornus florida 'Pink Flame' ▶

This flowering dogwood is a deciduous shrub grown for its boldly variegated foliage edged in cream and turning pink as the season progresses. The bracts also are pink.

Large; sun or partial shade; flowers late spring to early summer; fertile, preferably acid soil

Locate where there is good air circulation. Zone 5

Cornus florida 'Rainbow' ▲

This flowering dogwood is a deciduous shrub grown for its variegated foliage, edged in cream yellow and turning pink as the season progresses, becoming entirely red in autumn. The bracts are white.

Medium to large; sun or partial shade; flowers late spring to early summer; fertile, preferably acid soil

Locate where there is good air circulation. Zone 5

Cornus florida f. *rubra* ▼

The pink dogwood is a deciduous shrub or small tree grown for its pink to rose pink bracts followed by red autumn foliage.

Large; sun or partial shade; flowers late spring to early summer; fertile, preferably acid soil

Locate where there is good air circulation. Zone 5

Cornus florida 'Sunset' ◀

This flowering dogwood is a deciduous shrub or small tree grown for its variegated foliage, boldly edged yellow margins but turning pink and red as the season progresses. The bracts are pink.

Large; sun or partial shade; flowers late spring to early summer; fertile, preferably acid soil

Locate where there is good air circulation. Zone 5

Cornus kousa ◀ ▲

The kousa dogwood is a deciduous shrub or small tree grown for its creamy white bracts that turn pink with age, followed by strawberry-like red fruits and deep maroon red autumn foliage. **AGM**

Large; sun or partial shade; flowers early summer; fertile, preferably acid soil

Zone 5

▲ *Cornus kousa* var. *chinensis* 'Wisley Queen' ageing bracts

Cornus kousa var. *chinensis* 'Wisley Queen' ▼ ▼ ▶

This Chinese kousa dogwood is a slow-growing shrub or small tree grown for its creamy white bracts that turn pink with age and are followed by strawberry-like red fruits, deep maroon red autumn foliage, and flaking bark on older trees.

Large; sun or partial shade; flowers early summer; fertile, preferably acid soil

Zone 5

Cornus kousa 'Goldstar' ▲

This kousa dogwood is a deciduous shrub or small tree grown for its variegated foliage with a prominent golden yellow blotch in the centre of the leaf. The blotch turns red during the autumn.

Large; sun or partial shade; flowers early summer; fertile, preferably acid soil

Zone 5

Cornus kousa 'John Slocock' ▼

This kousa dogwood is an upright deciduous shrub or small tree grown for its greenish white pointed bracts, red strawberry-like fruits, and golden brown autumn foliage.

Large; sun or partial shade; flowers early summer; fertile, preferably acid soil

Zone 5

Cornus kousa 'Miss Satomi' ▲

This kousa dogwood is a broad-spreading deciduous grown for its rounded deep rose pink bracts, red strawberry-like fruits, and rich purple-red autumn foliage. AGM

Medium to large; sun or partial shade; flowers early summer; fertile, preferably acid soil

Zone 5

Cornus kousa 'Wolf Eyes' ▶

This kousa dogwood is a broad-spreading shrub grown for its variegated creamy white leaf margins and creamy white bracts.

Medium; sun or partial shade; flowers early summer; fertile, preferably acid soil

Zone 5

Cornus mas ▼

This spreading deciduous shrub is grown for its clusters of yellow flowers, bright red fruits, and deep reddish purple autumn foliage.

Large; sun or partial shade; flowers late winter; fertile soil

Zone 5

Cornus 'Norman Hadden' ▲▼

A large deciduous shrub or small tree grown for its prolific large white bracts that turn a deep pink on arching branches, followed by strawberry-like red fruits and red autumn foliage. **AGM**

Large; sun or partial shade; flowers late spring to early summer; fertile, neutral to acid soil

Zone 7

Cornus mas 'Aureoelegantissima' ▲

A spreading deciduous shrub grown for its variegated foliage with yellow margins that turn pink as the season progresses.

Medium; sun or partial shade; flowers late winter; fertile soil

Zone 5

Cornus mas 'Hillier's Upright' ▼

This form of the cornelian cherry is a deciduous shrub grown for its upright habit, clusters of yellow flowers, bright red fruits, and deep reddish purple autumn foliage.

Large; sun or partial shade; flowers late winter; fertile soil

Zone 5

Cornus nuttallii ▼

The mountain dogwood is a small deciduous tree or large shrub and is grown for its large creamy white bracts that are sometimes tipped green.

Large; sun or partial shade; flowers late spring; fertile, neutral to acid soil

Zone 7

Cornus officinalis ▲▶

The Japanese cornelian cherry is a spreading deciduous shrub grown for its clusters of bright yellow flowers, red fruits, and rich bronze-red autumn foliage.

Large; sun or partial shade; flowers late winter; fertile, neutral to acid soil

Zone 6

Cornus 'Ormonde' ▼▶

A deciduous, initially upright shrub grown for its large rounded white bracts followed by brilliant pinkish red autumn foliage.

Large; sun or partial shade; flowers late spring to early summer; fertile, neutral to acid soil

Zone 7

Cornus 'Porlock' ▲

A large deciduous shrub or small tree grown for its prolific large white bracts that turn a rich deep pink on arching branches, followed by strawberry-like red fruits, and red autumn foliage. AGM

Large; sun or partial shade; flowers late spring to early summer; fertile, neutral to acid soil

Zone 7

▲ *Cornus* 'Porlock' young bracts

▼ *Cornus* 'Porlock' ageing bracts

Cornus Ruth Ellen 'Rutlan' ▼▶

This Stellar Series dogwood is a deciduous shrub or small tree with an upright habit, spreading with age. It is grown for its white bracts and rich bronze autumn foliage.

Large; sun or partial shade; flowers late spring to early summer; fertile, neutral to acid soil

Zone 5

Cornus sanguinea 'Magic Flame' ▼

This common dogwood is a deciduous shrub grown for its winter stems that are generally orange-yellow at the base and glossy red for the top one-third, followed by rich peachy orange autumn foliage.

Small (when grown for coloured stems); sun; flowers early summer (if left unpruned); fertile soil

Prune hard in early spring to encourage the growth of new coloured stems the following winter. Zone 5

Cornus sanguinea 'Anny's Winter Orange' ▼

This form of common dogwood is a deciduous shrub grown for its winter stems that are orange at the base and generally coral red elsewhere. Autumn foliage is orange-yellow.

Small (when grown for coloured stems); sun; flowers early summer (if left unpruned); fertile soil

Prune hard in early spring to encourage the growth of new coloured stems the following winter. Zone 5

Cornus sanguinea 'Compressa' ▲

A dwarf form of the common dogwood grown for its compressed dark green leaves and upright habit.

Compact; sun; flowers early summer; any fertile, well-drained soil

Slow-growing. Suitable for the rock garden. Zone 5

Cornus sanguinea 'Midwinter Fire' ▼

This form of common dogwood is a deciduous shrub grown for its winter stems that are generally a pale orange-yellow at the base and wine red at the top, followed by orange-yellow autumn foliage.

Small (when grown for coloured stems); sun; flowers early summer (if left unpruned); fertile soil

Prune hard in early spring to encourage the growth of new coloured stems the following winter. Zone 5

Cornus sanguinea Winter Flame 'Anny' ◄

This common dogwood is a deciduous shrub grown for its winter stems that are generally bright yellow at the base and red at the top, followed by orange-yellow autumn foliage.

Small (when grown for coloured stems); sun; flowers early summer (if left unpruned); fertile soil

Prune hard in early spring to encourage the growth of new coloured stems the following winter. Zone 5

Cornus sericea 'Flaviramea' ▼

This American dogwood is a deciduous shrub grown for its winter stems that are generally a bright light green. AGM

Medium (when grown for coloured stems); sun; flowers early summer (if left unpruned); fertile soil

Prune hard in early spring to encourage the growth of new coloured stems the following winter. Zone 2

Cornus sericea Kelsey's Gold 'Rosco' ▲

This form of American dogwood is a dwarf deciduous shrub grown for its golden yellow foliage.

Compact (when grown for summer foliage effect); sun; flowers early summer (if left unpruned); fertile soil

Prune hard in early spring to encourage the growth of new stems for summer foliage effect. Zone 2

Cornus sericea 'Hedgerows Gold' ◄

This American dogwood is a deciduous shrub grown for its variegated foliage. The leaf margins start out golden and turn cream as the season progresses.

Medium (when grown for coloured stems); sun; flowers early summer (if left unpruned); fertile soil

Prune hard in early spring to encourage the growth of new coloured stems the following winter. Zone 2

Cornus sericea 'Silver and Gold' ▲

This American dogwood is a deciduous shrub grown for its variegated foliage with white leaf margins.

Medium (when grown for summer foliage effect); sun; flowers early summer (if left unpruned); fertile soil

Prune hard in early spring to encourage the growth of new stems for summer foliage effect. Zone 2

Corokia buddlejoides ▼

The korokio is an evergreen shrub grown for its small starlike yellow flowers, red fruits, and leathery olive green leaves that are silvery grey on the underside.

Medium; sun; flowers late spring; fertile, well-drained soil

Zone 8

Corokia cotoneaster ▼

The wire-netting bush is an evergreen shrub grown for its small starry yellow flowers, tangled mass of wiry stems, and red fruits.

Small to medium; sun; flowers late spring; fertile, well-drained soil

Zone 8

Coronilla valentina subsp. *glauca* ▲

An evergreen shrub grown for its fragrant rich yellow pealike flowers and glaucous blue-green leaves. **AGM**

Small; sun; flowers mid spring; well-drained soil

Prune after flowering to maintain habit. Zone 8

Correa 'Mannii' ▶

An evergreen shrub grown for its pendulous tubular red flowers and small glossy green leaves. **AGM**

Small; sun; flowers spring to autumn; fertile, well-drained, acid soil

Can be grown in a conservatory and will flower in winter. Zone 8

Correa 'Marian's Marvel' ▼

An evergreen shrub grown for its pendulous tubular flowers, pink at the base and yellow-green at the tips, accompanied by small glossy green leaves. **AGM**

Small; sun; flowers spring to autumn; fertile, well-drained, acid soil

Can be grown in a conservatory and will flower in winter. Zone 8

Correa pulchella ▲

The Australian fuchsia is an evergreen shrub grown for its pendulous tubular salmon or almond pink flowers and small matt green leaves. **AGM**

Small; sun; flowers erratically from spring to autumn; fertile, well-drained, acid soil

Can be grown in a conservatory and will flower in winter. Zone 8

Corylopsis coreana ▲

A deciduous shrub grown for its pendent racemes of fragrant primrose yellow flowers and greenish red new leaves that turn green followed by bronze-yellow in autumn.

Medium to large; sun or partial shade; flowers mid spring; fertile, acid to neutral soil

Zone 6

Corylopsis glabrescens ▼

A deciduous shrub grown for its pendent racemes of fragrant primrose yellow flowers and bright yellow autumn foliage.

Medium to large; sun or partial shade; flowers mid spring; fertile, acid to neutral soil

Zone 6

Corylopsis pauciflora ▲◀

The buttercup witch-hazel is a deciduous shrub grown for its short racemes of fragrant pale yellow flowers and small green leaves that have a hint of pink when young and become bronze-yellow in autumn. **AGM**

Small to medium; sun or partial shade; flowers early to mid spring; fertile, acid to neutral soil

Zone 7

Corylopsis sinensis ▲▶▶▼

A deciduous shrub grown for its long pendent racemes of fragrant pale, lemon yellow flowers with yellowish bronze foliage sometimes orange and purple in autumn. **AGM**

Large; sun or partial shade; flowers mid spring; fertile, acid to neutral soil

Zone 6

Corylopsis sinensis var. *sinensis* 'Spring Purple' ▶

A deciduous shrub grown for its rich purple new growth. Otherwise similar to *C. sinensis*.

Medium to large; sun or partial shade; flowers mid spring; fertile, acid to neutral soil

Zone 6

Corylus avellana 'Contorta' ▼

Harry Lauder's walking stick hazel is grown for its twisted spirally arranged stems and yellowish green pendent male catkins.

Large; sun or partial shade; flowers late winter to early spring; fertile soil

Prune out old wood from the centre of the plant to make room for contorted stems to grow. Zone 4

Corylus tibetica ▼

The Tibetan hazel is a deciduous shrub or small tree grown for its brownish pink catkins and clusters of nuts enclosed in burrlike husks.

Large; sun or partial shade; flowers late winter to early spring; fertile soil

Zone 7

Cotinus coggygria Golden Spirit 'Ancot' ▶

A deciduous shrub grown for its yellow foliage that turns a pale, lime green and eventually becomes bronze in autumn.

Medium to large; sun; flowers early to mid summer; fertile, well-drained soil

Prune in early spring to restrict growth. Maintain best yellow foliage by planting in full sun. Zone 7

Cotinus coggygria 'Red Beauty' ▼

A deciduous shrub grown for its purplish red foliage that turns shades of purple, orange, and red in autumn, and for its plumes of pink flowers.

Medium to large; sun; flowers early to mid summer; fertile, well-drained soil

Prune in early spring to restrict growth. Zone 7

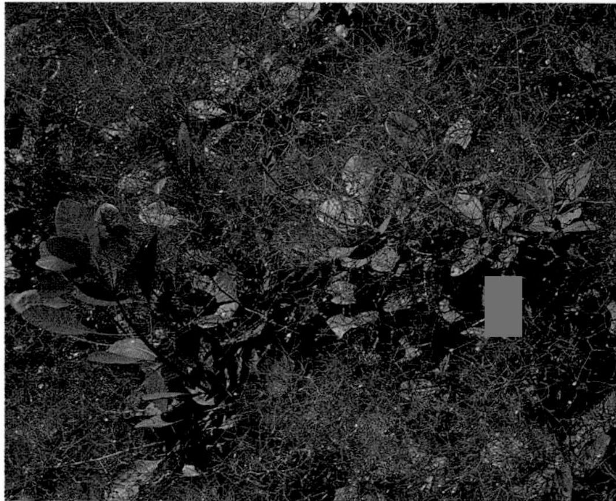

Cotinus coggygria ▲▼

The smoke tree is a deciduous shrub grown for its bright green leaves that turn a rich orange in autumn and for its plumes of bronze-pink flowers that fade to a greyish purple. **AGM**

Medium to large; sun; flowers early to mid summer; fertile, well-drained soil

Prune in early spring to restrict growth. Zone 5

Cotinus coggygria 'Royal Purple' ▲▼

A deciduous shrub grown for its deep purple leaves that turn purple-red in autumn and for its plumes of deep pink-purple flowers. **AGM**

Medium to large; sun; flowers early to mid summer; fertile, well-drained soil

Prune in early spring to restrict growth. Zone 7

Cotinus 'Flame' ▶

A deciduous shrub grown for its green leaves that turn a brilliant orange-red in autumn and for its plumes of pink flowers that fade to greyish pink. **AGM**

Large; sun; flowers early to mid summer; fertile, well-drained soil

Prune in early spring to restrict growth. Zone 7

Cotinus 'Grace' ▲▶▼

A deciduous shrub grown for its large rich purple leaves that turn shades of orange, yellow, purple, and red in autumn, and for its large plumes of greyish purple flowers.

Large; sun; flowers early to mid summer; fertile, well-drained soil

Prune hard periodically in early spring to produce strong vigorous growth. Zone 7

Cotinus obovatus ▲▼

The American smokewood is a deciduous shrub grown for its large green leaves that turn a bright orange in autumn, and for its plumes of greyish pink flowers that fade to purple. **AGM**

Large; sun; flowers early to mid summer; fertile, well-drained soil

Zone 5

Cotoneaster conspicuus 'Decorus' ◀ ▼

An evergreen shrub grown for its masses of small bright red fruits, mat-forming glossy, dark green leaves, and white flowers. **AGM**

Compact to small; sun or partial shade; flowers early summer; fertile soil

Zone 6

Cotoneaster 'Cornubia' ▲

A semievergreen shrub grown for its large bunches of bright red fruits and sprays of milk white flowers.

Large; sun or partial shade; flowers early summer; fertile soil

Zone 6

Cotoneaster 'Coral Burst' ▼

A semievergreen shrub grown for its bunches of bright apricot-coloured fruits.

Medium to large; sun or partial shade; flowers early summer; fertile soil

Zone 5

Cotoneaster 'Exburiensis' ▲

A deciduous shrub grown for its bunches of warm apricot yellow fruits and sprays of milk white flowers.

Large; sun or partial shade; flowers early summer; fertile soil

Zone 6

Cotoneaster frigidus ◀ ▼

A deciduous shrub grown for its large bunches of red fruit and sprays of white flowers.

Large; sun or partial shade; flowers early summer; fertile soil

Zone 7

Cotoneaster frigidus 'St. Monica' ▲

A deciduous shrub grown for its large bunches of red fruits and sprays of milk white flowers.

Large; sun or partial shade; flowers early summer; fertile soil

Zone 6

Cotoneaster induratus ▲

A deciduous shrub grown for its clusters of bright red fruits and white flushed pink flowers.

Small to medium; sun or partial shade; flowers early summer; fertile soil

Zone 6

Cotoneaster horizontalis ▲▼

A deciduous shrub grown for its bright scarlet fruits, orange-red autumn foliage, pale pink flowers, and herring-bone stem arrangement. **AGM**

Prostrate to compact; sun or partial shade; flowers early summer; fertile soil

Can be trained against a wall. Zone 4

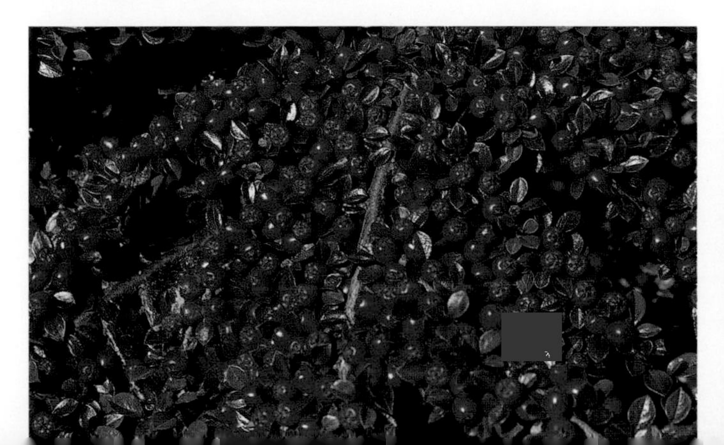

Cotoneaster lacteus ▼

An evergreen shrub grown for its late ripening red fruits and its milky white flowers. **AGM**

Medium to large; sun or partial shade; flowers early summer; fertile soil

Zone 6

▼ *Cotoneaster lacteus* hedge at Cambridge University Botanic Garden, England.

Cotoneaster pluriflorus ▲▼

An evergreen shrub grown for its masses of bright apricot red fruits.

Small; sun or partial shade; flowers early summer; fertile soil
Zone 7

Cotoneaster poluninii ▼

A deciduous shrub grown for its red fruits, grey-green leaves, and pinkish white flowers.

Prostrate; sun or partial shade; flowers early summer; fertile soil
Zone 7

Cotoneaster rehderi ▼

A deciduous shrub grown for its deep red fruits and dark green, deep-veined leaves that turn a rich bronze-yellow in autumn.

Medium to large; sun or partial shade; flowers early summer; fertile soil
Zone 5

Cotoneaster 'Rothschildianus' ▲

A semievergreen shrub grown for its large bunches of creamy yellow fruits and milk white flowers. AGM

Large; sun or partial shade; flowers early summer; fertile soil
Zone 6

Cotoneaster salicifolius 'Fructu Luteo' ▼

An evergreen shrub grown for its bunches of yellow fruits, narrow glossy green leaves, and milky white flowers.

Large; sun or partial shade; flowers early summer; fertile soil
Zone 6

Cotoneaster salicifolius 'Gnom' ▲

A low-growing evergreen shrub grown for its dark green leaves that turn purple-bronze in winter, red fruits, and pinkish white flowers.

Prostrate; sun or partial shade; flowers early summer; fertile soil

Useful for ground cover. Zone 6

Cotoneaster shannanensis ▼

A deciduous shrub grown for its small bright red fruits, pinkish white flowers, and greyish green leaves.

Medium; sun or partial shade; flowers early summer; fertile soil

Zone 6

Cotoneaster shansiensis ►

A deciduous shrub grown for its translucent red fruits and pinkish white flowers.

Medium; sun or partial shade; flowers early summer; fertile soil

Zone 7

Cotoneaster 'Streib's Findling' ▲

An evergreen shrub grown for its prostrate habit, small green leaves, red fruits, and white flowers.

Prostrate; sun or partial shade; flowers early summer; fertile soil

Useful for ground cover. Zone 5

Cotoneaster ×*suecicus* 'Juliette' ▲

A variegated evergreen shrub grown for its coral pink fruits set against creamy variegated foliage.

Compact; sun or partial shade; flowers early summer; fertile soil

Zone 5

Cotoneaster veitchii ▼

A deciduous shrub grown for its bright crimson fruits

Medium to large; sun or partial shade; flowers early summer; fertile soil

Zone 5

Cotoneaster ×watereri 'John Waterer' ◄ ▲

A semievergreen shrub grown for its profuse bunches of bright red fruits and sprays of milk white flowers. AGM

Large; sun or partial shade; flowers early summer; fertile soil

Zone 6

Cotoneaster ×watereri 'Pink Champagne' ◄ ▼

A semievergreen shrub grown for its bunches of yellowish orange fruits and milk white flowers.

Large; sun or partial shade; flowers early summer; fertile soil

Zone 6

Crinodendron hookerianum ▼

The Chile lantern tree is an evergreen shrub grown for its bright carmine red waxy lantern-shaped flowers and narrow dark green leaves. AGM

Large; partial shade; flowers late spring; fertile, acid to neutral soil

Needs a sheltered position. Zone 8

Crinodendron patagua ▼

An evergreen shrub grown for its white bell-shaped flowers held on red petiole stalks and its glossy, dark green leaves.

Large; partial shade; flowers late summer; fertile, acid to neutral soil

Needs a sheltered position. Zone 8

Croton alabamense ▲▶

A deciduous shrub grown for its small yellow flowers and pale green leaves with silvery grey undersides.

Small to medium; sun; flowers early to late spring; fertile, well-drained soil

Zone 7

Cyathodes colensoi ▲

An evergreen shrub grown for its greyish green heatherlike foliage, white flowers, and white or pinkish red fruits.

Prostrate; sun or partial shade; flowers mid spring; fertile, acid soil

Suitable for a rock garden. Zone 7

Cyrilla racemiflora ▼▶

The leatherwood or black titi is a deciduous shrub grown for its racemes of white flowers, leaves that turn orange-red in autumn, and persistent yellowish brown seed capsules.

Small to medium; sun; flowers late summer; fertile, well-drained, neutral to acid soil

Zone 5

Cytisus battandieri ▼

A deciduous shrub with large pineapple-scented yellow flowers and greenish silvery grey new foliage. **AGM**

Large; sun; flowers mid summer; well-drained soil

Can be trained against a south-facing wall. When grown as a free-standing shrub, periodically remove old stems in early spring. Zone 8

Cytisus ×beanii ▲
A floriferous shrub grown for its bright golden yellow pea-like flowers. AGM

Compact; sun; flowers late spring; well-drained soil
Prune one-year-old stems immediately after flowering. Zone 6

Cytisus 'Golden Carpet' ▼
A low-growing shrub grown for its large bright yellow pea-like flowers.

Prostrate; sun; flowers late spring; well-drained soil
Prune immediately after flowering. Zone 5

Cytisus 'Jessica' ▲
A hybrid of the common broom grown for its large bright yellow flowers and red wings.

Small to medium; sun; flowers mid spring; well-drained soil
Prune one-year-old wood immediately after flowering. Zone 6

Cytisus ×kewensis ▼
A floriferous shrub with pale cream-coloured flowers. AGM

Compact; sun; flowers late spring; well-drained soil
Prune one-year-old stems immediately after flowering. Zone 6

Cytisus nigricans ▼
An upright shrub grown for its racemes of yellow flowers.

Small; sun; flowers mid to late summer; well-drained soil
Prune in early spring to maintain habit. Zone 5

Cytisus 'Palette' ▶

A hybrid of the common broom grown for its yellow, pink, and vermillion flowers.

Medium; sun; flowers late spring; well-drained soil

Prune one-year-old wood immediately after flowering. Zone 6

Cytisus ×*praecox* 'Allgold' ▼

A floriferous shrub grown for its pale yellow flowers. **AGM**

Small; sun; flowers mid spring; well-drained soil

Prune one-year-old stems immediately after flowering. Zone 6

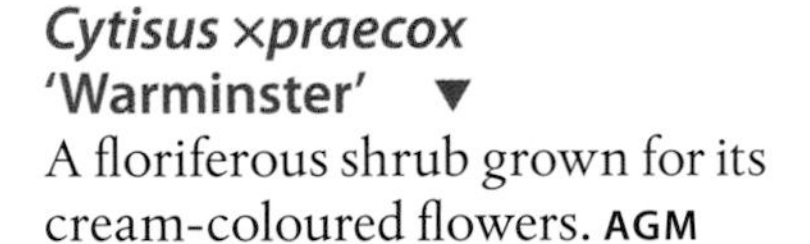

Cytisus ×*praecox* 'Warminster' ▼

A floriferous shrub grown for its cream-coloured flowers. **AGM**

Small; sun; flowers mid spring; well-drained soil

Prune one-year-old stems immediately after flowering. Zone 6

Daboecia cantabrica 'Bicolor' ▼

An evergreen shrub grown for its white, pink, and sometimes striped white and pink, nodding urn-shaped flowers, all seen on the same plant. **AGM**

Compact; sun or partial shade; flowers early summer to mid autumn; fertile, acid soil

Trim back old flowering shoots in spring. Zone 6

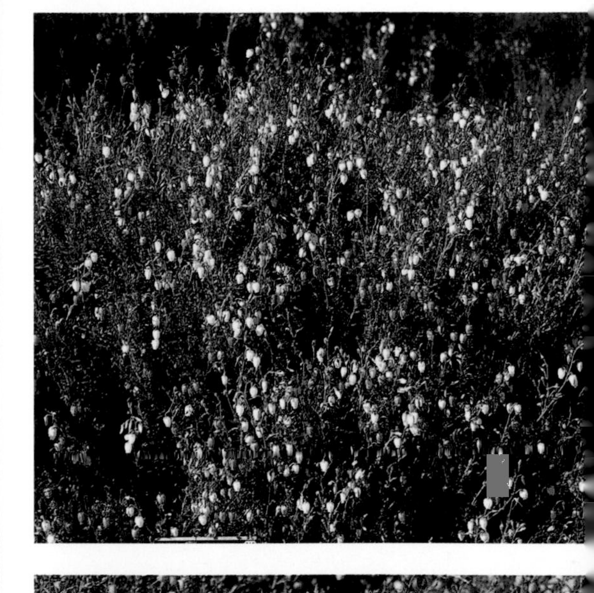

Daboecia cantabrica 'Lilac Osmond' ▲

An evergreen shrub grown for its lilac nodding urn-shaped flowers.

Compact; sun or partial shade; flowers early summer to mid autumn; fertile, acid soil

Trim back old flowering shoots in spring. Zone 6

Daboecia cantabrica subsp. *scotica* 'William Buchanan' ◄

An evergreen shrub grown for its prolific rich purple nodding urn-shaped flowers. **AGM**

Compact; sun or partial shade; flowers early summer to mid-autumn; fertile, acid soil

Trim back old flowering shoots in spring. Zone 6

Daboecia cantabrica 'Snowdrift' ▼

An evergreen shrub grown for its pure white nodding urn-shaped flowers.

Compact; sun or partial shade; flowers early summer to mid-autumn; fertile, acid soil

Trim back old flowering shoots in spring. Zone 6

Daphne albowiana ▼

An evergreen shrub grown for its fragrant soft yellowish green flowers, small fleshy red fruits, and glossy, dark green leaves.

Small; sun or partial shade; flowers mid to late spring; fertile, well-drained soil

Zone 6

Daphne arbuscula ▲

A floriferous small evergreen shrub grown for its beautifully fragrant deep pink (but can also be white to pale pink) flowers and narrow glossy, dark green leaves. **AGM**

Compact; sun or partial shade; flowers early to mid spring; fertile, well-drained soil

Suitable for growing on raised beds. Zone 6

Daphne bholua var. *glacialis* 'Gurkha' ▼

A semievergreen shrub grown for its fragrant pink flowers, purple-pink in bud.

Medium; sun or partial shade; flowers mid to late winter; fertile soil

Zone 7

Danae racemosa ◄

The Alexandrian laurel is a shrubby evergreen woody perennial grown for its arching glossy, light green leaves, and its racemes of tiny cream-coloured flowers followed by yellow fruits that turn orange-red.

Small; sun or shade; flowers early summer; fertile soil

Cut back older shoots in spring. Zone 7

Daphne bholua 'Jacqueline Postill' ▲▶

An evergreen shrub grown for its fragrant purplish pink flowers, mauve-purple in bud, and for its green leaves which can defoliate in hard winters. AGM

Medium; sun or partial shade; flowers mid to late winter; fertile soil

Vigorous-growing. Can be reduced in size by pruning after flowering. Zone 7

Daphne blagayana ▼

A prostrate evergreen shrub grown for its beautifully fragrant creamy white flowers.

Compact; partial shade; flowers early to mid spring; fertile, well-drained soil

Suitable for growing on raised beds. Zone 5

Daphne ×burkwoodii 'Golden Treasure' ▼

A semievergreen shrub grown for its strongly variegated foliage characterized by a bright yellow centre surrounded by a narrow green margin. The richly scented pale pink flowers are deeper pink in bud and as the flowers age.

Small; sun; flowers late spring to early summer; fertile, well-drained soil

Zone 5

Daphne ×burkwoodii 'G. K. Argles' ▲◀

A semievergreen shrub grown for its golden variegated foliage and richly scented pale pink flowers, deeper pink both in bud and as the flowers age. AGM

Small; sun; flowers late spring to early summer; fertile, well-drained soil

Zone 5

Daphne ×burkwoodii 'Somerset' ◄

A semievergreen shrub grown for its beautifully fragrant pink flowers, rosy purple in bud and deeper pink as the flowers age.

Small; sun; flowers late spring to early summer; fertile, well-drained soil

Zone 5

Daphne calcicola 'Sichuan Gold' ▼

An evergreen shrub grown for its golden yellow flowers.

Compact; sun or partial shade; flowers late spring to early summer; fertile, well-drained soil

Suitable for growing on raised beds. Zone 6

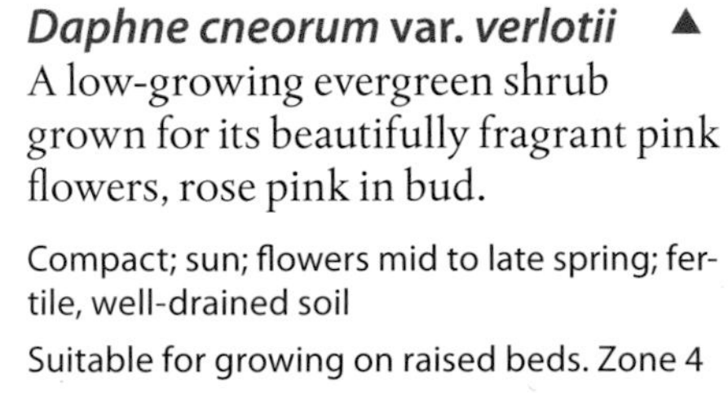

Daphne cneorum var. *verlotii* ▲

A low-growing evergreen shrub grown for its beautifully fragrant pink flowers, rose pink in bud.

Compact; sun; flowers mid to late spring; fertile, well-drained soil

Suitable for growing on raised beds. Zone 4

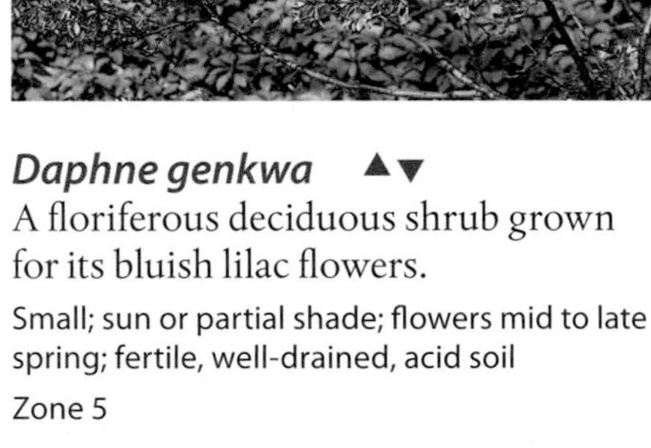

Daphne genkwa ▲▼

A floriferous deciduous shrub grown for its bluish lilac flowers.

Small; sun or partial shade; flowers mid to late spring; fertile, well-drained, acid soil

Zone 5

Daphne cneorum 'Puszta' ◄▲

A floriferous low-growing evergreen shrub grown for its beautifully fragrant deep rose pink flowers, carmine red in bud.

Compact; sun; flowers mid to late spring; fertile, well-drained soil

Suitable for growing on raised beds. Zone 4

Daphne glomerata ▶

A semievergreen suckering shrub grown for its scented creamy white flowers and its glossy green leaves.

Prostrate; sun; flowers early summer; fertile, well-drained soil

Suitable for growing on raised beds. Zone 6

Daphne ×hendersonii 'Jeanette Brickell' ▲

A dwarf evergreen shrub grown for its richly fragrant bright pink flowers, deeper pink in bud, and for its small glossy green leaves.

Compact; sun; flowers late spring; fertile, well-drained soil

Suitable for growing on raised beds. Zone 5

Daphne ×houtteana ▶

A semievergreen shrub grown for its glossy purple foliage (when grown in full sun) and slightly fragrant rose-purple flowers.

Small; sun or partial shade; flowers mid spring; fertile, well-drained soil

Zone 6

Daphne laureola ▶

The spurge laurel is an evergreen shrub grown for its honey-scented lime-green flowers and its glossy green leaves.

Small; shade or partial shade; flowers late winter to early spring; fertile, well-drained soil

Zone 7

Daphne mezereum ◀▲

The mezereon is a deciduous shrub grown for its beautifully fragrant bright magenta flowers and its fleshy red fruits. **AGM**

Small; sun or partial shade; flowers late winter to early spring; fertile, well-drained, preferably alkaline soil

Zone 5

Daphne mezereum f. *alba* ▲

This form of mezereon is a deciduous shrub grown for its beautifully fragrant white flowers and its fleshy yellow fruits.

Small; sun or partial shade; flowers late winter to early spring; fertile, well-drained, preferably alkaline soil

Zone 5

Daphne odora f. *alba* ▲

An evergreen shrub grown for its beautifully fragrant white flowers and its glossy green leaves.

Small; partial shade; flowers late winter to early spring; fertile, well-drained, acid soil

Zone 7

Daphne odora 'Geisha Girl' ▲

A variegated evergreen shrub grown for its pale yellow-and-green leaves and its beautifully fragrant lilac-pink flowers, rose-purple in bud.

Small; partial shade; flowers late winter to early spring; fertile, well-drained soil

Zone 7

Daphne odora ▲

An evergreen shrub grown for its beautifully fragrant lilac-pink flowers, rose-purple in bud, and its glossy green leaves.

Small; partial shade; flowers late winter to early spring; fertile, well-drained, acid soil

Zone 7

Daphne odora 'Walberton' ◄

This variegated evergreen shrub is grown for its glossy green leaves which have a golden yellow margin, and for its beautifully fragrant lilac-pink flowers, rose-purple in bud.

Small; sun; flowers late winter to early spring; fertile, well-drained, acid soil

Zone 7

Daphne petraea 'Grandiflora' ▲

This tiny evergreen shrub is grown for its beautifully fragrant rich rose pink flowers and its small glossy green leaves.

Prostrate; sun; flowers late spring and early summer; fertile, well-drained soil

Suitable for growing on raised beds. Zone 6

Daphne pontica ▼

An evergreen shrub grown for its scented soft yellowish green flowers, its blue-black fruits, and its glossy green leaves. **AGM**

Small; sun or partial shade; flowers mid to late spring; fertile, well-drained soil

Zone 6

Daphne ×*susannae* 'Cheriton' ▲

A slow-growing evergreen shrub grown for its strongly fragrant deep rosy purple flowers and its glossy, dark green leaves.

Compact; sun or partial shade; flowers mid to late spring; fertile, well-drained soil

Suitable for growing on raised beds. Zone 6

Daphne tangutica ▼

An evergreen shrub grown for its richly scented rose-purple flowers, pale lilac within, and its dark green leaves. **AGM**

Small; sun; flowers early to mid spring, sometimes also in late summer; fertile, well-drained, acid soil

Zone 6

Daphne ×*rollsdorfii* 'Arnold Chlorz' ◄

A slow-growing evergreen shrub grown for its strongly fragrant reddish purple flowers and its glossy green leaves.

Compact; sun; flowers late spring to early summer; fertile, well-drained soil

Suitable for growing on raised beds and may require winter protection. Zone 5

Daphniphyllum macropodum ▲▶

An evergreen shrub grown for its striking green foliage borne on a red petiole stalk, glaucous on the underside and pale yellow-green flush when emerging. The pungent male flowers are purple and the female flowers are green.

Large; partial shade; flowers late spring; fertile, preferably acid soil

Prune only when necessary to maintain shape. Zone 6

Decaisnea fargesii ◀▼

A deciduous shrub grown for its architectural foliage that is bluish green when young, for its pendulous racemes of bell-shaped lime-green flowers, and for its metallic blue-black seed pods.

Medium to large; sun or partial shade; flowers late spring to early summer; fertile soil

May be affected by late spring frosts. Zone 5

Dendromecon rigidum ▼

The tree poppy is an evergreen shrub grown for its golden yellow flowers and its bluish green leaves.

Large; sun; flowers early to late summer; fertile soil

Cut back old flowering shoots to the ground in spring. Also grown as a conservatory plant. Zone 9

Desfontainia spinosa ▼

An evergreen shrub grown for its trumpet-shaped scarlet flowers with a yellow mouth and hollylike glossy, dark green leaves. **AGM**

Medium; partial shade; flowers mid summer to early autumn; fertile, acid soil

Plant in a sheltered site. Zone 8

Desmodium callianthum ►

A deciduous shrub grown for its pendulous racemes of lilac-pink flowers.

Small to medium; sun; flowers early to mid summer; fertile, well-drained soil

Remove any shoots damaged by frost in spring. Zone 8

Desmodium elegans ▼

A deciduous shrub grown for its arching stems of rose-lilac pea-shaped flowers and pale glaucous green leaves. AGM

Small to medium; sun; flowers mid summer; fertile, well-drained soil

Remove any shoots damaged by frost in spring. Zone 8

Desmodium sinuatum ▼

A deciduous shrub grown for its racemes of lilac-pink pea-shaped flowers.

Small to medium; sun; flowers mid summer to late summer; fertile, well-drained soil

Remove any shoots damaged by frost in spring. Zone 9

Desmodium yunnanense ▼

A deciduous shrub grown for its racemes of magenta pink flowers and large glaucous green leaves.

Large; sun; flowers late summer; fertile, well-drained soil

Remove any shoots damaged by frost in spring. Zone 9

Deutzia calycosa ▲

A deciduous shrub grown for its arching stems of white flowers that have a central pink tinge.

Medium; sun or partial shade; flowers early summer; fertile soil

Remove older branches after flowering. Zone 6

Deutzia compacta SBEC 604 ▼▶

A deciduous shrub grown for its large clusters of fragrant, pale pink flowers with rounded petals and dark purple filaments. The scent is similar to hawthorn (*Crataegus*).

Small to medium; sun or partial shade; flowers early summer; fertile soil

Remove older branches after flowering. Zone 6

Deutzia coreana ▼

A deciduous shrub grown for its pendent bell-shaped white flowers.

Medium; sun or partial shade; flowers early summer; fertile soil

Remove older branches after flowering. Zone 6

Deutzia discolor ▼

A deciduous shrub grown for its large clusters of lilac-pink to white flowers.

Small to medium; sun or partial shade; flowers early summer; fertile soil

Remove older branches after flowering. Zone 5

Deutzia discolor 'Major' ▶

A deciduous shrub grown for its clusters of white stained pink flowers with a deeper pink on the outside of the petals.

Small to medium; sun or partial shade; flowers early summer; fertile soil

Remove older branches after flowering. Zone 5

Deutzia ×*elegantissima* 'Rosealind' ▼

A deciduous species grown for its clusters of deep carmine-pink flowers. **AGM**

Small; sun or partial shade; flowers early summer; fertile soil

Remove older branches after flowering. Zone 6

Deutzia glomeruliflora ▲

A deciduous shrub grown for its white flowers that have a delicate shade of pink and for the elegant long pointed leaves which are greyish on the underside.

Small to medium; sun or partial shade; flowers early summer; fertile soil

Remove older branches after flowering. Zone 5

Deutzia gracilis ▼

A deciduous shrub grown for its short erect panicles of scented pure white flowers.

Medium; sun or partial shade; flowers early summer; fertile soil

Remove older branches after flowering. Protect from late spring frost. Zone 4

Deutzia ×hybrida 'Strawberry Fields' ▲◄

A floriferous deciduous shrub grown for its clusters of rich mauve-pink flowers, the petals edged in white with deep colours on the outside of the petal and intensifying with age. AGM

Medium; sun or partial shade; flowers early summer; fertile soil

Remove older branches after flowering. Zone 6

Deutzia longifolia ◄

A deciduous shrub grown for clusters of white flowers or pink tinged on arching stems.

Medium; sun or partial shade; flowers early to mid summer; fertile soil

Remove older branches after flowering. Zone 6

Deutzia longifolia var. *farreri* ▲

A deciduous shrub grown for its loose clusters of pure white flowers. AGM

Medium; sun or partial shade; flowers early to mid summer; fertile soil

Remove older branches after flowering. Zone 6

Deutzia longifolia 'Veitchii' ▲▼

A deciduous shrub grown for its clusters of rich lilac tinted pink flowers, rose pink in bud. AGM

Medium; sun or partial shade; flowers early to mid summer; fertile soil

Remove older branches after flowering. Zone 6

Deutzia ×*magnifica* 'Latiflora' ▶

A deciduous shrub grown for its clusters of pure white flowers.

Medium; sun or partial shade; flowers early summer; fertile soil

Remove older branches after flowering. Zone 5

Deutzia ×*magnifica* 'Nancy' ▼

A deciduous shrub grown for its large clusters of double white flowers.

Medium; sun or partial shade; flowers early summer; fertile soil

Remove older branches after flowering. Zone 5

Deutzia monbeigii ▲▼

A deciduous shrub grown for its pure white starlike flowers.

Small; sun or partial shade; flowers early to mid summer; fertile soil

Remove older branches after flowering. Zone 6

Deutzia ningpoensis ▲

A deciduous shrub grown for its panicles of white flowers, pink in bud, and for its narrow grey-green leaves. **AGM**

Medium; sun or partial shade; flowers early summer; fertile soil

Zone 5

Deutzia pulchra ▼

A deciduous shrub grown for its panicles of bell-shaped white flowers.

Medium to large; sun or partial shade; flowers early summer; fertile soil

Remove older branches after flowering. Zone 6

Deutzia purpurascens ▼▼

A scented deciduous shrub grown for its white flushed pink flowers. The outside of each petal has rich purple-magenta lines. *Deutzia purpurascens* Forrest 846 differs from the typical species by having a deeper purple centre surrounding the stamens and paler magenta colour on the back of the petal.

Small to medium; sun or partial shade; flowers early summer; fertile soil

Remove older branches after flowering. Zone 6

▼ *Deutzia purpurascens* Forrest 846

Deutzia scabra 'Codsall Pink' ▼

A deciduous shrub grown for its large honey-scented clusters of double pink flowers, deep pink on the outside and in bud, and for its peeling cinnamon-brown bark.

Medium; sun or partial shade; flowers early to mid summer; fertile soil

Zone 5

Deutzia ×rosea ▲

A floriferous deciduous shrub grown for its clusters of pinkish white flowers, pale pink on the outside. **AGM**

Compact; sun or partial shade; flowers early summer; fertile soil

Zone 5

Deutzia ×rosea 'Carminea' ▶

A floriferous shrub grown for its clusters of pinkish white flowers, carmine pink in bud and on the outside of the petals.

Compact; sun or partial shade; flowers early summer; fertile soil

Zone 5

Deutzia scabra 'Candidissima' ◀▼

A deciduous shrub grown for its large clusters of double pure white flowers and peeling cinnamon brown bark.

Medium; sun or partial shade; flowers early to mid summer; fertile soil

Zone 5

Diervilla sessilifolia ▲

The southern bush honeysuckle is a deciduous shrub grown for its sulphur yellow flowers, copper red new growth, and its bronze autumn foliage.

Small to medium; sun; flowers early to mid summer; fertile soil

Remove excess suckers. Zone 4

Dipelta floribunda ▲▼

A deciduous shrub grown for its profusion of fragrant white flowers flushed pink, yellow throat, and light papery brown peeling bark. AGM

Large; sun; flowers late spring to early summer; fertile soil

Zone 6

Deutzia setchuenensis var. *corymbiflora* ▲►

A floriferous deciduous shrub grown for its large clusters of small starlike pure white flowers. AGM

Small to medium; sun or partial shade; flowers mid to late summer; fertile soil

Zone 7

Dichroa febrifuga ◄

An evergreen shrub grown for its hydrangea-like bright blue to lavender flowers and light green leaves.

Medium; sun to partial shade; flowers late spring; fertile, neutral to slightly acid soil

Can be grown as a conservatory plant. Flowers may be pink when grown in alkaline soil. Zone 9

Dipelta ventricosa ▼

A deciduous shrub grown for its clusters of rich rose flowers with a custard yellow throat.

Medium to large; sun; flowers late spring to early summer; fertile soil

Zone 6

Dipelta yunnanensis ▲

A deciduous shrub grown for its clusters of cream-coloured flowers with a bright yellow throat.

Large; sun; flowers late spring; fertile soil

Zone 6

Disanthus cercidifolius ▶

A deciduous shrub grown for its bluish green leaves that turn shades of maroon purple, scarlet red, and orange during the autumn, preceded by small purple flowers. **AGM**

Medium to large; partial shade; flowers mid autumn; fertile, acid soil

Plant in a sheltered site. Zone 8

Disanthus cercidifolius 'Seiju Yamaguchi' ▲

A deciduous shrub grown for its variegated white mottled bluish green leaves that turn red and orange during autumn.

Medium; partial shade; flowers mid autumn; fertile, acid soil

Plant in a sheltered site. Zone 8

Discaria chacaye ▶

The tortosa is a spiny deciduous shrub grown for its clusters of small fragrant white flowers and small glossy, dark green leaves.

Medium; sun; flowers mid spring to early summer; fertile, well-drained soil

Prune after flowering if necessary to maintain shape. Zone 8

Distylium racemosum ▲

The isu tree is an evergreen shrub grown for its petal-less clusters of bright red stamens and glossy, dark green leaves.

Medium to large; partial shade; flowers mid to late spring; fertile, acid soil

Prune only if required to maintain shape. Zone 8

Dodonaea viscosa 'Purpurea' ▼

The hopbush is an evergreen shrub grown for its brownish purple leaves and its inflated seed capsules that are flushed bronze-red.

Medium; sun; flowers mid summer; fertile, well-drained soil

Grown as a conservtory plant. Zone 9

Drimys lanceolata ▼

The pepper tree is an evergreen shrub grown for its aromatic dark green leaves borne on purple-red side branches, and for its clusters of small greenish white flowers that are pink in bud.

Medium; partial shade; flowers mid to late spring; fertile, acid soil

Prune if necessary after flowering. Zone 8

Drimys latifolia ▼

An evergreen shrub or small tree grown for its clusters of fragrant creamy white flowers, its broad glossy green leaves, glaucous beneath, its black fruits, and its aromatic bark.

Large; partial shade; flowers late spring; fertile, acid soil

Prune if necessary after flowering. Zone 8

Dracophyllum latifolium ▶

The neinei or spiderwood is a slow-growing evergreen shrub grown for its grasslike green leaves that can be a rich reddish purple when young, and followed by clusters of small white flowers.

Medium to large; sun to partial shade; flowers summer; fertile, acid soil

Zone 9

Drimys winteri ▼▶

An evergreen shrub or small tree grown for its clusters of fragrant creamy white flowers, its narrow glossy green leaves which are glaucous white beneath, its black fruits, and its aromatic bark. AGM

Large; partial shade; flowers late spring; fertile, acid soil

Prune if necessary after flowering. Zone 8

Dryas octopetala ▼

The mountain avens is an evergreen mat-forming shrub grown for its white flowers with prominent yellow stamens followed by fluffy seed heads. The dark green leaves are glaucous on the underside. AGM

Prostrate; sun; flowers late spring to early summer; well-drained, neutral to alkaline soil

Zone 2

Echium candicans ▼

The pride of Madeira is an evergreen short-lived shrub with silvery green, lance-shaped foliage and thick spikes of purple flowers.

Small to medium; sun; flowers late spring to mid summer; well-drained soil

Tends to self-seed in temperate climates. Also grown as a conservatory plant. Zone 9

Edgeworthia chrysantha ◀▼

The paper bush is a deciduous shrub with tough, dark green leaves, papery bark, and spherical clusters of scented tubular, yellow flowers that age to creamy white.

Small to medium; sun or partial shade; flowers late spring to early summer; fertile, well-drained soil

Zone 8

Edgeworthia chrysantha 'Grandiflora' ▶

A deciduous shrub with tough, dark green leaves, papery bark, and spherical clusters of large, scented tubular, golden yellow flowers that age creamy white.

Small to medium; sun or partial shade; flowers late spring to early summer; fertile, well-drained soil

Remove suckers from grafted plants. Can be grown in a conservatory. Zone 8

Edgeworthia chrysantha 'Red Dragon' ▲▼

A deciduous shrub with tough, dark green leaves, papery bark, and spherical clusters of scented tubular, orange-red flowers.

Small to medium; sun or partial shade; flowers late spring to early summer; fertile, well-drained soil

Remove suckers from grafted plants. Can be grown in a conservatory. Zone 8

Elaeagnus ×ebbingei ▲

An evergreen shrub bearing leathery dark green leaves with silvery undersides, also highly scented creamy white flowers, followed by orange fruits in spring.

Large; sun or partial shade; flowers early to mid autumn; fertile, well-drained soil

Can be used as an informal hedging plant, including in coastal districts. Zone 6

Elaeagnus ×ebbingei 'Gilt Edge' ▲◀

An evergreen shrub with broad, glossy, dark green leaves edged with yellow, producing small, fragrant, silvery white flowers. AGM

Large; sun or partial shade; flowers early to mid autumn; fertile, well-drained soil

Zone 6

Elaeagnus ×ebbingei 'Limelight' ▲

An evergreen shrub with variegated leaves, dark green surrounding lime-green and yellow centres, and with fragrant creamy white flowers.

Large; sun or partial shade; flowers early to mid autumn; fertile, well-drained soil

To maintain variegation, remove any all-green shoots as they appear. Zone 6

Elaeagnus macrophylla ▼

A fast-growing evergreen shrub bearing broad leaves with a silvery sheen and fragrant, creamy white bell-shaped flowers.

Large; sun or partial shade; flowers early to mid autumn; fertile, well-drained soil

Can be used as a hedging plant. Zone 8

Elaeagnus multiflora ▶

A deciduous or semievergreen shrub bearing dark green leaves with silvery undersides, small fragrant cream flowers, and bright red fruits in summer.

Medium; sun; flowers mid to late spring; fertile, well-drained soil

Can be used as a hedging plant. Zone 6

Elaeagnus pungens 'Frederici' ▼

An evergreen shrub bearing long, narrow, creamy yellow leaves with green edges, small fragrant silvery white flowers, and brown berries (turning to red) in spring.

Medium; sun or partial shade; flowers early to mid autumn; fertile, well-drained soil

To maintain variegation, remove any all-green shoots as they appear. Zone 7

Elaeagnus pungens 'Goldrim' ▼

A bushy, evergreen shrub bearing glossy green leaves narrowly edged with golden yellow, and with small fragrant white flowers in autumn followed by small red berries. AGM

Large; sun or partial shade; flowers early to mid autumn; fertile, well-drained soil

Zone 7

Elaeagnus 'Quicksilver' ▶

A deciduous shrub with silvery grey long and slender leaves and with small fragrant creamy yellow flowers followed by yellow fruits. AGM

Large; sun; flowers early summer; fertile, well-drained soil

Can be used as a hedging plant. Zone 3

Elaeagnus pungens 'Hosuba-fukurin' ▲

An evergreen shrub bearing glossy green leaves edged with yellow and small fragrant white flowers.

Medium; sun or partial shade; flowers early to mid autumn; fertile, well-drained soil

To maintain variegation, remove any all-green shoots as they appear. Zone 7

Elaeagnus pungens 'Maculata ▼

An evergreen shrub bearing attractive, glossy, dark green leaves with a bright golden centre and small fragrant white flowers followed by small orange fruits in spring.

Large; sun or partial shade; flowers early to mid autumn; fertile, well-drained soil

To maintain variegation, remove any all-green shoots as they appear. Zone 7

Elaeagnus ×*reflexa* ▲

A dense and vigorous evergreen shrub with long, dark green leaves that have scaly brown undersides, and with small, fragrant white flowers in autumn.

Large; sun or partial shade; flowers early to mid autumn; fertile, well-drained soil

Can be used as a hedging plant. Zone 7

Elaeagnus thunbergii ETOT 193 ◀

An evergreen shrub with large pale green leaves and fragrant milky white flowers.

Medium to large; sun or partial shade; flowers early autumn to early winter; fertile, well-drained soil

Zone 7

Eleutherococcus divaricatus ▲

A deciduous shrub grown for it clusters of glossy black fruits following small greenish white flowers. Synonym: *Acanthopanax* ×*henryi*.

Large; sun or partial shade; flowers late summer; fertile, well-drained soil

Zone 6

Eleutherococcus lasiogyne ▼

A deciduous shrub grown for its clusters of glossy black fruits following small white flowers. Synonym *Acanthopanax gracistyla*,

Large; sun or partial shade; flowers late summer to autumn; fertile, well-drained soil

Zone 6

Eleutherococcus sieboldianus 'Variegatus' ▶

An elegant, deciduous shrub bearing leaves divided into five lobe-shaped bright green leaflets edged with creamy white. Produces clusters of small white flowers in spring followed by black berries on female plants.

Medium; sun or partial shade; flowers late spring to early summer; fertile, well-drained soil

Plant in a sheltered position. Zone 4

Elliottia racemosa ▲▶

The Georgia plume is a deciduous shrub with elliptic or oval green leaves, turning to bright red in autumn, and four-petalled, white flowers borne in terminal racemes.

Medium; sun or partial shade; flowers late summer to early autumn; fertile, acid soil

Zone 8

Embothrium coccineum ◀▼

The Chilean fire bush is a semievergreen shrub grown for its clusters of orange-red flowers.

Large; sun or partial shade; flowers late spring to early summer; fertile, acid soil

Plant in a sheltered site. Zone 8

Embothrium coccineum Longifolium Group ▲

A selection of Chilean fire bush with longer evergreen leaves and with scarlet flowers.

Large; sun or partial shade; flowers late spring to early summer; fertile, acid soil

Plant in a sheltered site. Zone 8

Enkianthus campanulatus ▲▼

The furin-tsutsuji is a deciduous shrub with a profusion of cup-shaped, cream or red tinged waxy flowers and green foliage, turning to shades of reds, oranges, and yellows in autumn. AGM

Medium; sun or partial shade; flowers late spring; fertile, acid soil

Suitable for woodland conditions. Zone 5

Enkianthus campanulatus f. *albiflorus* ▲▲

A deciduous shrub grown for its creamy white flowers.

Medium; sun or partial shade; flowers late spring; fertile, acid soil

Suitable for woodland conditions. Zone 5

Enkianthus campanulatus var. *palbinii* ▼

A deciduous shrub grown for its deep red, paler within, cup-shaped flowers.

Medium; sun or partial shade; flowers late spring; fertile, acid soil

Suitable for woodland conditions. Zone 5

Enkianthus perulatus ▶▼

A dense and compact deciduous shrub with masses of cup-shaped white flowers and with attractive scarlet autumn foliage. **AGM**

Medium; sun or partial shade; flowers late spring; fertile, acid soil

Suitable for woodland conditions. Zone 6

Epacris paludosa ▲

The alpine heath is an evergreen shrub grown for its clusters of upward-facing tubular white flowers.

Small; sun to partial shade; flowers mid autumn to mid winter; fertile, acid soil

Do not allow soil to dry out if grown in sun. Suitable for the rock garden or conservatory. Zone 9

Epacris impressa var. *ovata* ▶

An evergreen shrub grown for its pendulous tubular bright red flowers.

Compact; sun to partial shade; flowers mid winter to mid spring; fertile, acid soil

Suitable for the rock garden or conservatory. Zone 9

Ephedra andina ▲

An evergreen shrub grown for its rushlike stems and yellow conelike flower clusters followed by fleshy red fruits.

Prostrate; sun; flowers early summer; well-drained soil

Useful for ground cover or in a rock garden or scree. Zone 6

Ephedra gerrardiana var. *sikkimensis* ◀

An evergreen shrub grown for its rushlike stems, yellow conelike flower clusters, and large fleshy red fruits.

Prostrate to compact; sun; flowers early summer; fertile, well-drained soil

Useful for ground cover or on a rock garden. Zone 7

Epigaea gaultherioides ◄

An evergreen shrub grown for its pale rose urn-shaped slightly fragrant flowers.

Prostrate; partial shade; flowers mid spring; fertile, acid soil

Suitable for a rock garden. Zone 4

Erica arborea 'Albert's Gold' ▼▼

An evergreen upright shrub with golden yellow foliage turning green as it matures, and sparse, fragrant, white flowers. AGM

Medium; sun; flowers early spring; fertile, well-drained, acid soil

Hard prune old plants after flowering to reduce size. Zone 8

Erica arborea 'Spring Smile' ▼

An evergreen shrub with light green foliage tipped pinkish yellow in early and mid winter, and with profuse fragrant white flowers. AGM

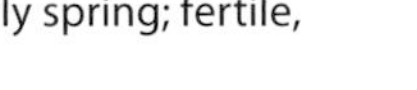

Medium; sun; flowers early spring; fertile, well-drained, acid soil

Hard prune old plants after flowering to reduce size. Zone 8

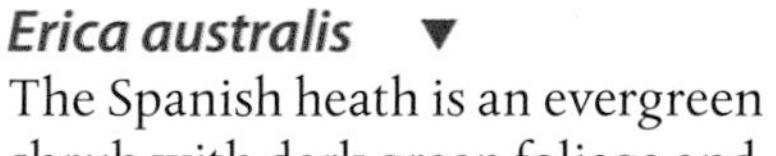

Erica australis ▼

The Spanish heath is an evergreen shrub with dark green foliage and abundant pink-purple flowers. AGM

Small to medium; sun; flowers mid to late spring; fertile, well-drained, acid soil

Hard prune old plants after flowering to reduce size. Zone 9

Erica carnea f. *alba* 'Golden Starlet' ▶

An evergreen shrub with yellow foliage in summer turning lime green in winter and with white flowers. **AGM**

Compact; sun; flowers mid winter to early spring; fertile, well-drained soil

Trim last year's growth after flowering with shears. Zone 5

Erica carnea f. *alba* 'Springwood White'

An evergreen shrub with bright green foliage and abundant pure white flowers. **AGM**

Compact; sun; flowers mid winter to early spring; fertile, well-drained soil

Trim last year's growth after flowering with shears. Zone 5

▼ *Erica carnea* f. *alba* 'Springwood White' at Rowallane Garden in County Down, northern Ireland.

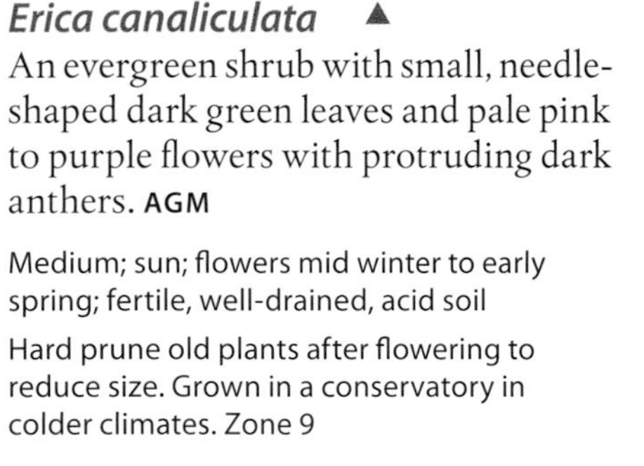

Erica canaliculata ▲

An evergreen shrub with small, needle-shaped dark green leaves and pale pink to purple flowers with protruding dark anthers. **AGM**

Medium; sun; flowers mid winter to early spring; fertile, well-drained, acid soil

Hard prune old plants after flowering to reduce size. Grown in a conservatory in colder climates. Zone 9

Erica carnea

The alpine heath is an evergreen shrub with needle-shaped dark green leaves and long-lasting purple, crimson, pink, and white flowers.

Compact; sun; flowers mid winter to early spring; fertile, well-drained soil

Trim last year's growth after flowering with shears. Zone 5

▼ *Erica carnea* seedlings sown and planted at Windsor Great Park show the range of flower colour.

Erica carnea f. *alba* 'Winter Snow' ▼

An evergreen shrub with bright green foliage and white flowers.

Compact; sun; flowers mid winter to early spring; fertile, well-drained soil

Trim last year's growth after flowering with shears. Zone 5

Erica carnea f. *aureifolia* 'Bell's Extra Special' ►

An evergreen shrub with whisky-coloured foliage flecked with orange and gold, and bearing long-lasting pink-purple flowers.

Compact; sun; flowers late winter to mid spring; fertile, well-drained soil

Trim last year's growth after flowering with shears. Zone 5

Erica carnea f. *aureifolia* 'Foxhollow'

An evergreen shrub with bright yellow foliage tinged red in winter, and with flowers white fading to pink. **AGM**

Prostrate; sun; flowers mid summer to early autumn; fertile, well-drained soil

Trim last year's growth in early spring with shears. Zone 5

▼ *Erica carnea* f. *aureifolia* 'Foxhollow' with purple-flowered *E. cinerea* 'Pentreath' and sparsely mauve-flowered *E. cinerea* f. *aureifolia* 'Apricot Charm'.

Erica carnea 'Challenger' ▼

An evergreen shrub with dark green foliage and abundant pink-magenta flowers. **AGM**

Compact; sun; flowers mid winter to early spring; fertile, well-drained soil

Trim last year's growth after flowering with shears. Zone 5

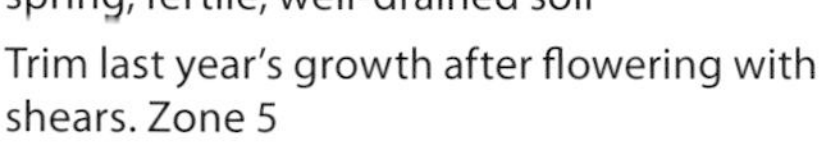

Erica carnea f. *aureifolia* 'Westwood Yellow' ▼

An evergreen shrub with bright yellow foliage and deep pink flowers. **AGM**

Compact; sun; flowers late winter to mid spring; fertile, well-drained soil

Trim last year's growth after flowering with shears. Zone 5

Erica carnea 'Eileen Porter' ▼

An evergreen shrub with dark green foliage and magenta-pink flowers in spring.

Compact; sun; flowers mid winter to mid spring; fertile, well-drained soil

Trim last year's growth after flowering with shears. Zone 5

Erica carnea 'Myretoun Ruby' ▶

An evergreen shrub with deep green foliage and long-lasting, purple through to magenta and crimson flowers. **AGM**

Compact; sun; flowers late winter to mid spring; fertile, well-drained soil

Trim last year's growth after flowering with shears. Zone 5

Erica carnea 'Rosalie' ▼

An evergreen shrub with green-bronze foliage and bright, deep pink flowers. **AGM**

Compact; sun; flowers mid winter to early spring; fertile, well-drained soil

Trim last year's growth after flowering with shears. Zone 5

Erica carnea 'Vivelli' ▼

An evergreen shrub with deep bronze-green foliage and deep purple-pink flowers. **AGM**

Compact; sun; flowers mid winter to early spring; fertile, well-drained soil

Trim last year's growth after flowering with shears. Zone 5

▲ *Erica ciliaris* 'Mrs. C. H. Gill' with lavender-flowered *E. cinerea* 'Hookstone Lavender'

Erica ciliaris 'Mrs. C. H. Gill'

An evergreen shrub with dark green foliage and deep red flowers. **AGM**

Compact; sun; flowers mid summer to early autumn; fertile, well-drained, acid soil

Trim last year's growth in early spring with shears. Zone 7

Erica ciliaris 'Wych' ▶

An evergreen shrub with apple green foliage and large shell pink flowers.

Compact; sun; flowers mid summer to early autumn; fertile, well-drained, acid soil

Trim last year's growth in early spring with shears. Zone 7

▲ *Erica cinerea* in Galloway, Scotland, where sections of moorland are control burned to maintain plant vigour.

Erica cinerea

The bell heather is an evergreen shrub generally seen with red flowers, sometimes with pink or white flowers. **AGM**

Compact; sun; flowers early summer to early autumn; fertile, well-drained, acid soil

Trim back last year's growth in early spring with shears. Zone 5

Erica cinerea f. *aureifolia* 'Ann Berry' ▲

An evergreen shrub with yellow-green foliage tipped bronze and with amethyst flowers.

Compact; sun; flowers early summer to early autumn; fertile, well-drained, acid soil

Trim back last year's growth in early spring with shears. Zone 5

Erica cinerea f. *aureifolia* 'Windlebrooke' ▶

An evergreen, mat-forming shrub with small golden yellow leaves turning red-orange in winter and with pink-purple flowers. **AGM**

Compact; sun; flowers early summer to early autumn; fertile, well-drained, acid soil

Trim back last year's growth in early spring with shears. Zone 5

Erica cinerea 'C. D. Eason' ▲

An evergreen shrub with dark green foliage and long-lasting bright magenta flowers. **AGM**

Compact; sun; flowers early summer to early autumn; fertile, well-drained, acid soil

Trim back last year's growth in early spring with shears. Zone 5

Erica cinerea 'Cevennnes' ▼

An evergreen shrub with green foliage and long-lasting mauve flowers.

Compact; sun; flowers mid summer to early autumn; fertile, well-drained, acid soil

Trim back last year's growth in early spring with shears. Zone 5

▲ *Erica cinerea* 'Hardwick's Rose' at the Royal Horticultural Society's Garden Wisley.

Erica cinerea 'Hardwick's Rose'

An evergreen shrub with dark green foliage and long-lasting magenta flowers.

Compact; sun; flowers early summer to early autumn; fertile, well-drained, acid soil

Trim back last year's growth in early spring with shears. Zone 5

Erica cinerea 'Pentreath' ▼

An evergreen shrub with dark green foliage and long-lasting rich, deep purple flowers. **AGM**

Compact; sun; flowers early summer to early autumn; fertile, well-drained, acid soil

Trim back last year's growth in early spring with shears. Zone 5

Erica cinerea 'Stephen Davis' ▲

An evergreen shrub with green foliage and long-lasting bright pink flowers. **AGM**

Compact; sun; flowers early summer to early autumn; fertile, well-drained, acid soil

Trim back last year's growth in early spring with shears. Zone 5

Erica ×*darleyensis* f. *albiflora* 'Silberschmelze' ◄

An evergreen shrub with green foliage tipped cream in spring and with white flowers.

Compact; sun; flowers early to late winter; fertile, well-drained soil

Trim back last year's growth after flowering with shears. Zone 6

Erica ×*darleyensis* f. *albiflora* 'White Perfection' ▼

An evergreen shrub with bright green foliage tipped yellow in spring and with pure white flowers. **AGM**

Compact; sun; flowers early to late winter; fertile, well-drained soil

Trim back last year's growth after flowering. Zone 6

Erica ×darleyensis 'Arthur Johnson' ▶

An evergreen shrub with green foliage tipped cream in spring and with long racemes of bright lilac-pink flowers.

AGM

Compact; sun; flowers early to late winter; fertile, well-drained soil

Trim back last year's growth after flowering with shears. Zone 6

Erica ×darleyensis 'J. W. Porter' ▼

An evergreen shrub producing dark green foliage tipped with red and cream in spring and bearing bright purplish pink flowers.

Compact; sun; flowers early to late winter; fertile, well-drained soil

Trim back last year's growth after flowering with shears. Zone 6

Erica erigena f. *alba* 'Brian Proudley' ▶

An evergreen shrub with bright green foliage and long-lasting white flowers.

Compact; sun; flowers early to late spring; fertile, well-drained, acid soil

Trim back last year's growth after flowering with shears. Zone 9

Erica erigena f. *alba* 'Nana Compacta' ▼

An evergreen shrub with bright green foliage and white flowers in spring.

Compact; sun; flowers early to late spring; fertile, well-drained, acid soil

Trim back last year's growth after flowering with shears. Zone 9

Erica ×darleyensis 'Kramer's Rote' ▼

An evergreen shrub with dark bronze-green foliage and deep rose-purple flowers.

Compact; sun; flowers early to late winter; fertile, well-drained soil

Trim back last year's growth after flowering with shears. Zone 6

Erica erigena 'Irish Salmon' ▶
An evergreen shrub with dark green foliage and salmon to rose pink flowers.

Compact; sun; flowers early to late spring; fertile, well-drained, acid soil

Trim back last year's growth after flowering with shears. Zone 9

Erica erigena 'Maxima' ▼
An evergreen shrub with dark green foliage and abundant pinky purple flowers.

Compact; sun; flowers early to late spring; fertile, well-drained, acid soil

Trim back last year's growth after flowering with shears. Zone 9

Erica ×griffithsii 'Valerie Griffiths' ▼
A bushy shrub with yellow-golden foliage deepening in colour in winter and with long-lasting pale pink flowers.

Compact; sun; flowers late summer to early autumn; fertile, well-drained, acid soil

Trim back last year's growth in early spring with shears. Zone 6

Erica lusitanica ◀ ▲
The Portuguese heath is an evergreen shrub with woody stems bearing needle-shaped green foliage and clusters of tubular, white, fragrant flowers. **AGM**

Medium; sun; flowers late winter to late spring; fertile, well-drained, acid soil

Old plants can be hard pruned after flowering. Zone 8

Erica lusitanica f. *aureifolia* 'George Hunt' ▼
An upright evergreen shrub with bright yellow foliage throughout the year and pink buds opening to fragrant white flowers.

Medium; sun; flowers late winter to late spring; fertile, well-drained, acid soil

Old plants can be hard pruned after flowering. Zone 8

Erica mackayana f. *eburnea* 'Doctor Ronald Gray' ▲

An evergreen shrub with dark green foliage and white flowers.

Compact; sun; flowers mid summer to early autumn; fertile, well-drained, acid soil

Trim back last year's growth in early spring with shears. Zone 3

Erica ×oldenburgensis 'Ammerland' ▲

An evergreen shrub producing shiny green foliage tipped orange in spring and bearing soft pink flowers.

Small; sun; flowers early to late spring; fertile, well-drained, acid soil

Trim back last year's growth after flowering with shears. Zone 6

Erica scoparia ▶

The besom heath is an evergreen shrub with greenish yellow flowers displaying prominent brown anthers.

Medium; sun; flowers late spring to early summer; fertile, well-drained, acid soil

Trim back last year's growth after flowering with shears. Zone 9

Erica spiculifolia ▼

The spike heath is an evergreen shrub with bright green foliage and short racemes of pale pink flowers.

Compact; sun; flowers early summer; fertile, well-drained, acid soil

Trim back last year's growth after flowering with shears. Zone 9

Erica ×stuartii 'Connemara' ▼

An evergreen shrub with bright green foliage and bright pink flowers.

Compact; sun; flowers late summer; fertile, well-drained, acid soil

Trim back last year's growth in early spring with shears. Zone 9

Erica tetralix f. *alba* ▲

The cross-leaved heath is an evergreen shrub with greenish grey foliage and dense heads of white flowers.

Compact; sun; flowers mid summer to early autumn; fertile, well-drained, acid soil

Trim back last year's growth in early spring with shears. Zone 3

Erica vagans f. *aureifolia* 'Valerie Proudley' ▲

An evergreen shrub with yellow-golden foliage and sparse white flowers. **AGM**

Compact; sun; flowers mid summer to early autumn; fertile, well-drained, acid soil

Trim back last year's growth in early spring with shears. Zone 5

Erica vagans f. *alba* 'Diana's Gold'

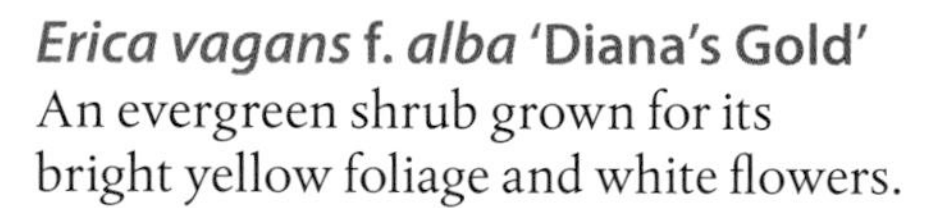

An evergreen shrub grown for its bright yellow foliage and white flowers.

Compact; sun; flowers mid summer to early autumn; fertile, well-drained, acid soil

Trim back last year's growth in early spring with shears. Zone 5

▶ *Erica vagans* f. *alba* 'Diana's Gold' with rosy pink-flowered *E. cinerea* 'Joseph Rock'.

Erica vagans f. *alba* 'White Giant'

An evergreen shrub grown for its large spikes of white flowers that age a golden brown. **AGM**

Compact; sun; flowers mid summer to early autumn; fertile, well-drained, acid soil

Trim back last year's growth in early spring with shears. Zone 5

▼ *Erica vagans* f. *alba* 'White Giant' in winter.

Erica vagans 'Charm' ▶

An evergreen shrub grown for its spikes of white flowers that age a golden brown.

Compact; sun; flowers mid summer to early autumn; fertile, well-drained, acid soil

Trim back last year's growth in early spring with shears. Zone 5

Erica vagans 'Hookstone Rose' ▼

An evergreen shrub with green foliage and bright pink flowers that age a golden brown.

Compact; sun; flowers mid summer to early autumn; fertile, well-drained, acid soil

Trim back last year's growth in early spring with shears. Zone 5

Erica ×watsonii ▲

An evergreen shrub grown for its long-lasting rose pink flowers and yellow new foliage growth.

Compact; sun; flowers mid summer to early autumn; fertile, well-drained, acid soil

Trim back last year's growth in early spring with shears. Zone 5

Erica ×veitchii 'Exeter' ▲

An evergreen shrub with bright green foliage and plenty of sweetly scented white flowers. **AGM**

Medium; sun; flowers mid to late spring; fertile, well-drained, acid soil

Old plants can be hard pruned after flowering. Zone 8

Erinacea anthyllis ▲▶

The hedgehog broom or branch thorn is a rounded evergreen shrub with spiny, green foliage and violet-blue flowers. **AGM**

Compact; sun; flowers mid to late spring; well-drained soil

Suitable for the rock garden or scree. Zone 8

Eriobotrya japonica ◄▼

The loquat is an evergreen shrub with big, leathery, deep green leaves that have pale brown, furry undersides. It produces small fragrant white flowers and orange, edible fruits. **AGM**

Large; sun or partial shade; flowers late autumn to early spring; fertile, well-drained soil

Thrives when grown against a south- or west-facing wall. Zone 7

Erythrina crista-galli ◄

The coral tree is a deciduous shrub or tree with irregular, spiny branches and large terminal racemes of deep red flowers.

Large; sun or partial shade; flowers early to mid summer; fertile, well-drained soil

Cut last season's growth down to ground level or on a short stem in early spring to encourage vigorous growth. Zone 9

▼ *Escallonia* can be grown as a hedge in maritime districts and should be pruned immediately after flowering.

Escallonia 'Apple Blossom' ▲

A slow-growing, compact, evergreen shrub displaying glossy, dark green foliage and pale pink flowers with white centres. **AGM**

Small to medium; sun to partial shade; flowers early to mid summer; well-drained soil

Useful as a hedge. Tolerates coastal conditions. Prune immediately after flowering. Zone 8

Escallonia 'C. F. Ball' ▼

An evergreen shrub with aromatic large dark green leaves and deep red flowers.

Medium; sun to partial shade; flowers early to mid summer; well-drained soil

Useful as a hedge. Tolerates coastal conditions. Prune immediately after flowering. Zone 8

Escallonia 'Donard Radiance' ▲

An evergreen shrub with glossy, dark green leaves and deep rose pink chalice-shaped flowers. **AGM**

Medium; sun to partial shade; flowers early to mid summer; well-drained soil

Useful as a hedge. Tolerates coastal conditions. Prune immediately after flowering. Zone 8

Escallonia 'Donard Seedling' ▼

An evergreen shrub with glossy, rounded deep green leaves and white flowers, pink in bud. **AGM**

Medium; sun to partial shade; flowers early to mid summer; well-drained soil

Useful as a hedge. Tolerates coastal conditions. Prune immediately after flowering. Zone 8

Escallonia 'Iveyi' ►

A rounded evergreen shrub with glossy green foliage and large panicles of fragrant white flowers. **AGM**

Medium to large; sun to partial shade; flowers mid summer; well-drained soil

Useful as a hedge. Tolerates coastal conditions. Prune immediately after flowering. Zone 8

Escallonia laevis 'Gold Brian' ▼

An evergreen shrub with bright yellow-golden foliage turning green as it matures and rose-red flowers.

Small to medium; sun to partial shade; flowers mid summer; well-drained soil

Useful as a hedge. Tolerates coastal conditions. Prune immediately after flowering. Zone 8

Escallonia 'Saint Keverne' ▼

An evergreen shrub with small leaves on arching stems and a profusion of large pink flowers in summer. **AGM**

Medium; sun to partial shade; flowers early to mid summer; well-drained soil

Useful as a hedge. Tolerates coastal conditions. Prune immediately after flowering. Zone 8

Escallonia 'Slieve Donard' ▲

A compact evergreen shrub with glossy green foliage and abundant long-lasting panicles of shell pink flowers.

Medium; sun to partial shade; flowers early to mid summer; well-drained soil

Useful as a hedge. Tolerates coastal conditions. Prune immediately after flowering. Zone 8

Eucryphia cordifolia ◄▲

The roble de Chile is an elegant evergreen shrub bearing ivory-white flowers with a prominent boss of stamens and glossy, dark green leaves that are grey and downy on the underside.

Large; sun to partial shade; flowers late summer to early autumn; fertile, well-drained, acid soil

Zone 9

Eucryphia glutinosa ◄

The nirrhe is a deciduous shrub with green pinnate leaves that turn a rich russet brown in autumn, and white flowers that can often be double when raised from seed. **AGM**

Large; sun to partial shade; flowers mid to late summer; fertile, well-drained, acid soil

Zone 8

Eucryphia ×*intermedia* ▲

An evergreen shrub or small tree with dark green simple and pinnate leaves and with delicately scented, white flowers.

Large; sun to partial shade; flowers late summer to early autumn; fertile, well-drained, acid soil

Zone 7

Eucryphia ×*intermedia* 'Rostrevor' ▼

An upright evergreen shrub or small tree with glossy, dark green simple and pinnate leaves and with delicately fragrant white flowers bearing prominent yellow stamens. **AGM**

Large; sun to partial shade; flowers late summer to early autumn; fertile, well-drained, acid soil

Zone 7

Eucryphia lucida 'Pink Cloud' ▲

This leatherwood is an upright evergreen shrub with dark green, glossy foliage and pale pink flowers that age white with a crimson centre.

Large; sun to partial shade; flowers early to mid summer; fertile, well-drained, acid soil

Zone 8

Eucryphia milliganii ▼

An evergreen upright slow-growing shrub with glossy, dark green leaves and small white cup-shaped flowers.

Small; sun to partial shade; flowers mid summer; fertile, well-drained, acid soil

Zone 8

Eucryphia moorei ▼

The pinkwood is an evergreen shrub bearing bright green pinnate leaves and white cup-shaped flowers on bright red stalks.

Medium to large; sun to partial shade; flowers late summer; fertile, well-drained, acid soil

Zone 10

Eucryphia ×nymansensis 'Nymansay' ▲▼

An upright evergreen shrub with glossy, dark green leaves and abundant, white flowers with prominent yellow stamens. **AGM**

Large; sun to partial shade; flowers late summer to early autumn; fertile, well-drained soil

More lime-tolerant than other Eucryphia species. Zone 8

Euonymus alatus ◀▼

The winged spindle tree is a deciduous shrub with many ridged branches bearing dark green foliage that turns brilliant fiery red in autumn, and small, insignificant green flowers. **AGM**

Medium; sun or partial shade; flowers early summer; fertile soil, but best in alkaline soils

Can be pruned as a hedge in early spring. Zone 3

Euonymus carnosus ▼

A deciduous shrub grown for its vibrant red autumn foliage and its pink fruits with orange- or red-coated seeds.

Medium to large; sun or partial shade; flowers late summer; fertile soil, but best in alkaline soils

Zone 8

Euonymus alatus 'Compactus' ▼

A dense, compact shrub with prominent, corky ridges on its branches and bright fiery red foliage in autumn. **AGM**

Small; sun or partial shade; flowers early summer; fertile soil, but best in alkaline soils

Can be pruned as a hedge in early spring. Zone 3

Euonymus cornutus var. *quinquecornutus* ▲▼

A semievergreen shrub with narrow green leaves, delicate pink-red flowers, and unusually shaped pink fruits with five horns and bright orange-red seed coats.

Small to medium; sun or partial shade; flowers early summer; fertile soil, but best in alkaline soils

Zone 9

Euonymus europaeus f. *albus* ▲

This spindle tree is a deciduous shrub with leaves that turn deep red in autumn and masses of milky white seed capsules that split open to reveal orange-coated seeds.

Large; sun or partial shade; flowers early summer; fertile soil, but best in alkaline soils

Self-fertile but best fruit seen when planted in a group. Zone 3

Euonymus europaeus 'Atropurpureus' ▼

This spindle tree is a deciduous shrub with dull purple leaves turning brilliant red in autumn and rose-red seed capsules and bright orange-coated seeds.

Large; sun or partial shade; flowers early summer; fertile soil, but best in alkaline soils

Zone 3

Euonymus europaeus 'Fructu-coccineo' ▶

The spindle tree is a deciduous shrub with leaves that turn red in autumn and with bright red seed capsules that reveal orange-coated seeds.

Large; sun or partial shade; flowers early summer; fertile soil, but best in alkaline soils

Best fruit seen when planted in a group. Zone 3

Euonymus europaeus 'Red Cascade' ▶

A deciduous shrub with scalloped, dark green leaves turning deep red in autumn and masses of rose-red seed capsules that split open, bearing bright orange-coated seeds. AGM

Large; sun or partial shade; flowers early summer; fertile soil, but best in alkaline soils

Self-fertile but best fruit seen when planted in a group. Zone 3

Euonymus fortunei Blondy 'Interbolwi' ▲▼

An evergreen shrub with variegated leaves that have dark green margins and large bright yellow centres. AGM

Small; sun or partial shade; flowers early summer; fertile soil

Suitable for ground cover. Zone 5

Euonymus fortunei 'Silver Queen' ▶

An evergreen shrub with variegated green leaves that open a rich creamy yellow and mature to a green centre with attractive creamy white margins.

Small to medium; sun or partial shade; flowers early summer; fertile soil

To maintain variegation, remove any all-green shoots as they appear.
Zone 5

Euonymus fortunei 'Sunshine' ▼▼

An attractive evergreen shrub with striking variegated foliage, green in the centre with bright yellow margins.

Small; sun or partial shade; flowers early summer; fertile soil

Zone 5

Euonymus grandiflorus ▼

A semievergreen shrub with deep reddish purple autumn foliage that appears very late in the season and straw-coloured flowers.

Large; partial shade; flowers early summer; fertile soil

Zone 9

Euonymus grandiflorus subsp. *morrisonensis* ETOT 57 ▼▶

A semievergreen shrub grown for its reddish purple autumn foliage and masses of straw-coloured flowers. **AGM**

Large; sun or partial shade; flowers early summer; fertile soil

Zone 9

Euonymus hamiltonianus var. *maackii* ▶
A deciduous shrub with vibrant red autumn foliage and red seed capsules containing red-coated seeds. **AGM**

Large; sun or partial shade; flowers early summer; fertile soil
Zone 4

Euonymus japonicus ▼
An evergreen shrub with green leaves and yellowish green young growth.

Large; sun or shade; flowers early summer; fertile soil
Readily pruned into a hedge. Prune during early spring. Zone 7

Euonymus japonicus 'Chollipo' ◀▼
An evergreen shrub bearing variegated leaves with a deep green centre and a broad cream margin. **AGM**

Large; sun or partial shade; flowers early summer; fertile soil
Zone 7

Euonymus myrianthus ▼
A slow-growing evergreen shrub with leathery bright green leaves and attractive orange fruit.

Large; sun or partial shade; flowers early summer; fertile soil
Zone 9

Euonymus nanus var. *turkestanicus* ▶

An erect, semievergreen shrub producing long, thin, bright green leaves and small golden flowers followed by bright pink fruit with red seed.

Compact; sun or partial shade; flowers early summer; fertile soil

Zone 2

Euonymus oxyphyllus ▼

A deciduous shrub with rich red to purple autumn foliage complemented by carmine red capsules containing orange-red coated seed.

Medium to large; sun or partial shade; flowers early summer; fertile soil

Zone 5

Euonymus phellomanus ▼

A deciduous shrub with young stems marked by conspicuous corky margins and with bright red fruit containing seed coated orange-red. **AGM**

Large; sun or partial shade; flowers early summer; fertile soil

Zone 5

Euonymus planipes ▼

A handsome deciduous shrub with red autumn foliage and abundant purple-red fruit that split to reveal orange seeds. **AGM**

Large; sun or partial shade; flowers early summer; fertile soil

Zone 4

Euonymus planipes 'Sancho' ▼

A deciduous shrub grown for its vibrant red autumn foliage and purple-red fruit that split to reveal orange-coated seeds.

Medium to large; sun or partial shade; flowers early summer; fertile soil

Zone 4

Euonymus vagans Lancaster 551 ▲

An evergreen shrub with broad glossy green leaves and pale greenish brown flowers that lie flat over the leaf surface.

Prostrate; sun or partial shade; flowers early summer; fertile soil

Useful for ground cover. Zone 6

Euphorbia amygdaloides 'Craigieburn' ▲

An evergreen woody perennial with dark maroon foliage and lime-green flowers.

Compact; sun to shade; flowers early to late spring; fertile, well-drained soil

Useful for ground cover in shade. Zone 7

Euphorbia amygdaloides 'Purpurea' ▼

An evergreen woody perennial with whorled purple-brown foliage and acid lime-green flowers.

Compact; sun to shade; flowers early to late spring; fertile, well-drained soil

Useful for ground cover in shade. Zone 7

Euphorbia amygdaloides var. *robbiae* ▼

An evergreen woody perennial with glossy, bright green foliage and upright spikes of lime-green flowers. **AGM**

Compact; sun to shade; flowers early to late spring; fertile, well-drained soil

Useful for ground cover in shade. Zone 7

Euphorbia amygdaloides var. *robbiae* 'Blue Dragon' ▲

An evergreen woody perennial with dark blue-green leaves with yellowish green flowers.

Small; sun to partial shade; flowers mid spring to early summer; fertile, well-drained soil

Useful for ground cover. Zone 7

Euphorbia characias Silver Swan 'Wilcott' ▼

An elegant evergreen woody perennial with variegated blue-green foliage edged with white and with green-striped white flowers.

Compact to small; sun or partial shade; flowers late spring to mid summer; fertile, well-drained soil

Prune out old flower stems the following spring, avoiding sap. Zone 8

Euphorbia characias subsp. *wulfenii* 'John Tomlinson' ▼▶

A robust, upright evergreen woody perennial with blue-green foliage and large, bright lime-yellow flowers. **AGM**

Compact to small; sun to partial shade; flowers late spring to mid summer; fertile, well-drained soil

Prune out old flower stems the following early spring. Zone 7

Euphorbia characias subsp. *wulfenii* 'Lambrook Gold' ◀

An evergreen woody perennial with blue-green foliage and tall heads of chartreuse-yellow trumpet-shaped flowers. **AGM**

Compact to small; sun or partial shade; flowers late spring to mid summer; fertile, well-drained soil

Prune out old flower stems the following early spring, avoiding sap. Zone 7

Euphorbia characias subsp. *wulfenii* 'Purple and Gold' ▲

An evergreen woody perennial grown for its greenish purple foliage and yellow flowers.

Compact to small; sun or partial shade; flowers late spring to mid summer; fertile, well-drained soil

Prune out old flower stems the following spring. Zone 7

Euphorbia ×*martinii* ▼

An evergreen subshrub bearing rosettes of narrow grey-green leaves and sprays of greenish yellow flowers with reddish purple eyes that often turn reddish pink. **AGM**

Compact; sun to partial shade; flowers mid spring to early summer; fertile, well-drained soil

Zone 7

Euphorbia mellifera ▶

An erect evergreen shrub producing narrow, green leaves with cream midribs and reddish brown tinted, honey scented flowers.

Small to medium; sun to partial shade; flowers late spring; fertile, well-drained soil

Zone 9

Euphorbia rigida ▼

An evergreen plant with narrow, pointed bluish grey-green leaves and bright yellow flowers. **AGM**

Compact; sun to partial shade; flowers late winter to late spring; well-drained soil

Prune out old flowering stems the following early spring, avoiding sap. Zone 8

Euphorbia stygiana ▼▶

An evergreen shrub producing bright green leaves with a conspicuous white midrib and grey undersides, the leaves becoming bright red with age. Flowers are green.

Compact to small; sun to partial shade; flowers mid spring to early summer; fertile, well-drained soil

Can be pruned in early spring to control size. Zone 9

Euryops acraeus ▲▼

An evergreen subshrub with silver-grey foliage and an abundance of bright yellow daisy-shaped flowers. **AGM**

Compact; sun; flowers late spring to early summer; fertile, well-drained, neutral to acid soil

Can survive in hot, dry situations. Best grown on a raised bed or rock garden. Zone 8

Euryops candollei

An evergreen subshrub with bright yellow flowers and apple green foliage.

Compact; sun; flowers mid summer; fertile, well-drained, neutral to acid soil

Best grown on a raised bed or rock garden. Zone 8

▼ *Euryops candollei* at Drakensburg, South Africa.

Euryops pectinatus ▼▼

An evergreen shrub with lobed grey-green leaves and bright yellow daisylike flowers. AGM

Small; sun; flowers late spring to mid summer; fertile, well-drained soil

Zone 9

Euscaphis japonica ▲▼

A deciduous shrub with yellowish green flowers and bright red fruit containing shiny blue-black seeds.

Large; sun or partial shade; flowers mid to late spring; fertile, well-drained soil

Can also be grown as a tree. Drought tolerant. Needs a hot summer to produce seeds. Zone 7

Exochorda giraldii var. *wilsonii* ▲

A hardy upright deciduous shrub with mid-green foliage and paper white flowers.

Medium to large; sun or partial shade; flowers mid to late spring; fertile soil

May become chlorotic on chalky soils. Zone 5

Exochorda ×*macrantha* 'The Bride' ▼▶

A deciduous shrub with arching branches bearing abundant racemes of small, pure white flowers whose petals fall like confetti. AGM

Medium to large; sun or partial shade; flowers mid to late spring; fertile, well-drained soil

May become chlorotic on alkaline soils. Prune immediately after flowering to control size. Zone 5

Fabiana imbricata f. *violacea* ▶▲

This form of pichi is an evergreen shrub with soft, needlelike bright green foliage and striking tubular lavender flowers. AGM

Small; sun; flowers early summer; fertile, well-drained soil

Zone 8

Fallugia paradoxa ▲

The Apache plume is a showy shrub with finely cut grey-green foliage, white, roselike flowers, and feathery pink seed heads after flowering.

Medium; sun; flowers mid summer; well-drained soil

Zone 8

Fascicularia bicolor ▲

A woody perennial herb with rosettes of long, leathery, narrow sage-green leaves, brownish on the undersides and red in the centre of the rosette. Flowers sky blue.

Compact; sun or partial shade; flowers mid summer; well-drained soil
Suitable on a raised bed or rock garden. Zone 8

Fatsia japonica ▼

The Japanese fatsia is an evergreen shrub with large, glossy green palmate leaves and clusters of creamy white flowers followed by green fruit that turn black. **AGM**

Medium; sun or partial shade; flowers early to mid autumn; fertile soil
Zone 7

Fatsia japonica 'Spider's Web' ▼

A rare form of the Japanese fatsia bearing variegated, shiny green palmate leaves with attractive white speckling. Clusters of white flowers are followed by black fruit.

Medium; partial shade; flowers early to mid autumn; fertile soil
Zone 8

Ficus pumila

The creeping fig is a climbing, woody evergreen. In its juvenile phase it spreads over surfaces while in its adult phase it has leathery green foliage with green fruit that ripen to a purplish green. **AGM**

Prostrate; sun or shade; flowers early to mid autumn; fertile soil
Can be grown as an epiphyte in its juvenile phase. Zone 9

▼ *Ficus pumila* at Isola Madre gardens, Lake Maggiore, Italy.

Fontanesia phillyreoides subsp. *fortunei* ◄

A deciduous shrub with narrow green foliage and racemes of greenish white flowers.

Medium; sun or partial shade; flowers mid summer; fertile soil
Zone 6

Forsythia 'Beatrix Farrand' ▲
A dense, upright deciduous shrub that is covered in large bright yellow bell-shaped flowers.

Medium to large; sun or partial shade; flowers early to mid spring; fertile soil

Produces flowers more freely in full sun. Prune out old stems after flowering. Zone 5

Forsythia 'Golden Nugget' ▼
A vigorous, bushy deciduous shrub with toothed, green foliage and masses of large, golden yellow trumpet-shaped flowers.

Medium to large; sun or partial shade; flowers early to mid spring; fertile soil

Produces flowers more freely in full sun. Prune out old stems after flowering. Zone 5

Forsythia ×intermedia 'Karl Sax' ▶
A dense and vigorous upright deciduous shrub with an abundance of deep canary yellow flowers.

Medium to large; sun or partial shade; flowers early to mid spring; fertile soil

Produces flowers more freely in full sun. Prune out old stems after flowering. Zone 5

Forsythia ×intermedia 'Lynwood Variety' ▼
A vigorous, deciduous shrub with upright branches, ovate leaves with toothed edges, and an abundance of large rich golden yellow flowers. AGM

Medium to large; sun or partial shade; flowers early to mid spring; fertile soil

Produces flowers more freely in full sun. Prune out old stems after flowering. Zone 5

Forsythia ×intermedia Minigold 'Flojor' ▼
A compact deciduous shrub with a profusion of golden flowers.

Medium; sun or partial shade; flowers early to mid spring; fertile soil

Produces flowers more freely in full sun. Prune out old stems after flowering. Zone 5

Forsythia ×intermedia 'Spectabilis' ▼▶

A showy and vigorous, deciduous shrub with an abundance of comparatively large, deep yellow flowers.

Medium to large; sun or partial shade; flowers early to mid spring; fertile soil

Produces flowers more freely in full sun. Prune out old stems after flowering. Zone 5

Forsythia ×intermedia 'Spring Glory' ▼

A deciduous shrub with attractive, upright branches and abundant pale yellow flowers along dark brown branches.

Medium to large; sun or partial shade; flowers early to mid spring; fertile soil

Produces flowers more freely in full sun. Prune out old stems after flowering. Zone 5

Forsythia ×intermedia Week-End 'Courtalyn' ▲

A deciduous compact forsythia with upright, arching branches and a profusion of rich yellow flowers. **AGM**

Small; sun or partial shade; flowers early to mid spring; fertile soil

Produces flowers more freely in full sun. Prune out old stems periodically after flowering. Zone 5

Forsythia mandschurica ▼▶

An upright deciduous shrub with bright yellow flowers.

Medium; sun or partial shade; flowers early spring; fertile soil

Produces flowers more freely in full sun. Prune out old stems after flowering. Zone 5

Forsythia ovata ▲

The Korean forsythia has a dense, bushy habit, ovate, dark green leaves, and bright yellow flowers.

Small; sun or partial shade; flowers early spring; fertile soil

Produces flowers more freely in full sun. Prune out old stems after flowering. Zone 5

Forsythia suspensa ▼

Golden bells is a rambling, deciduous shrub with trailing branches bearing broad, mid-green leaves and yellow flowers in spring.

Medium to large; sun or partial shade; flowers early to mid spring; fertile soil

Produces flowers more freely in full sun. Prune out old stems after flowering. Can be trained against a wall or cascading over a bank. Zone 5

Forsythia suspensa 'Nymans' ▶

This weeping forsythia or golden bells is a deciduous shrub with pendulous dark purple branches and large, pale yellow flowers.

Medium to large; sun or partial shade; flowers early to mid spring; fertile soil

Produces flowers more freely in full sun. Prune out old stems after flowering. Can be trained against a wall or cascading over a bank. Zone 5

Forsythia viridissima var. *koreana*

A deciduous species grown for its yellow flowers and golden brown autumn foliage.

Medium; sun or partial shade; flowers late spring; fertile soil

Produces flowers more freely in full sun. Prune out old stems after flowering. Zone 5

▼ *Forsythia viridissima* var. *koreana* in the wild with *Rhododendron mucronulatum*

Forsythia viridissima var. *koreana* 'Hgwang' ▼

A deciduous species grown for its variegated pale yellow leaves with a small central green area, its golden-brown autumn foliage, and its yellow flowers.

Medium; sun or partial shade; flowers late spring; fertile soil

To maintain variegation, remove any all-green shoots as they appear. Zone 6

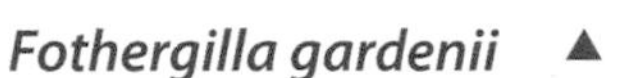

Fothergilla gardenii ▲

The witch alder is a pretty, deciduous shrub with brush-shaped white flower clusters and excellent autumn foliage. The leaves turn all shades of yellow, orange, red, and burgundy.

Small; sun or partial shade; flowers mid to late spring; fertile, acid soil

Produces best flowers in full sun. Zone 5

Fothergilla major ▼▶▶

An upright deciduous shrub with white flowers before the leaves emerge and with excellent multicoloured autumn foliage like the other fothergillas. **AGM**

Medium; sun or partial shade; flowers mid to late spring; fertile, acid soil

Flowers more freely in full sun. Zone 5

Fothergilla major Monticola Group ▲

An upright shrub with showy, white bottle-brush flowers in spring and leaves that are green on both sides, turning red, orange, and yellow in autumn.

Medium; sun or partial shade; flowers mid to late spring; fertile, acid soil

Zone 5

Franklinia alatamaha ▲▼

The Franklin tree is a deciduous shrub with large green leaves turning crimson in autumn. It has large, fragrant, cup-shaped white flowers which are seen at the same time as the leaves are turning colour.

Medium to large; sun or partial shade; flowers late summer to early autumn; fertile, acid soil

Needs a hot summer to flower freely. Zone 5

Fremontodendron 'California Glory' ▲▼

This flannel bush is an attractive, semi-evergreen shrub with rounded, three-lobed deep green leaves and large, long-lasting yellow flowers. **AGM**

Large; full sun; flowers early to mid summer; well-drained, neutral soil

Grows well against a wall. Tiny dustlike golden yellow hairs on the foliage are a skin irritant. Zone 9

Fuchsia 'Baby Blue Eyes' ▲

A deciduous, hardy fuchsia bearing flowers with red sepals and bluish lilac petals, followed by decorative fruit. **AGM**

Small; sun or partial shade; flowers mid summer to early autumn; fertile, well-drained soil

Cut back old stems in spring once new growth has started. Plant in a sheltered site. Zone 8

Fuchsia 'Blue Bush' ▶

A deciduous hardy shrub with flowers bearing rose-red sepals and mauve-blue petals.

Small; sun or partial shade; flowers mid summer to early autumn; fertile, well-drained soil

Cut back old stems in spring once new growth has started. Plant in a protected site. Zone 8

Fuchsia 'Charming' ▶

An attractive, upright deciduous bush bearing drooping flowers with reflexed, red sepals and pinkish purple petals beneath.

Small; sun or partial shade; flowers mid summer to early autumn; fertile, well-drained soil

Cut back old stems in spring once new growth has started. Plant in a protected site. Zone 9

Fuchsia 'Flocon de Neige' ▲

A deciduous shrub displaying flowers with red sepals and single white petals.

Small; sun or partial shade; flowers mid summer to early autumn; fertile, well-drained soil

Cut back old stems in spring once new growth has started. Plant in a sheltered site. Zone 9

Fuchsia 'Globosa' ▲

A deciduous fuchsia bearing plenty of flowers with bright red sepals and single purple petals.

Small; sun or partial shade; flowers mid summer to early autumn; fertile, well-drained soil

Cut back old stems in spring once new growth has started. Plant in a sheltered site. Zone 9

Fuchsia 'Lady Boothby' ▶

A vigorous, "climbing," deciduous fuchsia shrub bearing abundant flowers with bright pinkish red sepals and deep purple petals beneath.

Small to medium; sun or partial shade; flowers mid summer to early autumn; fertile, well-drained soil

Cut back old stems in spring once new growth has started. Plant in a sheltered site. Zone 9

Fuchsia magellanica var. *gracilis* ▼

A deciduous shrub with profuse pendent flowers marked by bright magenta sepals and dark purple petals. **AGM**

Medium; sun or partial shade; flowers mid summer to early autumn; fertile, well-drained soil

Cut back old stems in spring once new growth has started. Plant in a sheltered site. Zone 7

Fuchsia magellanica var. *gracilis* 'Variegata' ▼

An attractive deciduous shrub with variegated leaves, pale green edged in cream. The sparse pendent flowers have bright magenta sepals and dark purple petals. **AGM**

Medium; sun or partial shade; flowers mid summer to early autumn; fertile, well-drained soil

Cut back old stems in spring once new growth has started. Plant in a sheltered site. Zone 7

Fuchsia regia subsp. *reitzii* ▲

A vigorous, climbing deciduous shrub with bright red sepals and dark purple petals.

Large; sun or partial shade; flowers mid summer to early autumn; fertile, well-drained soil

Grown as a conservatory plant. Zone 10

Fuchsia 'Riccartonii' ▼

A versatile deciduous shrub of arching stems covered with an abundance of slender flowers. The sepals are bright red and the petals purple. AGM

Large; sun or partial shade; flowers mid summer to early autumn; fertile, well-drained soil

Cut back old stems in spring once new growth has started. Plant in a sheltered site. Zone 7

Fuchsia 'Saturnus' ▶

A versatile deciduous shrub bearing long-lasting flowers with bright red sepals and lilac-purple petals.

Small; sun or partial shade; flowers mid summer to early autumn; fertile, well-drained soil

Cut back old stems in spring once new growth has started. Plant in a sheltered site. Zone 8

Fuchsia 'Wharfedale' ▼

A deciduous attractive bushy shrub grown for its flowers with reflexed, white to palest pink sepals and bright cerise pink petals. AGM

Small; sun or partial shade; flowers mid summer to early autumn; fertile, well-drained soil

Cut back old stems in spring once new growth has started. Plant in a sheltered site. Zone 9

Garrya elliptica ▼▲

The catkin bush is an evergreen shrub grown for its long greyish green male catkins and greyish green leaves.

Large; sun or partial shade or shade; flowers mid to late winter; fertile, well-drained soil

Can be grown as a free-standing shrub or on a north-facing wall. Tolerates coastal conditions. Zone 7

Garrya ×issaquahensis 'Glasnevin Wine' ▼

An evergreen shrub with wine red male catkins and glossy green leaves.

Medium to large; sun or partial shade; flowers mid to late winter; fertile, well-drained soil

Can be grown as a free-standing shrub or on a west-facing wall. Tolerates coastal conditions. Zone 8

Gaultheria depressa var. *nova-zealandii* ▲

An evergreen shrub grown for its white to deep pink fleshy fruits, small white bell-shaped flowers, and its small dark green leaves which are deep red in winter and spring.

Prostrate; sun to partial shade; flowers late spring to early summer; fertile, acid soil

Grown on a raised bed. Zone 9

Gaultheria forrestii ▼

An evergreen shrub grown for its racemes of delicately fragrant white flowers followed by fleshy blue fruits.

Small; partial shade; flowers late spring to early summer; fertile, acid soil

Suitable for a woodland or shaded rock garden. Zone 6

Garrya ×issaqualiensis 'Pat Ballard' ▼

A floriferous evergreen shrub grown for its long green male catkins tinged with red and for its green leaves.

Large; sun or partial shade or shade; flowers mid to late winter; fertile, well-drained soil

Can be grown as a free-standing shrub or on a north-facing wall. Tolerates coastal conditions. Zone 8

Gaultheria fragrantissima HWJCM 149 ◀

An evergreen shrub grown for its pendulous fragrant racemes of yellowish white flowers followed by fleshy blue fruits. A form collected in Nepal can be white turning to pale blue.

Medium; partial shade; flowers late spring to early summer; fertile, acid soil

Suitable for a woodland or shaded rock garden. Zone 8

Gaultheria hookeri ▲

An evergreen shrub grown for its dense racemes of pinkish white flowers followed by fleshy blue fruits.

Compact to small; partial shade; flowers late spring; fertile, acid soil

Suitable for a woodland or shaded rock garden. Zone 6

Gaultheria itoana ▼

An evergreen shrub grown for its clusters of white flowers and brown-red fruits.

Prostrate; partial shade; flowers late spring; fertile, acid soil

Suitable for a woodland or shaded rock garden. Zone 6

Gaultheria miqueliana ▼

An evergreen shrub grown for its short racemes of white flowers followed by white flushed pink fruit. Foliage is a glossy green.

Compact; partial shade; flowers early summer; fertile, acid soil

Suitable for a woodland or shaded rock garden. Zone 6

Gaultheria mucronata 'Cherry Ripe' ▲

An evergreen shrub grown for its bright cherry red fruits preceded by small white flowers. Other cultivars of the species produce white, lilac, purple, or red fruits. **AGM**

Compact; sun or partial shade; flowers late spring to early summer; fertile, acid soil

To ensure fruiting, plant in groups and include male plants for pollination. Zone 6

Gaultheria semi-infera ◄

An evergreen shrub grown for its indigo blue fruit which follow short racemes of white often flushed pink flowers.

Small; partial shade; flowers late spring to early summer; fertile, acid soil

Suitable for a woodland or shaded rock garden. Zone 8

Gaultheria shallon ▼

The shallon is an evergreen shrub grown for its bold foliage and its pendulous racemes of white flowers flushed with pink.

Small; partial shade; flowers late spring to early summer; fertile, acid soil

Used as ground cover. Zone 5

Gaultheria trichophylla ▼

An evergreen shrub with iridescent fleshy blue fruits preceded by pinkish white flowers.

Prostrate to compact; partial shade; flowers late spring; fertile, acid soil

Grown on a shaded raised bed or rock garden. Zone 8

Gaultheria ×*wisleyensis* ▲

An evergreen shrub with clusters of white or pinkish white flowers and ruby-red to oxblood-red fruit.

Small; sun or partial shade; flowers late spring summer; fertile, acid soil

Zone 6

Gaylussacia brachysera ▶

The box huckleberry is an evergreen shrub grown for its racemes of white tinged with red flowers.

Compact; partial shade; flowers late spring to early summer; fertile, acid soil

Suitable for the rock garden. Zone 5

Genista aetnensis ▶

The Mount Etna broom is a deciduous shrub with loose racemes of fragrant golden yellow flowers. AGM

Large; sun; flowers mid to late summer; well-drained soil

Zone 8

Genista canariensis ▼

An evergreen shrub grown for its masses of bright golden yellow flowers.

Medium; sun; flowers late spring to early summer; well-drained soil

Prune after flowering. Zone 9

Genista hispanica ▲

The Spanish gorse is a deciduous shrub with masses of golden yellow flowers.

Compact; sun; flowers late spring to early summer; well-drained soil

Prune after flowering. Zone 6

Genista lydia ▼

A deciduous shrub with arching stems grown for its masses of golden yellow flowers. **AGM**

Prostrate to compact; sun; flowers late spring to early summer; well-drained soil

Can be used to clothe a low wall. Prune after flowering. Zone 7

Genista 'Porlock' ▼

A semievergreen shrub grown for its masses of fragrant butter yellow flowers. **AGM**

Large; sun; flowers early to mid spring; well-drained soil

Will flower in winter if grown in a conservatory. Prune after flowering. Zone 9

Gevuina avellana ▼

The Chilean hazelnut is an evergreen shrub or small tree grown for its glossy green pinnate leaves, which are rusty red as they unfurl, with ivory white flowers followed by red fruits that ripen black.

Large; partial shade and shade; flowers mid summer; fertile, well-drained soil

Can be grown in a woodland garden. Zone 8

Grevillea 'Canberra Gem' ▲▼

An evergreen shrub with aromatic foliage and spiderlike pink/red flowers. **AGM**

Medium; sun; flowers early spring to mid summer; well-drained, acid, phosphorus-deficient soil

Prune to reduce plant size after main flush of flowers. Zone 8

Grevillea juniperina 'Sulphurea' ▲▶

An evergreen shrub grown for its cluster of light yellow flowers.

Medium; sun; flowers early spring to mid summer; well-drained, acid, phosphorus-deficient soil

Prune to reduce plant size after main flush of flowers. Zone 9

Grindelia chiloensis ▼

The cabrera or gum weed is an evergreen subshrub grown for its large cornflower-like bright yellow flowers. The stems and leaves are covered with resinous glands.

Small; sun; flowers early to late summer; well-drained soil

Suitable for the rock garden or scree. Zone 6

Griselinia littoralis ▲▼

The kapuka is an evergreen shrub grown for its glossy apple green foliage. **AGM**

Large; sun to partial shade; flowers late spring; fertile, well-drained soil

Useful as a hedging plant, especially in coastal areas. Prune in early spring when planted as a hedge or to restrict size. Zone 8

Griselinia littoralis 'Dixon's Cream' ◀

This kapuka is an evergreen shrub grown for its creamy white and pale green variegated leaves.

Large; sun to partial shade; flowers late spring; fertile, well-drained soil

Prune in early to mid spring to restrict size. Zone 9

Hakea lissosperma ▼

The needlebush is a tall, upright evergreen shrub with scented greyish green needle-shaped leaves and white flowers.

Large; sun; flowers mid to late spring; well-drained, acid soil

Zone 8

Halesia diptera Magniflora Group ▲▼

The large-flowered silverbell is a deciduous shrub or small tree with toothed mid-green leaves and clusters of large, white, bell-shaped flowers.

Large; sun or partial shade; flowers late spring; fertile, acid soil

Zone 6

Halesia monticola ▼

A highly attractive deciduous shrub or small tree, the mountain silverbell has a profusion of white, bell-shaped flowers and greyish green leaves that turn yellow in autumn.

Large; sun or partial shade; flowers late spring; fertile, acid soil

Zone 6

Halesia monticola 'Silver Splash' ▼

A deciduous shrub bearing variegated leaves with splashes of white and cream, and plenty of white bell-shaped flowers.

Medium to large; sun or partial shade; flowers late spring; fertile, acid soil

Zone 7

Halesia monticola var. *vestita* ▲

A deciduous shrub with large hanging, bell-shaped flowers that are sometimes tinged with pink especially in bud, and are followed by wing-shaped fruits. AGM

Large; sun or partial shade; flowers late spring; fertile, acid soil
Zone 5

×*Halimiocistus* 'Ingwersenii' ▲

A short-lived evergreen spreading shrub with dense dark green leaves and saucer-shaped bright white flowers with a boss of yellow anthers, each flower lasting for a day but seen over a long period. AGM

Compact; sun; flowers late spring to mid summer; well-drained soil
Suitable for the rock garden. Prune lightly after flowering. Zone 8

×*Halimiocistus sahucii* ▶

A short-lived evergreen, spreading shrub bearing narrow, dark green leaves and plenty of bright white flowers with yellow anthers, each flower lasting for a day but seen over a long period. AGM

Compact; sun; flowers late spring to mid summer; well-drained soil

Suitable for the rock garden. Prune lightly after flowering. Zone 8

×*Halimiocistus wintonensis* ▼

A short-lived evergreen shrub bearing fuzzy, grey-green leaves and white saucer-shaped flowers with a dark maroon and yellow centre, each flower lasting for a day but seen over a long period. AGM

Compact; sun; flowers late spring to mid summer; well-drained soil
Suitable for the rock garden. Prune lightly after flowering. Zone 8

×*Halimiocistus wintonensis* 'Merrist Wood Cream' ▼

A short-lived evergreen shrub producing fuzzy, grey-green leaves and cream-coloured saucer-shaped flowers with a dark maroon and yellow centre, each flower lasting for a day but seen over a long period. AGM

Compact; sun; flowers late spring to mid summer; well-drained soil
Suitable for the rock garden. Prune lightly after flowering. Zone 8

Halimium atriplicifolium ▲
A short-lived evergreen shrub with saucer-shaped, plain, bright yellow flowers and silvery grey-green foliage, each flower lasting for a day but seen over a long period.

Medium; sun; flowers late spring to early summer; well-drained soil
Suitable for the rock garden. Prune lightly after flowering. Zone 8

Halimium calycinum ▼
A short-lived spreading, evergreen shrub with abundant yellow flowers, pink in bud, and narrow, linear mid-green leaves, each flower lasting for a day but seen over a long period.

Compact; sun; flowers early summer; well-drained soil
Suitable for the rock garden. Prune lightly after flowering. Zone 8

Halimium lasianthium 'Concolor' ▶
A short-lived spreading evergreen shrub with grey-green leaves and golden yellow flowers, each flower lasting for a day but seen over a long period.

Compact; sun; flowers late spring to early summer; well-drained soil
Suitable for the rock garden. Prune lightly after flowering. Zone 8

Halimium lasianthium subsp. *formosum* ▼
A short-lived handsome, low-spreading shrub bearing grey-green leaves and bright yellow flowers with maroon markings at the base of each petal, each flower lasting for a day but seen over a long period.

Compact; sun; flowers late spring to early summer; well-drained soil
Suitable for the rock garden. Prune lightly after flowering. Zone 8

Halimium ocymoides ▼
A short-lived evergreen shrub with small grey-green leaves and attractive saucer-shaped yellow flowers having dark brownish markings at the base of each petal, each flower lasting for a day but seen over a long period. AGM

Compact; sun; flowers early to mid summer; well-drained soil
Suitable for the rock garden. Prune lightly after flowering. Zone 8

Halimium ×pauanum ▶
A short-lived upright evergreen shrub with clear buttercup yellow flowers and greyish green leaves, each flower lasting for a day but seen over a long period.

Small to medium; sun; flowers late spring to early summer; well-drained soil

Suitable for the rock garden. Prune lightly after flowering. Zone 8

Halimium 'Sarah' ▼
A short-lived evergreen, spreading shrub with grey-green leaves and saucer-shaped yellow flowers with deepest maroon central markings, each flower lasting for a day but seen over a long period.

Compact; sun; flowers late spring to early summer; well-drained soil

Suitable for the rock garden. Prune lightly after flowering. Zone 8

Halimium umbellatum ▼
A short-lived dwarf, bushy rock rose bearing saucer-shaped white flowers with yellow centres and narrow, grey-green leaves, each flower lasting for a day but seen over a long period.

Compact; sun; flowers early to mid summer; well-drained soil

Suitable for the rock garden. Prune lightly after flowering. Zone 8

Hamamelis 'Brevipetala' ▼
This witch hazel is an upright then rounded, deciduous shrub, with distinctly spicy scented, short-petalled, golden yellow flowers and yellow autumn colour.

Medium to large; sun or partial shade; flowers mid to late winter; fertile, neutral to slightly acid soil

Spur prune last season's growth to three buds after flowering, if wanting to restrict growth. Zone 5

Hamamelis ×intermedia 'Angelly' ▼
This witch hazel is a deciduous upright-growing shrub with an abundance of scented bright citron yellow flowers and yellow autumn colour. **AGM**

Large; sun or partial shade; flowers late winter to early spring; fertile, neutral to acid soil

Spur prune last season's growth to three buds after flowering, if wanting to restrict growth. Zone 5

Hamamelis ×intermedia 'Aphrodite' ▼
This witch hazel is a deciduous shrub with clusters of beautiful burnt-orange flowers and a wide-spreading habit. **AGM**

Large; sun or partial shade; flowers mid to late winter; fertile, neutral to acid soil

Spur prune last season's growth to three buds after flowering, if wanting to restrict growth. Zone 5

Hamamelis ×intermedia 'Barmstedt Gold' ▶

A vigorous upright-growing witch hazel with abundant faintly scented, golden yellow flowers and striking yellow autumn colour. **AGM**

Large; sun or partial shade; flowers mid to late winter; fertile, neutral to slightly acid soil

Spur prune last season's growth to three buds after flowering, if wanting to restrict growth. Zone 5

Hamamelis ×intermedia 'Arnold Promise' ▲

This witch hazel is a vase-shaped deciduous shrub with delicately curled, lemon yellow, scented flowers and yellow, orange, and red autumn colour. **AGM**

Large; sun or partial shade; flowers late winter to early spring; fertile, neutral to acid soil

Spur prune last season's growth to three buds after flowering, if wanting to restrict growth. Zone 5

Hamamelis ×intermedia 'Aurora' ▼

An upright-growing witch hazel bearing beautifully scented, large yellow flowers with hints of orange and red, and with yellow foliage turning orange-red in autumn. **AGM**

Large; sun or partial shade; flowers mid to late winter; fertile, neutral to acid soil

Spur prune last season's growth to three buds after flowering, if wanting to restrict growth. Zone 5

Hamamelis ×intermedia 'Diane' ▲▼

A striking red-flowering witch hazel with crimped petals and excellent autumn colour ranging from yellow to orange and crimson. **AGM**

Large; sun or partial shade; flowers mid to late winter; fertile, neutral to acid soil

Spur prune last season's growth to three buds after flowering, if wanting to restrict growth. Zone 5

Hamamelis ×intermedia 'Georges' ▲

An upright deciduous witch hazel with crimped bright red flowers and maroon foliage changing to orange-yellow then crimson in autumn.

Large; sun or partial shade; flowers mid to late winter; fertile, neutral to acid soil

Spur prune last season's growth to three buds after flowering, if wanting to restrict growth. Zone 5

Hamamelis ×intermedia 'Harry' ▼

An upright deciduous witch hazel with an abundance of large yellowish orange flowers.

Large; sun or partial shade; flowers mid to late winter; fertile, neutral to slightly acid soil

Spur prune last season's growth to three buds after flowering, if wanting to restrict growth. Zone 5

Hamamelis ×intermedia 'Hiltingbury' ▶

A witch hazel with pale copper-red flowers and excellent red and orange then scarlet autumn foliage.

Large; sun or partial shade; flowers mid to late winter; fertile, neutral to acid soil

Spur prune last season's growth to three buds after flowering, if wanting to restrict growth. Zone 5

Hamamelis ×intermedia 'Jelena' ▶

A vigorous, spreading witch hazel with lovely, copper orange-coloured flowers and fiery autumn colours of red, orange, and scarlet. AGM

Large; sun or partial shade; flowers mid to late winter; fertile, neutral to acid soil

Spur prune last season's growth to three buds after flowering, if wanting to restrict growth. Zone 5

Hamamelis ×intermedia 'Livia' ▲▶

A spreading witch hazel with stunning, long-lasting, scented ruby red flowers and orange-red autumn foliage.

Large; sun or partial shade; flowers mid to late winter; fertile, neutral to acid soil

Spur prune last season's growth to three buds after flowering, if wanting to restrict growth. Zone 5

Hamamelis ×intermedia 'Pallida' ▼▶

A spreading deciduous shrub with branches covered in clusters of large, sulphur yellow, beautifully scented flowers followed by yellow autumn foliage. AGM

Large; sun or partial shade; flowers early to late winter; fertile, neutral to acid soil

Spur prune last season's growth to three buds after flowering, if wanting to restrict growth. Zone 5

Hamamelis ×intermedia 'Orange Peel' ▲▼

Named for its fragrant, orange petals that resemble shreds of orange peel, this upright-growing witch hazel also has excellent yellow, orange, and red autumn foliage.

Large; sun or partial shade; flowers mid to late winter; fertile, neutral to acid soil

Spur prune last season's growth to three buds after flowering, if wanting to restrict growth. Zone 5

Hamamelis ×intermedia 'Primavera' ▼

This witch hazel is a deciduous shrub with clusters of slightly fragrant, bright yellow flowers, purple-red at the base. It blooms later than the other cultivars. Foliage is yellow in autumn.

Large; sun or partial shade; flowers mid to late winter; fertile, neutral to acid soil

Spur prune last season's growth to three buds after flowering, if wanting to restrict growth. Zone 5

Hamamelis ×intermedia 'Robert' ▼

An attractive vase-shaped witch hazel with scented coppery orange-red flowers and yellow-orange then crimson foliage in autumn.

Large; sun or partial shade; flowers mid to late winter; fertile, neutral to acid soil

Spur prune last season's growth to three buds after flowering, if wanting to restrict growth. Zone 5

Hamamelis ×intermedia 'Ruby Glow' ▲

A large bushy witch hazel with leaves turning yellow-orange and red in autumn, and with crimped copper-red flower petals.

Large; sun or partial shade; flowers mid to late winter; fertile, neutral to acid soil

Spur prune last season's growth to three buds after flowering, if wanting to restrict growth. Zone 5

Hamamelis ×intermedia 'Sunburst' ▲▼

An upright witch hazel with large, unscented, lemon yellow flowers.

Large; sun or partial shade; flowers mid to late winter; fertile, neutral to acid soil

Spur prune last season's growth to three buds after flowering, if wanting to restrict growth. Zone 5

Hamamelis ×intermedia 'Treasure Trove' H11419

A horizontally spreading, vigorous witch hazel with late-flowering crimped deep golden yellow flowers and with greyish green young foliage that turns a sage green.

Large; sun or partial shade; flowers mid to late winter; fertile, neutral to acid soil

Spur prune last season's growth to three buds after flowering, if wanting to restrict growth. Zone 5

Hamamelis ×intermedia 'Vesna' ▼

An upright, sweetly scented witch hazel with orange and yellow flowers and dark green foliage turning yellow-orange and red in autumn. AGM

Large; sun or partial shade; flowers mid to late winter; fertile, neutral to acid soil

Spur prune last season's growth to three buds after flowering, if wanting to restrict growth. Zone 5

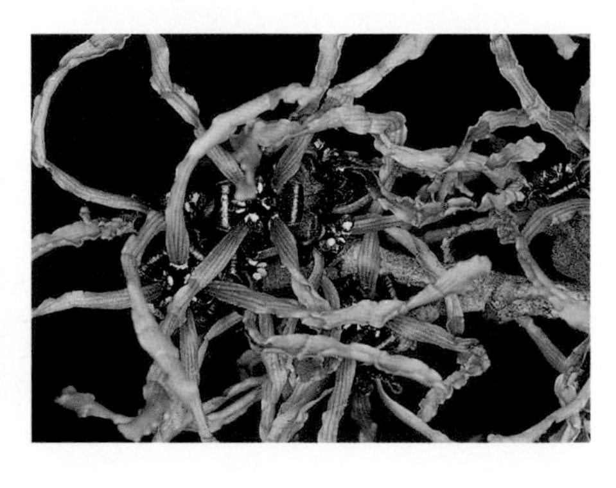

▲ *Hamamelis ×intermedia* 'Treasure Trove' H11419 at Hemelrijk, the Robert and Jelena de Belder estate in Kalmthout, Belgium.

Hamamelis japonica var. *flavopurpurascens* ▲

This deciduous, spreading witch hazel shrub bears smallish pale yellow flowers that turn red at the base of the petal, giving a bicoloured effect. Autumn foliage is yellow with a hint of orange-red.

Large; sun or partial shade; flowers mid to late winter; fertile, neutral to acid soil

Spur prune last season's growth to three buds after flowering, if wanting to restrict growth. Zone 5

Hamamelis japonica 'Superba' ▲

This Japanese witch hazel is a deciduous, spreading shrub with pale yellow crimped flowers and yellow foliage in autumn.

Large; sun or partial shade; flowers mid to late winter; fertile, neutral to acid soil

Spur prune last season's growth to three buds after flowering, if wanting to restrict growth. Zone 5

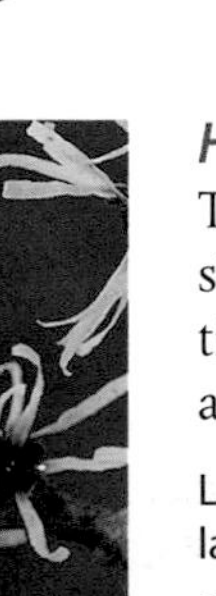

Hamamelis mollis ◄▼

The Chinese witch hazel is a deciduous shrub with bright golden yellow, distinctly scented flowers and yellow foliage in autumn. **AGM**

Large; sun or partial shade; flowers mid to late winter; fertile, neutral to acid soil

Spur prune last season's growth to three buds after flowering, if wanting to restrict growth. Zone 6

Hamamelis mollis 'Coombe Wood' ▼

This Chinese witch hazel is a spreading deciduous shrub with scented dark golden yellow flowers and lovely yellow to orange autumn colour.

Large; sun or partial shade; flowers mid to late winter; fertile, neutral to acid soil

Spur prune last season's growth to three buds after flowering, if wanting to restrict growth. Zone 6

Hamamelis mollis 'Wisley Supreme' ▼

This Chinese witch hazel is a vigorous, upright deciduous shrub with richly scented, large bright yellow spidery flowers, one of the earliest to be seen, and attractive dark green foliage turning yellow in autumn.

Large; sun or partial shade; flowers mid to late winter; fertile, neutral to acid soil

Spur prune last season's growth to three buds after flowering, if wanting to restrict growth. Zone 6

Hamamelis virginiana ▶

The Virginia witch hazel is a deciduous, spreading shrub with crimped pale yellow, spidery, subtly sweetly scented flowers and yellow autumn foliage.

Large; sun or partial shade; flowers early to late autumn; fertile, neutral to acid soil

Spur prune last season's growth to three buds after flowering, if wanting to restrict growth. Zone 5

Hamamelis vernalis 'Sandra' ▲

This Ozark witch hazel has green leaves that are purple when young and fiery red, orange, and scarlet in autumn. The small deep yellow flowers are scented.

Large; sun or partial shade; flowers mid to late winter; fertile, neutral to acid soil

Spur prune last season's growth to three buds after flowering, if wanting to restrict growth. Zone 5

Hamamelis vernalis 'Squib' ▼

This Ozark witch hazel is an upright, rounded shrub with small pale yellow flowers and yellow autumn colour.

Large; sun or partial shade; flowers mid to late winter; fertile, neutral to acid soil

Spur prune last season's growth to three buds after flowering, if wanting to restrict growth. Zone 5

Hebe 'Autumn Glory' ▲

An open, evergreen shrub with racemes of rich violet flowers and rounded green leaves edged with red.

Small; sun; flowers late summer to early autumn; fertile, well-drained soil

Zone 9

Hebe cupressoides 'Boughton Dome' ▼

This whipcord hebe is an evergreen shrub bearing dense, light greyish green foliage with paler juvenile leaves and pale blue flowers only rarely.

Compact; sun; flowers early to mid summer; fertile, well-drained soil

Suitable for the rock garden or scree. Zone 7

Hebe 'Great Orme' ▲

An evergreen bush with long racemes of bright pink flowers and long, shiny green leaves. AGM

Small; sun; flowers early to late summer; fertile, well-drained soil

Zone 9

Hebe 'Headfortii' ▼

A spreading evergreen shrub with racemes of blue-purple flowers and spear-shaped green leaves.

Small; sun; flowers mid to late summer; fertile, well-drained soil

Zone 9

Hebe 'Heartbreaker' ▼

An evergreen shrub grown for its cream-coloured variegated foliage which has pink and green young growth.

Compact; sun; flowers early to late summer; fertile, well-drained soil

Can be grown in containers. Zone 9

Hebe macrantha ▲

An upright evergreen shrub with toothed, leathery leaves and clusters of large pure-white flowers. AGM

Compact; sun; flowers early to mid summer; fertile, well-drained soil

Zone 8

Hebe 'Midsummer Beauty' ▼

A handsome, vigorous, evergreen shrub with spear-shaped green leaves, plum-coloured new growth, and long racemes of violet flowers fading to white. AGM

Small to medium; sun; flowers mid summer to early autumn; fertile, well-drained soil

Prune lightly in early spring to restrict size. Zone 7

Hebe 'Pink Elephant' ▲

An evergreen shrub bearing lovely grey-green leaves that have broad pale yellow margins and are flushed and edged pink. Short spikes of white flowers. **AGM**

Compact; sun; flowers early to mid summer; fertile, well-drained soil

Suitable for the rock garden. Zone 8

Hebe ochracea 'James Stirling' ▲

A slow-growing shrub with golden green foliage that intensifies in colour during winter. White flowers are borne in small racemes. **AGM**

Compact; sun; flowers late spring to early summer; fertile, well-drained soil

Suitable for a rock garden or scree. Zone 7

Hebe 'Pewter Dome' ▼

A dense evergreen shrub with grey-green foliage and short spikes of white flowers. **AGM**

Compact; sun; flowers late spring to early summer; fertile, well-drained soil

Suitable for the rock garden. Zone 7

Hebe recurva 'Aoira' ▲

A dense evergreen shrub with long, spear-shaped, grey-green leaves and racemes of white flowers.

Small; sun; flowers mid to late summer; fertile, well-drained soil

Zone 7

Hebe 'Red Edge' ▼

An evergreen, mound-forming shrub with grey-green leaves, edged with red especially so in winter, and racemes of pale lilac flowers. **AGM**

Compact; sun; flowers early to mid summer; fertile, well-drained soil

Suitable for the rock garden. Zone 7

Hebe salicifolia ▲

The koromiko is a bushy, upright, evergreen shrub with light green, spear-shaped leaves and racemes of white flowers tinted lilac.

Medium; sun; flowers mid to late summer; fertile, well-drained soil

Prune lightly in early spring to restrict size. Suitable for maritime exposure. Zone 7

Hebe speciosa ▼

A dense, rounded shrub with leathery bright green leaves and dark purplish red flowers.

Small to medium; sun; flowers mid summer to early autumn; fertile, well-drained soil

Suitable for maritime exposure in mild areas. Prune in early spring to restrict size. Zone 9

Hebe venustula ▼

A rounded evergreen bush with arching branches bearing glossy green leaves edged yellow. White flowers on short racemes have a hint of violet as they age.

Compact to small; sun; flowers early to mid summer; fertile, well-drained soil

Zone 7

Hebe 'Winter Glow' ▲

An evergreen shrub grown for its light green foliage with a fine creamy coloured margin that is pink on opening.

Compact; sun; flowers early to mid summer; fertile, well-drained soil

Suitable for the rock garden. Zone 8

Hebe 'Youngii' ◀

An evergreen shrub producing small leaves edged with red and abundant short racemes of violet flowers with a central white eye. **AGM**

Compact; sun; flowers early to late summer; fertile, well-drained soil

Suitable for the rock garden or as ground cover. Zone 8

Heimia salicifolia ▶

A bushy deciduous or semievergreen shrub with narrow green leaves and yellow flowers. AGM

Small to medium; sun; flowers mid summer to early autumn; fertile, well-drained soil

Prune lightly in early spring. Zone 7

Helianthemum 'Ben Ledi' ▼

This sun or rock rose is a dwarf, spreading, evergreen shrub with glossy green foliage and carmine-rose flowers with a deeper coloured centre fading pale pink.

Prostrate; sun; flowers late spring to mid summer; fertile, well-drained soil

Useful rock garden plant. Prune lightly after flowering. Zone 7

Helianthemum 'Golden Queen' ▼

This sun or rock rose is a spreading, evergreen shrub with glossy green foliage and saucer-shaped bright golden yellow flowers.

Prostrate; sun; flowers late spring to mid summer; fertile, well-drained soil

Useful rock garden plant. Prune lightly after flowering. Zone 7

Helianthemum 'Henfield Brilliant' ▲

This sun or rock rose is a vigorous, evergreen shrub with grey-green leaves and saucer-shaped bright orange-red flowers with yellow anthers at the centre. AGM

Prostrate; sun; flowers late spring to mid summer; fertile, well-drained soil

Useful rock garden plant. Prune lightly after flowering. Zone 7

Helianthemum nummularium

In the wild the sun or rock rose is a compact evergreen shrub with bright yellow flowers and small glossy green leaves.

Prostrate; sun; flowers late spring to mid summer; well-drained soil

Useful rock garden plant. Prune lightly after flowering. Zone 5

▼ *Helianthemum nummularium* in its native habitat at Picos de Europa.

Helianthemum 'Rhodanthe Carneum' ▲

This sun rose or rock rose is a dwarf evergreen shrub with silvery grey leaves and pink flowers with orange centres. AGM

Prostrate; sun; flowers late spring to mid summer; fertile, well-drained soil

Useful rock garden plant. Prune lightly after flowering. Zone 7

Helianthemum 'Ruth' ▼

This sun or rock rose is a vigorous spreading evergreen shrub grown for its grey-green leaves and its bright red flowers.

Prostrate; sun; flowers late spring to mid summer; well-drained soil

Useful rock garden plant. Prune lightly after flowering. Zone 7

Helianthemum 'Wisley White' ▲

This attractive sun or rock rose is an evergreen shrub with spreading, grey-green foliage and bright white flowers with conspicuous yellow anthers.

Prostrate; sun; flowers late spring to mid summer; fertile, well-drained soil

Useful rock garden plant. Prune lightly after flowering. Zone 7

Helichrysum splendidum ▶

An evergreen shrub with bright silvery grey foliage and yellow-gold, "everlasting" flowers. AGM

Small; sun; flowers mid summer to early autumn; fertile, well-drained soil

Prune lightly in early spring. Zone 8

Helwingia japonica ▲

A deciduous shrub with glossy bright green leaves pale green flowers and black berries found on the upper surface of the leaf.

Medium; partial shade; flowers early to mid summer; fertile, well-drained soil

Male and female flowers on separate plants. Zone 8

Heptacodium miconioides ▲▶▼

The seven son flower of Zhejiang is a vigorous, upright deciduous shrub with fragrant white flowers after which the calyces turn a rose pink. As the shrub ages, the pale brown bark peels off in strips.

Large; sun or partial shade; flowers late summer to early autumn; fertile soil

Zone 6

Heteromeles salicifolia ▲

The California holly or toyon is an evergreen shrub producing honey-scented flattened creamy white panicles of flowers followed by bright red fruits.

Large; sun or partial shade; flowers late summer; fertile soil

Zone 8

Hibiscus sinosyriacus 'Autumn Surprise' ▲

A vigorous, deciduous shrub with sage green foliage and white flowers showing feathered cerise markings at the base of each petal.

Medium; sun; flowers late summer to early autumn; fertile soil

Prune in early spring. Zone 8

Hibiscus sinosyriacus 'Lilac Queen' ▶

A vigorous, deciduous shrub with sage green leaves, grown for its soft pink flowers which have cerise markings at the base of each petal.

Medium; sun; flowers late summer to early autumn; fertile soil

Prune in early spring. Zone 8

Hibiscus syriacus WHITE CHIFFON 'Notwoodtwo' ▲

This rose of sharon is a vigorous, deciduous shrub with green lobed leaves and large semidouble pure white flowers. **AGM**

Medium; sun; flowers late summer to early autumn; fertile soil

Prune in early spring. Zone 5

Hibiscus syriacus 'Aphrodite' ▲

This rose of Sharon is a deciduous shrub grown for its large deep clear pink trumpet-shaped flowers with red markings at the base of each petal.

Medium; sun; flowers late summer to early autumn; fertile soil

Prune in early spring. Zone 5

Hibiscus syriacus 'Shintaeyang' ▲

This rose of sharon is a deciduous shrub grown for its white flowers with a hint of pink in each petal and feathered cerise markings at the base of each petal.

Medium; sun; flowers late summer to early autumn; fertile soil

Prune in early spring. Zone 5

Hibiscus syriacus 'Woodbridge' ▼

This rose of sharon is a vigorous, deciduous shrub grown for its large pink-mauve flowers with crimson centres. **AGM**

Medium; sun; flowers late summer to early autumn; fertile soil

Prune in early spring. Zone 5

Hibiscus syriacus 'Hamabo' ▼

This rose of sharon is a deciduous shrub with green leaves and striking blush-pink flowers with feathered dark red markings. The floral buds are pink. **AGM**

Medium; sun; flowers late summer to early autumn; fertile soil

Prune in early spring. Zone 5

Hippocrepis balearica ▲

The horseshoe vetch is a deciduous shrub grown for its bright yellow vetchlike flowers and its light green leaflets.

Compact; sun; flowers early summer; well-drained, preferably alkaline soil

Suitable for the rock garden or scree. Zone 8

Hippocrepis emerus ▲▶

The scorpion senna is a deciduous shrub grown for its clusters of bright yellow flowers.

Medium; sun; flowers late spring to early summer; well-drained soil

Prune lightly after flowering. Zone 7

Hoheria 'Glory of Amlwch' ▲▼

A semievergreen shrub with serrated green leaves and many clusters of honey-scented pure white flowers. **AGM**

Large; sun to partial shade; flowers mid summer; fertile soil

Zone 8

Hoheria angustifolia ▲
The narrow-leaved lacebark is a slender, upright, evergreen tree with small, toothed leaves and abundant star-shaped, white flowers.

Large; sun to partial shade; flowers mid summer; fertile soil
Zone 8

Hoheria populnea ▲
The lacebark is an evergreen tree bearing pointed, oval leaves with serrated edges and clusters of starry white, scented flowers.

Large; sun to partial shade; flowers mid to late summer; fertile soil
Zone 9

Hoheria populnea 'Alba Variegata' ▼
A lacebark cultivar with evergreen variegated dark green foliage with irregular creamy white margins and scented, white flowers.

Large; sun to partial shade; flowers mid to late summer; fertile soil
Zone 9

Hoheria lyallii ▼
The mountain riverwood or lacebark is a deciduous shrub or small tree with toothed, green leaves, often grey on the underside, and clusters of large white flowers. AGM

Large; sun to partial shade; flowers mid summer; fertile soil
Zone 8

Hoheria populnea 'Moonlight' ◄
An evergreen cultivar with irregular pale and dark green marked leaves and scented white flowers.

Large; sun to partial shade; flowers mid to late summer; fertile soil
Zone 9

Hoheria sexstylosa 'Stardust' ▲▶

An upright evergreen shrub or small tree with an abundance of white, star-shaped flowers. **AGM**

Large; sun to partial shade; flowers mid to late summer; fertile soil

Zone 8

Holodiscus discolor ▲

The creambush is a handsome deciduous shrub with green leaves, greyish beneath, and large feathery, drooping panicles of creamy white flowers.

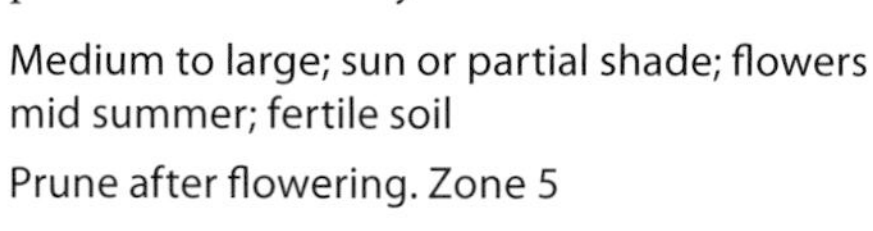

Medium to large; sun or partial shade; flowers mid summer; fertile soil

Prune after flowering. Zone 5

Hydrangea arborescens 'Annabelle' ▶

This smooth hydrangea is a rounded, deciduous shrub with large globes of densely packed, pale green then creamy white flower heads, fading to green with age. **AGM**

Medium; sun to partial shade; flowers mid to late summer; fertile soil

Prune during early spring. Zone 3

Hydrangea aspera Kawakamii Group ▶

A spreading deciduous shrub bearing soft, narrow hairy leaves and flattened lacecaps of violet flowers with long, deep violet stamens and surrounded with white florets.

Medium; partial shade; flowers late summer to early autumn; fertile, acid soil

Zone 7

Hydrangea aspera 'Macrophylla' ▶

A deciduous shrub with large, hairy or velvety, dark green leaves and small, blue-purple, flat flower heads surrounded with white florets. **AGM**

Medium; partial shade; flowers mid to late summer; fertile, acid soil

Zone 7

Hydrangea aspera subsp. *robusta* ▲▶

A spreading deciduous shrub with soft hairy leaves and one-year-old stems with flattened lacecaps of pinkish violet flowers. Long violet stamens are surrounded by soft pink florets. Old plants have flaking light brown bark.

Medium; partial shade; flowers mid to late summer; fertile, acid soil

Zone 7

Hydrangea aspera Villosa Group ▲▼

This rough-leaf hydrangea is a deciduous shrub with rough, hairy leaves and flat flower heads of small, pale mauve flowers with pink florets. **AGM**

Medium; partial shade; flowers mid to late summer; fertile, acid soil

Zone 7

Hydrangea aspera subsp. *sargentiana* ▲▶

An upright, rounded, deciduous shrub with velvety, very large dark green leaves and flat heads of small, purple-blue flowers surrounded with pale, bluish white florets. **AGM**

Medium to large; partial shade; flowers mid to late summer; fertile, acid soil

Zone 7

Hydrangea heteromalla 'Jermyns Lace' ▲▼

A deciduous shrub grown for its broad lacecap white flower heads that turn pink as they age.

Medium to large; sun to partial shade; flowers mid summer; fertile, acid soil

Zone 7

Hydrangea involucrata 'Hortensis' ▶

An attractive deciduous shrub with dark green leaves that are suedelike to the touch. The double, creamy white florets are tinged with rose pink. **AGM**

Small; sun to partial shade; flowers mid to late summer; fertile soil

Zone 7

Hydrangea macrophylla 'Altona' ▶

One of the mophead hydrangeas, this deciduous shrub has broad, green leaves and rounded flower heads with purplish pink florets that turn blue when grown in acid soils. **AGM**

Small; sun to partial shade; flowers mid to late summer; fertile soil

Colour of flowers is affected by soil acidity (smoky blue), alkalinity (plum), and other soil nutrients, and may change as the long-lasting flowers age. Dead-head and remove several stems on mature plants in mid spring. Tolerates maritime exposure. Zone 6

Hydrangea macrophylla 'Ayesha' ◀▲

The most distinctive of the mophead hydrangeas, this deciduous shrub has glossy green leaves and flattened, dense flower heads of lightly scented, thick-petalled pink or lilac (acid soil) florets.

Small; sun to partial shade; flowers mid to late summer; fertile soil

Colour of flowers is affected by soil acidity (pale blue to white to pink) and other soil nutrients, and may change as the long-lasting flowers age. Dead-head and remove a number of the stems on mature plants in mid spring. Zone 6

Hydrangea macrophylla Blue Tit 'Blaumeise' ▲

One of the Teller series of lacecap hydrangeas, this deciduous shrub has flattened lilac-blue flower heads.

Small; sun to partial shade; flowers mid to late summer; fertile soil

Colour of flowers is affected by soil acidity (rich blue) and other soil nutrients, and may change as the long-lasting flowers age (ageing pink). Dead-head and remove a number of the stems on mature plants in mid spring. Zone 6

Hydrangea macrophylla 'Générale Vicomtesse de Vibraye' ▼

A dense, free-flowering mophead with dark green leaves and rounded flower heads of pink flowers on alkaline soil, rich blue on acid soil. **AGM**

Small; sun to partial shade; flowers mid to late summer; fertile soil

Flower colour may be affected by soil acidity and other soil nutrients, and may change as the long-lasting flowers age. Dead-head and remove some stems from mature plants in mid spring. Tolerates maritime exposure. Zone 6

Hydrangea macrophylla 'Buntspecht' ▲

One of the Teller series of lacecap hydrangeas, this deciduous shrub has flattened deep rose-red flower heads.

Small; sun to partial shade; flowers mid to late summer; fertile soil

Colour of flowers is affected by soil acidity (plum red) and other soil nutrients, and may change as the long-lasting flowers age. Dead-head and remove a number of the stems on mature plants in mid spring. Zone 6

Hydrangea macrophylla 'Frillibet' ▼

An attractive deciduous shrub with frilly mopheads of white-cream florets, fading to an attractive sky blue on acid soils. Uniquely for a mophead, the sepals reverse colour in autumn.

Small; sun to partial shade; flowers mid to late summer; fertile soil

Flower colour is affected by soil acidity (pale, powder blue, and white) and other soil nutrients, and may change as the long-lasting flowers age. Dead-head and remove a number of the stems on mature plants in mid spring. Zone 6

Hydrangea macrophylla 'Geoffrey Chadbund' ▲

A spreading, deciduous shrub with large, light green leaves and flat, lacecap flower heads that are brick red in alkaline soil and purple-blue in acid soil. **AGM**

Small; position; flowers mid to late summer; fertile soil

Colour of flowers is affected by soil acidity (plum lilac) and alkalinity (red) as well as other soil nutrients, and may change as the long-lasting flowers age. Dead-head and remove a number of the stems on mature plants in mid spring. Zone 6

Hydrangea macrophylla 'Merveille Sanguine' ▼

A beautiful mophead hydrangea with brownish purple foliage tinted red and with rounded plum-red flower heads turning deep purple on acid soil.

Small; sun to partial shade; flowers mid to late summer; fertile soil

Colour of flowers is affected by soil acidity (deep purple) and alkalinity (plum red), and other soil nutrients, and may change as the long-lasting flowers age. Dead-head and remove a number of the stems on mature plants in mid spring. Zone 6

Hydrangea macrophylla 'Maculata' ▲

A deciduous variegated cultivar bearing attractive green leaves with irregular white edge markings and blue lacecap flower heads surrounded with white florets.

Small; sun to partial shade; flowers mid to late summer; fertile soil

Colour of flowers is affected by soil acidity (blue), alkalinity, and other soil nutrients, and may change as the long-lasting flowers age. Dead-head and remove a number of the stems on mature plants in mid spring. Zone 6

Hydrangea macrophylla 'Mariesii Grandiflora' ▲

A deciduous shrub with glossy, dark green leaves and flat, lacecap blue-pink flower heads surrounded with white florets. During autumn, the petals reverse, showing the underside which is a beautiful shell pink. Synonym: *Hydrangea macrophylla* 'White Wave'. **AGM**

Small; sun to partial shade; flowers mid to late summer; fertile soil

Dead-head and remove a number of the stems on mature plants in mid spring. Zone 6

Hydrangea macrophylla 'Veitchii' ▶

A rounded, deciduous shrub with dark green foliage and lacecap blue-lilac flower heads surrounded with large white florets that turn pink with age. **AGM**

Small to medium; sun to partial shade; flowers mid to late summer; fertile soil

Colour of flowers is affected by soil acidity (blue) and alkalinity (pink), and other soil nutrients. Dead-head and remove one-third of the stems on established plants in mid spring. Zone 6

Hydrangea paniculata 'Big Ben' ▶

An attractive, upright, spreading shrub with large panicles of large scented, free-flowering white flowers opening with a hint of green and turning pink with age. **AGM**

Medium; sun to partial shade; flowers late summer to mid autumn; fertile soil

Prune hard in early spring to obtain smaller plants and later, larger flowers. Zone 4

Hydrangea paniculata 'Floribunda' ◄

A deciduous shrub with a loose habit, large dark green leaves, and large, slender pointed conical flower heads of creamy white flowers. AGM

Medium to large; sun to partial shade; flowers mid summer to early autumn; fertile soil

Prune hard in early spring to obtain smaller plants and later, larger flowers. Zone 4

Hydrangea paniculata 'Grandiflora' ▼▼▼

A rounded, deciduous shrub with bluish green foliage and very dense tapered panicles of flower heads consisting of long-lasting white flowers that fade to pink with age. AGM

Medium; sun to partial shade; flowers late summer to mid autumn; fertile soil

Prune hard in spring to obtain smaller plants and later, larger flowers. Zone 4

Hydrangea paniculata 'Kyushu' ▼

An upright, deciduous shrub with glossy light green foliage and narrow, tapered panicles of frothy, greenish white flowers fading to white. AGM

Medium to large; sun to partial shade; flowers mid summer to early autumn; fertile soil

Prune hard in early spring to obtain smaller plants and later, larger flowers. Zone 4

Hydrangea paniculata Pink Diamond 'Interhydia' ◀

A tall, spreading deciduous shrub with glossy, dark green leaves and large, dense conical tapered clusters of creamy white flowers turning pink with age. **AGM**

Medium to large; sun to partial shade; flowers mid summer to mid autumn; fertile soil

Prune hard in spring to obtain smaller plants and later, larger flowers. Zone 4

Hydrangea paniculata 'Silver Dollar' ▼

A deciduous shrub with dense broadly conical spikes of creamy white flowers gradually turning pink with age. **AGM**

Medium; sun to partial shade; flowers mid summer to early autumn; fertile soil

Prune hard in spring to obtain smaller plants and later, larger flowers. Zone 4

Hydrangea paniculata 'Unique' ◀

A deciduous shrub with glossy, dark green leaves and large conical flower heads of white-cream flowers that turn purple-pink with age. **AGM**

Large; sun to partial shade; flowers mid summer to mid autumn; fertile soil

Prune hard in spring to obtain smaller plants and later, larger flowers. Zone 4

Hydrangea paniculata 'White Moth' ▼

An open shrub with large, pointed, dark green leaves and large rounded panicles of creamy white flowers, turning green with age.

Medium to large; sun to partial shade; flowers early to late summer; fertile soil

Prune hard in spring to obtain smaller plants and later, larger flowers. Zone 4

Hydrangea quercifolia Little Honey 'Brihon' ▼

A rounded shrub with attractive, lobed, oaklike golden yellow leaves turning green and then red with age. White flowers are borne in panicles. **AGM**

Small; sun to partial shade; flowers mid to late summer; fertile soil

Dead-head in mid spring. Zone 6

Hydrangea quercifolia SNOWFLAKE 'Brido' ▲▼

An oak-leafed hydrangea with lobed, dark green leaves, good orange, red, and purple autumn colour, and large conical flower heads bearing white, double star-shaped florets. Young stems are cinnamon coloured, and older stems are flaky. **AGM**

Medium; sun to partial shade; flowers mid to late summer; fertile soil

Dead-head in mid spring. Zone 5

Hydrangea serrata 'Bluebird' ▼

A deciduous shrub with dome-shaped lacecap flower heads surrounded by florets that are sea blue in acid soil and pink-purple on alkaline soils. **AGM**

Small; partial shade; flowers mid summer to mid autumn; fertile soil

Colour of flowers is affected by soil acidity (sea blue), alkalinity (reddish purple), and other soil nutrients, and may change as the long-lasting flowers age. Dead-head and remove some stems each year in spring. Zone 6

Hydrangea serrata 'Grayswood' ▼

An attractive shrub with flat blue lacecap flower heads, surrounded with white florets that turn pink and then deep red with age. **AGM**

Small; partial shade; flowers mid summer to mid autumn; fertile soil

Colour of flowers is affected by soil acidity (brilliant red florets) and other soil nutrients, and may change (brilliant crimson) as the long-lasting flowers age. Dead-head and remove some stems each year in spring. Zone 6

Hydrangea serrata 'Kurohime' ▼

A deciduous shrub grown for its bluish pink flower heads and bluish pink or blue florets. **AGM**

Compact to small; partial shade; flowers mid to late summer; fertile soil

Colour of flowers is affected by soil acidity and other soil nutrients, and may change as the long-lasting flowers age. Dead-head and remove some stems each year in spring. Zone 6

Hydrangea serrata 'Kyosumi' ▶

An attractive rounded lacecap hydrangea with green leaves, tinted purple-bronze on new growth, and for its flat creamy white flower heads surrounded with white florets edged with pink. **AGM**

Compact to small; partial shade; flowers mid to late summer; fertile soil

Colour of flowers is affected by soil acidity and other soil nutrients. Dead-head and remove some stems each year in spring. Zone 6

Hydrangea serrata 'Little Geisha Meiko' ▼

A sport of 'Maiko' grown for its marbled white and green young foliage ultimately reverting to green.

Compact to small; partial shade; flowers mid to late summer; fertile soil

Dead-head and remove some stems each year in spring. Zone 6

Hydrangea serrata 'Rosalba' ▲

A deciduous shrub with large dark green leaves and large white lacecap flower heads that quickly flush crimson with age. **AGM**

Small; partial shade; flowers mid to late summer; fertile soil

Colour of flowers is affected by soil acidity and other soil nutrients, and may change as the long-lasting flowers age. Dead-head and remove some stems each year in spring. Zone 6

Hydrangea serrata 'Preziosa' ▼

An upright shrub with globular, rose pink flower heads turning darker red ultimately reddish purple with age. On more acid soil, flower colour is blue to mauve. **AGM**

Small; partial shade; flowers mid to late summer; fertile soil

Colour of flowers is affected by soil acidity (pink to violet on the same plant) and other soil nutrients, and may change (reddish purple) as the long-lasting flowers age. Dead-head and remove some stems each year in spring. Zone 6

Hydrangea serrata 'Shirofuji' ▼

An attractive lacecap cultivar with white flower heads surrounded with white, starlike, double florets.

Compact to small; partial shade; flowers mid to late summer; fertile soil

Colour of flowers is affected by soil acidity and other soil nutrients, and may change as the long-lasting flowers age. Dead-head each year in spring. Zone 6

***Hydrangea serrata* 'Tiara'** ▲
A rounded shrub with green foliage tinted reddish purple and blue lacecap flower heads surrounded with paler blue florets that turn a beautiful mauve-pink. AGM

Small; partial shade; flowers mid to late summer; fertile soil

Colour of flowers is affected by soil acidity and other soil nutrients, and may change as the long-lasting flowers age. Dead-head and remove some stems each year in spring. Zone 6

***Hypericum androsaemum* 'Albury Purple'** ▲▼
This purple-leaved form of the tutsan is a bushy deciduous shrub with young leaves tinted purple. The small bright yellow flowers are followed by red-brown then black berries.

Compact; sun to shade; flowers mid to late summer; fertile soil

Useful for ground cover. Trim during spring. Zone 6

***Hypericum androsaemum* f. *variegatum* 'Mrs. Gladis Brabazon'** ▼
This variegated form of the tutsan is a bushy deciduous shrub with young leaves mottled green and creamy white. The small bright yellow flowers are followed by red berries that turn black.

Compact; partial shade; flowers mid to late summer; fertile soil

Useful for ground cover. Trim during early spring. Zone 7

***Hypericum ×dummeri* 'Peter Dummer'** ▲
A rounded semievergreen shrub with green leaves tinted red and purple, and large saucer-shaped golden yellow flowers with orange anthers followed by red-tinged fruits.

Compact; sun to partial shade; flowers mid summer to early autumn; fertile soil

Shorten stems and remove older stems in early spring. Zone 7

Hypericum forrestii ▲

A dense, rounded semievergreen shrub with mid-green foliage and bright golden yellow saucer-shaped flowers. **AGM**

Small; sun to partial shade; flowers mid summer to early autumn; fertile soil

Shorten stems and remove older stems in early spring. Zone 5

Hypericum frondosum 'Sunburst' ▲

A rounded deciduous shrub producing blue-green foliage and golden yellow flowers with prominent bushy central stamens.

Small; sun to partial shade; flowers mid to late summer; fertile soil

Remove older stems in early spring. Zone 5

Hypericum 'Hidcote' ▶

A bushy, semievergreen shrub with dense, green foliage and abundant lovely, long-lasting, saucer-shaped, large golden yellow flowers. **AGM**

Small to medium; sun to partial shade; flowers mid summer to early autumn; fertile soil

Shorten stems and remove older stems in early spring. Zone 7

Hypericum hircanum subsp. *albimontanum* ▲

A deciduous shrub bearing bluish green foliage and pale yellow flowers with prominent starlike stamens. **AGM**

Small; sun to partial shade; flowers mid to late summer; fertile soil

Remove older stems in early spring. Zone 7

Hypericum ×*inodorum* 'Elstead' ▼

A deciduous or semievergreen shrub with dark green leaves and clusters of star-shaped yellow flowers followed by rosy red fruits.

Small; sun to partial shade; flowers mid to late summer; fertile soil

Shorten stems and remove older stems in spring. Zone 7

Hypericum olympicum ▶

A deciduous, spreading shrub with grey-green foliage and open, bright yellow, star-shaped flowers. **AGM**

Compact; sun; flowers early to late summer; well-drained soil

Suitable for a rock garden or scree. Zone 6

Hypericum reptans ▼

A ground-covering deciduous shrub with green leaves, reddish yellow buds, and golden yellow flowers.

Prostrate; sun; flowers early to late summer; well-drained soil

Suitable for a rock garden or scree. Zone 7

Iberis sempervirens ▶▼

The evergreen candytuft is an attractive, low, mound-forming plant with glossy green foliage and heads of small, sweetly scented white flowers. **AGM**

Compact; sun; flowers mid winter to early spring; well-drained soil

Suitable for the rock garden or alpine house. Remove flower heads after flowering. Zone 8

Hypericum 'Rowallane' ▲▶

An upright, semievergreen shrub with arching branches that bear dark green leaves and wide, deep golden yellow, cup-shaped flowers. **AGM**

Small to medium; sun to partial shade; flowers mid summer to early autumn; fertile soil

Shorten stems and remove older stems in early spring. Zone 8

Ilex ×altaclerensis 'Belgica Aurea' ▲

A slow-growing, upright evergreen shrub that bears dark green leaves broadly edged with creamy yellow and bright orange-red fruits. AGM

Large; sun or shade; flowers late spring to early summer; fertile soil

Requires a male cultivar as a pollinator for production of fruit. Zone 7

Ilex ×altaclerensis 'Camelliaefolia Variegata' ▲◀

An attractive compact evergreen shrub. The glossy, dark green leaves have paler green markings and creamy golden edges which are variable in width. Fruits are red. AGM

Large; sun or shade; flowers late spring to early summer; fertile soil

Requires a male cultivar as a pollinator for production of fruit. To maintain variegation, remove any all-green shoots as they appear. Zone 7

Ilex ×altaclerensis 'Golden King' ▶

A handsome variegated holly bearing almost spineless, glossy, dark green leaves irregularly edged with golden yellow and producing clusters of red berries. AGM

Large; sun or shade; flowers late spring to early summer; fertile soil

Requires a male cultivar as a pollinator for production of fruit. Can be used as a hedging plant and for topiary. Zone 7

Ilex ×altaclerensis 'Hodginsii' ▼

A vigorous, upright, male evergreen holly with dark green, oval leaves that are normally free of spines in older specimens. Young shoots are purple. AGM

Large; sun or shade; flowers late spring to early summer; fertile soil

Suitable as a pollinator for female plants. Can be used as a hedging and screening plant. Zone 7

Ilex ×altaclerensis 'Lawsoniana' ▼

An attractive bushy holly bearing lovely variegated spineless leaves that are dark green with paler green and golden yellow central markings. Fruits are brownish red. AGM

Large; sun or shade; flowers late spring to early summer; fertile soil

Suitable as a pollinator for female plants. Can be used as a hedging and screening plant. Zone 7

Ilex aquifolium 'Elegantissima' ▼

An upright evergreen golden holly bearing spiny variegated glossy green leaves with creamy white margins.

Large; sun or shade; flowers late spring to early summer; fertile soil

Suitable as a pollinator for female plants. Can be used for topiary. Zone 6

Ilex aquifolium 'Argentea Marginata Pendula' ▲

A slow-growing weeping holly bearing evergreen variegated leaves which are dark green edged with yellow. The shrub produces abundant red berries.

Large; sun or shade; flowers late spring to early summer; fertile soil

Requires a male cultivar as a pollinator for production of fruit. To maintain variegation, remove any all-green shoots as they appear. Zone 6

Ilex aquifolium 'Bacciflava' ▼

A slow-growing evergreen cultivar with glossy, dark-green almost spineless leaves and clusters of yellow fruits.

Large; sun or shade; flowers late spring to early summer; fertile soil

Requires a male cultivar as a pollinator for production of fruit. Can be used as a hedging plant. Zone 6

Ilex aquifolium 'Green Pillar' ▲

An upright, architectural holly with dark green, spiny leaves and lots of bright red fruits.

Large; sun or shade; flowers late spring to early summer; fertile soil

Requires a male cultivar as a pollinator for production of fruit. Can be used as a hedging plant. Zone 6

Ilex aquifolium 'Handsworth New Silver' ▼

An attractive purple-stemmed evergreen cultivar bearing variegated, dark green leaves edged with creamy white. The small leaves are not particularly spiny. The free-fruiting shrub produces bright red berries. **AGM**

Large; sun or shade; flowers late spring to early summer; fertile soil

Requires a male cultivar as a pollinator for production of fruit. Can be used as a hedging plant. To maintain variegation, remove any all-green shoots as they appear. Zone 6

Ilex aquifolium 'Harpune' ▲

An upright evergreen holly with almost spineless, narrow glossy green leaves and bright red berries.

Large; sun or shade; flowers late spring to early summer; fertile soil

Requires a male cultivar as a pollinator for production of fruit. Can be grown as a container plant. Zone 6

Ilex aquifolium 'J. C. van Tol' ▲

An evergreen conical holly with less spiny, glossy green leaves. This shrub reliably produces quantities of large shiny red fruits. **AGM**

Large; sun or shade; flowers late spring to early summer; fertile soil

Unlike other fruit-bearing hollies, this one does not require a male cultivar as a pollinator for production of fruit. Can be used as a hedging plant. Zone 6

Ilex aquifolium 'Madame Briot' ▼

A broad, evergreen holly with bright golden yellow variegated glossy green spiny leaves and bright red berries. **AGM**

Large; sun or shade; flowers late spring to early summer; fertile soil

Requires a male cultivar as a pollinator for production of fruit. Can be used as a hedging plant. To maintain variegation, remove any all-green shoots as they appear. Zone 6

Ilex aquifolium 'Ovata Aurea' ▼

An evergreen male holly bearing variegated deep green leaves with golden margins which contrast well against the purple stems.

Large; sun or shade; flowers late spring to early summer; fertile soil

Suitable as a pollinator for female plants. Can be used as a hedging plant. To maintain variegation, remove any all-green shoots as they appear. Zone 7

Ilex aquifolium 'Silver Milkmaid' ▼

An evergreen shrub that produces twisted spiny, dark green leaves with silvery central markings, grey bark, and an abundance of red fruits.

Medium; sun or shade; flowers late spring to early summer; fertile soil

Requires a male cultivar as a pollinator for production of fruit. To maintain variegation, remove any all-green shoots as they appear. Zone 7

Ilex aquifolium 'Silver Queen' ▲

An evergreen male holly bearing dark green leaves marbled with grey edged with creamy white suffused with pink on opening. **AGM**

Large; sun or shade; flowers late spring to early summer; fertile soil

Suitable as a pollinator for female plants. Can be used as a hedging plant. To maintain variegation, remove any all-green shoots as they appear. Zone 7

Ilex aquifolium 'Silver van Tol' ▼

An evergreen conical holly bearing variegated, almost spineless leaves that are glossy green edged irregularly with cream. The large fruits are a bright red.

Large; sun or shade; flowers late spring to early summer; fertile soil

Unlike other fruit-bearing hollies, this one does not require a male cultivar as a pollinator for production of fruit. Can be used as a hedging plant. To maintain variegation, remove any all-green shoots as they appear. Zone 7

Ilex ×*attenuata* 'Howard' ▲

This topal holly has an upright multistemmed habit with almost spineless leaves and red fruits.

Large; sun to partial shade; flowers late spring to early summer; fertile soil

Zone 7

Ilex ×*attenuata* 'Sunny Foster' ▶

An upright evergreen shrub, bearing glossy golden yellow leaves that turn pale green with age. Fruits are red.

Medium; sun; flowers late spring to early summer; fertile soil

Requires a male cultivar as a pollinator for production of fruit. To maintain variegation, remove any all-green shoots as they appear. Zone 7

Ilex 'Bonfire' ▲

This deciduous shrub is a hybrid between *Ilex verticillata* and *I. serrata*. It has toothed, bright green leaves, white flowers, and an abundance of red berries.

Medium; sun to partial shade; flowers late spring to early summer; fertile, acid soil

Zone 4

Ilex cornuta ▼

The Chinese holly is a broad-spreading evergreen shrub with distinctive trapezoidal spiny glossy green leaves and red fruits.

Medium; sun to partial shade; flowers mid to late spring; well-drained, neutral to acid soil

Zone 7

Ilex cornuta 'Anicet Delcambre' ▶

The needlepoint holly is an evergreen with a compact rounded habit. It has glossy green leaves with distinctive, pointed ends and abundant dark red berries.

Medium to large; sun to partial shade; flowers mid to late spring; fertile, neutral to acid soil

Zone 7

Ilex cornuta 'Gay Blade' ▲▼

An evergreen shrub with glossy, dark green leaves on pendulous branches and abundant large decorative bright red berries.

Medium; sun to partial shade; flowers mid to late spring; fertile, neutral to acid soil

Zone 7

Ilex crenata 'Convexed Gold' ▶

This box holly is a slow-growing evergreen shrub with small, spineless, yellow leaves and black fruits.

Medium; sun; flowers late spring to early summer; fertile soil

Requires a male cultivar as a pollinator for production of fruit. Zone 7

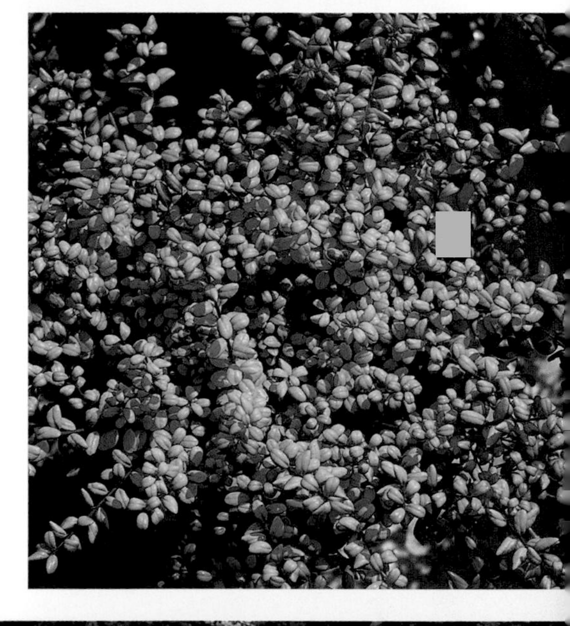

Ilex crenata 'Golden Gem' ▼

This box holly is a slow-growing spreading evergreen shrub with golden yellow, non-prickly leaves turning greener with age. Fruits are black. **AGM**

Small; sun; flowers late spring to early summer; fertile soil

Requires a male cultivar as a pollinator for production of fruit. Zone 6

Ilex fargesii ▲

An evergreen shrub with narrow, oblong green leaves and small, red fruits following greenish yellow flowers.

Large; partial shade; flowers late spring to early summer; fertile soil

Zone 7

Ilex ×koehneana 'Adonis' ▼▶

A narrowly upright evergreen male holly with spiny leaves.

Large; sun or shade; flowers late spring to early summer; fertile soil

Can be grown as a container plant. Zone 7

Ilex ×meserveae Blue Princess 'Conapry' ▶

An evergreen holly with dark foliage that appears blue in winter and with abundant bright red fruit.

Small to medium; sun to partial shade; flowers late spring to early summer; fertile soil

Requires a male cultivar as a pollinator for production of fruit. Zone 6

Ilex 'Nellie R. Stevens' ▶

A vigorous, upright evergreen holly with lovely, glossy toothed green leaves and abundant bright red fruit.

Large; sun and shade; flowers late spring to early summer; fertile soil

Requires a male cultivar as a pollinator for production of fruit. Zone 6

Ilex opaca

The American holly is a low-growing, spreading shrub with spiny toothed, dark olive green leaves and inconspicuous green-white flowers followed by sparsely produced red fruits.

Small; sun to partial shade; flowers late spring to early summer; fertile, acid soil

Makes a good ground cover plant. Zone 5

▼ *Ilex opaca* 'Maryland Dwarf' at Bernheim Arboretum, Clermont, Kentucky.

Ilex pedunculosa ▲

The longstalk holly is an upright evergreen shrub with glossy green, spineless leaves and bright red berries hanging from long stalks.

Large; sun to partial shade; flowers late spring to early summer; fertile, acid soil

Zone 6

Ilex perado subsp. *platyphylla* ▼

The Canary Island holly is a bushy shrub with large, leathery, dark green, slightly toothed leaves and dark red fruits.

Large; sun to shade; flowers late spring to early summer; fertile soil

Zone 8

Ilex verticillata ◀ ▼

The winterberry or black alder is a deciduous holly with a dense shrubby habit, bearing purple-tinted dark green leaves that turn yellow with age. The bright red fruits are long-lasting.

Medium; sun to partial shade; flowers late spring to early summer; fertile, acid soil

Requires a male cultivar as a pollinator for production of fruit. Zone 3

Ilex verticillata 'Red Sprite' ▲

A rounded, deciduous holly with glossy, dark green leaves and masses of large bright-red berries.

Small to medium; sun; flowers late spring to early summer; fertile, acid soil

Requires a male cultivar as a pollinator for production of fruit. Zone 4

Illicium anisatum ▼

The Japanese star anise is a dense evergreen shrub with pointed, leathery, dark green leaves, small, pale yellowish white flowers, and star-shaped fruits.

Medium to large; partial shade; flowers mid to late spring; fertile, acid soil

Pruning only required to maintain shape. Zone 8

Illicium floridanum ▲▼

The Florida anise is a fragrant, evergreen shrub with dark green, leathery, oval leaves and reddish purple flowers.

Medium; partial shade; flowers mid spring to early summer; fertile, acid soil

Pruning only required to maintain shape. Zone 8

Illicium floridanum 'Halley's Comet' ▼

A handsome evergreen shrub with attractive, large fragrant, deep red, star-shaped flowers.

Medium; partial shade; flowers mid spring to early summer; fertile, acid soil

Pruning only required to maintain shape. Zone 8

Illicium simonsii ▲

An evergreen shrub with oval, green, leathery leaves and clusters of small creamy yellow, star-shaped flowers.

Small to medium; partial shade; flowers mid spring; fertile, acid soil

Pruning only required to maintain shape. Zone 8

Illicium 'Woodland Ruby' ▼

A vigorous, evergreen shrub with abundant pinkish red, large star-shaped flowers over a long period.

Medium; partial shade; flowers mid spring to early summer; fertile, acid soil

Pruning only required to maintain shape. Zone 8

Indigofera amblyantha ▲

An attractive, deciduous shrub with bright green pinnate foliage, racemes of light pink, pealike flowers, and dark purple seed pods. **AGM**

Small to medium; sun; flowers early to late summer; fertile, well-drained soil

Reduce last season's growth in early spring. Zone 5

Indigofera hebepetala ▼

A spreading shrub bearing green leaves with furry undersides and racemes of purplish pink flowers.

Small; sun; flowers mid summer to early autumn; fertile, well-drained soil

Reduce last season's growth in early spring. Zone 8

Indigofera pendula ▼

A beautiful, arching shrub with pinnate, blue-green foliage and long, pendulous racemes of pink-purple, pealike flowers.

Small to medium; sun; flowers late summer to early autumn; fertile, well-drained soil

If cut back by a severe winter, will usually regrow from base in spring. Zone 9

Indigofera potaninii ▼

A lovely, deciduous shrub with grey-green pinnate leaves and long racemes of bright pink flowers.

Small; sun; flowers early to late summer; fertile, well-drained soil

Reduce last season's growth in early spring. Zone 5

Indigofera setchuenensis

SICH1038 ▲

A floriferous deciduous shrub with short racemes of rich purplish pink flowers.

Medium; sun; flowers late spring to mid summer; fertile, well-drained soil

Prune after flowering. Zone 7

Iochroma australe ▼

The mini angel's trumpet is an evergreen shrub covered with blue-purple trumpet-shaped flowers.

Medium; sun; flowers early to late summer but almost all year round if grown indoors; fertile, well-drained soil

Prune during early to mid spring. May be grown in a large container. Zone 10

Itea virginica 'Henry's Garnet' ▲▶▼

This Virginia sweetspire is a deciduous shrub with bright green leaves that turn red in autumn, and with long racemes of fragrant white flowers.

Medium; sun or partial shade; flowers mid summer; fertile, acid soil

May sucker freely. Prune out old shoots in early spring. Zone 5

Itea ilicifolia ▲▼

The holly-leaved sweetspire is an evergreen shrub with bright green, glossy, toothed leaves and long racemes of greenish white, scented flowers. **AGM**

Medium to large; sun to partial shade; flowers late summer; fertile soil

Prune in mid spring. Grows well against a wall. Zone 7

Jamesia americana ▶

The cliffbush is a deciduous shrub with soft, serrated, grey-green leaves and clusters of white flowers.

Medium; sun or partial shade; flowers mid summer; fertile, acid soil

May sucker freely. Prune out shoots in early spring. Zone 5

Jasminum fruticans ▲

The bush jasmine is a semievergreen shrub with clusters of bright yellow flowers followed by black fruits.

Small to medium; sun; flowers early to late summer or throughout the year in frost-free climates; fertile soil

Prune in early spring. Zone 8

Jasminum humile ▲

The yellow jasmine is a semievergreen shrub with bushy green foliage and clusters of bright yellow, lightly scented flowers.

Small to medium; sun; flowers early to mid summer; fertile soil

Prune in early spring. Zone 8

Jasminium nudiflorum ▶

This yellow jasmine is a semievergreen shrub with bushy green foliage and clusters of bright yellow, lightly scented flowers. **AGM**

Medium to large; sun and partial shade; flowers late autumn to late winter; fertile soil

Best seen when planted against a wall. Prune immediately after flowering. Zone 6

Jasminum parkeri ▲

An evergreen shrub bearing dense, untidy foliage and tiny, fragrant yellow flowers.

Prostrate; sun; flowers late spring to early summer; fertile, free-draining soil

May be grown in a rock garden or raised bed. Zone 8

Jovellana punctata ▼

An evergreen shrub bearing clusters of white flowers spotted pink in the throat.

Small; sun or partial shade; flowers early to mid summer; fertile soil

Suitable for a cool greenhouse or sheltered site. Zone 10

Jovellana violacea ▲▼

A charming, evergreen shrub bearing small toothed leaves and abundant delicate violet flowers with darker markings in the throat. **AGM**

Small; sun or partial shade; flowers early to mid summer; fertile soil

Suckering. Zone 9

Kalmia angustifolia ▼

A spreading evergreen shrub with deep green, narrow leaves and clusters of rosy red flowers. **AGM**

Compact to small; sun to partial shade; flowers late spring to early summer; fertile, acid soil

Zone 2

Kalmia latifolia ▼

The mountain laurel or calico bush is a handsome, evergreen shrub with glossy foliage and clusters of cup-shaped pink flowers. **AGM**

Medium; sun to partial shade; flowers late spring to early summer; fertile, acid soil

Can be used as an informal hedge. Zone 2

Kalmia latifolia f. *myrtifolia* ▲

This form of mountain laurel has smaller green leaves but the clusters of cup-shaped, pink flowers resemble those of the species.

Small; sun to partial shade; flowers late spring to early summer; fertile, acid soil

Zone 2

Kalmia polifolia ▶

The bog laurel is a dense, wiry, evergreen shrub with narrow glossy, dark green leaves and terminal clusters of purple-pink cup-shaped flowers.

Compact; sun to partial shade; flowers late spring to early summer; fertile, acid soil

Useful in boggy situations where the water table is high. Zone 2

Kalmia polifolia 'Olympic Fire' ▲

This evergreen shrub has glossy green leaves with rich rose pink flowers that are pale pink in the centre and open from red buds. **AGM**

Medium; sun to partial shade; flowers late spring to early summer; fertile, acid soil

Can be grown where the water table is high. Zone 2

Kalmia polifolia 'Pink Charm' ▼

An evergreen shrub with glossy green leaves and a profusion of rich pink flowers opening from red buds. **AGM**

Compact; sun to partial shade; flowers mid spring; fertile, acid soil

Can be grown where the water table is high. Zone 2

Kalmiopsis leachiana ▲

An evergreen shrub with thick, glossy, oval, dark green leaves and racemes of cup-shaped pink flowers. **AGM**

Compact; partial shade; flowers mid to late spring; fertile, acid soil

Grow in a rock garden. Zone 7

Kalmiopsis leachiana 'Glendoick' ▶

An evergreen shrub with thick, glossy, oval, dark green leaves and profuse racemes of cup-shaped pink flowers.

Compact; partial shade; flowers mid to late spring; fertile, acid soil

Grow in a rock garden. Zone 7

Kerria japonica 'Pleniflora' ▲▼

This Japanese rose is a deciduous shrub with bright green, toothed, oval leaves and double, golden yellow flowers. AGM

Small to medium; sun to partial shade; flowers mid to late spring; fertile soil

Remove excess suckering stems after flowering. Zone 5

Kerria japonica 'Simplex' ▲▼

This Japanese rose is a graceful, arching deciduous shrub covered with beautiful, single bright yellow flowers.

Small; sun to partial shade; flowers mid to late spring; fertile soil

Remove unwanted suckering shoots after flowering. Zone 5

Kolkwitzia amabilis ▲

The beauty bush is a deciduous bushy shrub with arching branches bearing masses of dark pink buds that open to bell-shaped, pale pink flowers. The pale brown bark is flaky.

Medium; sun to partial shade; flowers late spring to early summer; fertile soil

Thin out unwanted shoots after flowering. Zone 4

Kolkwitzia amabilis 'Maradco' ▲

A selection of beauty bush that produces yellowish green new growth.

Medium; sun to partial shade; flowers late spring to early summer; fertile soil

Thin out unwanted shoots after flowering. Zone 4

Kolkwitzia amabilis 'Pink Cloud' ▲

This attractive beauty bush is a deciduous shrub with arching branches and clusters of large bell-shaped pink flowers with a yellowish pink throat. **AGM**

Medium; sun to partial shade; flowers late spring to early summer; fertile soil

Thin out unwanted shoots after flowering. Zone 4

Kunzea ericoides ▼

The white tea-tree is a bushy, spreading, evergreen shrub covered with small, pointed, dark green leaves and plenty of small, scented white flowers.

Medium to large; sun; flowers mid to late summer; fertile, free-draining, neutral to acid soil

Prune early to mid spring to maintain habit. Zone 9

▲ *Lagerstroemia fauriei* 'Fantasy' at the J. C. Raulston Arboretum in North Carolina.

Lagerstroemia fauriei 'Fantasy'

A vigorous, deciduous, vase-shaped shrub or small tree of the copperbark crape myrtle with a beautiful patchwork of cinnamon-, grey-, and red-coloured bark, white flowers, and green foliage turning a lovely yellow in autumn.

Large; sun; flowers mid to late summer; fertile soil

Prune side shoots when young to produce a clean stem. Spur prune in early spring. Zone 7

Lagerstroemia fauriei 'Town House' ▲

This multistemmed, deciduous shrub of the copperbark crape myrtle has attractive grey and deep red-brown bark, white flowers, and dark green leaves with good autumn colour.

Large; sun; flowers mid to late summer; fertile soil

Prune side shoots when young to produce a clean stem. Spur prune in early spring. Zone 7

Lagerstroemia 'Sioux' ▲

This hybrid crape myrtle is an upright, deciduous shrub with ornamental bark, panicles of bright pink flowers, and attractive, deep red foliage in autumn.

Large; sun; flowers mid to late summer; fertile soil

Prune side shoots when young to produce a clean stem. Spur prune in early spring. Zone 7

Lagerstroemia 'Tuscarora' ◄

This hybrid crape myrtle is an attractive, upright deciduous shrub with a patchwork of grey-, pink-, and cinnamon-coloured bark, panicles of deep pinkish lilac, crinkled flowers, and small leaves that turn red and yellow in autumn.

Medium to large; sun; flowers mid to late summer; fertile soil

Prune side shoots when young to produce a clean stem. Spur prune in early spring. Zone 7

Laurus azorica ▲

The Canary Island laurel is an evergreen shrub with aromatic glossy, dark green leaves and yellow flowers followed by black fruit.

Large; sun; flowers mid spring; fertile, well-drained soil
Can be grown in a container. Zone 9

Laurus nobilis ▼

The bay tree is an architectural, evergreen shrub with aromatic, leathery, dark green leaves and clusters of yellow flowers followed by black fruit. **AGM**

Large; sun; flowers mid spring; fertile, well-drained soil
Can be grown as a hedge, clipped to shape. Useful in a container. Zone 8

Laurus nobilis 'Angustifolia' ▼

A narrow evergreen with aromatic narrow, wavy-edged leaves that give its common name of willow-leaf bay. Yellow flowers are borne in clusters.

Medium to large; sun; flowers mid spring; fertile, well-drained soil
Useful in a container. Zone 8

Lavandula angustifolia 'Folgate' ▼

A bushy evergreen form of English lavender with narrow, grey-green leaves and scented spikes of lavender blue-purple flowers.

Compact; sun; flowers mid summer; fertile, well-drained soil
Clip after flowering to maintain shape. Zone 7

Lavandula angustifolia 'Hidcote'

The best-known form of English lavender is an evergreen shrub with narrow, silvery grey-green leaves and masses of deep blue-purple flower spikes. **AGM**

Compact; sun; flowers mid summer; fertile, well-drained soil
Clip after flowering to maintain shape. Zone 7

▼ *Lavandula angustifolia* 'Hidcote' at Cambridge Botanic Garden, England.

Lavandula pedunculata subsp. _pedunculata_ ▲

An attractive form of French lavender with grey-green evergreen foliage and rounded purple flower spikes topped with long, paler purple, earlike bracts. AGM

Compact; sun; flowers mid summer; well-drained soil

Clip after flowering to maintain shape. Zone 8

Lavatera ×clementii 'Barnsley' ▲

A subshrub bearing velvety grey-green foliage and light pink flowers with a red eye.

Medium; sun; flowers early to late summer; well-drained soil

Reduce plant size in autumn. Cut stems down to ground level in early spring to encourage new growth. Zone 8

Lavatera ×clementii 'Blushing Bride' ▼

A subshrub with lobed, soft grey-green leaves and soft clear pink flowers with slightly deeper pink centres.

Medium; sun; flowers early to late summer; well-drained soil

Reduce plant size in autumn. Cut stems down to ground level in early spring to encourage new growth. Zone 8

Lavatera ×clementii 'Bredon Springs' ▼

A vigorous semievergreen subshrub with lobed, grey-green leaves and deep pink, five-petalled flowers. AGM

Medium; sun; flowers early to late summer; well-drained soil

Reduce plant size in autumn. Cut stems down to ground level in early spring to encourage new growth. Zone 8

Lavatera maritima ▲

The sea mallow is a rounded, deciduous shrub with grey-green foliage and large saucer-shaped pink flowers with a central area of purple-lilac. AGM

Small to medium; sun; flowers early to late summer; well-drained soil

Reduce plant size in autumn. Cut stems down to ground level in early spring to encourage new growth. Zone 9

Lavatera oblongifolia ▲

An upright semievergreen shrub with silvery grey-green leaves and mauve-pink flowers.

Small to medium; sun; flowers early to late summer; well-drained soil

Grow in a sunny yet sheltered site. Zone 10

Lavatera olbia ▲

An evergreen shrub with soft, fuzzy, lobed, grey-green foliage and large, showy, reddish purple flowers.

Medium; sun; flowers early to late summer; well-drained soil

Reduce plant size in autumn. Cut stems down to ground level in early spring to encourage new growth. Zone 8

Leiophyllum buxifolium var. *prostratum* ▲

The Allegheny sand myrtle is an evergreen shrub with a cushion habit, bearing small, glossy, dark green leaves and clusters of star-shaped, pale pink flowers that fade to white.

Prostrate; partial shade; flowers late spring to early summer; fertile, acid soil

Suitable for the rock garden. Zone 5

Leptodactylon californicum ▼

The prickly phlox is an evergreen shrub covered with dense, spiny green leaves and a liberal covering of bright, dark pink flowers.

Compact; sun; flowers early spring to early summer; well-drained soil

Needs a hot, dry summer to thrive. Suitable for the rock garden or scree. Zone 8

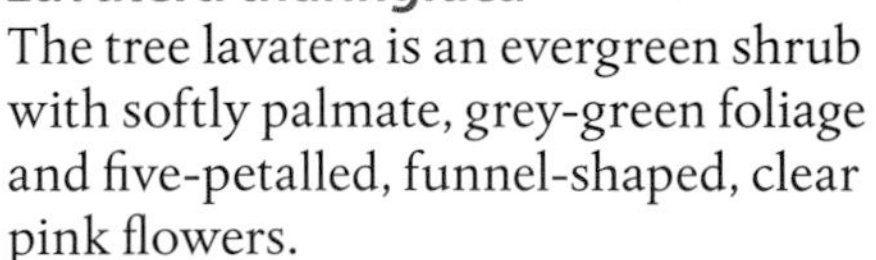

Lavatera thuringiaca ▲◀

The tree lavatera is an evergreen shrub with softly palmate, grey-green foliage and five-petalled, funnel-shaped, clear pink flowers.

Medium; sun; flowers early to late summer; well-drained soil

Reduce plant size in autumn. Cut stems down to ground level in early spring to encourage new growth. Zone 8

Leptodermis scabrida ▶

A deciduous shrub grown for its soft silvery pale pink tubular flowers which fade white.

Small to medium; sun; flowers late summer; well-drained soil

Suitable for the rock garden or scree. Zone 8

Leptospermum scoparium cultivar ▲▼

A cultivated variety of the manuka producing soft pink flowers with a prominent green centre and small heathlike evergreen leaves.

Medium; sun; flowers early summer; fertile, well-drained soil

Trim back after flowering to avoid plant becoming too leggy. Zone 10

Leptospermum scoparium 'Nichollsii' ▼▶

A cultivated variety of the manuka or tea tree with an arching, spreading habit, narrow, evergreen dark purple-green foliage, and attractive, cup-shaped, crimson flowers. AGM

Medium; sun; flowers early summer; fertile, well-drained soil

Trim back after flowering to avoid plant becoming too leggy. Zone 8

Leucadendron 'Safari Sunset' ▶

A dense, upright, evergreen shrub with purplish stems bearing leathery, green foliage ending in bright pink-red bracts.

Medium; sun; flowers early winter to early spring; well-drained, acid soil

Drought tolerant. Do not supplementary feed. Zone 9

Leucadendron 'Wilson's Wonder' ▼

A sprawling, evergreen shrub with reddish stems bearing thick, mid-green leaves topped with bright yellow bracts that turn orange with age.

Medium; sun; flowers early winter to early spring; well-drained, acid soil

Drought tolerant. Do not supplementary feed. Zone 9

Lespedeza bicolor ▲

The ezo-yama-hagi is an upright woody herbaceous plant with rounded, mid-green, trifoliate foliage and cascading spikes of bright pink-purple, pealike flowers.

Medium; sun; flowers late summer to early autumn; fertile soil

Cut stems back to ground level in spring. Provide plant supports for new growth in spring. Zone 5

Lespedeza thunbergii ▶

The miyagino-hagi is a woody herbaceous plant with arching branches bearing blue-green trifoliate foliage and large, terminal panicles of deep rose-purple, pealike flowers. **AGM**

Small to medium; sun; flowers late summer to early autumn; fertile soil

Cut stems back to ground level in spring. Provide plant supports for new growth in spring. Zone 5

Leucophyllum frutescens var. *compactum* ▲▼

A dense, rounded evergreen shrub with velvety silvery grey foliage and bright silvery pink flowers.

Medium; sun; flowers early winter to early spring; well-drained, acid soil

Drought tolerant. Do not supplementary feed. Zone 9

Leucothoe fontanesiana ▶

The drooping laurel is a spreading, evergreen shrub bearing leathery green leaves on arching branches, attractively tinted reddish purple in autumn. Bell-shaped white flowers are borne in racemes. **AGM**

Small to medium; shade to partial shade; flowers late spring; fertile, acid soil

Zone 5

Leucothoe fontanesiana 'Rainbow' ▶

A drooping laurel producing attractive, leathery, green foliage mottled with pink and white. Bell-shaped white flowers are borne in racemes.

Small to medium; shade to partial shade; flowers late spring; fertile, acid soil

Zone 5

Leycesteria crocothyrsos ▲

A deciduous shrub with large, pointed leaves and terminal racemes of bright yellow flowers.

Medium; sun or partial shade; flowers mid to late spring; fertile soil

Protect from frost in cold winters. Prune after flowering. Zone 9

Leycesteria formosa ▼

The Himalayan honesuckle is an upright, deciduous shrub with large, dark green, wavy-edged leaves and white flowers borne on drooping panicles of wine-red bracts followed by clusters of reddish purple berries. **AGM**

Medium; sun or partial shade; flowers early to late summer; fertile soil

Prune old stems in early spring. Zone 7

Ligustrum delavayanum ▲

The Delavay privet is a spreading, evergreen shrub with small, oval, glossy, dark green leaves and panicles of white flowers followed by black fruits.

Medium; sun or partial shade; flowers mid summer; fertile soil

Can be used as a hedging plant. Prune in early spring. Zone 7

Ligustrum lucidum ▲▼

The large-leaf privet is an evergreen shrub with large, pointed, glossy leaves and panicles of fluffy white flowers. **AGM**

Large; sun or partial shade; flowers mid to late summer; fertile soil

Can also be grown as a small tree. Zone 7

Ligustrum obtusifolium ▼

A spreading deciduous shrub with dense, oval-shaped, dark green foliage and panicles of small white flowers with an unpleasant smell.

Medium to large; sun or partial shade; flowers mid to late summer; fertile soil

Prune in early spring. Zone 3

Ligustrum quihoui ▼

A deciduous shrub noted for its long frothy panicles of scented creamy white flowers. It has very dark green leaves. **AGM**

Medium to large; sun or partial shade; flowers late summer to early autumn; fertile soil

Prune in early spring. Zone 5

Ligustrum sinense ▲

The Chinese privet is a spreading deciduous shrub with broadly oval, green leaves and many panicles of scented, star-shaped off-white flowers.

Large; sun or partial shade; flowers mid summer; fertile soil

Prune in early spring. Zone 7

Ligustrum sinense 'Wimbei' ▲

A Chinese privet with deciduous tiny, dark green, glossy leaves, making it a popular bonsai tree.

Compact to small; sun or partial shade; flowers mid summer; fertile soil

Zone 7

Lindera angustifolia ▶

A deciduous shrub grown for its narrow green leaves that turn a rich golden brown in the autumn and persist until growth starts in the spring.

Medium; sun or partial shade; flowers early to mid spring; fertile, acid soil

Zone 7

Lindera communis ▶

An evergreen shrub grown for its glossy green leaves and clusters of yellow flowers.

Medium to large; sun or partial shade; flowers early spring; fertile, acid soil

Zone 8

Lindera glauca ▼▶

A deciduous shrub with narrow, elliptical, blue-green leaves that are glaucous beneath and turn orange, red, and purple in autumn. Yellowish flowers are followed by small shiny black fruits.

Medium; partial shade; flowers early spring; fertile, acid soil

Zone 6

Lindera obtusiloba ▲▼▶▶

The Japanese spicebush is a deciduous shrub with bright green, three-lobed leaves, purplish green on opening and turning a lovely clear yellow in autumn. The small yellow flowers are star-shaped. **AGM**

Medium to large; partial shade; flowers early spring; fertile, acid soil

Zone 6

Lindera salicifolia ▶

The willow-leaf spicebush is a deciduous shrub with long, narrow leaves that turn shades of red, bronze, and orange in autumn. It bears small yellow flowers.

Large; sun to partial shade; flowers early spring; fertile, acid soil

Zone 6

Linum 'Gemmell's Hybrid' ▼

An evergreen shrub with grey-green leaves and bright golden yellow flowers. **AGM**

Compact; sun; flowers mid to late spring; well-drained soil

Suitable for the rock garden or alpine house.
Zone 8

Lithodora diffusa 'Heavenly Blue' ▶

A mat-forming evergreen shrub with small, hairy, dark green leaves and plenty of lovely, bright blue flowers. **AGM**

Prostrate to compact; sun or partial shade; flowers late spring to early summer; fertile, well-drained, acid soil

Suitable for the rock garden, scree, or wall. Zone 7

Lithodora oleifolia ▲

A low, spreading, evergreen shrub with smooth, dense, oval foliage and an abundance of azure blue, bell-shaped flowers. **AGM**

Prostrate to compact; sun or partial shade; flowers early to late summer; fertile, well-drained soil

Suitable for the rock garden or scree. Zone 8

Lithodora zahnii ▼

An evergreen shrub with hairy, grey-green foliage and long-lasting trumpet-shaped sky blue flowers.

Compact; sun; flowers late spring to early summer; fertile, well-drained soil

Zone 9

▲ *Loiseleuria procumbens* on Ben Alder, Scotland.

Loiseleuria procumbens

The mountain or alpine azalea is a mat-forming evergreen shrub with small glossy green leaves and pale soft pink flowers, pink in bud.

Prostrate; sun; flowers late spring to early summer; fertile, acid soil

Suitable for the rock garden or scree. Zone 2

Lomatia ferruginea ▲

An erect, evergreen shrub with beautiful deep green, fernlike leaves on red-brown velvety stems, and short racemes of deep golden yellow flowers with a red centre.

Large; sun or partial shade; flowers mid summer; fertile, acid soil

Zone 9

Lomatia silaifolia ▼

The crinkle bush is a spreading evergreen shrub with coarsely divided green leaves and large panicles of creamy white flowers.

Small to medium; sun or partial shade; flowers mid summer; fertile, acid soil

Prune occasionally in early spring to remove older stems. Zone 8

Lomatia tinctoria ▲

A dense shrub with dark green, pinnate, leathery leaves and long racemes of yellow to creamy white flowers.

Small to medium; sun or partial shade; flowers mid to late summer; fertile, acid soil

Prune occasionally in early spring to remove older stems. Zone 8

Lonicera ×amoena 'Rosea' ▼

A deciduous shrubby honeysuckle with an abundance of scented pink flowers.

Medium; sun to partial shade; flowers late spring to early summer; fertile soil

Thin out old wood after flowering. Zone 5

Lonicera bracteolaris ▼

A deciduous shrubby honeysuckle with paired pale yellow flowers set against rounded green leaves.

Large; sun or partial shade; flowers mid to late spring; fertile soil

Thin out older wood after flowering. Zone 5

Lonicera chaetocarpa ▼

An erect deciduous shrubby honeysuckle with green bristly foliage and bright cream-coloured, funnel-shaped flowers.

Small to medium; sun to partial shade; flowers late spring to early summer; fertile soil

Thin out older wood after flowering. Zone 5

Lonicera fragrantissima ◀ ▼

A beautifully flowering shrubby honeysuckle with a spreading, bushy habit with dainty, creamy white, scented flowers and oval, dark green leaves. The foliage is evergreen or deciduous according to the climate.

Medium; sun or partial shade; flowers late winter to early spring; fertile soil

Prune out older wood after flowering. Zone 5

Lonicera maackii ▲

A deciduous shrubby honeysuckle with long pointed green leaves and fragrant, creamy white flowers held above the stems and followed by ornamental dark red berries.

Large; sun or partial shade; flowers late spring to early summer; fertile soil

Prune out older wood after flowering. Zone 2

Lonicera maackii f. *podocarpa* ▼

A spreading deciduous shrubby honeysuckle with an abundance of fragrant yellow-white flowers and showy red berries.

Large; sun or partial shade; flowers late spring to early summer; fertile soil

Prune out older wood after flowering. Zone 2

Lonicera involucrata ▲

The twinberry is a vigorous, spreading deciduous shrubby honeysuckle with oval, green leaves and opposite pairs of yellow-orange tubular flowers, followed by shiny black berries.

Medium; sun or partial shade; flowers early summer; fertile soil

Prune out older wood after flowering. Zone 4

Lonicera mitis ▲

A deciduous shrubby honeysuckle grown for its grey-green leaves and its bluish purple first-year stems.

Medium; sun or partial shade; flowers late spring to early summer; fertile soil

Prune out older wood after flowering or cut stems down to ground level in early spring to encourage new growth. Zone 6

Lonicera morrowii ▼

A vigorous, deciduous shrubby honeysuckle with grey-green foliage and creamy white flowers which turn yellow with age and are followed by shiny dark red fruits.

Medium; sun or partial shade; flowers late summer to early autumn; fertile soil

Prune out older wood after flowering. Zone 3

Lonicera nitida 'Twiggy' ►

A bushy evergreen shrubby honeysuckle with dense, tiny golden leaves.

Compact; sun or partial shade; flowers mid spring; fertile soil

Can be clipped to shape. Zone 8

Lonicera pileata ▲▼

An evergreen shrub with glossy, bright green foliage turning darker with age and creamy white flowers followed by shiny bluish purple berries.

Compact to small; sun or partial shade; flowers mid spring; fertile soil

Can be grown as ground cover. Zone 5

Lonicera tatarica 'Hack's Red' ▼

A vigorous, shrubby honeysuckle with soft green, oval leaves and an abundance of pinky red flowers followed by red berries.

Large; sun or partial shade; flowers late spring to early summer; fertile soil

Prune out older wood after flowering. Zone 3

Lonicera ×purpusii ▲

A spreading deciduous or evergreen honeysuckle (depending on climate) with light green, oval leaves and fragrant, creamy white flowers.

Medium; sun or partial shade; flowers late winter to early spring; fertile soil

Prune out older wood after flowering. Zone 6

Lonicera quinquelocularis ▼

A deciduous shrub with oval green leaves and pairs of delicately fragrant creamy white flowers turning golden yellow, followed by translucent small white berries.

Large; sun or partial shade; flowers early summer; fertile soil

Prune out older wood after flowering. Zone 5

Lonicera setifera ▲

A shrubby honeysuckle with bristly stems and clusters of beautifully scented, pink and white, daphne-like flowers followed by red berries. AGM

Medium; sun or partial shade; flowers late winter to early spring; fertile soil

Prune out older wood after flowering. Zone 8

Lonicera trichosantha ▲

A deciduous shrubby honeysuckle with pale yellow flowers ageing golden yellow and followed by red berries.

Medium; sun or partial shade; flowers early summer; fertile soil

Prune out older wood after flowering. Zone 6

Lophomyrtus ×ralphii 'Variegata' ▶

A spreading, evergreen shrub of the New Zealand myrtle with variegated, rounded green foliage edged with white. The creamy white flowers are followed by red fruits.

Medium; sun; flowers early summer; fertile soil

To maintain variegation, remove any all-green shoots as they appear. Zone 9

Lophomyrtus ×ralphii 'Kathryn' ▲

This New Zealand myrtle is an evergreen shrub bearing glossy, rounded, reddish purple new foliage.

Medium; sun; flowers early summer; fertile soil

Zone 9

Lophomyrtus ×ralphii 'Red Wing' ▼

An evergreen shrub of the New Zealand myrtle bearing glossy, rounded, reddish purple new foliage.

Medium; sun; flowers early summer; fertile soil

Zone 9

▲ *Loropetalum chinense* in Kyoto Botanic Garden.

Loropetalum chinense ◀▼

The Chinese fringe flower is an evergreen shrub with an abundance of white or yellowish white flowers shaped like a witch hazel and oval, dark green, leathery foliage.

Medium; sun or partial shade; flowers late winter to mid spring; fertile soil

Prune after flowering to maintain size. Can be grown in a container in a cool greenhouse. Zone 9

Loropetalum chinense f. *rubrum* ▲

This form of the Chinese fringe flower is an evergreen shrub grown for its pink or reddish pink flowers and reddish purple new foliage ageing to purplish green.

Medium; sun or partial shade; flowers late winter to mid spring; fertile soil

Prune after flowering. Can be grown in a container in a cool greenhouse. Zone 9

Lotus hirsutus ▲

The hairy canary clover is a long-flowering semievergreen shrub with silvery grey leaves and pealike white flowers tinged pink followed by red-tinged seed pods. **AGM**

Prostrate; sun; flowers mid to late spring; well-drained soil

Suitable for the rock garden, scree, or alpine house. Zone 8

Luma apiculata ▲▶▼

The arrayan or Chilean myrtle or collimamol is an evergreen shrub with attractive, peeling, cinnamon brown and grey bark. It has small, glossy green leaves and white flowers followed by dark purple-black fruits. **AGM**

Large; sun; flowers mid to late summer; fertile soil

Prune lower shoots to reveal stems. Can be clipped to shape. Zone 8

Luma apiculata 'Glanleam Gold' ▼

An upright evergreen form of the arrayan bearing variegated, dark green leaves with creamy margins and white flowers. Young leaves are pink tinted. **AGM**

Medium to large; sun or partial shade; flowers mid to late summer; fertile soil

Can be clipped to shape. Zone 9

Lupinus arboreus ▲

The tree lupin is a bushy, evergreen shrub with greyish green foliage and erect dense racemes of scented, pealike bright yellow flowers. **AGM**

Medium; sun; flowers late spring to mid summer; well-drained soil

Plant out when young as they dislike root disturbance. Will naturalize if conditions allow. Zone 8

Lycium chinense ▲

The wolfberry or goji berry is a spreading shrub producing narrow, greyish green leaves and purple flowers with yellowish white on the outside. Pendulous red berries follow the flowers.

Medium; sun; flowers late spring to mid summer; well-drained soil

Good for seaside locations. Can be grown as a hedge or espaliered. Zone 6

Lyonia ligustrina ▲

The huckleberry is a deciduous shrub grown for its panicles of white flowers, shiny black fruits, and red autumn foliage.

Small to medium; sun to partial shade; flowers mid to late summer; fertile, acid soil

Prune out old stems in early spring. Zone 7

Maesa bullata ▼

A deciduous shrub with large glossy green leaves and racemes of small white flowers.

Medium to large; partial shade; flowers early to mid spring; fertile soil

Formative pruning after flowering. Zone 10

Magnolia 'Ann' ▼

One of eight hybrids from the U.S. National Arboretum known affectionately as the "Little Girls," this deciduous shrub has tulip-shaped pink flowers (rich reddish pink in the United States), pale on the inside. **AGM**

Medium to large; sun and partial shade; flowers mid to late spring; fertile soil

Formative pruning on young plants in late summer. Zone 5

Magnolia cylindrica ▲▼

A deciduous shrub or small tree grown for its beautiful pure white tulip-shaped flowers that have a hint of pink at the base of the tepals. Bright red fruiting cones are borne in autumn.

Large; sun and partial shade; flowers mid spring; fertile soil

Formative pruning on young plants in late summer. Crown reduction on mature specimens after flowering. Zone 6

▼ *Magnolia cylindrica* UBC 60714, a wild-collected form with beautiful rich rose-purple markings at the base of the tepals.

Magnolia 'David Clulow' ▼

This deciduous shrub has beautiful goblet-shaped large pure white flowers.

Large; sun and partial shade; flowers early to late spring; fertile soil

Formative pruning on young plants in late summer. Zone 5

Magnolia denudata ▼▶

The yulan is a deciduous broad-spreading shrub or small tree with lemon-scented pure white cup-shaped flowers. **AGM**

Large; sun and partial shade; flowers early spring; fertile, well-drained soil

Formative pruning on young plants in late summer. Crown reduction on mature specimens after flowering. Zone 6

Magnolia denudata 'Purple Eye' ▲

This yulan has a rich purple stain at the base of each pure white tepal.

Large; sun and partial shade; flowers early to mid spring; fertile soil

Formative pruning on young plants in late summer. Crown reduction on mature specimens after flowering. Zone 6

Magnolia 'George Henry Kern' ▲

A deciduous shrub with soft pink flowers, paler on the inside in Europe and lilac-red in the United States.

Small; sun and partial shade; flowers mid spring to early summer; fertile soil

Slow-growing with minimal pruning needs. Zone 5

Magnolia 'Gold Star' ▲

A deciduous shrub or small tree with pale yellow star-shaped flowers and light brown autumn colour.

Medium to large; sun and partial shade; flowers mid to late spring; fertile soil

Formative pruning on young plants in late summer. Zone 5

Magnolia 'Joe McDaniel' ▲

A broad-spreading deciduous shrub with large goblet-shaped flowers that are intense red-purple on the outside, pale pink within.

Large; sun and partial shade; flowers mid to late spring; fertile soil

Formative pruning in late summer. Crown reduction on mature specimens after flowering. Zone 5

Magnolia kobus ▲▼▼

The kobus magnolia or kobushi is a broad-spreading deciduous shrub or small tree grown for its delicately scented vase-shaped pure white flowers that have a hint of pink at the base of the tepals and are followed by bright orange seeds.

Large; sun and partial shade; flowers early to mid spring; fertile soil

Formative pruning on young plants in late summer. Crown reduction on mature specimens after flowering. Zone 5

Magnolia kobus 'Janaki Ammal' ▼▶

A broad-spreading deciduous shrub or small tree grown for its wide-opening pure white flowers.

Large; sun and partial shade; flowers early to mid spring; fertil soil

Formative pruning on young plants in late summer. Crown reduction on mature specimens after flowering. Zone 5

Magnolia kobus 'Norman Gould' ▶

A broad-spreading deciduous shrub or small tree grown for its cup-shaped pure white flowers.

Large; sun and partial shade; flowers early to mid spring; fertile soil

Formative pruning on young plants in late summer. Crown reduction on mature specimens after flowering. Zone 5

Magnolia laevifolia ▼

An evergreen shrub grown for its scented white or yellowish white flowers that have cinnamon-coloured coating when in bud. The green leaves sometimes have a velvety brown covering on the underside.

Medium to large; sun and partial shade; flowers early to mid spring; fertile soil

Limited pruning after flowering if necessary. Zone 8

Magnolia laevifolia 'Velvet and Cream' ▲▼

An evergreen shrub grown for is abundant cup-shaped scented white flowers. The floral buds have a cinnamon-coloured coating, and the green leaves have a velvety cinnamon-brown coating on the underside.

Medium to large; sun and partial shade; flowers early to late spring; fertile soil

Limited pruning after flowering if necessary. Zone 8

Magnolia 'Lileny' ▲

A deciduous shrub with soft pink flowers, paler on the inside, similar but larger than M. 'George Henry Kern'.

Medium; sun and partial shade; flowers mid to late spring; fertile soil

Slow growing with little pruning needs. Zone 5

Magnolia liliiflora ▼

The mulan or woody orchid is a deciduous shrub grown for its candle-shaped rich rose-red flowers, paler on the inside and sweetly scented on the first day of opening.

Medium; sun and partial shade; flowers mid spring to early summer; fertile soil

Limited pruning in late summer if necessary. Zone 6

Magnolia liliiflora 'Nigra' ▶

This form of the mulan is a compact, deciduous shrub grown for its dark reddish purple flowers that are pale purple on the inside and sweetly scented on the first day of opening. **AGM**

Medium; sun and partial shade; flowers mid spring to early summer; fertile soil

Limited pruning in late summer if necessary. Zone 6

Magnolia ×*loebneri* 'Ballerina' ▼

A twiggy deciduous shrub or small tree grown for its delicately scented white flowers with up to 30 tepals for each flower.

Medium; sun and partial shade; flowers early and mid spring; fertile soil

Formative pruning in late summer if necessary. Zone 5

Magnolia ×*loebneri* 'Donna' ▲

A twiggy deciduous shrub grown for its delicately scented broad-tepalled white flowers.

Medium; sun and partial shade; flowers mid spring; fertile soil

Limited pruning in late summer if necessary. Zone 5

Magnolia ×*loebneri* 'Leonard Messel' ▶

A twiggy deciduous shrub grown for its delicately scented pink flowers. **AGM**

Medium to large; sun and partial shade; flowers early to mid spring; fertile soil

Limited pruning in late summer if necessary. Zone 5

Magnolia ×*loebneri* 'Mags Pirouette' ▲

A twiggy deciduous shrub grown for its delicately scented white flowers.

Small to medium; sun and partial shade; flowers mid to late spring; fertile soil

Zone 5

Magnolia ×*loebneri* 'Merrill' ▼

A twiggy deciduous shrub or small tree grown for its delicately scented white flowers. **AGM**

Large; sun and partial shade; flowers mid spring; fertil soil

Limited pruning in late summer if necessary. Zone 5

Magnolia ×*loebneri* 'Raspberry Fun' ▼

A twiggy deciduous shrub grown for its delicately scented pink flowers.

Large; sun and partial shade; flowers mid spring; fertile soil

Limited pruning in late summer if necessary. Zone 5

Magnolia maudiae ▼

A broad-spreading or upright evergreen shrub or small tree grown for its beautifully scented pure white flowers and dark green leaves.

Large; sun and partial shade; flowers early to late spring; fertile soil

Limited pruning after flowering if necessary. Zone 9

Magnolia maudiae 'Golden Temple' ▲

An upright evergreen shrub or small tree grown for its beautifully scented large pure white flowers and dark green leaves.

Large; sun and partial shade; flowers early to mid spring; fertile soil

Limited pruning after flowering if necessary. Zone 9

Magnolia maudiae var. *platypetala* ▼▶

A broad-spreading shrub grown for its beautifully scented pure white flowers which appear as though they arranged on the top of branches.

Large; sun and partial shade; flowers early to mid spring; fertile soil

Limited pruning after flowering if necessary. Zone 9

Magnolia 'Pickard's Stardust' ▶

A deciduous shrub grown for its ivory white flowers which are slightly scented.

Medium to large; sun and partial shade; flowers early to mid spring; fertile soil

Formative pruning on young plants in late summer. Zone 5

Magnolia 'Pinkie' ▼

One of the eight "Little Girls," this deciduous round headed shrub has cup-shaped pink flowers (pale lilac-red in the United States), paler on the inside. AGM

Medium; sun and partial shade; flowers mid to late spring; fertile soil

Formative pruning on young plants in late summer. Zone 5

Magnolia sinensis ▶

A broad-spreading deciduous shrub grown for its beautifully sweetly scented pendent pure white flowers with a ring of magenta stamens and its green leaves which are grey on the underside.

Medium to large; partial shade; flowers late spring to early summer; fertile soil

Zone 7

Magnolia 'Randy' ▲

One of the eight "Little Girls," this deciduous upright shrub has rich pink flowers (red-purple in the United States), pale pink on the inside.

Medium; sun and partial shade; flowers mid spring; fertile soil

Formative pruning on young plants in late summer. Zone 5

Magnolia ×soulangeana ▲

A broad-spreading deciduous shrub grown for its tulip-, cup-and-saucer- and goblet-shaped white, pink, or purple flowers.

Large; sun and partial shade; flowers early to late spring; fertile soil

Formative pruning on young plants in late summer. Crown reduction on mature specimens after flowering. Zone 5

Magnolia ×soulangeana 'Alba Superba' ▼

A broad-spreading large deciduous shrub grown for its tulip-shaped white flowers with a hint of pink at the base of each flower.

Large; sun and partial shade; flowers early to mid spring; fertile soil

Formative pruning in late summer. Crown reduction on mature specimens after flowering. Zone 5

Magnolia sieboldii ▲

A broad-spreading deciduous shrub grown for its beautifully sweetly scented pure white nodding flowers with a ring of magenta or pink anthers.

Medium; partial shade; flowers late spring to mid summer; fertile soil

Zone 7

▶ *Magnolia ×soulangeana* 'Alexandrina' at the New York Botanical Garden.

Magnolia ×soulangeana 'Alexandrina'

A broad-spreading large deciduous shrub grown for its delicately fragrant tulip-shaped white or pale pink flowers with a hint of purple at the base of each flower.

Large; sun and partial shade; flowers mid to late spring; fertile soil

Formative pruning if necessary in late summer. Crown reduction on mature specimens after flowering. Zone 5

Magnolia ×soulangeana 'Brozzonii' ▲

A broad-spreading large deciduous shrub grown for its candlelike, ultimately cup-and-saucer-shaped large white flowers with pink at the base of each flower. One of the last soulangeana's to flower. **AGM**

Large; sun and partial shade; flowers early to mid spring; fertile soil

Formative pruning in late summer. Crown reduction on mature specimens after flowering. Zone 5

Magnolia ×soulangeana 'Coates' ▶

A broad-spreading large deciduous shrub grown for its cup-and-saucer-shaped rich rose pink flowers, pale pink inside.

Large; sun and partial shade; flowers mid to late spring; fertile soil

Formative pruning in late summer. Crown reduction on mature specimens after flowering. Zone 5

Magnolia ×soulangeana 'Lennei' ▶

A broad-spreading large deciduous shrub grown for its cup-shaped deep rose pink flowers, pale creamy white inside. **AGM**

Large; sun and partial shade; flowers mid to late spring; fertile soil

Formative pruning in late summer. Crown reduction on mature specimens after flowering. Zone 5

Magnolia ×soulangeana 'Lennei Alba' ▼

A broad-spreading deciduous shrub grown for its large goblet-shaped pure white flowers. **AGM**

Large; sun and partial shade; flowers mid to late spring; fertile soil

Formative pruning in late summer. Crown reduction on mature specimens after flowering. Zone 5

Magnolia ×soulangeana 'Picture' ▶

A broad-spreading deciduous shrub grown for its large cup-shaped white flowers with heavy staining of red purple on the outside of the flowers.

Large; sun and partial shade; flowers mid to late spring; fertile soil

Formative pruning in late summer. Crown reduction on mature specimens after flowering. Zone 5

Magnolia ×soulangeana 'Pickard's Opal' ▲

A broad-spreading large deciduous shrub grown for its goblet-shaped white flowers with a hint of rich pink at the base of each flower.

Large; sun and partial shade; flowers mid to late spring; fertile soil

Formative pruning in late summer. Crown reduction on mature specimens after flowering. Zone 5

Magnolia ×soulangeana 'Pickard's Schmetterling' ▼

An upright deciduous shrub or small tree grown for its large tulip-shaped white flowers with heavy rich rose-pink staining on the outside of the flowers.

Large; sun and partial shade; flowers mid to late spring; fertile soil

Formative pruning in late summer if necessary. Crown reduction on mature specimens after flowering. Zone 5

Magnolia ×soulangeana 'Rustica Rubra' ▲

A broad-spreading deciduous shrub grown for its large goblet-shaped rose purple flowers creamy white with a hint of pink within. **AGM**

Large; sun and partial shade; flowers mid to late spring; fertile soil

Formative pruning in late summer if necessary. Crown reduction on mature specimens after flowering. Zone 5

Magnolia ×soulangeana 'Verbanica' ▼

A spreading deciduous shrub grown for its cup-shaped rich clean pink flowers.

Large; sun and partial shade; flowers mid to late spring; fertile soil

Formative pruning in late summer if necessary. Crown reduction on mature specimens after flowering. Zone 5

Magnolia stellata ▲

A compact growing twiggy deciduous shrub grown for its delicately scented flowers which vary in colour and number of tepals. **AGM**

Medium; sun and partial shade; flowers early to mid spring; fertile soil
Zone 5

***Magnolia stellata* 'Centennial'** ▼

A compact growing twiggy deciduous shrub grown for its delicately scented pure white starlike flowers with about 30 tepals to each flower.

Medium; sun and partial shade; flowers early to mid spring; fertile soil
Zone 5

***Magnolia stellata* 'Dawn'** ▶

A compact growing twiggy deciduous shrub grown for its delicately scented rich pink, fading pale pink almost white starlike flowers with up to 45 tepals to each flower.

Medium; sun and partial shade; flowers early to mid spring; fertile soil
Zone 5

***Magnolia stellata* 'Jane Platt'** ▲

A compact growing twiggy deciduous shrub grown for its delicately scented rich pink, fading pale pink starlike flowers with 32 tepals to each flower.

Medium; sun and partial shade; flowers early to mid spring; fertile soil
Formative pruning in late summer if necessary. Zone 4

***Magnolia stellata* 'Royal Star'** ▼

A compact growing twiggy deciduous shrub grown for its delicately scented ice white flowers with up to 25 broad tepals to each flower.

Medium; sun and partial shade; flowers early to mid spring; fertile soil
Formative pruning in late summer if necessary. Zone 5

▲ *Magnolia stellata* 'Waterlily' at the New York Botanical Garden.

Magnolia stellata 'Water Lily' ▶

A compact growing twiggy deciduous shrub grown for its delicately scented white flowers with about 25 tepals to each flower. The European clone ('Water Lily') has white flowerrs, the American ('Waterlily'), pinkish. **AGM**

Medium; sun and partial shade; flowers early to mid spring; fertile soil
Zone 5

Magnolia 'Susan' ▶

One of the eight "Little Girls," this deciduous round-headed shrub has fragrant deep pink flowers (red-purple in the United States), paler pink on the inside. **AGM**

Medium; sun and partial shade; flowers mid spring; fertile soil
Formative pruning on young plants in late summer. Zone 5

Magnolia virginiana ▲

The sweet bay magnolia is a broad-spreading evergreen shrub or small tree (but can also be deciduous) grown for its sweetly scented white goblet-shaped flowers and its green leaves which are glaucous white beneath.

Medium to large; sun and partial shade; flowers early to late summer; fertile soil
Formative pruning in late summer if necessary. Zone 5

Magnolia ×wieseneri ▼

A broad-spreading deciduous shrub grown for its sweetly scented ivory white upward-facing flowers, each with a red boss of stamens.

Large; sun and partial shade; flowers early to mid summer; fertile soil
Formative pruning if necessary in late summer. Zone 7

Magnolia wilsonii ▲

Wilson's magnolia is a broad-spreading deciduous shrub grown for its beautifully sweetly scented pendent pure white flowers with a ring of magenta stamens and its green leaves which have cinnamon brown hairs on the underside of the main veins. AGM

Medium; partial shade; flowers late spring, early summer; fertile soil

Zone 7

×Mahoberberis aquisargentii ▼

An evergreen bi-generic hybrid upright shrub with bold shiny spiny green foliage and soft yellow flowers followed by black fruits.

Medium; sun to partial shade; flowers late winter to mid spring; fertile soil

Zone 6

Mahonia aquifolium 'Apollo' ▲

A dense low-growing form of the Oregon grape grown for its bright yellow flower clusters and deep green foliage with red stalks. AGM

Compact; sun and partial shade; flowers early to late spring; fertile soil

Useful as evergreen ground cover. Zone 5

Mahonia aquifolium 'Green Ripple' ▼

A dense low-growing form of the Oregon grape grown for its bold shiny wavy plum purple foliage during winter turning a bright, glossy green during summer.

Compact; sun and partial shade; flowers early to late spring; fertile soil

Useful as evergreen ground cover. Prune after flowering in early spring. Zone 5

Mahonia 'Arthur Menzies' ▲

An evergreen upright shrub with bold shiny blue-green foliage and lemon yellow racemes of flowers.

Medium; sun and partial shade; flowers early winter to early spring; fertile soil

Prune after flowering in early spring. Zone 7

Mahonia confusa ▼

A dense upright, unbranched evergreen shrub grown for its sea green pinnate foliage, its pale yellow racemes of flowers followed by blue-black fruits.

Small; partial shade; flowers early to late autumn; fertile soil

Prune in early spring. Zone 8

Mahonia fremontii ▲

A compact growing evergreen shrub grown for its glaucous blue foliage and its clusters of pale yellow flowers.

Small to medium; sun; flowers late spring to early summer; fertile, well-drained soil

Prune where necessary after flowering in early summer. Zone 8

Mahonia gracilipes ▼

A compact suckering evergreen shrub grown for its pinnate foliage, bluish green above and a bright glaucous grey beneath, which contrasts well with its light brown stems and its bicoloured maroon-and-white flowers.

Small; partial shade; flowers late summer to early autumn; fertile soil

Prune where necessary in early spring. Zone 7

Mahonia japonica ▼

An upright evergreen shrub grown for its bold glossy green pinnate foliage, often tinged red in winter, and for its long racemes of fragrant pale yellow flowers. AGM

Medium; partial shade; flowers mid winter to early spring; fertile soil

Prune where necessary after flowering. Zone 6

Mahonia lomariifolia ▼▼▼▶

An upright evergreen shrub grown for its bold, dark green pinnate foliage and long erect racemes of yellow flowers followed by glaucous blue-black fruit. **AGM**

Large; partial shade; flowers mid to late winter; fertile soil

Prune after flowering in early spring. Zone 7

Mahonia mairei ▲

A broad-spreading evergreen shrub grown for its bold green foliage and long erect racemes of bright orange-yellow flowers.

Medium; partial shade; flowers mid to late winter; fertile soil

Grow in a sheltered site. Prune after flowering in early spring. Zone 9

Mahonia ×*media* 'Charity' ▼

An upright evergreen shrub grown for its green pinnate foliage, bronze new growth and its erect racemes of delicately fragrant bright yellow flowers.

Medium to large; partial shade; flowers early winter to early spring; fertile soil

Prune older plants in early spring. Zone 7

Mahonia ×media 'Faith' ▲

An upright evergreen shrub grown for its long pinnate green foliage and its terminal racemes of bright yellow flowers.

Medium to large; partial shade; flowers early winter to early spring; fertile soil

Prune older plants in early spring. Zone 7

Mahonia ×media 'Roundwood' ▲

A broad-spreading evergreen shrub grown for its bold pinnate foliage and its profuse long racemes of rich yellow flowers.

Medium to large; partial shade; flowers early winter to early spring; fertile soil

Prune older plants in early spring. Zone 7

Mahonia ×media 'Lionel Fortescue' ▲

An upright evergreen shrub grown for its pinnate green foliage, bronze new growth and its terminal racemes of fragrant bright deep yellow flowers. **AGM**

Medium; partial shade; flowers early winter to early spring; fertile soil

Prune older plants in early spring. Zone 7

Mahonia ×media 'Underway' ◀▲

A broad-spreading evergreen shrub grown for its bold pinnate foliage, bronze new growth and its racemes of rich yellow flowers. **AGM**

Medium; partial shade; flowers early winter to early spring; fertile soil

Prune older plants in early spring. Zone 7

Mahonia ×media 'Winter Sun' ▲
An upright evergreen shrub grown for its bold pinnate foliage bronze new growth followed by fragrant rich yellow flowers which are often the first to open. **AGM**

Medium; partial shade; flowers mid autumn to early winter; fertile soil

Prune older plants in early spring. Zone 7

Mahonia nervosa ▼
A low-growing suckering evergreen shrub grown for its green leaves which turn reddish purple in winter, and for its racemes of yellow flowers followed by glaucous blue fruit.

Compact; partial shade; flowers late winter to early spring; fertile soil

Zone 6

Mahonia nevinii ▲
An upright evergreen shrub grown for its bluish green foliage and small clusters of yellow flowers.

Small; sun and partial shade; flowers mid to late autumn; fertile, well-drained soil

Prune where necessary in early spring. Zone 8

Mahonia nitens ▶
An evergreen shrub grown for its glossy green leaves which have a distinctive red colouration to the base of each leaflet, also copper red young foliage with racemes of pale yellow flowers with red stamens followed by purplish black fruits on red stalks.

Small; partial shade; flowers mid to late autumn; fertile soil

New to cultivation. Zone 8

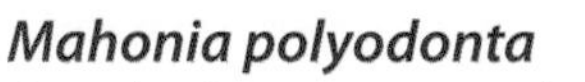

Mahonia polyodonta ▲
A suckering evergreen shrub grown for its glossy, dark green leaves and its terminal clusters of sulphur yellow flowers followed by bluish black fruits.

Compact to small; partial shade; flowers early to mid spring; fertile soil

Zone 7

Mahonia russellii JR442 ▼

An upright evergreen shrub with long drooping leaves which are pinkish red on opening with nodding small red, white and yellow flowers and small blue black fruits.

Medium; partial shade; flowers late winter and sometimes also in early winter and mid summer; fertile soil

Grows as a single stem if left unchecked. Pruning necessary in early spring. Zone 8

Mahonia ×wagneri 'Hastings Elegant' ◄

A compact evergreen shrub grown for its glossy, dark green leaves and bright yellow flowers seen in dense clusters.

Small; sun to partial shade; flowers early to mid spring; fertile soil

Zone 7

Mahonia ×wagneri 'Moseri' ▼

A compact evergreen shrub grown for its green foliage which turns a bright red in winter later bronze-red in new growth and compact clusters of bright yellow flowers.

Small; sun to partial shade; flowers early to mid spring; fertile soil

Zone 7

Mahonia ×savilliana 'Verderer' ▲

A compact evergreen shrub grown for its green leaflets, which are chalky white beneath, and their erect dense flowering racemes of orange-yellow flowers red in bud.

Medium; sun to partial shade; flowers late summer to early autumn; fertile soil

Zone 7

Mahonia ×wagneri 'Pinnacle' ▼

A spreading evergreen shrub grown for its copper-coloured new foliage and its clusters of yellow flowers. AGM

Small to medium; sun to partial shade; flowers early to mid spring; fertile soil

Zone 7

Mallotus japonica ▲

A large deciduous shrub or small tree grown for its rounded light green leaves which are red as they unfold with panicles of red female and yellow male flowers (on separate plants) followed by yellow autumn foliage.

Medium; sun or partial shade; flowers early to mid summer; well-drained soil

Thrives when grown against a south-facing wall. Zone 9

Matudaea trinervia ▼

A broad-spreading deciduous shrub or small tree grown for its rich purple new growth set against green foliage. Flowers are inconspicuous.

Large; sun and partial shade; flowers late winter to early spring; fertile, well-drained soil

Little pruning necessary, but stems could be cut down to the ground to encourage new growth. Zone 9

Medicago arborea ▶

A semievergreen shrub grown for its yellow pealike flowers and grey-green cloverlike leaves.

Small; sun; flowers early to late summer; well-drained soil

Suitable for coastal conditions. Zone 8

Melaleuca gibbosa ▼

The slender honey myrtle is an evergreen shrub grown for its small rounded purple-pink flowers and green needlelike leaves.

Small to medium; sun; flowers mid summer; well-drained, acid soil

Prune in early spring. Zone 9

Melaleuca squamea ▼

An upright evergreen shrub grown for its small white flowers and tiny dark green leaves.

Small to medium; sun; flowers late spring; well-drained, acid soil

Prune after flowering to maintain habit. Zone 9

Melianthus major ▼

The honey flower is an evergreen shrub grown for its glaucous grey-green leaves and racemes of brick red flowers. **AGM**

Small to medium; sun; flowers mid to late summer; fertile, well-drained soil

Can be treated as a herbaceous plant by pruning in the spring. May be cut back by severe winters. Zone 9

Melicytus angustifolius ▲

An evergreen shrub grown for its small yellow flowers, white fruits, and oblong grey-green leaves.

Small; sun or partial shade; flowers mid spring; fertile, well-drained soil

A male and a female plant are necessary to see fruits. Best grown in the rock garden. Zone 9

Menziesia ciliicalyx var. *purpurea* ▲

A spreading evergreen shrub grown for its nodding bell-shaped rose-purple flowers and green leaves.

Small; sun and partial shade; flowers late spring; fertile, acid soil

Best grown in a woodland garden or rock garden. Zone 6

Meterosideros robusta ►

The northern rata is a broad-spreading evergreen shrub grown for its dark scarlet bottlebrush-like flowers and dark green leaves.

Large; sun; flowers early to late summer; fertile, acid soil

Can be grown in a conservatory in colder climates. Where necessary, prune in early spring. Zone 9

Mitraria coccinea ▼

A low-spreading evergreen subshrub grown for its bright orange-red tubular flowers and dark green leaves.

Prostrate to compact; shade; flowers late spring to mid summer; fertile, acid soil

Succeeds when grown as an epiphyte in a woodland garden. Zone 9

Moltkia petraea ▲

A small deciduous spreading shrub grown for its tubular pale violet-blue flowers and narrow bright green leaves.

Compact; sun; flowers early to mid summer; well-drained, neutral to alkaline soil

Suitable for the rock garden or scree. Zone 6

Myrsine africana ▲▼

The Cape myrtle is an upright evergreen shrub grown for its tiny reddish brown flowers, small glossy green leaves, and lilac-black fruits.

Small; sun or partial shade; flowers late spring; fertile soil

Can be grown in a container or on the rock garden. Zone 9

Myrtus communis ▼

The common myrtle is an evergreen shrub grown for its conspicuous fragrant white flowers, aromatic green foliage, and conspicuous blue-black fruits. **AGM**

Large; sun; flowers mid to late summer; fertile, well-drained soil

Can be clipped to shape. Zone 8

Myrtus communis subsp. *tarentina* ▲

A compact evergreen shrub grown for its unscented pink tinged creamy white flowers and its aromatic narrow green foliage. **AGM**

Small to medium; sun; flowers mid to late summer; fertile, well-drained soil

Can be clipped to shape. Zone 8

Nandina domestica ◀▼

The heavenly bamboo is a decorative, evergreen shrub with long, erect stems bearing bright green leaves that have hints of red when young and turn reddish purple in autumn. The panicles of small white flowers are followed by red berries. **AGM**

Medium; sun; flowers mid summer; fertile, well-drained soil

Plant in groups to achieve good fruit set. Leggy plants can be cut back to get regrowth in spring. Zone 7

Nandina domestica 'Fire Power' ▲

A small rounded evergreen shrub with attractive, yellowish green leaves that turn fiery orange-red during winter. **AGM**

Small to medium; sun; flowers mid summer; fertile, well-drained soil

Zone 7

Nandina domestica 'Richmond' ▼

A vigorous, rounded evergreen cultivar with glossy, dark green leaves, reddish new growth, and purplish red autumn colour. The panicles of white flowers are followed by masses of bright red berries, which are produced without the need for a pollinator.

Medium; sun; flowers mid summer; fertile, well-drained soil

Does not need to be planted in a group to achieve fruit set. Leggy plants can be cut back to get regrowth in spring. Zone 7

Neillia thibetica ▶

An arching deciduous shrub that bears terminal racemes of pink flowers on reddish brown stems and lobed, green leaves with a crimped appearance. The foliage turns yellow in autumn.

Medium; sun or partial shade; flowers early summer; fertile, well-drained soil

Remove any older stems and excess suckers after flowering. Zone 6

Neolitsea sericea ▲▼

An evergreen shrub or small tree with aromatic foliage. Grown for its beautiful new leaves that are velvety, rusty brown with white, silky undersides, becoming dark green and more leathery with age. Flowers are yellowish green.

Medium to large; sun; flowers mid autumn; fertile, acid soil

Zone 9

▲ *Nerium oleander* at Varenna, on Lake Como in Italy.

Nerium oleander ▶

An evergreen shrub with leathery, long, narrow leaves and clusters of either single or double white, yellow, or pink flowers.

Medium to large; sun; flowers early summer to early autumn; fertile, well-drained soil

Can be grown in a container or a conservatory. Zone 8

Neviusia alabamensis ▼

The Alabama snow wreath is a suckering deciduous shrub with an arching habit and clusters of fluffy, white flowers.

Small to medium; sun or partial shade; flowers mid summer; fertile, well-drained soil

Remove excess suckers after flowering. Zone 5

Oemleria cerasiformis ▼

The Indian plum is a deciduous shrub bearing light green lance-shaped leaves with slightly furry undersides. The hanging racemes of white flowers are followed by purplish brown rounded fruit.

Medium; sun or partial shade; flowers early to mid spring; fertile soil

Can sucker freely. Zone 6

Olearia arborescens ▲

A bushy, spreading, evergreen shrub with oval leaves, glossy, dark green above and silvery below. White daisy-like flowers with yellow eyes are borne on branched flower heads.

Large; sun; flowers early to mid summer; fertile, well-drained soil

Zone 9

Olearia cheesmannii ▼

An upright evergreen shrub with thick, slightly serrated leaves, glossy green above and buff or silvery grey below, and covered by a profusion of large white daisylike flowers.

Medium to large; sun; flowers early summer; fertile, well-drained soil

Zone 9

Olearia erubescens ▲

A spreading shrub with toothed, glossy, dark green leaves and daisylike flowers.

Small; sun; flowers late spring to early summer; fertile, well-drained soil

Zone 9

Olearia ×haastii ▼

A rounded evergreen shrub bearing dark green, leathery, spear-shaped leaves with velvety white undersides, and an abundance of white daisylike flowers.

Small to medium; sun; flowers mid to late summer; fertile, well-drained soil

Useful for hedging. Zone 8

Olearia 'Henry Travers' ▶

An upright, bushy, evergreen shrub with narrow, spear-shaped, greyish green leaves, silvery on the underside, and with long-lasting daisylike lilac flowers with dark purple eyes.

Medium; sun; flowers mid summer; fertile, well-drained soil

Zone 9

Olearia ilicifolia ▼

The Marlborough rock daisy is an evergreen shrub with white-felted new growth, green leaves with white undersides, and white daisylike flowers with yellow centres.

Medium to large; sun; flowers early summer; fertile, well-drained soil

Zone 8

Olearia ×mollis ▼

A rounded evergreen shrub bearing silvery grey, gently toothed, wavy edged leaves and flower heads of white daisylike flowers.

Medium; sun; flowers late spring; fertile, well-drained soil

Zone 8

Olearia ×mollis 'Zennorensis' ▶

An evergreen shrub with attractive long, toothed leaves, dark green above and pale green below. Daisylike flowers are white and yellow.

Small to medium; sun; flowers mid summer; fertile, well-drained soil

Zone 8

Olearia nummularifolia ▼

A dense evergreen shrub with stiff branches bearing small, leathery, oval, yellowish green leaves and clusters of fragrant daisylike flowers.

Medium; sun; flowers mid summer; fertile, well-drained soil

Zone 8

Olearia phlogopappa ▲

The dusty daisy bush is an upright evergreen shrub with toothed, narrow, deep bluish green leaves and clusters of daisylike white, pink, mauve, or blue flowers.

Medium; sun; flowers late spring; fertile, well-drained soil

Reduce length of stems after flowering. Zone 9

Olearia paniculata ▲▶

A large shrub with oval, bright olive green, wavy-edged leaves and tiny, fragrant daisylike flowers.

Large; sun; flowers late autumn to early winter; fertile, well-drained soil

Can be used as a hedge. Prune in spring. Zone 9

Olearia phlogopappa 'Comber's Pink' ▲

An attractive cultivar of the dusty daisy bush with long, narrow, grey-green leaves and bright pink daisylike flowers.

Medium; sun; flowers late spring; fertile, well-drained soil
Reduce length of stems after flowering. Zone 9

Olearia ×scilloniensis ▼

A rounded, free-flowering evergreen shrub with greyish green leaves and white daisylike flowers.

Medium; sun; flowers late spring; fertile, well-drained soil
Zone 8

Olearia ×scilloniensis 'Master Michael' ▶

An attractive, compact shrub with grey-green leaves and plenty of mauve daisylike flowers.

Medium; sun; flowers late spring; fertile, well-drained soil
Zone 8

Olearia 'Waikariensis' ▼

An evergreen shrub with leaves olive green above and white below, and with clusters of white daisylike flowers.

Small to medium; sun; flowers summer; fertile, well-drained soil
Zone 8

Orixa japonica ▼

A deciduous shrub with bright green, fragrant leaves that turn yellow in autumn and small, greenish flowers. Female flowers are borne singly, while male flowers are borne in small panicles.

Medium; partial shade; flowers early to late spring; fertile soil
Used as a hedging plant in Japan. Zone 6

Osmanthus ×burkwoodii ▶

A rounded evergreen shrub with dense, dark green foliage and clusters of scented, white, tubular flowers. **AGM**

Medium; sun or partial shade; flowers late spring; fertile, well-drained soil

Can be used as a hedging plant. Zone 6

Osmanthus decorus ▼

An attractively rounded evergreen shrub with leathery leaves and clusters of white, scented flowers followed by purplish black fruit.

Medium; sun or partial shade; flowers mid to late spring; fertile soil

Can be used as a hedging plant. Zone 7

Osmanthus delavayi ▼

A lovely, small-leaved, rounded evergreen shrub producing smooth but serrately edged dark green leaves, paler beneath, with a profusion of scented white flowers. **AGM**

Medium; sun or partial shade; flowers mid to late spring; fertile soil

Zone 7

Osmanthus fragrans f. *auriantiacus* ▼

This form of the fragrant olive is an evergreen shrub with finely toothed, oblong, dark green foliage and clusters of small, beautifully scented yellow-orange flowers.

Large; sun or partial shade; flowers early to mid summer; fertile soil

Zone 9

Osmanthus heterophyllus ▼

A slow-growing, evergreen shrub with shiny dark green, hollylike leaves that can be spiny-toothed or entire, and with fragrant, white flowers.

Large; sun or partial shade; flowers early autumn; fertile soil

Useful as a hedging plant. Zone 6

Osmanthus heterophyllus 'Goshiki' ▲

A striking cultivar with variegated, mottled green and gold foliage, tinged pink when young, and with tiny, white flowers followed by black berries.

Medium; sun or partial shade; flowers early autumn; fertile soil
Zone 6

Osmanthus heterophyllus 'Variegatus' ▼

A variegated cultivar with shiny green leaves edged in creamy white and with small, scented white flowers followed by black berries. AGM

Medium; sun or partial shade; flowers early autumn; fertile soil
Used as a hedging plant. Zone 6

Osmanthus yunnanensis ►

An architectural evergreen shrub with olive green leaves being variously toothed, rounded, flat, or wavy-edged and with clusters of scented, white, tubular flowers.

Large; sun or partial shade; flowers late winter; fertile soil
Zone 7

Osteomeles schweriniae ▼

A semievergreen, arching shrub with glossy, fernlike, dark green foliage and clusters of hawthornlike white flowers followed by white berries.

Medium to large; sun; flowers early summer; fertile soil
Zone 8

Ozothamnus coralloides ▼

A rounded evergreen shrub with grey-green scalelike leaves, hairy beneath, and with pale yellow flowers. AGM

Compact; sun; flowers mid summer; well-drained soil
Suitable for the rock garden, scree, or trough. Zone 8

Ozothamnus ledifolius ▲▼

The kerosene bush is a rounded shrub with yellowish stems bearing dense, rounded, green leaves, ochre yellow beneath. Orange-red buds become scented, white flowers. AGM

Small to medium; sun; flowers mid summer; well-drained soil

Prune after flowering. Zone 8

▲ *Ozothamnus rosmarinifolius* at Kiftsgate Court Gardens, Gloucestershire, England.

Ozothamnus rosmarinifolius

A dense evergreen shrub grown for its dark green leaves and pink floral buds that open to scented white flowers.

Medium; sun; flowers mid summer; well-drained soil

Zone 8

Ozothamnus rosmarinifolius 'Silver Jubilee' ▼▶

A dense evergreen shrub with whitish stems bearing small silvery green leaves and pink flower buds that become scented white flowers. AGM

Medium; sun; flowers mid summer; well-drained soil

Prune after flowering. Zone 8

Ozothamnus leptophyllus Fulvidus Group ▼

The golden heather is a compact evergreen shrub with curry-coloured foliage and large panicles of white flowers.

Small; sun; flowers late summer to early autumn; well-drained soil

Prune in early spring. Zone 8

Ozothamnus selago ▲▼

A small evergreen shrub with tiny green scalelike leaves and small ball-shaped creamy yellow flowers.

Prostrate; sun; flowers summer; well-drained soil

Rarely flowering but impressive when it occurs. Suitable for the rock garden, scree, or trough. Zone 7

Pachysandra axillaris ▼

A dwarf evergreen shrub with large, glossy, dark green leaves and spikes of white flowers.

Prostrate; shade or partial shade; flowers mid spring; fertile soil

Useful as ground cover. Zone 6

Pachysandra procumbens ▼

A creeping, evergreen shrub with clusters of ovate, green leaves, pale green as they unfurl, and with spikes of white flowers.

Prostrate; shade or partial shade; flowers mid spring; fertile soil

Useful as ground cover. Zone 6

Pachysandra terminalis 'Variegata' ▼

A dwarf evergreen shrub with dense, variegated, green leaves edged with creamy white and short spikes of white flowers. AGM

Prostrate; shade or partial shade; flowers late winter to early spring; fertile soil

Useful as ground cover. Zone 5

▲ *Pachystegia insignis* at Dunedin Botanic Garden, South Island, New Zealand.

Pachystegia insignis

The Marlborough rock daisy is a dwarf evergreen shrub with white-felted new growth and white on the underside of green leaves. The white daisylike flowers have yellow centres. Synonym: *Olearia insignis*.

Medium; sun; flowers late summer; fertile, well-drained soil

Zone 9

Paeonia 'Bartzella' ▶

A hybrid between tree and herbaceous peonies, this deciduous, compact bush has large, delicately fragrant, double yellow flowers and deeply cut green foliage.

Medium; sun or partial shade; flowers late spring to early summer; fertile soil

Zone 7

Paeonia delavayi ▲▶

This tree peony is a handsome deciduous shrub producing deep crimson flowers with yellow stamens and deeply cut, dark green leaves tinted dark red in spring. **AGM**

Small to medium; sun or partial shade; flowers late spring to early summer; fertile soil

Zone 6

Paeonia ×*lemoinei* 'Souvenir de Maxime Cornu' ▶

A stunning tree peony bearing very large, delicately fragrant, double yellow flowers with ruffled margins that are flushed with orange and red.

Small to medium; sun or partial shade; flowers late spring to early summer; fertile soil

Zone 7

Paeonia ludlowii ▲▶

This tree peony is a handsome deciduous shrub with beautiful, deep yellow flowers and deeply cut leaves.

Small to medium; sun or partial shade; flowers late spring to early summer; fertile soil

Zone 6

***Paeonia ostii* 'Feng Dan Bai'** ▲

This tree peony is a handsome deciduous shrub with large white flowers, compound leaflets, and silvery, peeling bark.

Small to medium; sun or partial shade; flowers late spring to early summer; fertile soil

Zone 7

Paeonia rockii ◀▲

A lovely tree peony that makes a handsome branching deciduous shrub with green foliage and large silky, pale, pinkish white flowers with central maroon markings.

Small to medium; sun or partial shade; flowers late spring to early summer; fertile soil

Zone 7

▲ *Paeonia suffruticosa* cultivar

Paeonia suffruticosa ▲

Commonly called the Moutan peony, this is a handsome branching shrub with deeply cut leaves. The large flowers are semidouble or double and come in a range of colours, depending on the cultivar.

Small to medium; sun or partial shade; flowers late spring to early summer; fertile soil

Zone 7

▲▼▼▼▼ *Paeonia suffruticosa* cultivars

▲▼ *Paeonia suffruticosa* cultivars

Paeonia suffruticosa 'Godaishu' ▲

This tree peony has handsome deeply cut foliage and semi-double to double white flowers with yellow centres. **AGM**

Small to medium; sun or partial shade; flowers late spring to early summer; fertile soil

Zone 7

Paliurus spina-christi ▼

The Christ's thorn is a deciduous shrub with thorny stems bearing ovate, bright green leaves that turn golden yellow in autumn. Flowers are greenish yellow.

Medium to large; sun; flowers mid summer; fertile, well-drained soil

Can be used as a hedging plant. Prune after flowering. Zone 8

Paeonia suffruticosa 'Hakuo-jisi' ▲

An attractive tree peony with handsome deeply cut leaves and huge, silky, cup-shaped double white flowers.

Small to medium; sun or partial shade; flowers late spring to early summer; fertile soil

Zone 7

Paeonia suffruticosa 'Yachiyo-tsubaki' ▼

A beautiful tree peony producing silvery pink semidouble or double flowers with ruffled edges, and purplish green unfurling leaves.

Small to medium; sun or partial shade; flowers late spring to early summer; fertile soil

Zone 7

Parahebe formosa ▲

An evergreen shrub with violet buds that open to white flowers.

Compact; sun; flowers early to mid summer; fertile, well-drained soil

Suitable for the rock garden. Zone 9

◀ An 80-year-old *Parrotia persica* at the Royal Horticultural Society's Garden Wisley.

Parahebe hookeriana ▲

A low-growing, bushy shrub with toothed, leathery green leaves and pretty, pale lavender flowers.

Prostrate; sun; flowers early to mid summer; fertile, well-drained soil

Suitable for the rock garden. Zone 9

Parahebe perfoliata ▼

A small shrub with greyish green leaves that clasp the stem (and appear to be pierced by it), and arching racemes of blue-violet flowers. **AGM**

Compact; sun; flowers mid to late spring; well-drained soil

Suitable for the rock garden. Remove old stems after flowering. Zone 8

Parrotia persica ▶▶▶

The ironwood is a large spreading deciduous shrub or tree with flaking bark and bearing glossy green, wavy edged leaves with shades of red and gold in autumn, and clusters of small dark red flowers. **AGM**

Large; sun or partial shade; flowers mid to late winter; fertile soil

Zone 5

▲ *Parrotia persica* at the Royal Horticultural Society's Garden Wisley.

Penstemon newberryi ▼

A dwarf shrub with thick, toothed leaves and racemes bearing plenty of funnel-shaped, pinkish red flowers. **AGM**

Compact; sun; flowers early summer; well-drained soil

Suitable for the rock garden. Zone 8

Parrotiopsis jacquemontiana ◀▼

An upright, deciduous shrub with rounded, dark green leaves turning yellow in autumn and clusters of white flowering bracts surrounding yellow stamens.

Medium to large; sun or partial shade; flowers mid to late spring; fertile soil

Zone 7

Perovskia atriplicifolia

The Russian sage is a deciduous shrub with stiff grey-green, aromatic foliage, upright spikes of blue-violet flowers, and silvery grey stems in autumn.

Small; sun; flowers late summer to early autumn.; well-drained soil

Cut back old stems in spring. Zone 6

▼ *Perovskia atriplicifolia* in the Piet Oudolf border at the Royal Horticultural Society's Garden Wisley.

Perovskia atriplicifolia 'Little Spire' ▲

This Russian sage is a lovely, deciduous shrub with stiff, silvery, aromatic foliage, upright spikes of blue-violet flowers, and silvery grey stems in autumn. **AGM**

Compact; sun; flowers late summer to early autumn; well-drained soil

Cut back old stems in spring. Zone 6

Philadelphus argyrocalyx ▼

The silvercup mock orange is a graceful, deciduous shrub that produces slightly fragrant, white flowers having a woolly white calyx.

Small to medium; sun to partial shade; flowers early to mid summer; fertile soil

Prune after flowering to control size. Zone 7

Philadelphus 'Beauclerk' ▶

A deciduous shrub in the Purpureomaculatus Group with an arching habit and bearing toothed, ovate leaves and scented white flowers with pale pinkish purple central markings. **AGM**

Medium; sun to partial shade; flowers early to mid summer; fertile soil

Prune after flowering to control size. Zone 5

Philadelphus 'Belle Etoile' ▼

An arching deciduous shrub in the Purpureomaculatus Group, bearing oval, dark green foliage and beautifully fragrant white flowers with maroon central markings and yellow stamens. **AGM**

Small to medium; sun to partial shade; flowers early to mid summer; fertile soil

Prune after flowering to remove old stems. Zone 5

Philadelphus 'Bialy Karzel' ▼

A dense slow-growing deciduous shrub with slightly fragrant pure white flowers.

Small to medium; sun to partial shade; flowers early to mid summer; fertile soil

Prune after flowering to remove old stems. Zone 5

Philadelphus 'Bialy Sopel' ▶

An erect, vigorous, deciduous shrub grown for its fragrant creamy white flowers.

Medium; sun to partial shade; flowers early to mid summer; fertile soil

Prune after flowering to control size. Zone 5

Philadelphus 'Bicolore' ▼

A deciduous shrub in the Purpureomaculatus Group bearing scented cup-shaped, creamy white flowers with purple central markings.

Small to medium; sun to partial shade; flowers early to mid summer; fertile soil

Prune after flowering to remove old stems. Zone 5

Philadelphus delavayi f. *melanocalyx* ▼

A deciduous shrub bearing racemes of beautifully scented, pure white flowers with purple calyces.

Large; sun to partial shade; flowers early to mid summer; fertile soil

Prune after flowering to control size. Zone 7

Philadelphus coronarius 'Aureus' ▶

A deciduous shrub producing bright golden leaves that turn green with age, and scented, white flowers. **AGM**

Small to medium; partial shade; flowers early to mid summer; fertile, moisture-retentive soil

Keep plant out of full sun for best foliage colour. Zone 5

Philadelphus coronarius 'Variegatus' ▶

An attractive shrub bearing soft, green leaves with creamy white edge markings and strongly scented, white flowers. **AGM**

Medium; sun to partial shade; flowers early to mid summer; fertile soil

Prune after flowering to control size and remove all-green reverted foliage. Zone 5

Philadelphus 'Frosty Morn' ▼

A deciduous shrub in the Lemoinei Group with clusters of very fragrant, double, white flowers.

Small; sun to partial shade; flowers early to mid summer; fertile soil

Prune after flowering to remove old stems. Zone 5

Philadelphus 'Innocence' ▲

An arching deciduous shrub in the Burfordensis Group bearing variegated, green leaves with creamy gold mottled markings and cup-shaped, fragrant, white flowers.

Medium; sun to partial shade; flowers early to mid summer; fertile soil

Prune after flowering to remove old stems and all-green reverted foliage. Zone 5

Philadelphus 'Karolinka' ▼

A vigorous, deciduous shrub grown for its clusters of slightly fragrant double white flowers.

Medium to large; sun to partial shade; flowers early to mid summer; fertile soil

Prune after flowering to control size. Zone 5

Philadelphus madrensis ▲

The desert mountain mock orange is an arching deciduous shrub with oval greyish green leaves and small very fragrant white flowers.

Medium; sun to partial shade; flowers early to mid summer; fertile soil

Prune after flowering to remove old stems. Zone 9

Philadelphus mexicanus ▶

A semievergreen shrub bearing highly scented, single, cup-shaped, creamy white flowers with flushed pale purple markings in the centre of the flower.

Small to large; sun to partial shade; flowers early to mid summer; fertile soil

Can scramble into other large shrubs. Zone 9

Philadelphus 'Mont Blanc' ▼

A deciduous shrub with greyish green leaves and an abundance of single, snowy white scented flowers.

Medium; sun to partial shade; flowers early to mid summer; fertile soil

Prune after flowering to control size. Zone 5

Philadelphus 'Norma' ▲

A deciduous shrub in the Burfordensis Group producing single, subtly scented, white flowers with bright yellow anthers.

Medium; sun to partial shade; flowers early to mid summer; fertile soil

Prune after flowering to control size. Zone 5

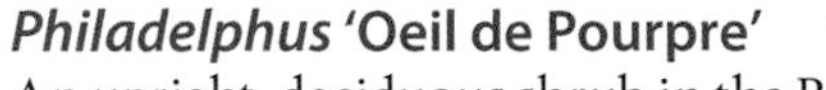

Philadelphus 'Oeil de Pourpre' ▼

An upright, deciduous shrub in the Purpureomaculatus Group bearing cup-shaped scented white flowers with a deep purple centre and prominent yellow stamens.

Small; sun to partial shade; flowers early to mid summer; fertile soil

Prune after flowering to remove old stems. Zone 5

Philadelphus palmeri ◀

A deciduous shrub grown for its scented white flowers with a mass of bright yellow stamens and its bright green leaves.

Medium to large; sun to partial shade; flowers early to mid summer; fertile soil

Prune after flowering to control size. Zone 8

Philadelphus 'Sybille' ◀▲

A lovely, deciduous shrub in the Purpureomaculatus Group with an arching habit and bearing sweetly scented, single, white flowers flushed pale purple in the centre. **AGM**

Small; sun to partial shade; flowers early to mid summer; fertile soil

Prune after flowering to remove old stems. Zone 5

Philesia magellanica ▲

An attractive evergreen, suckering shrub with dense, narrow, dark green leaves, paler on the undersides, and bright rosy red, tube-shaped flowers.

Compact; shade to partial shade; flowers summer to early autumn; fertile, acid soil

Plant in a sheltered woodland setting or on a rock garden. Zone 9

Phillyrea angustifolia ▲

An evergreen shrub with narrow, dark green leaves and clusters of small, scented, creamy yellow flowers followed by black berries.

Medium to large; sun or partial shade; flowers late spring to early summer; fertile, well-drained soil

Can be used as a hedging plant. Zone 7

Phlomis 'Edward Bowles' ►

An attractive evergreen shrub bearing large, heart-shaped, bright green leaves with silvery green new growth and whorls of bright sulphur yellow flowers.

Small to medium; sun; flowers late summer to early autumn; fertile, well-drained soil

Zone 7

Phlomis fruticosa ▼

The Jerusalem sage is an evergreen subshrub with long, narrow green leaves, grey-green on the underside, and whorls of bright yellow flowers. **AGM**

Small; sun; flowers mid to late summer; well-drained soil

Zone 7

Phlomis grandiflora ▼

An evergreen shrub with velvety, silvery grey foliage and whorls of golden yellow flowers sparsely produced.

Medium; sun; flowers late spring to mid summer; well-drained soil

Zone 8

Phlomis italica ▼

A dwarf evergreen shrub with hairy, grey-green foliage and spikes of pale, pinkish lilac flowers.

Compact; sun; flowers early to late summer; well-drained soil

Plant on a rock garden or raised bed. Zone 8

Phlomis lanata ▲

A rounded evergreen shrub producing deeply veined, velvety, sage green foliage on yellow stems and whorls of golden yellow flowers. AGM

Compact; sun; flowers early to late summer; well-drained soil

Plant on a rock garden or raised bed. Zone 8

Phlomis longifolia var. *bailanica* ▶

A spreading evergreen shrub with bright green, deeply veined foliage and whorls of deep golden yellow flowers.

Small; sun; flowers early to late summer; well-drained soil

Zone 8

▼ *Phlomis longifolia* var. *bailanica* with *Cistus* ×*crispatus* 'Warley Rose'

▲ Cultivars of *Phormium cookianum* (foreground) and *P. tenax* at Dunedin Botanic Garden. The flax lilies are woody evergreen perennials with striking arching (*P. cookianum*) or upright (*P. tenax*) leaves and yellowish or bronze-red panicles of flowers followed by decorative seedpods.

▼ *Phormium cookianum* at Overbecks Garden in Devon, England.

Phormium cookianum

The mountain flax is an evergreen perennial with thinner, green arching leaves and panicles of yellow flowers. **AGM**

Medium; sun; flowers mid summer; well-drained soil

Useful in coastal areas and as an architectural feature. Zone 8

Phormium tenax 'Awahou' ▶

A woody evergreen New Zealand flax with stout grey-green leaves.

Compact to small; sun; flowers mid summer; fertile, well-drained soil

Useful in coastal areas. Zone 8

Phormium tenax 'Variegatum' ▶

A variegated cultivar of the woody evergreen perennial producing strap-shaped, green leaves with creamy yellow margins and tall panicles of red flowers. **AGM**

Medium; sun; flowers mid summer; fertile, well-drained soil

Useful in coastal areas and as an architectural feature. Zone 8

Phormium tenax 'Veitchii' ▲

A New Zealand flax cultivar with tall, strap-shaped green and creamy white striped foliage including in the middle of the leaves. **AGM**

Medium; sun; flowers mid summer; fertile, well-drained soil

Useful in coastal areas and as an architectural feature. Zone 8

Phormium 'Yellow Wave' ▲

A hybrid evergreen perennial with long, spiky, arching swordlike leaves with a bright yellow central stripe. **AGM**

Medium; sun; flowers mid summer; well-drained soil

Useful in coastal areas and as an architectural feature. Zone 8

◀ *Photinia beauverdiana* at Westonbirt Arboretum in Gloucestershire, England.

Photinia beauverdiana

A spreading deciduous shrub or small tree with dark green leaves and clusters of small white flowers followed by dark reddish orange fruits and rich orange-red autumn foliage.

Large; sun or partial shade; flowers late spring to early summer; fertile soil

Zone 6

Photinia beauverdiana var. *notabilis* ◀▲

A more upright form of the species with lovely creamy white clusters of hawthornlike flowers followed by clusters of orange-red berries and golden yellow autumn foliage.

Large; sun or partial shade; flowers late spring to early summer; fertile soil

Zone 6

▲ *Photinia davidiana* at Wakehurst Place, Sussex, England.

Photinia davidiana ▼

An evergreen shrub bearing green foliage and white flowers followed by large pendent clusters of matt red fruits. The leaves turn red with age.

Large; sun or partial shade; flowers late spring to early summer; fertile soil

Zone 8

Photinia davidiana 'Fructuluteo' ▶

An upright evergreen shrub with corymbs of small white flowers followed by clusters of yellow fruits.

Large; sun or partial shade; flowers late spring to early summer; fertile soil

Zone 8

Photinia ×fraseri 'Red Robin' ▲▼

An evergreen shrub grown for its glossy, dark green foliage and striking red younger leaves which turn a copper red before changing to green. Flowers are a dull white. **AGM**

Medium to large; sun or partial shade; flowers late spring to early summer; fertile soil

Prune in early spring to deliver striking young growth colour. Zone 8

▶ *Photinia glabra* hedge at Lake Orta in northern Italy.

Photinia glabra

An evergreen shrub grown for its reddish bronze new growth and clusters of white flowers.

Small, medium to large; sun or partial shade; flowers late spring to early summer; fertile soil

Can be maintained as a hedge, by pruning in early spring. Zone 7

Photinia serratifolia ▼

A handsome evergreen shrub bearing leathery, coarsely toothed leaves with coppery red young foliage and large corymbs of white flowers followed by red fruits.

Large; sun or partial shade; flowers mid to late spring; fertile soil

Zone 7

Photinia villosa var. *laevis* ▼

A form of the species with ascending branches bearing green leaves that turn a bright orange-yellow or red in autumn. Corymbs of small white flowers are followed by orange-red fruits.

Large; sun or partial shade; flowers late spring; fertile soil

Zone 4

Photinia villosa ◀▼

A deciduous shrub with dark green leaves turning orange and red in autumn, and corymbs of small white flowers followed by bright red fruits. **AGM**

Large; sun or partial shade; flowers late spring; fertile soil

Zone 4

Phygelius aequalis 'Yellow Trumpet' ▲

A bushy evergreen shrub with light green leaves and one-sided panicles of tubular trumpet-shaped, creamy yellow flowers.

Small; sun; flowers mid summer to early autumn; fertile, well-drained soil

May die back in cold winters but will regrow from base; otherwise prune in early spring. Zone 8

Phygelius capensis ▼▶

The Cape figwort or Cape fuchsia forms a shrub with upright spikes of drooping, orange-red, tubular flowers. **AGM**

Small; sun; flowers mid summer to early autumn; fertile, well-drained soil

May die back in cold winters but will regrow from base; otherwise prune in mid spring. Zone 8

Phygelius ×rectus 'African Queen' ▼

An upright, bushy evergreen shrub with dark green leaves and panicles of pendulous tubular red flowers. **AGM**

Small; sun; flowers mid summer to early autumn; fertile, well-drained soil

May die back in cold winters but will regrow from base; otherwise prune in mid spring. Zone 8

Phygelius ×rectus 'Devils Tears' ▲

An upright, bushy evergreen shrub with dark green foliage and panicles of large, pendulous, tubular trumpet-shaped, dark pink-red flowers with yellow throats. **AGM**

Small; sun; flowers mid summer to early autumn; fertile, well-drained soil

May die back in cold winters but will regrow from base; otherwise prune in mid spring. Zone 8

Phygelius ×rectus 'Salmon Leap' ▼

An upright, bushy evergreen shrub with dark green, oval foliage and upright panicles of pendulous tubular orange flowers. **AGM**

Small; sun; flowers mid summer to early autumn; fertile, well-drained soil

May die back in cold winters but will regrow from base; otherwise prune in mid spring. Zone 8

×*Phylliopsis hillieri* 'Pinocchio' ▲

A dwarf mound-forming evergreen shrub with shiny heath-like dark green foliage and spikes of pinky mauve bell-shaped flowers.

Compact; sun or partial shade; flowers late spring and sometimes also in early autumn; fertile, acid soil

Suitable for the rock garden. Do not allow to dry out. Zone 6

Phyllodoce caerulea ▼

A dwarf evergreen shrub with small, thick, heathlike leaves and bell-shaped purple-blue flowers. **AGM**

Prostrate; sun or partial shade; flowers late spring to early summer; fertile, acid soil

Suitable for the rock garden. Do not allow to dry out. Zone 2

Phyllodoce ×*intermedia* 'Fred Stoker' ▼

A compact mat-forming shrub with heathlike dark green, glossy leaves and small, bell-shaped, rich pinkish purple flowers. **AGM**

Prostrate; sun or partial shade; flowers late spring to early summer; fertile, acid soil

Suitable for the rock garden. Do not allow to dry out. Zone 3

×*Phyllothamnus erectus* ▲

A dwarf evergreen shrub grown for its funnel-shaped rich rose pink flowers and glossy heathlike foliage.

Compact; sun or partial shade; flowers late spring to early summer; fertile, acid soil

Suitable for the rock garden. Do not allow to dry out. Zone 3

Physocarpus opulifolius 'Dart's Gold' ▶

A bushy, deciduous shrub with lobed, golden yellow leaves turning green with age and clusters of small white flowers tinged with pink. AGM

Medium; sun or partial shade; flowers early summer; fertile soil

Zone 2

Physocarpus opulifolius 'Diabolo' ▼

A striking deciduous shrub with lobed, dark purple foliage and clusters of small white flowers, pink in bud. AGM

Medium; sun or partial shade; flowers early summer; fertile soil

Prune after flowering to control size. Zone 2

Pieris 'Bert Chandler' ▶

An evergreen shrub bearing glossy green leaves that are a salmon pink changing to creamy white when young. The shrub also bears a few panicles of small white flowers.

Small to medium; sun to partial shade; flowers early to mid spring; fertile, acid soil

Zone 6

Physocarpus opulifolius 'Luteus' ▼

A deciduous shrub grown for its clear yellow new foliage turning pale green with age and its clusters of white flowers. AGM

Medium; sun or partial shade; flowers early summer; fertile soil

Prune after flowering. Zone 2

Pieris 'Brouwer's Beauty' ▼

An upright evergreen shrub with dense, glossy, dark green foliage and panicles of lily-of-the-valley indigo purple flowers, a deep dull red in bud.

Medium; sun to partial shade; flowers mid to late spring; fertile, acid soil

Zone 7

Pieris 'Firecrest' ▲▶▼

An upright evergreen shrub bearing glossy green leaves that are a bright glossy red when new, ageing pink then green. There are large drooping panicles of white lily-of-the-valley flowers. **AGM**

Medium to large; sun to partial shade; flowers mid to late spring; fertile, acid soil

Zone 7

Pieris 'Flaming Silver' ▲▼

An evergreen shrub bearing clear red young foliage, turning green with silvery white margins, and panicles of small tightly packed lily-of-the-valley white flowers. **AGM**

Small to medium; sun to partial shade; flowers mid to late spring; fertile, acid soil

Prune out all-green reverted stems. Zone 7

Pieris formosa ▼

An evergreen shrub grown for its large panicles of lily-of-the-valley white flowers and bronze-red new growth.

Medium to large; sun to partial shade; flowers mid to late spring; fertile, acid soil

Zone 7

Pieris formosa Forrestii Group ▲▶

An evergreen shrub grown for its bright red new growth ageing pink before green, and for its large panicles of lily-of-the-valley white flowers.

Medium; sun to partial shade; flowers mid to late spring; moisture-retentive but well-drained, acid soil

Zone 7

Pieris formosa (Forrestii Group) 'Henry Price' Forrest 8945 ▼

An evergreen shrub with dark vinous red new foliage, turning green with age, and with upright panicles of white flowers.

Medium to large; sun to partial shade; flowers mid to late spring; fertile, acid soil

Zone 8

Pieris formosa (Forrestii Group) 'Jermyns' ▲▼

A broad, arching, evergreen shrub with dark vinous red new foliage turning green with age, and with drooping panicles of white lily-of-the-valley flowers that are a distinctive rich reddish brown in bud.

Medium; sun to partial shade; flowers mid to late spring; fertile, acid soil

Zone 8

Pieris japonica 'Blush' ▶

An evergreen shrub bearing glossy, dark green leaves with reddish young growth and dark pink buds opening to pale pink lily-of-the-valley flowers. AGM

Medium; sun to partial shade; flowers early to mid spring; fertile, acid soil

Zone 6

Pieris japonica 'Cavatine' ▼

A dense evergreen shrub with glossy green leaves and a profusion of bell-shaped creamy white flowers. AGM

Compact to small; sun to partial shade; flowers early to mid spring; fertile, acid soil

Zone 6

Pieris japonica 'Christmas Cheer' ▼

An evergreen shrub with pale pink lily-of-the-valley flowers with a magenta calyx and dark green foliage, tinted reddish bronze when young.

Medium; sun to partial shade; flowers early to mid spring; fertile, acid soil

Zone 6

Pieris japonica 'Dorothy Wyckoff' ▶

An attractive, upright, evergreen shrub with deeply veined, dark green leaves and deep reddish purple buds opening to pinkish white then white flowers.

Medium; sun to partial shade; flowers early to mid spring; fertile, acid soil

Zone 6

Pieris japonica 'Grayswood' ▼

An evergreen shrub bearing dark green foliage, reddish bronze new growth, and free-flowering large panicles of white flowers. AGM

Small to medium; sun to partial shade; flowers early to mid spring; fertile, acid soil

Zone 6

Pieris japonica 'Katsura' ▼

A rounded evergreen shrub with rich, glossy burgundy-red new growth turning dark green with age. Pale pink flowers are borne in arching racemes.

Small; sun to partial shade; flowers early to mid spring; fertile, acid soil

Zone 7

Pieris japonica 'Little Heath' ▼

A dwarf shrub bearing small green leaves with silver cream edges. New growth is pink tinted. Panicles of pale pink buds open to white flowers. **AGM**

Compact to small; sun to partial shade; flowers early to mid spring; fertile, acid soil

Prune out reverted green stems. Zone 6

Pieris japonica 'Scarlett O'Hara' ▲▼

An upright evergreen shrub bearing green, glossy foliage, deep reddish bronze new growth, and dense panicles of white flowers.

Medium; sun to partial shade; flowers early to mid spring; fertile, acid soil

Zone 7

Pieris japonica 'Sinfonia' ▼

A dwarf rounded shrub with glossy, dark green leaves and abundant panicles of white flowers.

Small; sun to partial shade; flowers early to mid spring; fertile, acid soil

Zone 6

Pieris japonica 'Temple Bells' ▲
A dense evergreen shrub with orange-red young foliage turning dark green with age, and panicles of white lily-of-the-valley flowers.

Medium; sun to partial shade; flowers early to mid spring; fertile, acid soil

Zone 5

Pieris japonica 'Valley Valentine' ▼
A bushy evergreen shrub with green leaves and abundant racemes of deep reddish pink flowers. **AGM**

Small to medium; sun to partial shade; flowers early to mid spring; fertile, acid soil

Zone 6

Pieris 'Tilford' ▲
An evergreen shrub grown for its bright, glossy red new growth ageing bronzy pink then bronzy cream before green and for its white lily-of-the-valley flowers.

Small to medium; sun to partial shade; flowers early to mid spring; fertile, acid soil

Zone 5

Pittosporum eugenioides 'Variegatum' ▼
An evergreen shrub producing glossy green leaves with creamy white edges and a honey scent, and star-shaped pale yellow flowers. **AGM**

Medium; sun or partial shade; flowers mid spring; fertile soil

Prune after flowering to maintain size. Prune out reverted all-green stems. Zone 9

Pittosporum tenuifolium ◄
The kohuhu is an evergreen shrub with black stems bearing bright green leaves and small, brownish purple, honey-scented flowers. **AGM**

Large; sun to partial shade; flowers mid spring; fertile soil

Good as a hedging plant. Useful for cut foliage. Zone 9

Pittosporum tenuifolium 'Irene Paterson' ▲

A slow-growing evergreen shrub bearing roundish green leaves with mottled white markings that are pink tinged in winter. There are honey-scented, purple flowers. **AGM**

Medium; sun to partial shade; flowers mid spring; fertile soil

Zone 9

Pittosporum tenuifolium 'Tom Thumb' ▼

A slow-growing evergreen shrub with deep reddish purple leaves that are green when young. **AGM**

Compact; sun to partial shade; flowers mid spring; fertile soil

Zone 9

Plagianthus regius ▼▶

The ribbonwood is a graceful, deciduous shrub with olive green leaves and massed panicles of pale yellow flowers.

Medium to large; sun or partial shade; flowers late spring; fertile soil

Zone 8

Platycrater arguta ▶

A low-growing deciduous shrub with a lovely, elegant habit and clusters of nodding, white flowers with the outer ones pale green and disclike.

Compact; shade to partial shade; flowers late summer; fertile, well-drained soil

Suitable for the rock garden. Zone 8

Plumbago auriculata ▼

The Cape leadwort is an evergreen climbing shrub with a scrambling habit. It bears bright green leaves and clusters of sky-blue flowers. **AGM**

Medium; sun or partial shade; flowers early summer to mid autumn; fertile, well-drained soil

Useful as a conservatory plant. Plant against a wall. Prune in early to mid spring. Zone 9

Polygala chamaebuxus var. *grandiflora* ▼▶

A low-growing evergreen shrub with dark green ovate leaves and racemes of pinkish purple and yellow flowers. **AGM**

Prostrate to compact; sun or partial shade; flowers mid spring to early summer; fertile, well-drained soil

Suitable for the rock garden. Zone 6

Pomaderris apetala ▼

An evergreen shrub with wrinkly, toothed leaves and large panicles of small pale yellow flowers.

Large; sun; flowers mid summer; fertile, well-drained soil

Zone 9

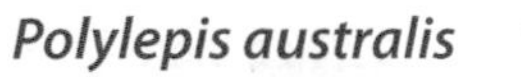

Polylepis australis ▼▶

An attractive deciduous shrub grown for its peeling rich reddish brown bark, pale green leaves, and small green flowers with reddish purple stamens.

Medium to large; sun or partial shade; flowers late spring; fertile soil

Zone 8

Polygala ×*dalmaisiana* ▲

An evergreen shrub with oval green foliage and pinkish purple pealike flowers. **AGM**

Small; sun or partial shade; flowers seen for most of the year, main flush in spring; fertile, well-drained soil

Can be grown in a container or in a conservatory. Zone 10

Poncirus trifoliata ▲

The Japanese bitter orange is a deciduous, spiny-stemmed shrub grown for its scented white flowers, green ultimately orange fruits, and trifoliate green leaves that turn a butter yellow in autumn.

Large; sun; flowers late spring to early summer; fertile, well-drained soil

Forms an effective spiny barrier when grown as an informal hedge. Prune after flowering. Zone 5

Potentilla fruticosa 'Goldstar' ▲

A bushy deciduous shrub with grey-green pinnate leaves and saucer-shaped large golden yellow flowers.

Compact; sun to partial shade; flowers early summer to early autumn; fertile soil

Trim in early spring. Zone 4

Potentilla fruticosa 'Hopley's Orange' ▶

A deciduous shrub with bright green leaves and orange-yellow, saucer-shaped flowers often with an orange outer margin. **AGM**

Compact; sun to partial shade; flowers early summer to early autumn; fertile soil

Trim in early spring. Zone 4

Potentilla fruticosa 'Limelight' ▼

An upright, bushy, deciduous shrub bearing bright green leaves and pale lemon yellow flowers with a deeper yellow centre. **AGM**

Compact; sun to partial shade; flowers early summer to early autumn; fertile soil

Trim in early spring. Zone 4

Potentilla fruticosa Marian Red Robin 'Marrob' ▼

A spreading deciduous shrub grown for its bright ruby red flowers. **AGM**

Compact; sun to partial shade; flowers early summer to early autumn; fertile soil

Trim in early spring. Zone 4

Potentilla fruticosa 'New Dawn' ▲

A bushy deciduous shrub with dark green leaves and deep rich pink flowers.

Compact; sun to partial shade; flowers early summer to early autumn; fertile soil

Trim in early spring. Zone 4

Potentilla fruticosa 'Snowbird' ▼

A rounded deciduous shrub with bright green foliage and abundant white semidouble flowers.

Compact; sun to partial shade; flowers early summer to early autumn; fertile soil

Trim in early spring. Zone 4

Potentilla 'Rhodocalyx' ▲

An upright deciduous shrub grown for its nodding cup-shaped white flowers and contrasting magenta calyces. **AGM**

Small; sun or partial shade; flowers early to late summer; fertile soil

Trim in early spring. Zone 4

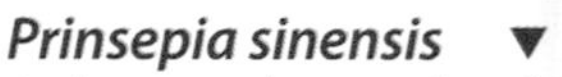

Prinsepia sinensis ▼

A dense and spiny deciduous shrub with bright green leaves and clusters of small yellow flowers followed by red fruits.

Small to medium; sun or light shade; flowers early spring; fertile soil

Prune after flowering. Zone 4

Potentilla fruticosa 'Pink Beauty' ▲

A mound-forming deciduous shrub with small, bushy green foliage and dusky pink saucer-shaped flowers. **AGM**

Compact; sun to partial shade; flowers early summer to early autumn; fertile soil

Retains flower colour throughout the season. Trim in early spring. Zone 4

Prinsepia utilis ◄

A vigorous, spiny, deciduous shrub with an arching habit and bearing racemes of small white flowers.

Small to medium; sun or light shade; flowers late winter to early spring; fertile soil

Prune after flowering. Zone 5

Prostanthera cuneata ▶

The alpine mint bush is an evergreen shrub bearing rounded, dark green leaves and small white flowers that are flushed pale lilac and have purple inside the throat. **AGM**

Compact; sun; flowers late spring to early summer; fertile, well-drained soil

Zone 8

Prostanthera incisa 'Rosea' ▼

The cut-leafed mint bush is an aromatic evergreen shrub with greyish green leaves and pinky lilac flowers.

Small; sun; flowers late spring to early summer; fertile, well-drained soil

Can be grown in a conservatory. Prune after flowering. Zone 9

Prunus laurocerasus 'Otto Luyken' ▲

A low, spreading, bushy evergreen shrub with shiny, narrow dark green leaves and racemes of small white flowers followed by red-black fruits. **AGM**

Compact to small; sun or shade; flowers mid spring; fertile soil

Useful for ground cover. Zone 7

Prunus laurocerasus 'Latifolia' ▼

This cherry laurel is a tall, vigorous, evergreen shrub with large, glossy, leathery green leaves and racemes of small, white flowers.

Large; sun or shade; flowers mid spring; fertile soil

Good as a hedging plant. Zone 7

Prunus laurocerasus 'Zabeliana' ▼

A low, spreading evergreen shrub with long, narrow, willowlike leaves and racemes of small white flowers.

Compact; sun or shade; flowers mid spring; fertile soil

Useful for ground cover. Zone 7

Prunus lusitanica ▲

The Portugal laurel or Azores laurel cherry is an evergreen shrub with ovate, dark green leaves on reddish petioles and with long racemes of white, hawthorn-scented flowers. **AGM**

Large; sun or partial shade; flowers early summer; fertile soil

Good as a hedging plant. Zone 7

Prunus tenella 'Fire Hill' ▼

This dwarf Russian almond is an upright deciduous shrub with dark green foliage and a profusion of beautiful rose-red flowers.

Small; sun; flowers mid spring; fertile soil

Zone 2

Prunus tomentosa ▶

An upright deciduous shrub with a woolly underside to the foliage and with white flowers, pink in bud, followed by red fruits.

Medium; sun; flowers early to mid spring; fertile soil

Zone 2

Pseudopanax (Adiantifolius Group) 'Cyril Watson' ▲

A bushy evergreen shrub with leathery, lobed or unlobed, slightly serrated, glossy green leaves marked by a prominent midrib and veins. **AGM**

Large; sun or partial shade; flowers (male) early to mid spring; fertile soil

Zone 9

Pseudopanax ferox ▶

The toothed lancewood is a slender shrub generally seen in its juvenile foliage form with long narrow coarsely toothed leaves that are dark bronze-green with an orange midrib.

Large; sun or partial shade; flowers spring; fertile, well-drained soil

Juvenile foliage form grown. Zone 9

Pseudopanax laetus ▲

A handsome tropical-looking shrub with glossy green leaves marked by a prominent midrib and with deep purple berries.

Large; sun or partial shade; flowers mid to late spring; fertile, well-drained soil

Zone 10

Pseudowintera colorata ▲▼

An evergreen shrub grown for its unusually coloured foliage. The oval, leathery leaves are yellowish green, tinted pink, with dark purple edges and glaucous undersides. Star-shaped greenish yellow flowers are borne in small clusters.

Compact to small; sun to partial shade; flowers late spring; fertile soil

Needs full sun for best foliage colour. Zone 8

Pseudowintera colorata 'Marjorie Congreve' ▼

An evergreen shrub grown for its coloured foliage. The greenish yellow leaves are glaucous on the underside, and new growth is deep purplish red.

Compact to small; sun or partial shade; flowers late spring; fertile soil

Needs full sun for best foliage colour. Zone 8

Punica granatum 'Hazel Hyde' ▼

This pomegranate is a deciduous shrub with shiny, deep green leaves that turn golden yellow in autumn. Shrimp pink flowers are followed by brown-yellow to purple-red fruits.

Small to medium; sun; flowers mid summer to early autumn; fertile, well-drained soil

Grows well against a warm south-facing wall. Fruits require a long hot summer to ripe. Zone 9

Punica granatum 'Rubrum Flore Pleno' ▶

This pomegranate is a deciduous shrub with shiny green leaves that turn golden yellow in autumn and with double bright orange-red flowers. AGM

Medium; sun; flowers mid summer to early autumn; fertile, well-drained soil

Grows well against a warm south-facing wall. Zone 9

Puya chilensis ▲▼

A woody perennial forming a dense rosette of narrow triangular spiny leathery leaves with a tall flowering stem of striking greenish yellow flowers.

Small to medium; sun; flowers early summer; well-drained soil

Zone 8

Pyracantha atalantioides 'Aurea' ▼▼

A vigorous evergreen shrub with large, dark green, glossy leaves and large clusters of white flowers followed by golden yellow fruits.

Large; sun or partial shade; flowers early summer; fertile soil

Grow against an east- or north-facing wall. Prune after flowering. Zone 7

▶ *Pyracantha coccinea* at Villa Melzi on Lake Como in Italy.

Pyracantha coccinea

A vigorous evergreen shrub with narrow dark green leaves and large clusters of white flowers followed by orange-red fruits.

Large; sun or partial shade; flowers early summer; fertile soil

Grow against an east- or north-facing wall. Prune after flowering. Zone 5

Pyracantha 'Golden Charmer' ▲▼

An upright evergreen shrub with thorny arching branches bearing glossy, dark green leaves and large clusters of white flowers followed by a profusion of golden orange-yellow fruits. **AGM**

Large; sun or partial shade; flowers early summer; fertile soil

Grow against an east- or north-facing wall. Prune after flowering. Zone 5

Pyracantha 'Orange Charmer' ▶

An evergreen shrub with glossy, dark green leaves and clusters of white flowers followed by bunches of bright orange fruits.

Large; sun or partial shade; flowers early summer; fertile soil

Grow against an east- or north-facing wall. Prune after flowering. Zone 5

Pyracantha 'Rosedale' ▼

An evergreen shrub with shiny, dark green leaves and large clusters of white flowers followed by an abundance of large bright red fruits.

Large; sun or partial shade; flowers early summer; fertile soil

Grow against an east- or north-facing wall. Prune after flowering. Resistant to firelight. Zone 7

Pyracantha Saphyr Orange 'Cadange' ▲▼

An upright, spreading evergreen shrub with dark green leaves and clusters of white flowers followed by a profusion of attractive, bright orange fruits. **AGM**

Medium; sun or partial shade; flowers early summer; fertile soil

Grow against an east- or north-facing wall. Prune after flowering. Resistant to scab and canker. Can be grown in a container. Zone 5

Pyracantha 'Watereri' ▼

An evergreen shrub with arching branches of dark green, glossy leaves and large clusters of white flowers followed by a liberal covering of red fruits.

Medium; sun or partial shade; flowers early summer; fertile soil

Grow against an east- or north-facing wall. Prune after flowering. Zone 5

Raphiolepis ×delacourii 'Spring Song' ▼▼

An evergreen shrub bearing glossy green, toothed leaves and panicles of apple-blossom pink flowers.

Small to medium; sun; flowers mid to late spring; fertile soil

Zone 8

Rhamnus alaternus 'Argenteovariegatus' ▲

A bushy evergreen shrub bearing variegated green leaves, marbled grey centres with creamy edges, and small yellowish flowers followed by red fruits that turn black with age. **AGM**

Medium; sun or partial shade; flower mid spring; fertile, well-drained soil

Zone 8

Rhaphithamnus spinosus ▼

A dense evergreen shrub bearing clusters of sharply toothed leaves with sharp spines, and small, tubular, pale blue flowers followed by deep blue berries.

Medium to large; sun; flowers mid spring; fertile, well-drained soil

Select a sunny yet sheltered site. Zone 9

▲ Three *Rhododendron* shrubs at Mount Congreve gardens, County Waterford, southeastern Ireland: 'Bad Eilsen', a dwarf, spreading evergreen with funnel-shaped deep red flowers; 'Fragrantissimum', dark green corrugated leaves and funnel-shaped extremely fragrant white flowers flushed with rose, AGM; and 'Roza Stevenson', loose trusses of saucer-shaped lemon yellow flowers with dark green leaves.

Rhododendron albrechtii ▼

A lovely deciduous azalea with an open habit and clusters of deep rose pink flowers fading to clear pink. The green leaves turn yellow in autumn.

Small to medium; sun or partial shade; flowers mid to late spring; fertile, acid soil

Zone 5

Rhododendron 'Alice de Stuers' ▶

A deciduous Mollis hybrid azalea producing obovate, green leaves and showy clusters of yellowish pink flowers with a deep orange blotch. **AGM**

Medium; sun or partial shade; flowers late spring to early summer; fertile, acid soil

Zone 6

***Rhododendron* 'Ann Lindsay'** ▲
An evergreen *R. yakushimanum* hybrid grown for its dark green leaves with a woolly indumentum on the underside, and large trusses of red flowers shading inward to a white throat.

Small; sun or partial shade; flowers late spring to early summer; fertile, acid soil

Zone 7

***Rhododendron atlanticum* Choptank River hybrids** ▲
Deciduous azalea with an open habit and bearing beautifully fragrant, shell pink, trumpet-shaped flowers and green foliage that turns shades of yellow and orange in autumn.

Small; sun or partial shade; flowers late spring to early summer; fertile, acid soil

Zone 6

Rhododendron augustinii ▲
An evergreen shrub with small leaves and masses of beautiful funnel-shaped blue-purple flowers.

Medium; sun or partial shade; flowers mid to late spring; fertile, acid soil

Zone 6

Rhododendron augustinii* var. *hardyi Rock 195 ▼
An upright deciduous shrub with glossy green leaves and funnel-shaped white flowers that have a prominent orange-yellow blotch.

Medium; sun or partial shade; flowers mid to late spring; fertile, acid soil

Zone 6

Rhododendron 'Babette' ▲

A rounded evergreen shrub bearing mid-green, glossy leaves and clusters of pink-tinted, very pale creamy yellow flowers with a red blotch.

Small; sun or partial shade; flowers late spring; fertile, acid soil

Zone 7

Rhododendron barbatum ▼

An attractive, spreading evergreen shrub with bristly young foliage and rounded trusses of crimson-scarlet flowers.

Large; sun or partial shade; flowers early spring; fertile, acid soil

Remove dead flower heads to improve flowering in the following year. Zone 7

Rhododendron 'Beatrice Keir' ▶

A bushy, upright evergreen shrub with glossy, dark green foliage and thick trusses of funnel-shaped lemon yellow flowers.

Large; sun or partial shade; flowers mid spring; fertile, acid soil

Remove dead flower heads to improve flowering in the following year. Zone 7

Rhododendron 'Beaulieu Manor' ▼

A bushy, upright deciduous azalea in the Solent Series of Exbury hybrids bearing showy clusters of vivid red flowers with a strong orange centre.

Small; sun or partial shade; flowers late spring; fertile, acid soil

Zone 6

Rhododendron 'Bo-peep' ▲

A slender shrub with a loose habit, bearing glossy green leaves and clusters of funnel-shaped primrose yellow flowers with darker spotting.

Small; sun or partial shade; flowers early spring; fertile, acid soil

Best grown on a rock garden. Zone 7

Rhododendron 'Britannia' ▲

A rounded evergreen shrub with dull, green leaves and dense clusters of bright crimson-scarlet flowers.

Small to medium; sun or partial shade; flowers late spring to early summer; fertile, acid soil

Remove dead flower heads to improve flowering in the following year.
Zone 6

Rhododendron campylocarpum Spring-Smyth 32A ▲

An evergreen shrub with small glossy green leaves, glaucous green beneath, with trusses of bell-shaped clear yellow flowers.

Medium; sun or partial shade; flowers mid to late spring; fertile, acid soil

Zone 7

Rhododendron canadense ▲

An upright deciduous azalea with sea green, oval leaves and rosy purple flowers.

Small; sun or partial shade; flowers mid spring; fertile, acid soil

Zone 3

Rhododendron 'Caroline de Zoete' ▼

An evergreen shrub grown for its slightly scented pure white trusses of flowers and green foliage.

Small; sun or partial shade; flowers mid to late spring; fertile, acid soil

Zone 6

Rhododendron 'Champagne' ◄

An upright evergreen shrub grown for its trusses of lemon yellow flowers tinged with pink. **AGM**

Small; sun or partial shade; flowers late spring to early summer; fertile, acid soil

Zone 7

Rhododendron Comely Group ▶

An upright evergreen shrub with trusses of clear yellow tubular flowers and glossy, bluish green leaves.

Medium; sun or partial shade; flowers late spring to early summer; fertile, acid soil

Zone 7

Rhododendron 'Chapeau' ▲

An upright evergreen shrub with matt green leaves and trusses of pinkish purple flowers with a maroon blotch, becoming darker purple with age.

Small; sun or partial shade; flowers late spring; fertile, acid soil

Zone 6

Rhododendron 'Chikor' ▼

A dwarf evergreen shrub with clusters of pale greenish yellow flowers and glossy, dark green leaves turning bronze with age.

Compact; sun or partial shade; flowers mid spring; fertile, acid soil

Best grown on a rock garden. Zone 6

Rhododendron 'Curlew' ▲

An evergreen shrub bearing dark green leaves and clusters of funnel-shaped light yellow flowers with greenish brown markings. **AGM**

Compact; sun or partial shade; flowers mid spring to early summer; fertile, acid soil

Best grown on a rock garden. Zone 6

Rhododendron dauricum 'Midwinter' ▼

A semievergreen shrub with funnel-shaped, bright pinkish purple flowers and elliptic green leaves. **AGM**

Small to medium; sun or partial shade; flowers mid winter to early spring; fertile, acid soil

Zone 5

Rhododendron davidsonianum ▶

An evergreen shrub with an upright, open habit bearing clusters of funnel-shaped flowers varying in colour from soft pink to lavender pink-purple and often spotted. **AGM**

Medium; sun or partial shade; flowers mid to late spring; fertile, acid soil

Zone 7

Rhododendron decorum ▲

An attractive evergreen shrub bearing matt green, oblong leaves with paler undersides and large trusses of funnel-shaped, white or shell pink flowers, pink in bud. **AGM**

Large; sun or partial shade; flowers late spring to early summer; fertile, acid soil

Zone 7

Rhododendron 'Diana Colville ▼

A vigorous evergreen shrub grown for its dome-shaped trusses of pale lilac flowers.

Large; sun or partial shade; flowers late spring to early summer; fertile, acid soil

Remove dead flower heads to improve flowering in the following year. Zone 6

Rhododendron Duke of Cornwall Group ▼

An upright, vigorous evergreen shrub, bearing large dome-shaped trusses of bright crimson flowers and conspicuously veined green leaves.

Medium to large; sun or partial shade; flowers late spring to early summer; fertile, acid soil

Zone 7

Rhododendron 'Edelweiss' ▼

A hybrid of *R. yakushimanum* grown for its greenish white thick indumentum and dome-shaped trusses of white flowers opening from pink buds and showing yellowish green markings in the throat. **AGM**

Small; sun or partial shade; flowers late spring to early summer; fertile, acid soil

Zone 7

Rhododendron 'Elizabeth' ▶

An evergreen shrub grown for its free-flowering trusses of funnel-shaped bright red flowers.

Medium; sun or partial shade; flowers mid to late spring; fertile, acid soil

Zone 7

Rhododendron 'Exbury Lady Chamberlain' ▲

An upright shrub with pendulous clusters of tubular pinkish orange flowers and waxy green leaves.

Medium; sun or partial shade; flowers late spring to early summer; fertile, acid soil

Zone 8

▶ *Rhododendron falconeri* at Logan Botanic Garden in southwestern Scotland.

Rhododendron falconeri ▼

An evergreen shrub with large matt, dark green leaves marked by deeply indented veins and a rusty red indumentum on the undersides, as well as beautifully exhibited with cinnamon brown on new growth and large, rounded trusses of creamy yellow flowers with purple blotches. **AGM**

Large; partial shade; flowers mid to late spring; fertile, acid soil

Remove dead flower heads to help flowering in the following year. Zone 8

Rhododendron 'Fantastica' ▶

A rounded evergreen hybrid of *R. yakushimanum* bearing dark green foliage, woolly beneath, and clusters of bright pink flowers with paler centres, fading to white with age. **AGM**

Small; sun or partial shade; flowers late spring to early summer; fertile, acid soil

Zone 7

Rhododendron 'Fireman Jeff' ▼

An evergreen shrub with trusses of large bright, fiery red flowers and green leaves.

Small; sun or partial shade; flowers late spring to early summer; fertile, acid soil

Best on a rock garden. Zone 7

▲ *Rhododendron forrestii* var. *repens* on the Doshong La in southeastern Tibet.

Rhododendron forrestii var. *repens*

A creeping shrub producing dark green leaves with paler undersides and large bell-shaped scarlet flowers. **AGM**

Prostrate to compact; partial shade; flowers mid to late spring; fertile, acid soil

Best on a rock garden. Zone 6

Rhododendron fortunei ▶

A spreading evergreen shrub with matt green leaves and large trusses of fragrant bell-shaped lilac-pink flowers. **AGM**

Large; sun or partial shade; flowers late spring; fertile, acid soil

Remove dead flower heads to improve flowering in the following year. Zone 6

Rhododendron 'Fred Wynniatt' ▲

An evergreen shrub bearing trusses of large peach-coloured flowers with ruffled, pinkish edges.

Large; sun or partial shade; flowers late spring to early summer; fertile, acid soil

Remove dead flower heads to improve flowering in the following year. Zone 6

Rhododendron 'Furnivall's Daughter' ▼

A vigorous evergreen shrub bearing large trusses of funnel-shaped pale pink flowers with bold, darker markings. **AGM**

Large; sun or partial shade; flowers late spring to early summer; fertile, acid soil

Remove dead flower heads to improve flowering in the following year. Zone 6

Rhododendron 'Golden Torch' ▲

An evergreen hybrid of *R. yakushimanum* with trusses of bell-shaped, pale yellow flowers, salmon pink in bud. **AGM**

Small; sun or partial shade; flowers late spring to early summer; fertile, acid soil

Zone 7

Rhododendron 'Glory of Littleworth' ▲

A semievergreen shrub (Azaleodendron) bearing bluish green leaves and scented clusters of funnel-shaped creamy flowers with a prominent coppery orange blotch.

Small to medium; sun or partial shade; flowers late spring; fertile, acid soil

Zone 6

Rhododendron 'Golden Oriole' ▼

An upright, bushy, deciduous Knaphill hybrid azalea with green leaves, bronze-tinted when young, and clusters of deep golden yellow flowers.

Small; sun or partial shade; flowers mid spring; fertile, acid soil

Zone 6

Rhododendron 'Greenway' ▲

A bushy evergreen Kurume azalea with glossy green foliage and floriferous clusters of funnel-shaped pink flowers.

Compact; sun or partial shade; flowers mid to late spring; fertile, acid soil

Zone 7

Rhododendron griersonianum ▶

An attractive evergreen shrub bearing long, matt green leaves with woolly, brownish indumentum on the undersides and trusses of funnel-shaped bright scarlet flowers.

Medium; sun or partial shade; flowers early summer; fertile, acid soil

Zone 8

Rhododendron groenlandicum ▲▼

The Labrador tea is a low-growing, evergreen shrub with narrow, leathery, green leaves and ball-shaped clusters of small white flowers.

Compact; sun or partial shade; flowers mid spring to early summer; fertile, acid soil

Best on a rock garden. Zone 2

Rhododendron 'Hachmann's Charmant' ◀

A hybrid of *R. yakushimanum* bearing clusters of white flowers with pink, ruffled edges and a prominent dark stain at the base of the flower.

Small; sun or partial shade; flowers late spring to early summer; fertile, acid soil

Zone 7

Rhododendron 'Hachmann's Marlis' ▼

A vigorous, upright, evergreen hybrid of *R. yakushimanum* grown for its green foliage that unfurls a silvery green, and its large funnel-shaped clusters of rose pink flowers with a white eye. **AGM**

Small; sun or partial shade; flowers late spring; fertile, acid soil

Zone 7

Rhododendron 'Hinode-giri' ▶

A bushy, upright, evergreen Kurume azalea bearing small, bright olive-green leaves and copious clusters of small funnel-shaped, bright crimson flowers.

Compact; sun or partial shade; flowers mid to late spring; fertile, acid soil

Zone 7

Rhododendron 'Hinomayo' ▼

A bushy evergreen Kurume azalea with small green leaves and copious clusters of small funnel-shaped clear pink flowers. **AGM**

Compact; sun or partial shade; flowers mid to late spring; fertile, acid soil

Zone 7

Rhododendron hodgsonii ▼

An evergreen shrub bearing handsome, wide dark green leaves with silvery to cinnamon brown indumentum on the underside and large rounded trusses of magenta-purple to pink flowers.

Large; partial shade; flowers mid spring; fertile, acid soil

Remove dead flower heads to improve flowering in the following year. Zone 9

▼ *Rhododendron* 'Hinomayo' surrounding the white-flowered evergreen Vuyk hybrid *R.* 'Palestrina'.

Rhododendron 'Hydon Hunter' ▼

A bushy, evergreen *R. yakushimanum* hybrid bearing slightly glossy, dark green leaves and rounded trusses of bell-shaped, bright pink flowers with spotty, orange markings on the inside. **AGM**

Small to medium; sun or partial shade; flowers late spring; fertile, acid soil

Zone 7

▲ *Rhododendron indicum*, showing how one plant has "sported" to produce a range of coloured flowers.

Rhododendron indicum

The Indian evergreen azalea is a tender species that has yielded an assortment of pot plants used by florists.

Small; sun or partial shade; flowers mid to late spring; fertile, acid soil

Best in a conservatory in cold climates. Zone 10

Rhododendron 'Jack Skilton' ▲

An upright evergreen shrub grown for its large funnel-shaped trusses of creamy yellow flowers with red spots in the throat.

Medium to large; sun or partial shade; flowers late spring; fertile, acid soil

Remove dead flower heads to improve flowering in the following year. Zone 6

Rhododendron 'Jingle Bells' ▲

An evergreen bushy shrub bearing deep red buds that open to orange flowers with a red-tinted centre, fading to yellow with age.

Small; sun or partial shade; flowers late spring to early summer; fertile, acid soil

Best grown on a rock garden. Zone 6

Rhododendron 'Jolie Madame' ◀

An upright deciduous azalea with clusters of scented pink flowers blotched with orange markings.

Medium; sun or partial shade; flowers early summer; fertile, acid soil

Zone 6

Rhododendron keiskei 'Yaku Fairy' ▲

A mounded evergreen shrub with dense, olive-green foliage and trusses of creamy yellow flowers. **AGM**

Prostrate to compact; sun or partial shade; flowers early to mid spring; fertile, acid soil

Best grown in a rock garden. Zone 5

Rhododendron kiusianum ▲

A dense evergreen azalea bearing small dark green leaves and flowers varying from salmon red to reddish purple. **AGM**

Compact; sun or partial shade; flowers late spring to early summer; fertile, acid soil

Zone 7

Rhododendron, Kurume Hybrids

Low-growing evergreen shrubs with dense foliage and variously coloured flowers.

Small; sun and partial shade; flowers late spring; fertile, acid soil

Zone 7

◀ *Rhododendron*, Kurume hybrids, at Ashland Hollow, Maryland. Whether grown in the United Kingdom or the United States, these evergreen azaleas are ideally suited to providing excellent colour during spring.

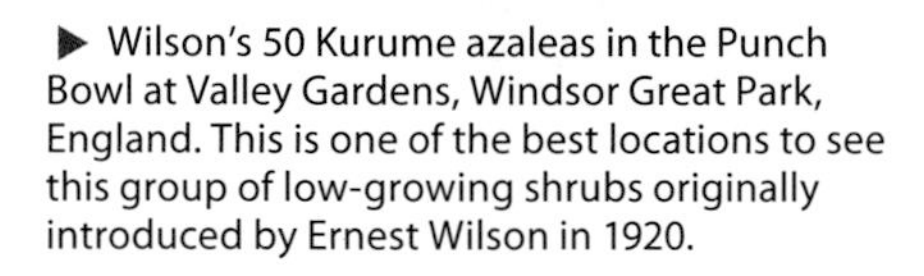

▶ Wilson's 50 Kurume azaleas in the Punch Bowl at Valley Gardens, Windsor Great Park, England. This is one of the best locations to see this group of low-growing shrubs originally introduced by Ernest Wilson in 1920.

Rhododendron 'Lady Alice Fitzwilliam' ▲

An evergreen shrub bearing dark green leaves with deeply cut veins. The beautifully scented, white flowers have yellow markings in the throat and are pink in bud. **AGM**

Small; sun or partial shade; flowers mid spring; fertile, acid soil
Cultivate in a conservatory, or outside in a sheltered site. Zone 9

Rhododendron 'Lampion' ▲

A hybrid of *R. yakushimanum* grown for its trusses of vivid red to deep pink flowers with a light brownish indumentum on the underside of the leaf.

Compact; sun or partial shade; flowers late spring; fertile, acid soil
Zone 7

Rhododendron 'Lavender Girl' ▶

A vigorous evergreen shrub with large mid-green leaves and trusses of lightly scented, funnel-shaped, lilac flowers. **AGM**

Small to medium; sun or partial shade; flowers late spring to early summer; fertile, acid soil
Zone 6

Rhododendron 'Lem's Cameo' ▼

An attractive, upright shrub bearing glossy, dark green leaves and large trusses of creamy apricot flowers with ruffled, pink edges. **AGM**

Medium; sun or partial shade; flowers late spring; fertile, acid soil
Zone 7

Rhododendron 'Lem's Stormcloud' ▼

A rounded evergreen shrub grown for its large funnel-shaped trusses of deep red flowers. **AGM**

Medium; sun or partial shade; flowers late spring to early summer; fertile, acid soil
Zone 7

Rhododendron lepidostylum ▲

An evergreen shrub with a dense, mounding habit of bristly blue-green leaves and funnel-shaped pale yellow flowers.

Compact to small; sun or partial shade; flowers late spring to early summer; fertile, acid soil

Best grown on a rock garden. Zone 7

▲ *Rhododendron* 'Loderi King George' at Savill Garden in Windsor Great Park, Egham, England.

Rhododendron 'Loch Tummel' ▼

An evergreen shrub grown for its large trusses of funnel-shaped pure white flowers, dark purplish pink in bud. The green leaves are silvery green when young and have a light brown indumentum on the underside.

Compact; sun or partial shade; flowers early to mid spring; fertile, acid soil

Zone 6

Rhododendron 'Loderi King George' ▲

A beautiful, tall, evergreen shrub with large green leaves and enormous trusses of sweetly scented white, trumpet-shaped flowers, soft pink in bud. **AGM**

Large; sun or partial shade; flowers late spring; fertile, acid soil

Remove dead flower heads to improve flowering in the following year. Zone 8

Rhododendron luteum ▲

A deciduous azalea with beautifully scented, funnel-shaped, yellow flowers and mid-green leaves with rich golden yellow to orange and red autumn colour. **AGM**

Medium; sun or partial shade; flowers late spring; fertile, acid soil

Zone 5

▼ *Rhododendron luteum* in the wild in north-eastern Turkey.

▲ *Rhododendron macabeanum* at Trewithen Gardens, Cornwall, England.

Rhododendron macabeanum ▶

A rounded shrub bearing large, shiny, dark green leaves with woolly, grey or greyish white indumentum on the undersides and large trusses of funnel-shaped, lemon yellow flowers with purple markings. **AGM**

Large; partial shade; flowers early to mid spring; fertile, acid soil

Remove dead flower heads to improve flowering in the following year. Zone 8

Rhododendron 'Maricee' ▼

An evergreen shrub with small leathery foliage and clusters of small tubular funnel-shaped pure white flowers.

Compact; sun or partial shade; flowers mid to late spring; fertile, acid soil

Suitable for the rock garden. Zone 6

Rhododendron 'Markeeta's Prize' ▼

A vigorous broad-spreading evergreen shrub with green leathery leaves and trusses of large, frilly edged, scarlet red flowers. **AGM**

Medium; sun or partial shade; flowers late spring to early summer; fertile, acid soil

Remove dead flower heads to improve flowering in the following year. Zone 6

Rhododendron 'Mary Swaythling' ▼

A broad-spreading evergreen shrub with trusses of soft, sulphur yellow flowers.

Medium; sun or partial shade; flowers late spring; fertile, acid soil

Remove dead flower heads to improve flowering in the following year. Zone 7

▲ *Rhododendron molle* subsp. *japonicum* on Mount Akagi, Japan.

Rhododendron molle subsp. *japonicum*

A compact deciduous azalea grown for its fragrant trusses of funnel-shaped orange to salmon red flowers and its golden yellow to orange-red autumn foliage.

Medium; sun or partial shade; flowers late spring; fertile, acid soil

Zone 7

Rhododendron 'Mother's Day' *Rhododendron* 'Palestrina'

Under optimal growing conditions, these compact, evergreen, floriferous azaleas provide spectacular results in even the smallest of gardens.

Compact; partial shade; flowers late spring; fertile, acid soil

Zone 7

▼ *Rhododendron* 'Mother's Day' (red) and *R.* 'Palestrina' (white, AGM) with other azaleas at the Royal Horticultural Society's Garden Wisley.

Rhododendron 'Mrs. Davies Evans' ▲

A vigorous, upright, evergreen shrub bearing green leaves and rounded trusses of purple flowers with frilly edges and white markings. **AGM**

Medium; sun or partial shade; flowers late spring to early summer; fertile, acid soil

Remove dead flower heads to improve flowering in the following year. Zone 6

***Rhododendron mucronulatum* 'Cornell Pink'** ▲▶

An open, rounded, deciduous shrub bearing green leaves with red, orange, and yellow autumn colour, and funnel-shaped, clear pink flowers. **AGM**

Medium; sun or partial shade; flowers mid winter to early spring; fertile, acid soil

Zone 4

***Rhododendron* 'Norma'** ▼

An upright, rounded, deciduous Rustica azalea bearing green leaves with good autumn colours in shades of red, orange, and yellow, and clusters of sweetly scented, double, salmon-coloured flowers. **AGM**

Small; sun or partial shade; flowers late spring to early summer; fertile, acid soil

Zone 6

***Rhododendron* 'Nancy Evans'** ▲

An evergreen shrub grown for its dark green leaves, bronze-tinted new growth, and floral trusses of orange buds that open to yellow flowers with shades of orange. **AGM**

Small to medium; sun or partial shade; flowers mid to late spring; fertile, acid soil

Zone 7

***Rhododendron* 'Naomi Astarte'** ▶

A broad-spreading evergreen shrub bearing large trusses of pale pink flowers with yellow shading towards the centre.

Large; sun or partial shade; flowers mid to late spring; fertile, acid soil

Remove dead flower heads to improve flowering in the following year.
Zone 7

Rhododendron occidentale ▼

A deciduous azalea with glossy green leaves that turn a rich golden yellow, orange, and red in autumn. The sweetly scented cream to pale pink flowers have golden yellow blotches. **AGM**

Small to medium; sun or partial shade; flowers early summer; fertile, acid soil

Zone 6

Rhododendron 'Odee Wright' ▲

An evergreen shrub with glossy, dark green leaves and peach-coloured buds that open to pale yellow flowers tinted with light pink.

Small to medium; sun or partial shade; flowers mid to late spring; fertile, acid soil

Zone 6

Rhododendron 'Olin O. Dobbs' ▼

An evergreen shrub with dark green leaves and rounded trusses of funnel-shaped deep reddish purple flowers.

Small to medium; sun or partial shade; flowers late spring to early summer; fertile, acid soil

Remove dead flower heads to improve flowering in the following year. Zone 6

Rhododendron occidentale 'Irene Koster' ▲

A deciduous azalea bearing glossy green leaves with paler undersides that turn a rich golden yellow and orange in autumn. Showy trusses bear sweetly scented, creamy pink flowers with a prominent golden yellow blotch. **AGM**

Small; sun or partial shade; flowers early summer; fertile, acid soil

Zone 6

Rhododendron Oreocinn Group ▲

An upright evergreen shrub with sea green leaves and clusters of tubular pale rose pink flowers. **AGM**

Medium; sun or partial shade; flowers mid to late spring; fertile, acid soil

Zone 7

Rhododendron 'Orpheus' ▲

An erect deciduous Ghent azalea, with clusters of scented deep orange-red flowers. The green leaves turn a rich golden orange and red in autumn.

Small; sun or partial shade; flowers late spring to early summer; fertile, acid soil

Zone 6

Rhododendron 'Paprika Spiced' ▲

An evergreen shrub bearing waxy, green leaves and large funnel-shaped trusses of pale peach-coloured wavy edged flowers with paprika-red markings.

Small; sun or partial shade; flowers late spring; fertile, acid soil

Zone 7

Rhododendron 'Peeping Tom' ▲

An evergreen shrub bearing dark green leaves and trusses of funnel-shaped white flowers with deep purple blotches.

Small; sun or partial shade; flowers late spring to early summer; fertile, acid soil

Zone 6

Rhododendron 'Persil' ▶

A bushy, deciduous Knaphill azalea bearing mid-green leaves and beautiful clusters of white flowers with a golden yellow-orange flare. **AGM**

Small; sun or partial shade; flowers late spring; fertile, acid soil

Zone 6

Rhododendron 'Peter John Mezitt' ▼

A rounded evergreen shrub with glossy, slightly aromatic dark green leaves turning mahogany in autumn, and clusters of pinkish purple flowers. **AGM**

Small to medium; sun or partial shade; flowers mid winter to mid spring; fertile, acid soil

Zone 6

Rhododendron 'Point Defiance' ▲

An evergreen shrub bearing dull, mid-green leaves and large funnel-shaped trusses of deep pink buds opening to pink flowers with a paler centre.

Medium; sun or partial shade; flowers late spring; fertile, acid soil

Remove dead flower heads to improve flowering in the following year. Zone 6

Rhododendron 'Princess Anne' ▼

An attractive shrub bearing bronze-tinted young foliage changing to dark green with age, and trusses of funnel-shaped pale, greenish yellow flowers. **AGM**

Compact; sun or partial shade; flowers mid to late spring; fertile, acid soil

Best grown on a rock garden. Zone 6

Rhododendron prinophyllum 'Marie Hoffman' ▲

A deciduous azalea with bright green leaves and clusters of clove-scented, funnel-shaped clear pink flowers.

Medium; sun or partial shade; flowers late spring; fertile, acid soil

Zone 6

Rhododendron 'Queen Elizabeth II' ▶

An evergreen shrub with glossy green leaves and trusses of funnel-shaped, clear yellow flowers. **AGM**

Medium; sun or partial shade; flowers late spring to early summer; fertile, acid soil

Remove dead flower heads to improve flowering in the following year. Zone 8

Rhododendron 'Raspberry Ripple' ▼

A hybrid of *R. yakushimanum* bearing glossy green leaves and conical trusses of funnel-shaped white flowers with broad flushes of purplish red fading to pink.

Small; sun or partial shade; flowers late spring; fertile, acid soil

Zone 7

Rhododendron 'Red Carpet' ▶

A low-growing evergreen shrub with small glossy, dark green leaves and small trusses of vivid red flowers.

Compact; sun or partial shade; flowers mid to late spring; fertile, acid soil

Suitable for the rock garden. Zone 6

Rhododendron 'Renoir' ▼

An upright evergreen hybrid of R. *yakushimanum* bearing long, dark green leaves and rounded trusses of bell-shaped, deep purplish pink flowers with a white throat. **AGM**

Small; sun or partial shade; flowers late spring to early summer; fertile, acid soil

Zone 7

Rhododendron 'Rosemary Hyde' ▼

A dense evergreen azalea with purplish pink flowers.

Compact; sun or partial shade; flowers late spring; fertile, acid soil

Zone 7

Rhododendron reticulatum ◀

A deciduous azalea producing purple-tinted young leaves and bright purple, funnel-shaped flowers.

Small to medium; sun or partial shade; flowers mid to late spring; fertile, acid soil

Zone 6

Rhododendron 'Rothenburg' ▶

An evergreen shrub with large, glossy, dark green leaves and trusses of pale, creamy yellow flowers.

Small to medium; sun or partial shade; flowers mid to late spring; fertile, acid soil

Remove dead flower heads to improve flowering in the following year. Zone 7

Rhododendron 'September Song' ▼

An evergreen shrub with glossy green leaves and open trusses of funnel-shaped flowers in a fusion of orange-yellow and pink.

Small; sun or partial shade; flowers late spring to early summer; fertile, acid soil

Zone 6

Rhododendron 'Silver Slipper' ▼

A bushy, deciduous Knaphill azalea producing large trusses of white flowers with a pink tint and a vivid yellow blotch. The green leaves are coppery coloured when young. **AGM**

Small; sun or partial shade; flowers late spring early summer; fertile, acid soil

Zone 6

Rhododendron sichotense ▼

An evergreen shrub grown for its funnel-shaped rich rose-purple flowers.

Medium; sun or partial shade; flowers mid to late spring; fertile, acid soil

Zone 7

Rhododendron sinogrande ▼

A magnificent evergreen shrub producing huge glossy, dark green leaves with a silvery grey or fawn indumentum on the underside and huge, rounded trusses of creamy white flowers with red markings. **AGM**

Large; partial shade; flowers mid spring; fertile, acid soil

Remove dead flower heads to improve flowering in the following year. Zone 8

▶ *Rhododendron* Solent Series at Exbury gardens with Edmund de Rothschild, who developed these hybrids.

Rhododendron Solent Series

A group of deciduous azaleas raised at Exbury for their larger flowers which fade less quickly in the sun, are longer lasting, and have better wind resistance.

Small; sun or partial shade; flowers late spring early summer; fertile, acid soil

Zone 5

Rhododendron 'Solent Swan' ▲▼

A tall, evergreen shrub with trusses of large fragrant funnel-shaped, pure white flowers with green markings in the throat.

Large; sun or partial shade; flowers late spring to early summer; fertile, acid soil

Remove dead flower heads to help flowering in the following year. Zone 8

Rhododendron 'Sunset over Harkwood' ▶

An evergreen shrub bearing olive green leaves and funnel-shaped trusses of brilliant yellow flowers with a deep red blotch in the throat.

Small; sun or partial shade; flowers late spring early summer; fertile, acid soil

Zone 7

Rhododendron 'Sylphides' ▼

A bushy, upright, deciduous Knaphill azalea bearing glossy, mid-green foliage and large trusses of trumpet-shaped white flowers with a purple-pink tint and a prominent yellow blotch.

Small; sun or partial shade; flowers late spring early summer; fertile, acid soil

Zone 6

Rhododendron 'Taurus' ▲

A sturdy, upright, evergreen shrub producing pointed green leaves and clusters of deep vibrant red funnel-shaped flowers with black speckles on the upper lobes. **AGM**

Large; partial shade; flowers mid to late spring; fertile, acid soil

Remove dead flower heads to improve flowering in the following year. Zone 6

Rhododendron trichostomum ▲

An evergreen shrub bearing small glossy, dark green leaves with whitish brown undersides, and rounded heads of small, tubular daphnelike pink flowers.

Small; sun or partial shade; flowers mid to late spring; fertile, acid soil

Best grown on a rock garden. Zone 6

Rhododendron 'Vanessa' ▶

A spreading, evergreen shrub producing soft pink flowers with carmine spots at the base of the throat. **AGM**

Small to medium; sun or partial shade; flowers late spring to early summer; fertile, acid soil

Zone 8

▼ *Rhododendron vaseyi* with its compact, white-flowered selection 'White Find'

Rhododendron vaseyi

A deciduous shrub grown for its funnel-shaped pale to rosy pink flowers and for its oval leaves which turn a rich orange-red in autumn.

Medium; sun or partial shade; flowers mid to late spring; fertile, acid soil

Zone 6

Rhododendron 'Vintage Rosé' ▼

A hybrid of *R. yakushimanum* with dark green leaves and dome-shaped trusses of lovely, white flushed rose pink flowers. **AGM**

Small; sun or partial shade; flowers late spring to early summer; fertile, acid soil

Zone 7

Rhododendron 'Virginia Richards' ▲

A dense evergreen shrub with dark green leaves and ball-shaped trusses that open to funnel-shaped pink-tinted, apricot-coloured flowers.

Small to medium; sun or partial shade; flowers late spring to early summer; fertile, acid soil

Remove dead flower heads to improve flowering in the following year. Zone 7

Rhododendron Walloper Group ▼

A rounded evergreen shrub grown for its large funnel-shaped trusses of deep pink flowers that fade to pale pink and have some spotting on the inside. **AGM**

Medium; sun or partial shade; flowers mid spring; fertile, acid soil

Zone 7

Rhododendron 'Wally Miller' ▲

An evergreen shrub bearing dark green leaves with a pale indumentum on the underside and trusses of deep pink flowers fading to pale pink.

Small to medium; sun or partial shade; flowers late spring; fertile, acid soil

Zone 7

Rhododendron wardii ▶

An evergreen shrub producing rounded, green leaves, somewhat glaucous on the underside, and trusses of saucer-shaped, clear yellow flowers, sometimes with a bright crimson blotch.

Medium; sun or partial shade; flowers late spring; fertile, acid soil

Zone 7

▼ *Rhododendron wardii* in the wild on the Doshong La in southeastern Tibet.

Rhododendron williamsianum ▶

A lovely spreading evergreen shrub with a rounded habit, rounded, small, heart-shaped, leathery leaves, and trusses of two or three bell-shaped, shell pink flowers. **AGM**

Compact to small; sun or partial shade; flowers mid spring; fertile, acid soil

Zone 7

Rhododendron 'Windsor Apple Blossom' ▲▶

A bushy upright deciduous Knaphill azalea with two-toned apple-blossom pink and white flowers marked by a conspicuous orange blotch. The leaves turn orange-red in autumn.

Medium; sun or partial shade; flowers mid to late spring; fertile, acid soil

Zone 6

▼ *Rhododendron yakushimanum* was hybridized during the 1950s by Waterers Nursery, resulting in a number of hybrids, seen here at the Royal Horticultural Society's Garden Wisley: 'Chelsea Seventy', salmon-pink; 'Golden Torch', salmon-pink, AGM; 'Sneezy', pink with a red spot; 'Percy Wiseman', creamy pink, AGM; and 'Hoppy', pale lilac fading to white.

Rhododendron yakushimanum 'Koichiro Wada' ▼▶

An evergreen shrub with leathery, glossy, dark green leaves, a beautiful pale, fawn brown on the underside and also on new growth. Rounded trusses bear bell-shaped flowers that open apple-blossom pink and become paler and finally white. **AGM**

Compact; sun or partial shade; flowers late spring; fertile, acid soil

Zone 7

Rhododendron yunnanense ▶

This beautiful semievergreen shrub has plenty of funnel-shaped, pink flowers with darker spotted markings.

Medium; sun or partial shade; flowers late spring; fertile, acid soil

Zone 7

▼ *Rhododendron yunnanense* in the wild on the Bei-ma Shan in northwestern Yunnan, China.

Rhodoleia championii ▲

An evergreen shrub bearing glossy, dark green leaves with glaucous undersides, and drooping clusters of rose pink flowers with black anthers.

Large; partial shade; flowers early to mid spring; fertile, acid soil

Zone 10

Rhodothamnus chamaecistus ▶

An evergreen shrub bearing small ovate, dark green leaves with paler undersides and hairy edges, and clusters of pale pink, saucer-shaped flowers.

Compact; sun and partial shade; flowers mid to late spring; fertile, acid soil

Suitable for the rock garden or scree. Zone 6

Rhodotypos scandens ▶

A twiggy, deciduous shrub with plenty of large, paper white flowers followed by shiny black berries.

Medium; sun to partial shade; flowers late spring to early summer; fertile soil

Zone 5

Rhus copallina ▼

The mountain sumach or dwarf sumac is a deciduous shrub with pinnate leaves that turn red and purple in autumn. Clusters of greenish yellow flowers are followed by red fruits.

Small to medium; sun; flowers late summer; fertile soil

Zone 5

Rhus glabra ▼

The smooth sumach is a spreading deciduous shrub with pinnate leaves that turn beautiful shades of red and orange in autumn. The dense panicles of tiny green flowers are followed by plumelike clusters of orange-red fruits.

Medium; sun; flowers late summer; fertile soil

Zone 2

Rhus ×*pulvinata* 'Red Autumn Lace' ◀▼

A spreading deciduous shrub with green pinnate leaves, glaucous on the underside, and turning fiery orange-red in autumn. The erect panicles of greenish flowers are followed by erect clusters of red fruits. **AGM**

Medium to large; sun; flowers mid summer; fertile soil

Zone 3

Rhus typhina 'Dissecta' ▶▼

The cut-leaved stag horn sumach is a deciduous spreading shrub with velvety branches bearing pinnate leaves that turn fiery shades of orange, red, and purple in autumn. The upright panicles of greenish yellow flowers are followed by erect clusters of red fruits. **AGM**

Medium to large; sun; flowers mid summer; fertile soil

Strongly suckering. Zone 3

Ribes ×gordonianum ▲

A vigorous, deciduous shrub with drooping racemes of bronzy red and yellow flowers.

Medium; sun; flowers mid spring; fertile soil

Prune out older stems after flowering. Zone 6

Ribes himalayense ▶

A deciduous shrub grown for its pendent racemes of small greenish yellow flowers and lobed leaves.

Small; sun or partial shade; flowers mid to late spring; fertile soil

Prune out older stems after flowering. Zone 6

Ribes magellanicum ▼

A deciduous shrub with mid-green, lobed leaves and long racemes of creamy yellow flowers followed by edible, black-red berries.

Medium to large; sun or partial shade; flowers mid spring; fertile soil

Prune out older stems after flowering. Zone 6

Ribes odoratum ▲

The buffalo currant is an upright deciduous shrub with a loose habit. It bears shiny green, lobed leaves and scented racemes of bright yellow flowers followed by black berries.

Small to medium; sun; flowers mid spring; fertile soil

Prune out older stems after flowering. Zone 5

Ribes sanguineum 'King Edward VII' ▲▼

This flowering currant is a deciduous shrub with aromatic foliage and drooping racemes of bright crimson flowers.

Medium; sun; flowers mid spring; fertile soil

Prune out older stems after flowering. Zone 6

Ribes sanguineum 'Koja' ▲

This flowering currant is an upright deciduous shrub with aromatic, lobed, green leaves and long drooping clusters of pinkish red flowers.

Medium; sun; flowers mid spring; fertile soil

Prune out older stems after flowering. Zone 6

Ribes sanguineum 'Brocklebankii' ▲

A flowering currant that makes a deciduous shrub with a slender habit. It bears aromatic, lobed, bright yellow then yellowish green leaves and racemes of pink flowers.

Medium; sun or partial shade; flowers mid spring; fertile soil

Prune out older stems after flowering. Zone 6

Ribes sanguineum 'Plenum' ▲
A flowering currant that produces aromatic foliage and short pendent racemes of attractive, double, pinkish red flowers.

Medium; sun; flowers mid spring; fertile soil

Prune out older stems after flowering. Zone 6

Ribes sanguineum 'Red Pimpernel' ▼
This flowering currant is a bushy, deciduous shrub with aromatic foliage and an abundance of rich rose-red flowers with a distinctive white tube.

Medium; sun; flowers mid spring; fertile soil

Prune out older stems after flowering. Zone 6

Ribes sanguineum White Icicle 'Ubric' ▶
This flowering current is a vigorous, deciduous shrub bearing lobed, aromatic leaves and pendent racemes of white flowers. **AGM**

Medium; sun; flowers mid spring; fertile soil

Prune out older stems after flowering. Zone 6

Ribes speciosum ▲
The fuchsia-flowered gooseberry is a semievergreen shrub with spiny branches bearing shiny green, lobed leaves and clusters of fuchsia-like, red flowers that are often seen hanging in rows. **AGM**

Small to medium; sun; flowers mid to late spring; fertile soil

Fan train against a wall. Prune out older stems after flowering. Zone 7

Richea scoparia ▶
The kerosene bush is an upright, evergreen shrub with tapering, dark green sharply pointed leaves and erect spike-like panicles of reddish pink or orange flowers.

Compact; partial shade; flowers late spring; fertile, acid soil

Zone 8

Rosa 'Beau Narcisse' (gallica) ▶
A shrub with strongly fragrant, crimson flowers speckled with purple.

Medium; sun; flowers early summer; fertile soil

Prune in late winter. Dead-head in growing season. Zone 5

Rosa Amber Queen 'Harroony' (floribunda) ▲
A low, spreading shrub bearing glossy, dark green leaves with bronze-tinted new growth, and large clusters of fragrant double, amber yellow flowers.
AGM

Compact; sun; flowers early to late summer; fertile soil

Prune in mid winter. Dead-head in growing season. Zone 6

Rosa 'Andersonii' (*canina* hybrid) ▼
A shrub with arching, prickly branches bearing green leaves and scented, single, clear, rich pink flowers followed by red hips.

Medium; sun; flowers early to late summer; fertile soil

Prune in late winter. Dead-head in growing season. Zone 6

Rosa Bonica 'Meidomonac' (ground cover shrub) ▲▼
A sturdy shrub that produces an abundance of long-lasting bright rose pink flowers followed by bright red hips.
AGM

Compact to small; sun; flowers early to late summer; fertile soil

Needs minimal pruning in late winter. Zone 6

Rosa **Britannia** 'Frycalm' (hybrid tea) ▶

An upright deciduous shrub with glossy green leaves and apricot-coloured, double flowers.

Small; sun; flowers early to late summer; fertile soil

Prune in late winter. Dead-head in growing season. Zone 6

Rosa **'Cantabrigiensis'** (shrub) ▼

A bushy shrub with arching stems bearing small leaves and saucer-shaped pale yellow, slightly scented flowers in great profusion. **AGM**

Medium to large; sun; flowers late spring to early summer; fertile soil

Needs minimal pruning in late winter. Zone 6

Rosa **Charles Austin** 'Ausles' (English) ▼

A tall shrub bearing lovely, double, full petalled apricot yellow, fruity fragrant flowers.

Small; sun; flowers early to late summer; fertile soil

Prune in late winter. Dead-head in growing season. Zone 6

Rosa **Chianti** 'Auswine' (shrub) ▲

A tall, shrubby rose with strongly fragrant, dark crimson flowers ageing to purple maroon.

Medium; sun; flowers early to late summer; fertile soil

Prune in late winter. Dead-head in growing season. Zone 6

Rosa 'Cornelia' (hybrid musk) ▲
An old-fashioned-looking rose with an arching habit, bearing dark green leaves and strongly fragrant, double, pink-tinted apricot flowers that become a creamy pink. **AGM**

Medium; sun to partial shade; flowers early summer and early autumn; fertile soil

Prune in late winter. Dead-head in growing season. Zone 7

Rosa Edith Holden 'Chewlegacy' (floribunda) ▲
An upright rose bearing shiny, dark green leaves and clusters of semi-double, reddish brown flowers with golden centres.

Medium; sun; flowers early to late summer; fertile soil

Prune in late winter. Dead-head in growing season. Zone 6

Rosa Eye Paint 'Maceye' (floribunda) 
A tall, vigorous rose bearing large clusters of single, vivid scarlet red flowers with a white eye.

Medium; sun; flowers early to late summer; fertile, moisture-retentive soil

Prune in late winter. Dead-head in growing season. Zone 6

Rosa Fellowship 'Harwelcome' (floribunda) ▼
A shrub producing glossy, mid-green leaves and clusters of scented double orange flowers that fade to apricot. **AGM**

Compact; sun; flowers early to late summer; fertile soil

Prune in late winter. Dead-head in growing season. Zone 6

Rosa foetida (species) ▶
The Australian copperbriar is an upright, prickly shrub with bright green leaves and single, rich sulphur yellow flowers.

Small; sun; flowers late spring to early summer; fertile soil

Needs minimal pruning in late winter. Zone 4

***Rosa foetida* 'Bicolor'** (species) ▼

An attractive, upright shrub with an arching habit, bearing bright coppery red flowers, coloured yellow on the reverse of the petals.

Small; sun; flowers late spring to early summer; fertile soil

Needs minimal pruning in late winter. Zone 4

***Rosa* 'Fritz Nobis'** (modern shrub)

A lovely shrub bearing abundant beautifully clove-scented, clear pink, semi-double flowers. **AGM**

Medium; sun; flowers early to late summer; fertile soil

Prune in late winter. Dead-head in growing season. Zone 6

▼ *Rosa* 'Fritz Nobis' at Tatton Park, Cheshire, England.

***Rosa* 'Geranium'** (*moyesii* hybrid) ▲

A more compact form of *R. moyesii* with an arching habit, and bearing geranium red flowers followed by red hips that are larger than those of the species. **AGM**

Medium; sun; flowers early to mid summer; fertile soil

Needs minimal pruning in late winter. Zone 5

***Rosa* Graham Thomas 'Ausmas'** (English) ▶

A popular rose that makes an excellent climber as well as a shrub, with a vigorous and arching habit and bearing double, cupped, deep yellow flowers with a lovely tea rose fragrance. **AGM**

Small; sun; flowers early to late summer; fertile soil

Prune in late winter. Dead-head in growing season. Zone 6

***Rosa* 'Helen Knight'** (*ecae* hybrid) ▼

An upright shrub rose with small, single, saucer-shaped, bright deep yellow flowers. One of the earliest flowering roses.

Small to medium; sun; flowers mid to late spring; fertile soil

Needs minimal pruning in late winter. Zone 6

***Rosa* HYDE HALL** 'Ausbosky' (English) ▲
A notably hardy shrub rose bearing long-lasting, subtly fragrant, double pink flowers.

Large; sun; flowers early to late summer; fertile soil
Needs minimal pruning in late winter. Dead-head in growing season. Zone 6

***Rosa* ICEBERG** 'Korbin' (floribunda) ▲
A tall bushy, branching rose with light glossy green leaves and lightly double pure white delicately fragrant flowers. **AGM**

Small; sun; flowers early to late summer; fertile soil
Prune in late winter. Dead-head in growing season. Zone 6

***Rosa* INGRID BERGMAN** 'Poulman' (hybrid tea) ▶
A vigorous, upright rose with fully double pure dark red flowers. **AGM**

Small; sun; flowers early to late summer; fertile soil
Prune in late winter. Dead-head in growing season. Zone 6

***Rosa* INTRIGUE** 'Korlech' (floribunda) ▼
An upright shrub with leathery, dark green leaves and clusters of long-lasting, deep red, double flowers.

Compact; sun; flowers early to late summer; fertile soil
Prune in late winter. Dead-head in growing season. Zone 6

***Rosa* JENNY'S ROSE** 'Cansit' (floribunda) ▼
An upright rose with large clusters of double soft pink flowers that fade to white.

Small; sun; flowers early to late summer; fertile, acid soil
Zone 6

▶ *Rosa* KENT 'Poulcov' with *R.* PINK BELLS 'Poulbells' in a border.

Rosa KENT 'Poulcov' (ground cover shrub) ▼

A ground-covering rose with clusters of large double white flowers. **AGM**

Compact; sun; flowers early to late summer; fertile soil

Needs minimal pruning in late winter. Zone 6

Rosa L. D. BRAITHWAITE 'Auscrim' (English) ▼

A low-spreading, bushy rose with pale green leaves and fully double, brilliant crimson red flowers that become more scented with age. **AGM**

Small; sun; flowers early to late summer; fertile soil

Prune in late winter. Dead-head in growing season. Zone 6

Rosa LEANDER 'Auslea' (English) ▶

A tall shrub or climber with shiny green foliage and beautifully symmetrical, apricot-coloured, fully double blooms that have a raspberry tea rose scent.

Small to medium; sun; flowers early to late summer; fertile soil

Prune in late winter. Dead-head in growing season. Zone 6

Rosa LILLI MARLENE 'Korlima' (floribunda)

A rose with large clusters of double dark red flowers.

Compact to small; sun; flowers early to late summer; fertile soil

Prune in late winter. Dead-head in growing season. Zone 6

▼ *Rosa* LILLI MARLENE 'Korlima' at Savill Garden in Windsor Great Park, Egham, England.

Rosa macrophylla (species) ▲

A tall, vigorous shrub with large leaves and clusters of bright pink, single flowers followed by large bright red hips.

Medium to large; sun; flowers early summer; fertile soil

Needs minimal pruning in late winter. Zone 7

Rosa MARJORIE FAIR 'Harhero' (polyantha/modern shrub) ▼

A small bushy shrub grown for its glossy foliage and single, cup-shaped, deep carmine red flowers with a white eye. **AGM**

Small; sun; flowers early to late summer; fertile soil

Prune in late winter. Dead-head in growing season. Zone 6

Rosa 'Mevrouw Nathalie Nypels' (polyantha) ▶

A bushy shrub with glossy, dark green leaves and semidouble, scented, rose pink flowers fading to almost white. **AGM**

Compact; sun; flowers early to late summer; fertile soil

Prune in late winter. Dead-head in growing season. Zone 6

Rosa moyesii (species) ◀ ▼

A rose shrub with a loose habit and bearing single blood-red flowers and ornamental, urn-shaped, orange-red to crimson hips.

Medium; sun; flowers early to mid summer; fertile soil

Needs minimal pruning in late winter with removal of older stems. Zone 5

▶ *Rosa* 'Mrs. Anthony Waterer' at Cambridge University Botanic Garden, England.

Rosa 'Mrs. Anthony Waterer'
(rugosa)

A dense, arching shrub with abundant fragrant, double, crimson red flowers.

Small; sun; flowers early to mid summer; fertile soil

Prune in late winter. Dead-head in growing season. Zone 6

Rosa 'Mrs. Oakley Fisher' (hybrid tea) ▼

A shrub with dark green foliage, bronzy green as it unfurls, and single, subtly scented, deep orange-yellow flowers.

Compact; sun; flowers early to late summer; fertile soil

Prune in late winter. Dead-head in growing season. Zone 6

Rosa Paddy Stephens 'Macclack' (hybrid tea) ▼

A strong-growing rose with glossy, dark green leaves and double rich pink flowers that open silvery pink.

Small to medium; sun; flowers early to late summer; fertile soil

Prune in mid winter. Dead-head in growing season. Zone 6

Rosa ×*odorata* (Sanguinea Group) 'Bengal Crimson' (china) ▶

An upright species rose bearing long-lasting, large single, slightly fragrant, blood-red flowers that fade to crimson red.

Medium; sun; flowers early to mid summer; fertile soil

Needs minimal pruning in late winter. Zone 7

▲ *Rosa* 'Penelope' at the Royal Horticultural Society's Garden Wisley.

Rosa 'Penelope' (hybrid musk)
A vigorous, bushy shrub bearing glossy, dark green foliage and plenty of beautifully scented, semidouble pale pink flowers that open blush pink. **AGM**

Medium; sun; flowers early summer and early autumn; fertile soil

Prune in late winter. Dead-head in growing season. Zone 6

Rosa PERDITA 'Ausperd' (English musk) ▼
A bushy shrub with lovely, fully double pinkish apricot-coloured, strongly fragrant flowers.

Small; sun; flowers early to mid summer; fertile soil

Prune in late winter. Dead-head in growing season. Zone 6

Rosa 'Raubritter' ('Macrantha' hybrid) ▶▶
A sprawling, mounded bush with glossy, dark green, finely toothed leaves and cup-shaped, semidouble pink flowers.

Compact; sun; flowers early to mid summer; fertile soil

Needs minimal pruning in late winter. Dead-head in growing season. Zone 6

Rosa RED BELLS 'Poulred' (ground cover shrub)
A ground-covering rose with clusters of lightly fragrant, small, double, red flowers and small, mid-green leaves.

Compact; sun; flowers early to late summer; fertile soil

Needs minimal pruning in late winter. Zone 6

▼ *Rosa* RED BELLS 'Poulred' at the Royal Horticultural Society's Garden Wisley.

***Rosa* Rhapsody in Blue 'Frantasia' (shrub)** ▶

A bushy, upright shrub with bright green leaves and clusters of sweetly scented, mauve-purple flowers.

Small; sun; flowers early to late summer; fertile soil

Prune in mid winter. Dead-head in growing season. Zone 6

***Rosa* 'Robin Hood'** (hybrid musk) ▼

A shrub with large clusters of delicate, fragrant, pinkish red flowers.

Small to medium; sun; flowers early summer to early autumn; fertile soil

Prune in late winter. Dead-head in growing season. Zone 6

***Rosa* Rosemoor 'Austough'** (English) ▼

A bushy, upright, free-flowering shrub with medium-sized, strongly scented, soft pink flowers.

Small; sun; flowers early to late summer; fertile soil

Prune in mid winter. Dead-head in growing season. Zone 6

Rosa roxburghii* f. *normalis (species) ▼

A strong-growing very prickly shrub with twisted branches and flaky light brown bark, bearing fragrant single shell pink flowers followed by yellowish orange hips. **AGM**

Medium to large; sun; flowers late spring to early summer; fertile soil

Needs minimal pruning in late winter with removal of older stems. Zone 5

Rosa roxburghii* f. *roxburghii (species) ▼

The chestnut rose or chinquapin rose is a tender species that lacks vigour. It is grown for its beautiful fully double, scented, rich pink flowers.

Small to medium; sun; flowers late spring to early summer; fertile soil

Needs minimal pruning in late winter. Dead-head in growing season. Can be grown against a south-facing wall. Zone 8

Rosa sericea subsp. *omeiensis*

(species) ▶

A dense, spreading shrub with thorny branches and bearing single, four-petalled, white flowers followed by multicoloured crimson and yellowish green pear-shaped edible fruits.

Medium; sun; flowers late spring to early summer; fertile soil

Needs minimal pruning in late winter with removal of older stems. Zone 6

Rosa sericea subsp. *omeiensis* f. *pteracantha* (shrub) ◀

Grown for its large triangular red thorns that are translucent when young. The small flowers are white.

Medium; sun; flowers early to late summer; fertile soil

Prune out old wood in late winter. Zone 6

Rosa soulieana (species)

A mound-forming shrub with spreading, prickly branches bearing grey-green leaves and yellowish buds opening to single, creamy white flowers. **AGM**

Large; sun; flowers early to late summer; fertile soil

Needs minimal pruning in late winter with removal of older stems. Dead-head in growing season. Zone 7

▼ *Rosa soulieana* at Cambridge University Botanic Garden, England.

Rosa Summer Lady 'Tanydal' (hybrid tea) ▲

A bushy, upright rose with delicately fragrant double clear pink flowers.

Small; sun; flowers early to late summer; fertile soil

Prune in late winter. Dead-head in growing season. Zone 6

Rosa The Times Rose 'Korpeahn' (floribunda) ▼

A shrub rose with glossy, dark green leaves and clusters of bright red, semi-double blooms. **AGM**

Small to medium; sun; flowers early to late summer; fertile soil

Prune in late winter. Dead-head in growing season. Zone 6

Rosa webbiana (species) ▶

A graceful shrub with an arching habit and single, pale pink flowers followed by bottle-shaped, sealing wax red hips.

Medium; sun; flowers early summer; fertile soil

Needs minimal pruning in late winter with removal of older stems. Zone 6

Rosa 'Wickwar' (rambler shrub) ▼

A spreading shrub with clusters of large, highly fragrant, single, white flowers, contrasting nicely with grey-green foliage and orange fruits.

Medium to large; sun; flowers early to late summer; fertile soil

Prune in late winter by removing older stems. Zone 6

Rosa villosa (species) ▲

The apple rose is a shrub with bluish green leaflets and single, clear pink flowers followed by apple-shaped bristle-clad hips.

Medium; sun; flowers early summer; fertile soil

Zone 5

Rosa Warm Wishes 'Fryxotic' (hybrid tea) ▼

A small rose with glossy, dark green leaves and nicely scented, double, coral pink flowers. **AGM**

Compact; sun; flowers early to late summer; fertile soil

Prune in late winter. Dead-head in growing season. Zone 6

Rosa Wisley 'Ausintense' (English) ▼

A charming, vigorous shrub with an arching habit, bearing fully double, rosette-shaped, dark pink scented flowers.

Medium; sun to partial shade; flowers early to late summer; fertile soil

Prune in late winter. Dead-head in growing season. Zone 6

Rosa 'Zéphirine Drouhin'
(Bourbon) ▶

A climbing shrub but treated as a shrub. Has thornless stems bearing an abundance of fragrant, deep cerise carmine, semidouble flowers.

Medium to large; sun; flowers early to late summer; fertile soil

Prune in late winter. Dead-head in growing season. Zone 6

Rosmarinus eriocalyx ▼

A sprawling aromatic evergreen shrub with violet-blue flowers.

Prostrate to compact; sun; flowers mid to late spring; well-drained soil

Zone 8

Rosmarinus officinalis 'Miss Jessopp's Upright' ▼

A vigorous, upright evergreen shrub with aromatic, greyish green foliage and pale blue flowers. **AGM**

Small; sun; flowers mid to late spring; well-drained soil

Can be used as a small hedge and pruned after flowering. Zone 6

Rosmarinus officinalis 'Majorca Pink' ◀

An evergreen shrub with fragrant, dark green, needle-shaped leaves and erect spikes of pink flowers.

Small; sun; flowers mid to late spring; well-drained soil

Can be used as a small hedge and pruned after flowering. Zone 7

▲ *Rosmarinus officinalis* 'Mrs. McConnell' growing on a wall

Rosmarinus officinalis 'Mrs. McConnell'

A low-spreading evergreen shrub with aromatic, dark green foliage and dark blue flowers. AGM

Prostrate to compact; sun; flowers mid to late spring; well-drained soil

Prune after flowering. Can be grown over a low wall. Zone 7

Rostrinucula dependens ▼

An unusual, deciduous shrub with flaky bark, green leaves, grey on the underside, and long drooping racemes of tiny, pale pink flowers.

Small; sun or partial shade; flowers early autumn; fertile soil

May die back to ground level in winter. Zone 8

▲ *Rubus biflorus*, an outstanding collection by Christopher Brickell and Alan C. Leslie.

Rubus biflorus ▼

A prickly shrub with highly ornamental, waxy, white canes and bearing small white flowers followed by yellow edible fruits. AGM

Medium; sun or partial shade; flowers early summer; fertile soil

Cut back shoots in early spring. Zone 8

Rubus 'Benenden' ◀

A spreading deciduous shrub with an arching habit, bearing lobed, dark green leaves and plenty of large white, saucer-shaped flowers produced along the length of the stems. AGM

Medium; sun or partial shade; flowers late spring; fertile soil

Prune out old wood after flowering. Zone 5

Rubus cockburnianus 'Goldenvale' ▶

An upright prickly bramble bush with lovely, golden fernlike leaves borne on purple stems that turn white in winter. The small flowers are purple. **AGM**

Medium; sun or partial shade; flowers early summer; fertile soil

Cut back shoots to ground level annually in early spring. Zone 6

Rubus coreanus 'Dart's Mahogany' ▲

A deciduous shrub with arching mahogany-coloured branches bearing shining dark green leaflets, glaucous beneath, and small pink flowers.

Medium to large; sun or partial shade; flowers early to mid summer; fertile soil

Cut back shoots in early spring. Zone 6

Rubus odoratus ▶

A vigorous, bushy bramble with velvety, large palmate leaves and clusters of scented, pinkish purple flowers followed by edible red fruits.

Medium; sun or partial shade; flowers early to mid summer; fertile soil

Zone 3

Rubus spectabilis 'Olympic Double' ▲

A vigorous bramble bearing green foliage and striking, fully double, scented bright pink-purple flowers.

Medium; sun or partial shade; flowers mid to late spring; fertile soil

Can spread rapidly by suckers. Zone 5

Rubus tricolor ▼

A lovely ground-covering, evergreen shrub bearing glossy, dark green, deeply veined leaves with white-felted undersides and white flowers followed by bright red edible fruits.

Prostrate; sun or partial shade; flowers mid summer; fertile soil

Can be used for ground cover in shaded areas. Zone 7

Rubus 'Walberton' ▲

A spreading deciduous shrub with an arching habit, lobed green leaves, and plenty of large pink saucer-shaped flowers produced along the length of the stems. **AGM**

Medium; sun or partial shade; flowers mid summer; fertile soil

Zone 6

Ruscus aculeatus 'Sparkler' ▶

This butcher's broom or box holly is a small evergreen shrub that spreads by underground stems. It produces spine-tipped leaves and small self-fertile violet flowers that turn into large glossy, red cherrylike berries.

Compact; shade and partial shade; flowers late winter to mid spring; fertile soil

Zone 7

Ruscus colchicus ▼

A dwarf spreading shrub with arching stems, pale green leaves, and small violet flowers on the underside of the leaf. **AGM**

Compact; shade and partial shade; flowers mid winter to mid spring; fertile soil

Zone 7

Ruscus hypoglossum ▼

A low-growing evergreen shrub with glossy green leaves that are really flat stems. Tiny green flowers are borne on the upper surface of the leaf and on female plants are followed by red fruits.

Compact; shade and partial shade; flowers late winter to mid spring; fertile soil

Zone 7

Ruscus ×microglossus ▲

A ground-covering shrub bearing leaf-shaped stems with a whitish flower in the centre. **AGM**

Compact; shade and partial shade; flowers late winter to mid spring; fertile soil

Zone 7

Ruta chalepensis ▲

An aromatic evergreen shrub with thick, oval, bluish green leaves and fringed, yellow flowers.

Compact; sun; flowers early to late summer; well-drained soil
Zone 8

Ruta graveolens ▲

The rue or herb-of-grace is an evergreen shrub with divided, fernlike, blue-green leaves and small yellow flowers.

Compact; sun; flowers early to late summer; well-drained soil
Zone 5

Salix alba 'Golden Ness' ▼

A deciduous shrub that, when coppiced or pollarded, produces beautiful, golden yellow stems in winter. It bears silky green leaves.

Large unless pruned regularly; sun; flowers early to mid spring; fertile soil
Prune back hard in spring to encourage new coloured stems. Zone 2

Salix alba var. *vitellina* ▼

The golden willow is a deciduous shrub that, when coppiced or pollarded, produces golden yellow stems. The long, bright green leaves have silvery undersides. **AGM**

Large unless pruned regularly; sun; flowers early to mid spring; fertile soil
Prune back hard in spring to encourage new coloured stems. Zone 2

Salix alba var. *vitellina* 'Yelverton' ▶

A deciduous shrub that, when coppiced or pollarded, produces bright scarlet-orange stems and silky green leaves.

Large unless pruned regularly; sun; flowers early to mid spring; fertile soil

Prune back hard in spring to encourage new coloured stems. Zone 2

Salix apoda ▼

A compact, dwarf willow with glossy green leaves that turn yellow in autumn and silvery grey catkins that turn yellow when the anthers emerge.

Prostrate; sun; flowers late winter to mid spring; fertile soil

Suitable for the rock garden or scree. Zone 6

Salix caprea 'Curlilocks' ▼

A deciduous shrub with arching stems bearing silvery grey catkins which turn yellow when the anthers emerge.

Small to medium; sun or partial shade; flowers early spring; fertile soil

Grown as a weeping standard (on a single stem). Zone 3

Salix fargesii ▲

A deciduous shrub with mahogany coloured bark, dark red buds, and long, glossy green leaves.

Medium; sun or partial shade; flowers mid to late spring; fertile soil

Zone 6

Salix gracilistylla 'Melanostachys' ▼

The black pussy willow is an attractive shrub with very dark and shiny black catkins and red anthers.

Large unless pruned regularly; sun or partial shade; flowers early to mid spring; fertile soil

Prune out older stems in spring. Zone 6

Salix hastata 'Wehrhahnii' ▶▼

A slow-growing, spreading willow with purplish brown new shoots, attractive, silvery catkins, and green leaves with bluish grey undersides. **AGM**

Small; sun; flowers early to mid spring; fertile soil

Suitable for the rock garden. Zone 6

Salix helvetica ▼

The Swiss willow is a bushy shrub bearing soft, silvery grey catkins studded with yellow anthers and greyish green leaves with velvety, silvery undersides. **AGM**

Prostrate to compact; sun; flowers early to mid spring; fertile soil

Suitable for the rock garden. Zone 6

▲ *Salix herbacea* on Goat Fell, the highest point on the Isle of Arran, Scotland.

Salix herbacea

The dwarf willow has a creeping habit and bears little, rounded glossy green leaves.

Prostrate; sun; flowers early to mid spring; fertile, well-drained soil

Suitable for the rock garden or scree. Zone 2

Salix hookeriana ▶

The coastal willow has broad glossy green leaves with felty silvery white undersides and large silvery grey catkins turning yellow as the anthers open.

Small to medium; sun or partial shade; flowers early to mid spring; fertile soil

Prune out older stems in spring. Zone 6

Salix integra 'Hakuro-nishiki' ▼▶

An attractive shrub with a slightly weeping habit and bearing mottled, green and white foliage tinted pink when young. The slender catkins are yellow.

Small to medium; sun or partial shade; flowers early to mid spring; fertile soil

Prune out older stems in late winter. Zone 6

▲ *Salix phylicifolia* at the Royal Botanic Garden Edinburgh.

Salix irrorata ▲▶

An upright shrub with reddish brown new growth which when coppiced or pollarded turns purplish white in winter. The glossy, bright green leaves are glaucous beneath and the catkins are yellow.

Medium; sun; flowers early to mid spring; fertile soil

Prune back hard in spring to encourage coloured stems. Zone 5

Salix phylicifolia ▼

The tea-leaved willow is a deciduous shrub producing shiny, bright green leaves with greyish undersides and grey catkins that turn yellow with the emergence of the anthers.

Small to medium; sun; flowers early to mid spring; fertile soil

Zone 5

Salix reticulata ▶

A mat-forming shrub with rounded, dark green leaves which have an attractive net venation above and silvery undersides. The catkins are upright. **AGM**

Prostrate; sun; flowers mid spring; fertile, well-drained soil

Suitable for the rock garden or scree. Zone 1

Salix udensis 'Sekka' ▶

An unusual willow with flattened stems bearing narrow green leaves that turn yellow in autumn. The large catkins are silvery grey.

Large; sun or partial shade; flowers early to mid spring; fertile soil

Stems are used for floral decorations. Prune out older stems in spring. Zone 5

Salvia elegans ▼

Commonly called pineapple sage for its aromatic foliage, this subshrub has an upright habit, with yellowish green leaves and tubular, red flowers.

Small; sun; flowers mid summer to early autumn; fertile, well-drained soil

Tends to be short-lived so propagate regularly. Prune in spring to remove straggly and frost-damaged stems. Zone 9

Salvia gesneriiflora ▲

A subshrub with woody stems bearing mid-green, heart-shaped, aromatic leaves and showy, bright scarlet flowers.

Compact; sun; flowers late summer; fertile, well-drained soil

Tends to be short-lived so propagate regularly. Prune in spring to remove straggly and frost-damaged stems. Zone 9

Salvia greggii ▲

The autumn sage is a mound-forming shrub with small, narrow leaves and long-lasting rosy red flowers.

Compact; sun; flowers mid summer to early autumn; fertile, well-drained soil

Tends to be short-lived so propagate regularly. Prune in spring to remove straggly and frost-damaged stems. Zone 8

Salvia greggii 'Caramba' ▶

A cultivar of the autumn sage bearing variegated green foliage edged with white, and red flowers.

Compact; sun; flowers mid summer to early autumn; fertile, well-drained soil

Tends to be short-lived so propagate regularly. Prune in spring to remove straggly and frost-damaged stems. Zone 8

Salvia greggii 'Dark Dancer' ▲

This cultivar of the autumn sage has narrow, green, aromatic foliage and raspberry-coloured flowers.

Compact; sun; flowers mid summer to early autumn; fertile, well-drained soil

Tends to be short-lived so propagate regularly. Prune in spring to remove straggly and frost-damaged stems. Zone 8

Salvia greggii 'Peach' ▼

An autumn sage with peach-coloured flowers. **AGM**

Compact; sun; flowers mid summer to early autumn; fertile, well-drained soil

Tends to be short-lived so propagate regularly. Prune in spring to remove straggly and frost-damaged stems. Zone 8

Salvia guaranitica 'Blue Enigma' ▲

A perennial subshrub with aniseed-scented, wrinkly green foliage and upright stems of deep blue flowers with a green calyx. **AGM**

Small to medium; sun; flowers mid summer to early autumn; fertile, well-drained soil

Tends to be short-lived so propagate regularly. Prune hard in spring. Zone 9

Salvia ×jamensis 'Hot Lips' ▶

An evergreen shrub with small, oval-shaped, aromatic leaves and spikes of magenta-pink and white flowers.

Small; sun; flowers mid summer to early autumn; fertile, well-drained soil

Tends to be short-lived so propagate regularly. Prune in spring to remove straggly and frost-damaged stems. Zone 8

Salvia ×jamensis 'Pleasant Pink' ▲

An evergreen shrub with small oval aromatic leaves and spikes of soft pink flowers which contrast with the dark brownish purple calyces.

Small; sun; flowers mid summer to early autumn; fertile, well-drained soil

Tends to be short-lived so propagate regularly. Prune in spring to remove straggly and frost-damaged stems. Zone 8

Salvia leucantha ▲▼

The Mexican sage bush is a rounded shrub with narrow, green leaves and abundant, upright spikes of white flowers appearing from rich purple calyces. **AGM**

Compact to small; sun; flowers late summer to mid autumn; fertile, well-drained soil

If grown in a conservatory will continue to flower into winter. Propagate regularly. Zone 10

Salvia microphylla 'Cerro Potosi' ▼

The cherry sage has little, slightly scalloped, mid-green leaves and upright spikes of pink flowers.

Small; sun; flowers mid summer to early autumn; fertile, well-drained soil

Tends to be short-lived so propagate regularly. Prune in spring to remove straggly and frost-damaged stems. Zone 9

Salvia microphylla var. *microphylla* 'La Foux' ▼

This small-leaved sage has long-lasting spikes of red flowers.

Small; sun; flowers mid summer to early autumn; fertile, well-drained soil

Tends to be short-lived so propagate regularly. Prune in spring to remove straggly and frost-damaged stems. Zone 8

Salvia 'Silke's Dream' ▲

A shrub with green foliage and upright spikes of long-lasting coral-red flowers.

Compact; sun; flowers mid summer to early autumn; fertile, well-drained soil

Tends to be short-lived so propagate regularly. Prune in spring to remove straggly and frost-damaged stems. Zone 9

Salvia splendens 'Van-Houttei' ▼

The scarlet sage is a shrub bearing lance-shaped, toothed dark green foliage and upright spikes of wine-red flowers. **AGM**

Compact to small; sun to partial shade; flowers mid summer to early autumn; fertile, well-drained soil

Frost tender so propagate regularly in late summer. Zone 10

Salvia uliginosa ►

The bog sage is a perennial subshrub with an erect habit, bearing aromatic, oblong, toothed light green leaves and short spikes of turquoise-blue flowers. **AGM**

Small to medium; sun to partial shade; flowers mid summer to early autumn; fertile, well-drained soil

Treat as a perennial by hard cutting back in spring. Zone 9

Sambucus nigra Black Beauty 'Gerda' ▼

A common elder with gorgeous, dark burgundy, almost black, deciduous foliage and pale pink flowers opening from darker red buds and followed by black berries. **AGM**

Large; sun but can also grow in partial shade; flowers early summer; fertile soil

Prune stems in early spring for foliage effect. Zone 5

Sambucus nigra Black Lace 'Eva' ▼

An attractive common elder with dissected, very dark purple foliage and clusters of pinkish white flowers.

Large; sun but can also be grown in partial shade; flowers early summer; fertile soil

Prune stems in early spring for foliage effect. Zone 5

Sambucus nigra 'Guincho Purple' ▲

A spreading deciduous shrub with finely cut, green leaves that age bronze-purple, and with clusters of pale pink flowers.

Large; sun or partial shade; flowers early summer; fertile soil

Prune stems in early spring for foliage effect. Zone 5.

Sambucus nigra 'Marginata' ▼

A vigorous common elder that has attractive, dark green foliage edged with creamy white and clusters of cream flowers.

Large; sun or partial shade; flowers early summer; fertile soil

Prune stems in early spring for foliage effect. Zone 5

Sambucus nigra 'Thundercloud'

A handsome elder with brownish red to purple leaves and large clusters of pink flowers opening from rich pink buds and followed by black berries.

Large; sun or partial shade; flowers early summer; fertile soil

Prune stems in early spring for foliage effect. Zone 5

▲ *Sambucus nigra* 'Thundercloud' at Cally Gardens in southwestern Scotland.

Sambucus racemosa 'Plumosa Aurea'

An attractive shrub with deeply cut, deciduous golden yellow foliage and creamy yellow flowers.

Large; partial shade; flowers mid to late spring; fertile soil

Prune stems in early spring for foliage effect. Zone 4

▼ *Sambucus racemosa* 'Plumosa Aurea' with black-foliaged *S. nigra* Black Beauty 'Gerda'.

Santolina chamaecyparissus ▶

The lavender-cotton is an evergreen spreading shrub with woolly, silvery foliage and bright lemon yellow flowers. AGM

Compact; sun; flowers mid summer; well-drained soil

Prune in spring to retain compact habit. Zone 8

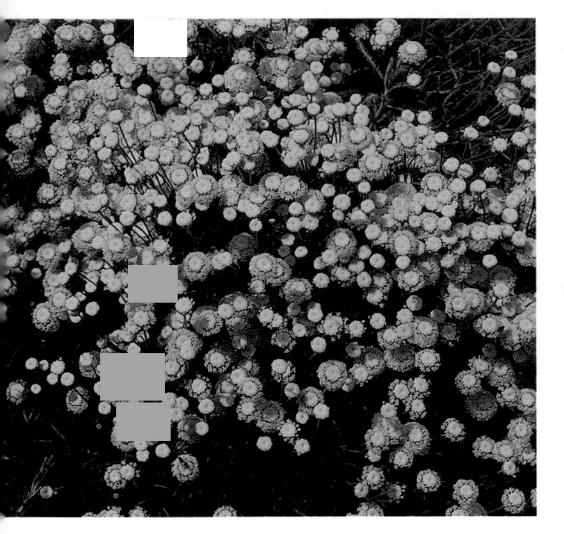

Santolina pinnata subsp. *neapolitana* ▲▼

An evergreen shrub with leathery, greyish green or green finely serrated leaves and yellow flower heads growing on long stalks. AGM

Compact; sun; flowers mid summer; well-drained soil

Prune in spring to retain compact habit. Zone 8

Santolina rosmarinifolia ▲

A shrub with bright green, dissected leaves and bright yellow flowers.

Compact; sun; flowers mid summer; well-drained soil

Prune in spring to retain compact habit. Zone 8

Sapium japonicum ▶

A deciduous shrub with dark green leaves that turn crimson in autumn, and small greenish yellow flowers.

Large; sun; flowers early summer; fertile soil

Zone 8

Sarcococca confusa ▲

The Christmas box is a dense, spreading, evergreen shrub with glossy, dark green, pointed leaves, and highly scented white flowers followed by black berries. **AGM**

Compact to small; shade or partial shade, will also tolerate sun; flowers late winter to early spring; fertile soil

Prune older plants after flowering. Zone 6

Sarcococca hookeriana Schilling 2083 ▶

An upright, mound-forming shrub with dark green, tear-shaped leaves and scented, white flowers.

Small; shade or partial shade; flowers late winter to early spring; fertile soil

Prune older plants after flowering. Zone 6

Sarcococca hookeriana var. *digyna* ▼

A more slender habit and narrower leaves than var. *hookeriana*. It bears clusters of scented, creamy white flowers followed by black berries. **AGM**

Small; shade or partial shade but also tolerant of sun; flowers late winter to early spring; fertile soil

Prune older plants after flowering. Zone 6

Sarcococca hookeriana var. *humilis* ◀▲

A dense Christmas box with glossy, dark green leaves and white flowers tinged pink followed by black berries.

Compact; shade or partial shade but also tolerant of sun; flowers late winter to early spring; fertile soil

Prune older plants after flowering. Zone 6

Sarcococca orientalis ▲
A vigorous, upright evergreen shrub with large green leaves and fragrant white flowers tinged pink.

Small; shade or partial shade; flowers late winter to early spring; fertile soil

Zone 6

Schefflera taiwaniana ▼
An upright evergreen shrub with attractive dark green leaves and contrasting orange petiole stalks.

Large; sun, partial shade, or shade; flowers late summer to early winter; fertile soil

Zone 9

Senecio petasitis ▲▼
Called velvet groundsel, this is an evergreen shrub with large, rounded, velvety leaves and orange-yellow flowers.

Small; sun; flowers late winter; fertile, well-drained soil

Tolerant of coastal conditions. Zone 9

Sibiraea laevigata ▼
A deciduous shrub with greyish green foliage and panicles of white flowers.

Small; sun; flowers early summer; fertile, well-drained soil

Prune after flowering. Zone 7

Sinocalycanthus chinensis ▶

A spreading deciduous shrub with large shiny green leaves turning yellow in autumn and large nodding, white cup-shaped flowers flushed with pink and displaying yellow inner tepals.

Medium to large; sun to partial shade; flowers early summer; fertile soil

Zone 5

Sinojackia rehderiana ▼

A deciduous shrub with a bushy, spreading habit bearing dark green leaves that turn orange-yellow in autumn and short racemes of white star-shaped flowers.

Medium to large; sun to partial shade; flowers mid to late spring; fertile soil

Zone 8

Skimmia ×confusa 'Kew Green' ▼

A rounded evergreen shrub with aromatic, glossy green leaves and large clusters of beautifully fragrant, greenish yellow male flowers. **AGM**

Small; sun to shade; flowers mid to late spring; fertile soil

Suitable as a pollinator for female plants.
Zone 7

Skimmia anquetilia ▼

An evergreen shrub grown for clusters of bright red fruits, following greenish yellow flowers, on female plants.

Compact; partial shade to shade; flowers mid to late spring; fertile soil

Both male and female plants are needed for the production of fruits on female plants.
Zone 7

Skimmia japonica ▼▶

An evergreen shrub with leathery leaves and panicles of fragrant, white flowers on male and female plants. Flower size varies. On female forms, clusters of usually red fruits follow the flowers.

Compact to small; partial shade to shade; flowers mid to late spring; fertile soil

Both male and female plants are needed for the production of fruits on female plants.
Zone 7

Skimmia japonica 'Bowles's Dwarf Female' ▲

A slow-growing evergreen shrub with dark green leaves and dense panicles of fragrant, white flowers followed by bright red fruits.

Compact; partial shade to shade; flowers mid to late spring; fertile soil
Male plants are needed for the production of fruits. Zone 7

Skimmia japonica 'Fragrans' ▲

A rounded, bushy shrub with glossy, dark green leaves and dense panicles of tiny, scented, white, male flowers. **AGM**

Small; partial shade to shade; flowers mid to late spring; fertile soil
Suitable as a pollinator for female plants. Zone 7

Skimmia japonica 'Fructu Albo' ▲

A low-growing cultivar bearing small leaves and fragrant creamy white flowers followed by white fruits.

Compact; partial shade to shade; flowers mid to late spring; fertile soil
Male plants are needed for the production of fruits. Zone 7

Skimmia japonica 'Red Princess' ▲

An evergreen shrub with red flower buds opening a fragrant creamy white followed by large bright red fruits.

Small; partial shade to shade; flowers mid to late spring; fertile soil
Male plants are needed for the production of fruits. Zone 7

Skimmia japonica 'Redruth' ▼

A vigorous, upright, evergreen shrub with clusters of creamy white flowers followed by bright red fruits.

Small; partial shade to shade; flowers mid to late spring; fertile soil
Male plants are needed for the production of fruits. Zone 7

Skimmia japonica subsp. *reevesiana* 'Chilan Choice' ▲▶

An upright-growing evergreen shrub bearing long, green leaves with pink-tinted undersides, and clusters of white flowers followed by bright red fruits.

Small; partial shade to shade; flowers mid to late spring; fertile soil

Male plants are needed for the production of fruits. Zone 7

Skimmia japonica subsp. *reevesiana* 'Robert Fortune' ▼

A low-growing evergreen shrub grown for its matt crimson red fruits following panicles of white flowers.

Compact; partial shade to shade; flowers mid to late spring; fertile soil

Male plants are needed for the production of fruits. Zone 7

Skimmia japonica 'Rubella' ◀

A male cultivar bearing dark green leaves margined with red. Large panicles of red buds are seen over a long period and open to fragrant white flowers. AGM

Small; partial shade to shade; flowers mid to late spring; fertile soil

Suitable as a pollinator for female plants. Zone 7

Skimmia japonica 'Ruby King' ▼

An evergreen shrub bearing narrow dark green leaves tinted red. Large conical red buds open to fragrant, white flowers.

Small; partial shade to shade; flowers mid to late spring; fertile soil

Suitable as a pollinator for female plants. Zone 7

Skimmia japonica 'Scarlet Dwarf' ▶

A low-growing, bushy, evergreen shrub with bright red berries following fragrant white flowers.

Compact; partial shade to shade; flowers mid to late spring; fertile soil

Male plants are needed for the production of fruits. Zone 7

Skimmia japonica 'Stoneham Red' ▲

A vigorous cultivar with large panicles of red buds opening to fragrant white flowers. The broad leathery leaves are evergreen.

Small; partial shade to shade; flowers mid to late spring; fertile soil

Suitable as a pollinator for female plants. Zone 7

Skimmia japonica 'Variegata' ▼

A cultivar with grey-green leaves edged in creamy white and with panicles of white flowers.

Compact to small; partial shade to shade; flowers mid to late spring; fertile soil

Both male and female plants are needed for the production of fruits on female plants. Zone 7

Skimmia japonica 'Veitchii' ▲

A vigorous, evergreen shrub with broad, waxy, dark green leaves and white star-shaped flowers followed by large clusters of bright red fruits.

Small; partial shade to shade; flowers mid to late spring; fertile soil

Male plants are needed for the production of fruits. Zone 7

Skimmia japonica 'Wakehurst White' ▶

A rounded, low-growing, evergreen shrub with leathery, dark green leaves and clusters of white, scented flowers followed by white fruits.

Compact; partial shade to shade; flowers mid to late spring; fertile soil

Male plants are needed for the production of fruits. Zone 7

Skimmia laureola subsp. *lancasteri* ▲

An open, evergreen shrub with leathery green leaves and small panicles of white flowers followed by black fruits.

Small; partial shade to shade; flowers mid to late spring; fertile soil

Male plants are needed for the production of fruits. Zone 7

Solanum valdiviense ▼

A vigorous, deciduous climbing shrub with an arching habit, bearing long, pointed leaves and pinkish lavender flowers.

Medium to large; sun to partial shade; flowers late spring; fertile soil

Tends to climb. Grow on a south- or west-facing wall. Spur prune in spring. Zone 9

Sophora davidii ▼

A bushy, deciduous shrub with green pinnate leaves and racemes of pale violet-white pealike flowers.

Medium; sun; flowers early summer; fertile, well-drained soil

Zone 6

Sophora microphylla ▲◄

An evergreen shrub with abundant, small, pinnate leaflets and short racemes of bright yellow, large pealike flowers.

Large; sun; flowers late spring to early summer; fertile, well-drained soil

Zone 8

Sophora microphylla Sun King 'Hilsop' ▲▼

A large evergreen shrub bearing racemes of large, dark yellow, pealike flowers. **AGM**

Large; sun; flowers late spring to early summer; fertile, well-drained soil

Zone 8

Sophora tetraptera ▶

The kowhai is a spreading, evergreen shrub with a drooping appearance, pinnate leaves, and tubular, pea-shaped, yellow flowers. **AGM**

Large; sun; flowers late spring; fertile, well-drained soil

Zone 8

▲ *Sorbaria sorbifolia* 'Sem', a compact form of the species.

Sorbaria sorbifolia ▼

An upright deciduous suckering shrub with green pinnate leaves that are flushed pink when young. White flowers are borne in erect panicles.

Medium; sun to partial shade; flowers mid to late summer; fertile soil

May sucker freely, so cut out older stems in spring. Zone 2

Sorbaria tomentosa var. *angustifolia* ▼

A spreading shrub bearing dark green, pinnate leaves and large frothy plumes of creamy white flowers. **AGM**

Large; sun; flowers mid to late summer; fertile soil

Cut out older stems in spring. Zone 6

Sorbus poteriifolia ▼

A rare ground-covering deciduous shrub with up to 15 dark green leaflets and clusters of rose-coloured flowers followed by white fruits.

Prostrate; partial shade; flowers late spring; fertile soil

Suitable for the rock garden or scree. Zone 7

Sorbus reducta ▲

A deciduous shrub bearing shiny green pinnate leaves that turn bronze and purple in autumn. Clusters of small white flowers are followed by pinkish white fruits. **AGM**

Compact; sun or partial shade; flowers late spring; fertile soil

Suitable for the rock garden or scree. Zone 6

Sparmannia africana ▶

The African hemp is a vigorous, deciduous shrub that produces large hairy leaves and white cup-shaped flowers with yellow stamens that change to reddish purple and reflex when touched. **AGM**

Large; sun or partial shade; flowers late spring early summer; fertile soil

Useful for a large conservatory in cold areas. Zone 9

Spartium junceum ▼

The Spanish broom is an upright shrub with a loose habit, bright green stems bearing small leaves, and racemes of fragrant, bright yellow, pea-like flowers. **AGM**

Medium; sun; flowers early to late summer; well-drained soil

Tolerant of coastal conditions. Prune back in spring to maintain shape. Zone 8

Sphaeralcea 'Hyde Hall' ▲

A short-lived deciduous subshrub with grey-green leaves and soft pink cup-shaped flowers with an inner flash of red on the petals.

Small; sun; flowers early to mid summer; well-drained soil

Prune straggly shoots and frost-damaged shoots in spring. Zone 9

Spiraea betulifolia var. *aemiliana* ▼

A deciduous shrub with masses of snow white flowers.

Compact; sun; flowers early summer; fertile soil

Prune out older stems after flowering. Zone 6

Spiraea cantoniensis ▶

A deciduous spreading shrub with arching branches bearing toothed, dark green leaves, paler on the underside, and with rounded clusters of white flowers along the branches.

Medium; sun; flowers early summer; fertile soil

Prune out older stems after flowering. Zone 6

Spiraea ×*fontenaysii* 'Rosea' ▼

A deciduous shrub with broad stubby clusters of white flowers opening a soft pink. Leaves are bluish green.

Medium; sun; flowers mid summer; fertile soil

Prune out older stems after flowering. Zone 6

Spiraea japonica 'Bullata' ▲

A slow-growing deciduous shrub bearing small leaves with a wrinkly, blistered appearance and flat-topped clusters of rose-red flowers.

Small; sun; flowers mid summer; fertile soil

Remove old flower heads to encourage new coloured foliage growth. Prune established plants in spring. Zone 5

Spiraea japonica 'Darts Red' ▲

A low-growing, rounded deciduous shrub bearing large clusters of fuchsia pink flowers. **AGM**

Small; sun; flowers mid summer; fertile soil

Remove old flower heads to encourage new coloured foliage growth. Prune established plants in spring. Zone 5

Spiraea japonica Golden Princess 'Lisp' ▼

An attractive, rounded deciduous shrub with golden bronze, toothed leaves turning greenish yellow then orange-gold during autumn. Pink flowers are borne in clusters. **AGM**

Small; sun; flowers mid summer; fertile soil

Remove old flower heads to encourage new coloured foliage growth. Prune established plants in spring. Zone 5

Spiraea japonica 'Little Princess' ▼

A mound-forming deciduous shrub with small, dark green leaves and clusters of rose pink flowers.

Small; sun; flowers early to mid summer; fertile soil

Remove old flower heads to encourage new coloured foliage growth. Prune established plants in spring. Zone 5

Spiraea japonica Magic Carpet 'Walbuma' ▲

A rounded, deciduous shrub with foliage bright red when young, becoming gold then lemon green and finally orange and red in autumn. Clusters of purplish pink flowers adorn the plant. **AGM**

Compact; sun; flowers early to mid summer; fertile soil

Remove old flower heads to encourage new coloured foliage growth. Prune established plants in spring. Zone 5

Spiraea japonica 'Nana' ▲

A deciduous shrub bearing toothed, green leaves with greyish undersides and many small clusters of deep pink flowers. AGM

Compact; sun; flowers early to mid summer; fertile soil

Remove old flower heads to encourage new coloured foliage growth. Prune established plants in spring. Zone 5

Spiraea nipponica 'Snowmound' ▲

A spreading deciduous shrub with dark green leaves and abundant arching sprays of snow white flowers. AGM

Medium; sun; flowers early summer; fertile soil

Prune out older stems after flowering on established plants. Zone 4

Spiraea ×*pseudosalicifolia* 'Triumphans' ▼

A lovely deciduous shrub with dense, upright panicles of rosy purple flowers and bluish green leaves.

Medium; sun; flowers mid summer; fertile soil

Prune established plants in spring. Zone 4

Spiraea sargentiana ▼

An attractive deciduous shrub with an arching habit, bearing toothed leaves and dense clusters of creamy white flowers.

Medium; sun; flowers early summer; fertile soil

Prune out older stems after flowering. Zone 6

Spiraea thunbergii ▲

A twiggy deciduous shrub bearing narrow, toothed leaves and dainty, pure white flowers. **AGM**

Small; sun; flowers early to mid spring; fertile soil

Prune out older stems after flowering. Zone 4

Spiraea veitchii ◄▲

A deciduous shrub with an upright arching habit, oval leaves, and dense clusters of white flowers.

Large; sun; flowers early to mid summer; fertile soil

Prune out older stems after flowering. Zone 5

Stachyurus chinensis ▲

A spreading deciduous shrub with dull green leaves changing to golden brown in autumn on branches that are purplish when young. Long drooping racemes bear cup-shaped yellow flowers.

Medium; sun or partial shade; flowers early to mid spring; fertile soil

Zone 7

▼ *Stachyurus chinensis* growing on a wall

Stachyurus himalaicus ▲
A spreading deciduous shrub with lance-shaped green leaves on red petioles and with racemes of dark rose-purple flowers fading to pale green.

Medium; sun or partial shade; flowers early to mid spring; fertile soil

Zone 9

***Stachyurus* 'Magpie'** ▼▶
A deciduous shrub with purple branches bearing variegated grey-green leaves irregularly edged with a cream colour and tinted pink then yellowish green when young. Creamy yellow flowers are borne on drooping racemes.

Medium; sun or partial shade; flowers early spring; fertile soil

Zone 7

Stachyurus praecox ▲▼
A deciduous shrub with a spreading habit and bearing oval, mid-green leaves and drooping racemes of pale yellow flowers. **AGM**

Medium; sun or partial shade; flowers early spring; fertile soil

Zone 7

***Stachyurus* 'Rubriflorus'** ▼
A spreading deciduous shrub with short pink-tinged drooping racemes of flowers and with green leaves on purplish brown branches when young.

Small to medium; sun or partial shade; flowers early spring; fertile soil

Zone 8

Stachyurus salicifolius ▲

An evergreen shrub with narrow, willowlike leaves that are bronzy pink on the underside. Long, thin racemes carry greenish yellow flowers.

Medium; sun or partial shade; flowers mid spring; fertile soil

Zone 9

Stachyurus sp. ETOT 72 ▼

A deciduous shrub with a spreading habit and long drooping racemes of greenish yellow flowers on purplish green young stems.

Medium; sun or partial shade; flowers mid spring; fertile soil

Zone 8

Staphylea bolanderi ▲◄

An upright shrub with drooping panicles of white flowers and green leaves that turn yellow in autumn.

Large; sun or partial shade; flowers mid to late spring; fertile soil

Zone 6

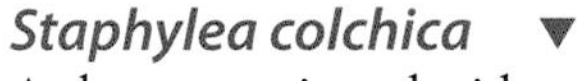

Staphylea colchica ▼

A slow-growing, deciduous shrub with an erect habit, bearing pinnate, shiny green leaves and upright panicles of white flowers which have a milky fragrance.

Large; sun or partial shade; flowers late spring; fertile soil

Zone 6

Staphylea colchica 'Hessei' ▶

A slow-growing deciduous erect shrub with shiny pinnate green leaves and clusters of white flowers opening from pinkish purple buds.

Small; sun or partial shade; flowers late spring; fertile soil

Suitable for the rock garden. Zone 6

Staphylea holocarpa

A deciduous shrub with trifoliate leaves and drooping racemes of white flowers developing from attractive pink buds.

Large; sun or partial shade; flowers mid to late spring; fertile soil

Zone 6

▼ *Staphylea holocarpa* at Kiftsgate Court Gardens, Gloucestershire, England

Staphylea pinnata ▼

The bladdernut is a vigorous, upright deciduous shrub bearing pinnate green leaves with paler undersides, and long drooping panicles of white flowers.

Large; sun or partial shade; flowers late spring to early summer; fertile soil

Zone 6

Staphylea holocarpa var. *rosea* ◀

A deciduous shrub with spreading branches bearing drooping clusters of rose pink flowers.

Large; sun or partial shade; flowers mid to late spring; fertile soil

Zone 6

▲ *Sutherlandia montana*, a wild-collected form

Stephanandra incisa 'Crispa' ▲

A dense, mound-forming shrub with crinkly fernlike leaves which turn purplish red then orange in autumn. Young stems are a rich brown in winter. Tiny greenish white flowers are carried in panicles.

Compact; sun or partial shade; flowers early summer; fertile soil

Cut back older stems after flowering if plant becomes straggly. Or, cut back hard to encourage coloured winter stems. Zone 5

Stephanandra tanakae ▼

An arching shrub bearing lobed, toothed dark green leaves that turn orange and red in autumn. Young stems are a rich brown in winter. Greenish white flowers are borne in panicles.

Medium; sun or partial shade; flowers early summer; fertile soil

Cut back older stems after flowering if plant becomes straggly. Zone 6

Sutherlandia montana ▼

The bergkanker bossie is a semi-evergreen shrub with delicate pinnate leaves on silvery grey branches. Bright red flowers are carried in large pendulous clusters.

Small; sun; flowers early summer; well-drained soil

Suitable for the rock garden or scree. Zone 8

Sycopsis sinensis ▲

A spreading evergreen shrub bearing blistered, leathery, dark green leaves that are paler beneath. The flowers lack petals but have yellow stamens with red anthers.

Large; partial shade; flowers late winter to early spring; fertile soil

Zone 8

Symphoricarpos ×doorenbosii 'White Hedge' ▲

An upright deciduous shrub with green foliage and small pink flowers followed by many clusters of white succulent berries.

Small to medium; sun or partial shade or shade; flowers late spring to early summer; fertile soil

Often grown as a low informal hedge. Prune in late winter or early spring. Zone 4

Symplocos sawafutagi ▶

The sapphire berry is a twiggy, deciduous shrub with panicles of fragrant white flowers. When two or more plants are present, the white flowers are followed by vivid, bright blue fruits.

Large; sun; flowers late spring to early summer; fertile soil

Zone 5

Symplocos tinctoria ▲

A deciduous shrub with panicles of fragrant white flowers. The glossy green leaves are slightly glaucous on the underside.

Large; sun to shade; flowers mid to late spring; fertile, neutral to acid soil

Zone 8

Syringa ×chinensis 'Saugeana' ▲▼

A spreading, bushy, deciduous shrub with an arching habit, bearing drooping rounded panicles of scented reddish lilac flowers.

Medium to large; sun; flowers late spring; fertile, preferably alkaline soil

Zone 4

Syringa emodi 'Aureovariegata' ▲

A deciduous shrub bearing pale lilac buds opening to white flowers. The variegated greenish yellow leaves have a green centre.

Large; sun; flowers early summer; fertile, preferably alkaline soil

Prune out old stems on a four- or five-year rotation on established plants. Zone 6

Syringa ×*hyacinthiflora* 'Buffon' ▲

A lilac with an upright, broad multi-stemmed habit, bronze new growth followed by purplish red autumn colour, and panicles of faintly scented, single shell pink flowers.

Large; sun; flowers late spring; fertile, preferably alkaline soil

Prune out older stems on a four- or five-year rotation on established plants. Zone 4

Syringa ×*hyacinthiflora* 'Maiden's Blush' ▶

A deciduous shrub with a broad habit, bluish green, heart-shaped leaves that are bronze as they open with autumn foliage colour, and upright panicles of scented, single pink flowers.

Large; sun; flowers late spring; fertile, preferably alkaline soil

Prune out older stems on a four- or five-year rotation on established plants. Zone 4

Syringa ×*hyacinthiflora* 'The Bride' ▲

A deciduous spreading shrub covered with large panicles of fragrant, white flowers.

Large; sun; flowers late spring; fertile, preferably alkaline soil

Prune out older stems on a four- or- five-year rotation on established plants. Zone 4

Syringa ×*hyacinthiflora* 'Pink Cloud' ▶

A lilac bearing plenty of large panicles of faintly scented pinkish lilac flowers. The foliage has a hint of bronze as it opens and turns purple-red in autumn.

Large; sun; flowers late spring; fertile, preferably alkaline soil

Prune out older stems on a four- or- five-year rotation on established plants. Zone 4

Syringa komarowii subsp. *reflexa* ▶

A tall, vigorous shrub with an arching habit. It bears long drooping panicles of rich purplish pink flowers which are pale pink within.

Medium to large; sun; flowers late spring to early summer; fertile, preferably alkaline soil

Prune out old stems on a four- or five-year rotation on established plants. Zone 5

Syringa oblata var. *oblata* ▲▼

The early or broadleaf lilac is a large, rounded, deciduous shrub with heart-shaped, bluish green leaves which are bronze tinted when opening. The lilac-blue flowers are borne in broad panicles.

Large; sun; flowers mid to late spring; fertile, preferably alkaline soil

Prune out older stems on a four- or five-year rotation on established plants. Zone 5

Syringa ×*laciniata* ▲

Called the cut-leaf lilac for its attractive foliage, this graceful, spreading shrub has pinnate leaves and panicles of lilac flowers.

Medium; sun; flowers late spring; fertile, preferably alkaline soil

Zone 5

Syringa meyeri 'Palibin' ▼

The dwarf Korean lilac is a dense, compact shrub with many clusters of faintly scented, pale lilac-pink flowers. Often flowers are seen twice during the season. **AGM**

Small; sun; flowers late spring; fertile, preferably alkaline soil

Zone 5

Syringa oblata var. *donaldii* ▼

A rounded deciduous shrub with leathery leaves, dark green above, pale beneath, opening a rich purple and deep purple, changing to red in autumn. The slightly scented pale lilac flowers are deep purple in bud.

Large; sun; flowers mid to late spring; fertile, preferably alkaline soil

Prune out older stems on a four- or five-year rotation on established plants. Zone 5

Syringa pinnatifolia Lancaster 1916 ▼

A tall lilac bearing unusual, pinnate leaves with up to 11 leaflets and small nodding panicles of pink-tinted white, tubular flowers.

Medium; sun; flowers late spring; fertile, preferably alkaline soil

Zone 6

Syringa ×*prestoniae* 'Ethel M. Webster' ▲

A vigorous, deciduous hardy hybrid grown for its erect then spreading panicles of lilac-pink flowers opening from pink buds.

Large; sun; flowers late spring to early summer; fertile, preferably alkaline soil

Prune out older stems on a four- or- five-year rotation on established plants. Zone 5

Syringa pubescens subsp. *julianae* 'George Eastman' ▼

A lovely, upright lilac bearing panicles of sweetly scented cerise-pink flowers opening from wine red buds. AGM

Medium; sun; flowers early summer; fertile, preferably alkaline soil

Zone 6

Syringa ×*prestoniae* 'Elinor' ▼

A deciduous shrub with large upright panicles of reddish purple buds opening to pale lavender flowers. AGM

Medium; sun; flowers late spring to early summer; fertile, preferably alkaline soil

Prune out older stems on a four- or- five-year rotation on established plants. Zone 4

Syringa pubescens subsp. *microphylla* Forrest 20336 ▶

Called the daphne lilac, this shrub has small dark green, oval leaves and clusters of fragrant rose pink, daphne-like flowers.

Medium; sun; flowers late spring; fertile, preferably alkaline soil

Zone 6

Syringa reticulata subsp. *pekinensis* China Snow 'Morton' ▲▼

This Japanese lilac is an upright, deciduous shrub or small tree with large panicles of fragrant, white flowers and rich chocolate brown peeling bark.

Large; sun; flowers early summer; fertile, preferably alkaline soil

Remove twiggy growth from main stems to reveal stem colour. Zone 6

Syringa vulgaris 'Aurea' ▶

This common lilac is a spreading deciduous shrub with yellowish green foliage contrasting nicely with the drooping panicles of purple flowers.

Large; sun; flowers late spring to early summer; fertile, preferably alkaline soil

Prune out older stems on a four- or- five-year rotation on established plants. Zone 5

Syringa vulgaris Beauty of Moscow 'Krasavitsa Moskvy' ▶

This Russian cultivar of the common lilac bears panicles of double, highly fragrant, white flowers opening from pink buds.

Large; sun; flowers late spring to early summer; fertile, preferably alkaline soil

Prune out older stems on a four- or- five-year rotation on established plants. Zone 5

Syringa vulgaris 'Decaisne' ▼

A deciduous shrub with panicles of scented single, blue-purple flowers.

Large; sun; flowers late spring to early summer; fertile, preferably alkaline soil

Prune out older stems on a four- or- five-year rotation on established plants. Zone 5

Syringa vulgaris 'Etna' ◄

A beautiful upright, spreading deciduous shrub with scented panicles of pinkish purple flowers.

Large; sun; flowers late spring to early summer; fertile, moisture-retentive yet well-drained, preferably alkaline soil

Prune out older stems on a four- or- five-year rotation. Zone 5

▼ *Syringa vulgaris* cultivars: 'Etna' (pinkish purple), 'Maréchal Foch' (carmine rose), and 'Volcan' (dark purple).

Syringa vulgaris 'Kardynal' ▲

A beautiful cultivar of the common lilac bred in Poland. Produces scented panicles of single rich purple flowers.

Large; sun; flowers late spring to early summer; fertile, preferably alkaline soil

Prune out older stems on a four- or five-year rotation on established plants. Zone 5

Syringa vulgaris 'Frank Paterson' ▼

A tall, spreading deciduous shrub with panicles of showy, scented single deep reddish purple flowers.

Large; sun; flowers late spring to early summer; fertile, preferably alkaline soil

Prune out older stems on a four- or- five-year rotation on established plants. Zone 5

Syringa vulgaris 'Maud Notcutt' ▲▼

A handsome, spreading deciduous shrub with large panicles of single pure white, fragrant flowers.

Large; sun; flowers late spring to early summer; fertile, preferably alkaline soil

Prune out older stems on a four- or- five-year rotation on established plants. Zone 5

Syringa vulgaris 'Monument' ▶

A very old introduction with large scented panicles of pure white flowers opening from creamy white buds.

Large; sun; flowers late spring to early summer; fertile, preferably alkaline soil

Prune out older stems on a four- or- five-year rotation on established plants. Zone 5

Syringa vulgaris 'Primrose' ▼

A dense deciduous shrub bearing panicles of fragrant, creamy yellow flowers.

Large; sun; flowers late spring to early summer; fertile, preferably alkaline soil

Prune out older stems on a four- or- five-year rotation on established plants. Zone 5

Syringa vulgaris 'Sensation' ▼

An attractive lilac bearing large panicles of scented purple flowers that are edged with white.

Large; sun; flowers late spring to early summer; fertile, preferably alkaline soil

Prune out older stems on a four- or- five-year rotation on established plants. Zone 5

Syringa vulgaris 'Professor Edmund Jankowski' ▶

A beautiful common lilac cultivar from Poland with dense, scented panicles of lilac flowers opening from purple buds.

Large; sun; flowers late spring to early summer; fertile, preferably alkaline soil

Prune out older stems on a four- or- five-year rotation on established plants. Zone 5

Syringa vulgaris 'Victor Lemoine' ▲

An attractive lilac named for the raiser. Produces dense panicles of fragrant, double, pinkish lavender flowers opening from mauve buds.

Large; sun; flowers late spring to early summer; fertile, preferably alkaline soil

Prune out older stems on a four- or- five-year rotation on established plants. Zone 5

Syringa vulgaris 'Volcan' ▶

A spreading shrub with panicles of scented dark purple flowers.

Large; sun; flowers late spring to early summer; fertile, preferably alkaline soil

Prune out older stems on a four- or- five-year rotation on established plants. Zone 5

Syringa vulgaris 'Yankee Doodle' ▼

A common lilac raised by John Fiala and grown for its scented panicles of lilac-purple flowers.

Large; sun; flowers late spring to early summer; fertile, preferably alkaline soil

Prune out older stems on a four- or- five-year rotation on established plants. Zone 5

Tamarix ramosissima 'Pink Cascade' ▲

Like the species but with bright pink flowers.

Large; sun; flowers mid summer to early autumn; well-drained soil

A useful coastal plant being wind- and salt-resistant. Prune after flowering to avoid becoming leggy. Zone 3

Tamarix ramosissima ▼

A graceful arching deciduous shrub with tiny scalelike leaves and masses of small light pink flowers in showy, feathery inflorescences.

Large; sun; flowers mid summer to early autumn; well-drained soil

A useful coastal plant being wind- and salt-resistant. Prune after flowering to avoid becoming leggy. Zone 3

Tamarix tetrandra ▼

A graceful arching deciduous shrub with tiny scalelike leaves and masses of tiny pink flowers in large, showy, feathery inflorescences. **AGM**

Large; sun; flowers late spring; well-drained soil

A useful coastal plant being wind- and salt-resistant. Prune after flowering to avoid becoming leggy. Zone 6

Telopea oreades ▶

The Gippsland waratah is an evergreen shrub grown for its deep crimson flower heads and narrow dark green leaves which are often glaucous on the underside.

Medium; sun or partial shade; flowers late spring to early summer; fertile, acid soil

Zone 9

Telopea truncata ▲

The Tasmanian waratah is an evergreen shrub with long, almost leathery leaves and dense heads of bright crimson flowers.

Medium; sun or light shade; flowers late spring to early summer; fertile, acid soil

Zone 9

Tetrapanax papyrifera ◀

The rice-paper plant is a striking evergreen grown for the enormous deeply lobed leaves, to 60 cm across, on leaf stalks even longer. Small white flowers are carried in flattened clusters. **AGM**

Large; sun or partial shade; flowers early to mid autumn; fertile, acid soil

Requires a sunny yet sheltered location to flourish wherre it can sucker in good growing conditions. Zone 8

Teucrium fruticans ▲

The shrubby germander is a bushy evergreen shrub producing aromatic, grey-green leaves and 2-lipped pale blue flowers with a long lower lip and prominently protruding stamens.

Small; sun; flowers early to late summer; well-drained soil

Prune to size and shape during early to mid spring. Zone 8

Thryptomene saxicola 'F. C. Payne' ▶

A wiry evergreen shrub grown for its tiny starlike pale pink or white flowers and its aromatic heathlike leaves.

Compact; sun; flowers late winter to early spring; well-drained, acid soil

Zone 8

Tripetaleia bracteata ▼

The hako-tsutsuji is a deciduous, slow-growing shrub with greenish or pinkish white flowers formed on erect branching stems. Autumn foliage is a yellowish brown.

Small; partial shade; flowers mid to late summer; fertile, acid soil

Grow on a rock garden. Zone 6

Trochodendron aralioides ▲▼

A slow-growing evergreen shrub or small tree with leathery fresh glossy green leaves on strikingly long stalks and erect clusters of small green flowers.

Large; sun, partial shade, and shade; flowers mid spring to early summer; fertile soil

Zone 8

Trochocarpa thymifolia ▼

An evergreen shrub grown for its nodding rich pink flowers, magenta in bud and white within once open, its fleshy blue fruits, and its heathlike leaves with pinkish green new growth.

Prostrate; sun; flowers early spring; fertile, acid soil

Requires alpine house conditions in cool climates. Zone 9

Ugni molinae ▲

A slow-growing evergreen shrub with stiffly erect branches, leathery leaves, and pink bell-shaped flowers followed by edible aromatic dark brownish red berries.

Medium; sun; flowers mid summer; fertile soil

Can be clipped to shape. Zone 9

Ulex europaeus 'Flore Pleno' ▲▼

This very spiny green-stemmed shrub has minute very short-lived leaves but is covered with bright golden yellow double, pea-shaped flowers. **AGM**

Small; sun; flowers mid to late spring; well-drained, acid soil

Prune after flowering to retain compactness. A sterile (non-invasive) cultivar. Zone 6

▲ *Ulex europaeus* can colonize hillsides as seen here in Scotland and is capable of regenerating after being burnt to control spread.

Ulex europaeus ▶

The gorse or whin is a very spiny green-stemmed shrub with minute very short-lived leaves and bright golden yellow, pea-shaped flowers. It is also known as the furze.

Small; sun; flowers mid to late spring mainly, but also intermittently throughout most of the year; well-drained, acid soil

Prune after flowering to retain compactness. Invasive in many regions. Zone 6

Vaccinium corymbosum ▲

The American blueberry is a deciduous erect shrub with leaves becoming bright red and orange in autumn. White flowers are followed by edible black fruits covered with a white bloom. **AGM**

Small to medium; sun or partial shade; flowers late spring; fertile, acid soil

Cultivated for the edible fruit. Zone 3

Vaccinium corymbosum 'Herbert' ▼

This blueberry is a deciduous erect shrub with leaves becoming bright red in autumn. The white flowers are followed by large dark blue edible fruits.

Small; sun or partial shade; flowers late spring; fertile, acid soil

Cultivated for its edible fruits which have an excellent flavor. Zone 3

Vaccinium cylindraceum ►▼

A deciduous erect shrub with leaves lasting well into early winter and with reddish buds opening to greenish white cylindrical flowers. The blue-black fruits are also cylindrical and are covered by a white bloom. **AGM**

Medium; sun or partial shade; flowers late summer; fertile, acid soil

Cut out older shoots close to the base in early spring to promote regeneration. Zone 9

Vaccinium floribundum ▲

An evergreen shrub with purplish red young leaves becoming dark green in summer. Dense clusters of pink flowers are followed by small red edible fruits.

Small to medium; sun or partial shade; flowers early summer; fertile, acid soil

Zone 9

Vaccinium glaucoalbum ▶

An evergreen shrub with leaves that are bright blue above and white below. Pink flowers in short pendulous clusters are followed by edible black fruits covered with a white bloom. **AGM**

Small; sun or partial shade; flowers late spring; fertile, acid soil

Zone 8

Vaccinium sikkimense ▼

A small evergreen shrub with dense clusters of white flowers that are flushed pink and followed by blue-black berries. The leaves are dark green.

Compact; sun or partial shade; flowers mid summer; fertile, acid soil

Zone 9

Vaccinium macrocarpon ▲

The American cranberry is a creeping evergreen shrub with wiry stems, tiny leaves, and pink pendant flowers followed by large globose red edible berries.

Prostrate; sun or partial shade; flowers mid summer; fertile, acid soil

Cultivated for its edible fruit. Zone 2

Vaccinium ovatum ▼

The Californian huckleberry is a small evergreen bushy shrub with leathery leaves, reddish tinged when young. The white bell-shaped flowers are followed by red fruits that mature to black.

Medium; sun or partial shade; flowers late spring to early summer; fertile, acid soil

Grown for its fruit which is made into jam. Zone 7

Vaccinium stamineum ▼

The deerberry is a deciduous shrub with bluish green foliage that turns orange in autumn. Clusters of pendant white bell-shaped flowers are followed by blue, green, and purple fruits.

Medium; sun or partial shade; flowers late spring to early summer; fertile, acid soil

Zone 5

Vestia foetida ▲

An erect, evergreen shrub with glossy, bright green, unpleasantly scented leaves and nodding tubular yellow flowers with swept-back petals and long protruding stamens, followed by greenish yellow non-edible fruits. **AGM**

Small; sun or partial shade; flowers mid spring to late summer; fertile, well-drained soil

Can be grown in a container or in the conservatory. Prune in spring to remove frosted stems. Zone 9

Viburnum awabuki ▼

An evergreen with large bold glossy, leathery leaves and large conical heads of scented white flowers followed by red fruits that mature to black.

Large; sun to partial shade; flowers late summer; fertile soil

Zone 9

Viburnum betulifolium ▼

An erect deciduous shrub with jagged-toothed leaves, white flowers, and profuse long-lasting clusters of globose red fruits. **AGM**

Large; sun to partial shade; flowers early to mid summer; fertile soil

Needs to be planted in a group for fruit to be set. Zone 5

Viburnum ×bodnantense 'Charles Lamont' ◄▼

A deciduous shrub with highly scented pale, silvery pink flowers produced well before the leaves unfold. **AGM**

Medium to large; sun to partial shade; flowers late autumn to early spring; fertile soil

Old stems can be pruned after flowering to maintain size and regenerate new growth. Zone 7

Viburnum ×*burkwoodii* 'Mohawk' ▲▶

A deciduous shrub with highly scented white flowers tinged pink and opening from bright red buds produced well before the leaves unfold.

Medium; sun to partial shade; flowers late winter to late spring; fertile soil

Zone 5

Viburnum carlesii ▼

A rounded deciduous shrub with rounded heads of sweetly scented pure white flowers opening from pink buds. The green leaves are greyish green beneath and change to a dull red in autumn.

Medium; sun to partial shade; flowers mid to late spring; fertile soil

Plant often grafted, in which case it is necessary to remove suckers from the rootstock.
Zone 8

Viburnum carlesii 'Aurora' ▼▶

A rounded deciduous shrub with rounded heads of sweetly scented pink flowers opening from carmine pink buds. AGM

Medium; sun to partial shade; flowers mid to late spring; fertile soil

Plant often grafted, in which case it is necessary to remove suckers from the rootstock.
Zone 8

Viburnum cassinoides ▲

A deciduous shrub with dull green leaves turning to scarlet in autumn. Creamy white heads of flowers are followed by red fruits that eventually turn black.

Medium; sun to partial shade; flowers early summer; fertile soil

Zone 2

Viburnum cylindricum ▼

An evergreen shrub with waxy leaves, flattened heads of tubular white flowers, and ovoid black fruits.

Large; sun to partial shade; flowers mid to late summer; fertile soil

Zone 6

Viburnum davidii ▼▶

David viburnum is an evergreen shrub grown for its glossy, dark green three-ribbed leaves and clusters of small white male or female flowers. Turquoise blue fruits are only formed on plants producing female flowers. **AGM**

Compact; sun to partial shade; flowers early summer; fertile soil

Grow several plants together to ensure good fruit set. Can be used as a ground cover.
Zone 7

Viburnum dilatatum ▲

A deciduous shrub bearing many heads of pure white strongly scented flowers followed by large bunches of long-lasting bright red fruits.

Medium; sun to partial shade; flowers late spring to early summer; fertile soil

Zone 5

Viburnum dilatatum 'Ogon' ▲

A deciduous shrub grown for its lemon yellow new growth that changes to a pale green.

Small to medium; partial shade; flowers late spring to early summer; fertile soil

Zone 5

Viburnum erubescens ▼

A deciduous shrub with fragrant pink-tinged white flowers in branching clusters followed by red fruits that eventually turn black.

Medium to large; sun to partial shade; flowers mid summer; fertile soil

Zone 6

Viburnum 'Eskimo' ▲

A dense semievergreen shrub with leathery, glossy, dark green leaves and balls of white flowers.

Small; sun to partial shade; flowers late spring; fertile soil
Zone 7

Viburnum farreri ▼

Named after Reginald Farrer, this deciduous erect shrub bears sweetly scented pale pink flowers in clusters well before the young bronze-coloured leaves unfold. AGM

Medium; sun to partial shade; flowers early to late winter; fertile soil
Zone 6

Viburnum farreri 'Candidissimum' ▼

A deciduous erect shrub with sweetly scented pure white flowers produced in clusters long before the green leaves unfold.

Medium; sun to partial shade; flowers early to late winter; fertile soil
Zone 6

Viburnum foetidum ▼

A semievergreen shrub with rounded heads of white flowers followed by scarlet red fruits.

Medium to large; sun to partial shade; flowers mid summer; fertile soil
Zone 8

Viburnum furcatum ▲

A deciduous shrub with conspicuously veined leaves that become purple before turning to brilliant red in autumn. White flowers are borne in flattened heads, the large sterile ones on the outside, and are followed by red fruits that turn to black. **AGM**

Large; sun to partial shade; flowers late spring; fertile, neutral to acid soil

Zone 6

Viburnum ×globosum 'Jermyn's Globe' ▼▶

A rounded evergreen shrub with leathery leaves on red stems and flattened heads of white flowers followed by blue-black fruits.

Small to medium; sun to partial shade; flowers late spring; fertile soil

Zone 7

Viburnum grandiflorum ▼

A deciduous shrub with a stiff erect habit grown for the dense clusters of very fragrant deep pink flowers gradually fading but opening from carmine pink buds formed well before the leaves unfold.

Medium; sun to partial shade; flowers late winter to mid spring; fertile soil

Zone 7

Viburnum grandiflorum f. *foetens* ▼

A deciduous spreading shrub with dense clusters of very fragrant white flowers opening from pink buds formed well before the leaves unfold.

Medium; sun to partial shade; flowers late winter to early spring; fertile soil

Zone 6

Viburnum ×*hillieri* 'Winton' ▲▶

A semievergreen shrub with leaves opening a reddish brown and tinged with red in winter, creamy white flowers, and fruits that are black when mature. **AGM**

Medium to large; sun to partial shade; flowers early summer; fertile soil

Zone 6

Viburnum ×*juddii* 'Arlene' ◀

A bushy deciduous shrub with clusters of highly scented white flowers.

Small to medium; sun to partial shade; flowers mid to late spring; fertile soil

Plant often grafted in which case it is necessary to remove suckers from the rootstock. Zone 5

Viburnum lantana 'Aureum' ▼

A deciduous shrub with leaves tinged with yellow when young, covered on the underside with white hairs, remaining light green, and turning red in autumn. The creamy white flowers are followed by fruits that eventually turn black.

Medium to large; sun to partial shade; flowers late spring to early summer; fertile soil

To enhance foliage colour, plant in partial shade. Zone 3

Viburnum lantanoides ▼▶

The wayfaring tree is a deciduous suckering shrub grown for the large heads of small white flowers surrounded by large sterile flowers and followed by small black fruits. Distinctly veined leaves have good autumn colour of orange and red.

Medium to large; sun to partial shade; flowers late spring to early summer; fertile soil

Zone 3

Viburnum lentago ▼

A vigorous, deciduous shrub or small tree with leaves rich orange-red and scarlet in autumn. Small creamy white flowers are followed by large blue-black fruits covered with a bloom.

Large; sun to partial shade; flowers late spring to early summer; fertile soil

Zone 2

Viburnum macrocephalum ▲◀

A semievergreen rounded shrub with rounded dense trusses of pure white sterile flower heads that open greenish white.

Medium; sun to partial shade; flowers late spring; fertile soil

Zone 7

Viburnum nudum 'Pink Beauty' ▲

An erect deciduous shrub with glossy, dark green leaves and good autumn colour. Clusters of pale pink flowers are followed by ovoid blue-black fruits.

Medium; sun to partial shade; flowers mid summer; fertile soil

Zone 6

Viburnum opulus 'Compactum' ▼

The guelder rose is a deciduous shrub with maplelike leaves that turn red before falling. White flowers are borne in flattened clusters with small central flowers surrounded by larger outer ones. Pendulous clusters of glistening, fleshy, red fruits follow. AGM

Small; sun to partial shade; flowers early to mid summer; fertile soil

Zone 3

Viburnum opulus 'Sunshine' ▲

A deciduous shrub with yellow-green maplelike leaves turning red before falling. White flowers are borne in flattened inflorescences with smaller central flowers surrounded by larger outer ones. Pendulous clusters of glistening, fleshy, red fruits follow.

Large; partial shade; flowers early to mid summer; fertile soil

Zone 3

Viburnum parvifolium ETOT 71 ▶

A deciduous shrub with white flowers followed by red fruits. Rarely seen in cultivation.

Medium; sun to partial shade; flowers early summer; fertile soil

Zone 7

Viburnum plicatum 'Popcorn' ▶▼

A deciduous shrub bearing large balls of pure white sterile flowers that do not produce fruits.

Medium; sun to partial shade; flowers late spring to early summer; fertile soil

Zone 4

Viburnum plicatum 'Rosace' ▶

A deciduous shrub with bronze new growth and large pink-and-white sterile flowers that do not produce fruits.

Medium; sun to partial shade; flowers late spring to early summer; fertile soil

Zone 4

Viburnum plicatum 'Sterile' ▼

A spreading deciduous shrub with large globular heads of pure white sterile flowers but no fruits.

Medium; sun to partial shade; flowers late spring to early summer; fertile soil

Zone 4

Viburnum plicatum f. *tomentosum* 'Dart's Red Robin' ▼

A wide-spreading deciduous shrub with flattened heads of flowers, the central ones small and creamy white surrounded by much large white flowers. Fruits are bright red. Free-flowering and free-fruiting.

Medium; sun to partial shade; flowers late spring to early summer; fertile soil

Zone 4

Viburnum plicatum f. *tomentosum* 'Lanarth' ▲

A vigorous, deciduous shrub with flattened erect heads of large pure white flowers surrounding small central ones and followed by black fruits.

Medium to large; sun to partial shade; flowers late spring to early summer; fertile soil

Zone 4

Viburnum plicatum f. *tomentosum* 'Nanum Semperflorens' ▶

A deciduous shrub similar to the species but more delicate and slowly upright growing, producing long-lasting flowers.

Small to medium; sun to partial shade; flowers late spring to early summer; fertile soil

Zone 4

Viburnum plicatum f. *tomentosum* 'Pink Beauty' ▲

A deciduous shrub with flattened heads of flowers similar to 'Lanarth' but opening white and maturing to pink. **AGM**

Small to medium; sun to partial shade; flowers late spring to early summer; fertile soil

Zone 4

Viburnum 'Pragense' ▼

A wide-spreading evergreen shrub with unusual slightly corrugated glossy, dark green leaves, white hairy below. Creamy white flowers open from pink buds. **AGM**

Medium to large; sun to partial shade; flowers late spring; fertile soil

Zone 6

Viburnum plicatum f. *tomentosum* 'St. Keverne' ▲

A deciduous shrub with arched flower heads of pure white sterile flowers contrasting with cream fertile flowers. Autumn foliage purple, then orange.

Compact; sun to partial shade; flowers late spring to early summer; fertile soil

Zone 4

Viburnum prunifolium ◄▲

The black haw is an upright, ultimately spreading deciduous shrub with shiny, bright green foliage that turns bright orange and red in autumn. Clusters of fertile flowers are white.

Large; sun to partial shade; flowers late spring; fertile soil

Zone 3

Viburnum sargentii ▼

A deciduous shrub with maplelike leaves that turn orange-red in autumn and globose, glossy, red translucent fruits following the white flowers in flattened heads, the outer ones being sterile.

Large; sun to partial shade; flowers early summer; fertile soil

Zone 4

Viburnum ×rhytidophylloides DART'S DUKE 'Interduke' ▲

A deciduous or semievergreen shrub with bold corrugated leaves and yellowish white flowers often flowering twice. The many red fruits turn black when ripe.

Large; sun to partial shade; flowers late spring to early summer and sometimes again in early autumn; fertile soil

Zone 5

▶ ▼ *Viburnum rhytidophyllum* Wilson 220 blossoms

Viburnum rhytidophyllum ▼

A vigorous evergreen often grown for the bold glossy, corrugated foliage but also for the creamy white flowers and red fruits that turn to black.

Large; sun to partial shade; flowers late spring; fertile, moisture-retentive soil

Zone 6

Viburnum setigerum ▲

A deciduous shrub with leaves turning from red tinged on opening to green and purple to red then orange-yellow in autumn. White flowers are followed by hanging clusters of striking oval reddish orange fruits.

Medium; sun to partial shade; flowers early summer; fertile soil

Zone 5

Viburnum sieboldii ▼

A deciduous shrub with attractive foliage bronze-coloured in spring and autumn, yellow-green in summer with an unpleasant scent. Creamy white flowers are followed by fruits that turn from pink through red to blue-black.

Medium to large; sun to partial shade; flowers late spring to early summer; fertile soil

Zone 4

Viburnum tinus ▲

The laurustinus is a bushy evergreen shrub with glossy, dark green leaves and flattened clusters of white flowers opening from pink buds.

Medium to large; sun to partial shade; flowers early winter to early spring; fertile soil

Prune severely in mid spring after flowering to control size. Zone 7

Viburnum tinus 'Eve Prince' ▼

A bushy but dense evergreen shrub with glossy, dark green leaves and flattened clusters of pink-tinged white flowers opening from deep pink buds.

AGM

Small to medium; sun to partial shade; flowers early winter to early spring; fertile soil

Zone 7

Viburnum trilobum 'Snowball' ▶

This American cranberry bush is a deciduous shrub with maple-shaped leaves that turn a rich red in autumn, and dense round trusses of pure white sterile flowers.

Medium; sun to partial shade; flowers early to mid summer; fertile soil

Zone 2

Viburnum utile ▲

An evergreen shrub with glossy, dark green leaves and rounded clusters of strongly scented white flowers.

Small to medium; sun to partial shade; flowers late spring; fertile soil

Zone 7

Viburnum wrightii 'Hessei' ▼

A deciduous shrub with clusters of white flowers but more often grown for the striking scarlet fruits.

Compact to small; sun to partial shade; flowers late spring; fertile soil

Zone 5

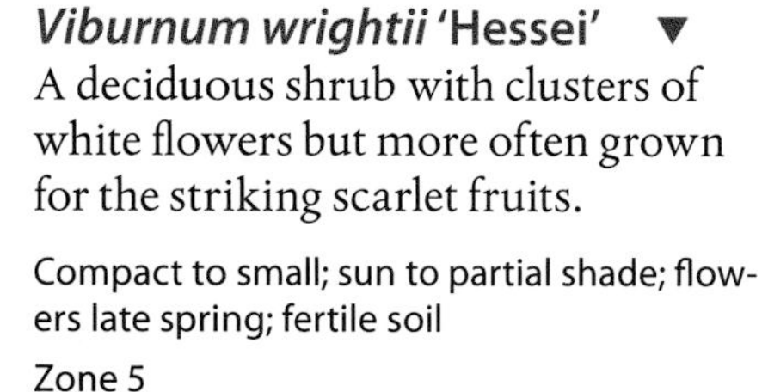

Vinca difformis ▼

An evergreen shrub that may behave as a herbaceous perennial in colder areas. Each petal of the pale blue flowers is slightly twisted. **AGM**

Prostrate to compact; sun or shade; flowers mid spring to mid summer; fertile soil

Makes a good ground cover but can spread readily. Zone 8

Vinca major 'Alba' ▼

A vigorous evergreen with long-lasting large white flowers, short erect stems, and creeping, self-rooting stems.

Prostrate to compact; sun or shade; flowers mid spring to mid summer; fertile soil

Makes a good ground cover but can spread readily. Zone 7

Vinca major 'Maculata' ▲

A very vigorous evergreen shrub with short erect stems that elongate and trail over long distances. Leaves have a central yellowish blotch, and the flowers are bright blue.

Prostrate; sun or shade; flowers mid spring to mid summer; fertile soil
Makes a good ground cover but can spread readily. Zone 7

Vinca major 'Variegata' ▼

A vigorous creeping evergreen grown for its leaves blotched and edged with creamy white and for its bright blue flowers produced over several months. **AGM**

Prostrate; sun or shade; flowers mid spring to mid summer; fertile soil
Makes a good ground cover but can spread readily. Zone 7

Vinca minor ►

The lesser periwinkle is an evergreen carpeting shrub with long, trailing, self-rooting stems and clear blue flowers.

Prostrate; sun or shade; flowers mid spring to mid summer; fertile soil
Makes a good ground cover but can spread readily. Zone 4

Vinca minor 'Argenteovariegata' ▼

A long-flowering evergreen shrub with trailing self-rooting stems that bear variegated with creamy white leaves and clear blue flowers. **AGM**

Prostrate; sun or shade; flowers mid spring to mid summer; fertile soil
Makes a good ground cover but can spread readily. Zone 6

Vinca minor 'Aureovariegata' ▼

An evergreen carpeting shrub with long, trailing, self-rooting stems that bear leaves blotched and spotted with yellow, sometimes completely yellow. The flowers are clear blue.

Prostrate; sun or shade; flowers mid spring to mid summer; fertile soil
Makes a good ground cover but can spread readily. Zone 6

Vitex agnus-castus var. *latifolia* ▲

A deciduous spreading shrub with compound aromatic leaves of about seven oval leaflets and with small rich violet flowers on erect stems.

Medium; sun; flowers mid to late summer; fertile, well-drained soil

Best against a warm wall. Prune back last season's growth in early spring to improve flower size. Zone 8

Vitex agnus-castus ▲

The chaste tree is a deciduous spreading shrub with compound aromatic leaves of about seven narrow leaflets and with small pale violet flowers on erect stems.

Medium; sun; flowers mid to late summer; fertile, well-drained soil

Best against a warm wall. Prune back last season's growth in early spring to improve flower size. Zone 7

Vitex agnus-castus 'Alba' ▼

A spreading deciduous shrub with compound aromatic leaves of about seven narrow leaflets and with small white flowers on erect stems.

Medium; sun; flowers mid to late summer; fertile, well-drained soil

Best against a warm wall. Prune back last season's growth in early spring to improve flower size. Zone 8

Weigela 'Abel Carrière' ▲

A bushy deciduous very free-flowering shrub with rose-red trumpet-shaped flowers marked with yellow in the throat and opening from purplish red buds.

Small to medium; sun or partial shade; flowers late spring to early summer; fertile soil

Thin out older shoots after flowering. Zone 5

Weigela BRIANT RUBIDOR 'Olympiade' ▶▼

A bushy deciduous shrub grown for both the carmine red trumpet-shaped flowers and the yellow-margined leaves best grown out of strong sunlight.

Medium; partial shade; flowers late spring to early summer; fertile soil

Thin out older shoots after flowering. Zone 5

Weigela CARNAVAL 'Courtalor' ▼

A bushy deciduous very floriferous shrub with trumpet-shaped flowers of two colours either pink or pink and white.

Medium; sun or partial shade; flowers late spring to early summer; fertile soil

Thin out older shoots after flowering. Zone 5

Weigela coraeensis ▼

A bushy deciduous shrub grown for its trumpet-shaped clear pink flowers, rich pink in bud.

Small to medium; sun or partial shade; flowers early summer; fertile soil

Thin out older shoots after flowering. Zone 6

Weigela 'Eva Rathke' ◀

A slow-growing deciduous free-flowering shrub with rich crimson red trumpet-shaped flowers and contrasting pale yellow anthers.

Small to medium; sun or partial shade; flowers late spring to early summer; fertile soil

Thin out older shoots after flowering. Zone 5

Weigela 'Féerie' ▲

A bushy deciduous very floriferous shrub with rose pink trumpet-shaped flowers formed in erect clusters.

Small; sun to partial shade; flowers late spring to early summer; fertile soil

Thin out older shoots after flowering. Zone 5

Weigela 'Florida Variegata' ▼

A bushy deciduous shrub grown both for the pink trumpet-shaped flowers and the variegated leaves margined with creamy white. **AGM**

Small to medium; sun or partial shade; flowers late spring to early summer; fertile soil

Zone 6

Weigela florida 'Versicolor' ▼

A bushy deciduous shrub grown for its trumpet-shaped greenish white flowers that become a rich wine red.

Small to medium; sun or partial shade; flowers late spring to early summer; fertile soil

Thin out older shoots after flowering. Zone 5

Weigela hortensis 'Nivea' ▲

A bushy deciduous floriferous shrub grown for its pure white trumpet-shaped flowers and green leaves with a striking white hairy underside.

Small to medium; sun or partial shade; flowers late spring to early summer; fertile soil

Thin out older shoots after flowering. Zone 5

Weigela 'Looymansii Aurea' ▼

A bushy deciduous shrub grown for its pink trumpet-shaped flowers contrasting with the golden yellow young foliage that becomes greener as it matures.

Small to medium; partial shade; flowers late spring to early summer; fertile soil

Thin out older shoots after flowering. Zone 5

Weigela 'Ruby Queen' ▶

A bushy deciduous shrub grown for its reddish purple new growth.

Small to medium; sun or partial shade; flowers late spring to early summer; fertile soil

Can be coppiced in early spring. Zone 5

Weigela 'Victoria' ▼

A bushy deciduous floriferous shrub with purplish pink trumpet-shaped flowers and purple to bronze leaves.

Small to medium; sun or partial shade; flowers late spring to early summer; fertile soil

Thin out older shoots after flowering. Zone 5

Weigela middendorffiana WHHD 4950 ▲

A bushy deciduous floriferous shrub with peeling bark and pale yellow bell-shaped flowers marked with a conspicuous orange-red blotch on the lower inner surface.

Small to medium; partial shade; flowers early to late spring; fertile soil

Thin out older shoots after flowering. Zone 5

Weigela 'Praecox Variegata' ▼

A bushy arching deciduous shrub with grey-green leaves margined with white, complemented by bright pink trumpet-shaped flowers. **AGM**

Small to medium; sun or partial shade; flowers late spring to early summer; fertile soil

Thin out older shoots after flowering. Zone 5

Weinmannia racemosa 'Harlequin' ▼

The kamahi is an evergreen shrub with simple serrated adult leaves that have a creamy pink margin and with white bottlebrush-like blooms.

Medium to large; sun or partial shade; flowers early summer; fertile soil

Zone 9

Weinmannia trichosperma ▲

The tineo or maden is a slow-growing evergreen shrub or small tree with graceful fernlike leaves of up to 19 small leaflets and unusual triangular wings between each leaflet. Dense clusters of white flowers are followed by small brownish red seed pods.

Large; sun or partial shade; flowers late spring to early summer; fertile soil

Zone 8

Westringia fruticosa ▼

The coastal rosemary is a bushy evergreen rosemary-like shrub with whorls of narrow leaves and white two-lipped flowers. **AGM**

Small; sun; flowers mid summer; well-drained soil

Tolerates coastal exposure and dry conditions. Grown as a conservatory plant in cool climates. Zone 9

Wigandia caracasana ▶

An evergreen shrub grown for its terminal clusters of violet-blue flowers and its large rough-textured green leaves with wavy edges and hairy white undersides.

Large; sun; flowers late winter to mid spring; well-drained soil

Can be grown as a container specimen. Zone 10

Wikstroemia gemmata ▼

A subshrub grown for its daphnelike pale yellow flowers, yellow in bud.

Compact; sun to partial shade; flowers midsummer; fertile soil

Suitable for a raised bed or alpine house conditions. Zone 9

Xanthoceras sorbifolium ▼

A deciduous shrub that can be trained into a small tree with attractive pinnate leaves and erect clusters of pure white flowers. The centre of the flower is a striking bright yellow that turns to carmine red as the flower ages. **AGM**

Medium to large; sun; flowers mid spring; fertile soil

Protect from late spring frosts. Needs a hot summer to flower well. Zone 6

Xanthorrhiza simplicissima ▲▶

A suckering deciduous carpet-forming shrub with divided leaves turning bronze in autumn and with loose clusters of tiny purple flowers.

Compact; sun or partial shade; flowers mid to late spring; fertile soil

Can be used for ground cover. Zone 4

Yucca filamentosa 'Variegata' ▲

An evergreen grown for the very long lance-shaped leaves, edged with curled threadlike filaments and margined with creamy white. The leaves are formed in a stemless rosette that produces very tall branching spikes bearing large creamy white bell-shaped flowers. AGM

Medium but much taller in flower; sun; flowers mid to late summer; fertile, well-drained soil

Of architectural value. Needs a hot sunny site. Zone 7

Yucca flaccida 'Golden Sword' ▼

Long lance-shaped evergreen leaves with a cream to yellow central variegation are produced in a stemless clump. Creamy white bell-shaped flowers are borne on very tall branching stems. AGM

Medium but much taller in flower; sun; flowers mid to late summer; well-drained soil

Of architectural value. Needs a hot sunny site. Zone 8

Yucca glauca ◀

An evergreen plant with long lance-shaped grey-green leaves edged with white and produced in a rosette atop a short stem. Large greenish white bell-shaped flowers are formed on tall unbranched stems.

Medium but much taller in flower; sun; flowers mid to late summer; well-drained soil

Of architectural value. Needs a hot sunny site. Zone 4

▶ *Yucca gloriosa* at the Royal Botanic Gardens, Kew.

Yucca gloriosa ▼

An evergreen plant with very long, spine-tipped, lance-shaped, blue-green leaves formed in a rosette at the top of a stout stem and with large creamy white, bell-shaped flowers borne on a tall branched spike. **AGM**

Medium but much taller in flower; sun; flowers mid to late summer; well-drained soil

Of architectural value. Needs a hot sunny site. Zone 8

Yucca gloriosa 'Variegata' ▼

An evergreen plant with lance-shaped, spine-tipped, blue-green leaves striped and edged with pale yellow when young but fading to creamy white. Tall branched spikes bear creamy white bell-shaped flowers. **AGM**

Medium but much taller in flower; sun; flowers mid to late summer; well-drained soil

Of architectural value. Needs a hot sunny site. Zone 8

Yucca recurvifolia ▲

Long, evergreen, lance-shaped leaves curve gracefully downwards and are bluish green when young becoming green as they mature. Large bell-shaped flowers are borne on tall branching stems. **AGM**

Medium but much taller in flower; sun; flowers late summer; well-drained soil

Of architectural value. Needs a hot sunny site. Zone 8

Yucca whipplei

A stemless clump-forming evergreen with long lance-shaped, spine-tipped, bluish green leaves and tall branching stems that bear large greenish white bell-shaped flowers margined with purple.

Medium but much taller in flower; sun; flowers late spring to early summer; well-drained soil

Of architectural value. Needs a hot sunny site. Zone 8

▼ *Yucca whipplei* at the Royal Botanic Gardens, Kew.

Zanthoxylum ailanthoides ▲

A vigorous, deciduous shrub or small tree grown for its aromatic bold fernlike pinnate leaves up to 60 cm long borne on stout thorny branches. Small greenish yellow flowers are formed in flattened heads.

Large; sun or partial shade; flowers late summer to early autumn; fertile soil

Zone 9

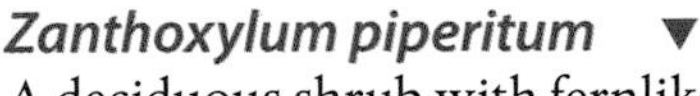

Zanthoxylum piperitum ▼

A deciduous shrub with fernlike pinnate leaves, flattened spines in pairs, greenish yellow flowers, and small red fruits.

Large; sun or partial shade; flowers late spring to early summer; fertile soil

Zone 6

Zanthoxylum americanum ▲▶

A deciduous shrub with stems bearing stout spines and large fernlike pinnate aromatic leaves. Clusters of yellow-green flowers are followed by glossy, red then black fruits.

Large; sun or partial shade; flowers mid spring; fertile soil

Zone 3

Zanthoxylum schinifolium ▲

A deciduous thorny shrub with fernlike pinnate leaves of up to 21 leaflets and with small clusters of greenish flowers followed by bright red fruits.

Large; sun or partial shade; flowers late summer; fertile soil

Zone 6

Zauschneria californica ▶

The California fuchsia is an upright suckering subshrub with silvery grey-green softly hairy narrow leaves and pendulous, scarlet red, narrow tubular flowers formed in spikes.

Compact; sun; flowers late summer to mid autumn; fertile, well-drained soil

Suitable for the rock garden. Cut back in early spring. Zone 8

Zauschneria californica subsp. *cana* 'Sir Cedric Morris' ▼

An upright subshrub with fine linear grey-green foliage and long tubular scarlet flowers.

Compact; sun; flowers late summer to mid autumn; fertile, well-drained soil

Suitable for the rock garden, scree, or wall. Cut back in early spring. Zone 8

Zauschneria californica 'Western Hills' ▼

An erect long flowering subshrub with narrow green leaves and spikes of tubular bright scarlet red flowers. **AGM**

Compact; sun; flowers late summer to mid autumn; fertile, well-drained soil

Suitable for the rock garden, scree, or wall. Cut back in early spring. Zone 8

Zenobia pulverulenta 'Blue Sky' ◀

A deciduous shrub with attractive blue-green leaves, glaucous on the underside when young, sometimes turning orange-red in autumn, and with hanging clusters of sweetly scented white bell-shaped flowers.

Small to medium; partial shade; flowers early to mid summer; fertile, acid soil

Zone 5

Table of Selected Shrubs by Key Design and Cultural Characteristics

FOLIAGE: = evergreen; = semievergreen; = deciduous; = variagated

FLOWER COLOUR: = yellow; = orange; = pink; = red; = purple; = blue; = green; = white; = black

SIZE: **P** = prostrate; **C** = compact; **S** = small; **M** = medium; **L** = large

LIGHT: = sun; = partial shade; = shade

FLOWERING SEASON: = winter; = spring; = summer; = autumn

SOIL: = acid; = alkaline; = fertile; = fertile, well drained; = well drained

NAME OF SHRUB	FOLIAGE	FLOWER COLOUR	SIZE	LIGHT	FLOWERING SEASON	SOIL	ZONE
Abelia chinensis			**M**				7
Abelia 'Edward Goucher'			**S**				7
Abelia floribunda			**S M**				9
Abelia ×*grandiflora*			**M**				7
Abelia mosanensis			**M L**				6
Abelia parvifolia			**S**				7
Abelia spathulata			**S**				8
Abelia triflora			**L**				7
Abeliophyllum distichum			**S M**				4
Abutilon 'Golden Fleece'			**M**				10
Abutilon megapotamicum			**P S M**				9
Abutilon 'Nabob'			**M**				10
Abutilon ×*suntense* 'Jermyns'			**M L**				8
Abutilon vitifolium cultivars			**M L**				8
Acca selloana			**M L**				7
Acradenia frankliniae			**M L**				7
Adenocarpus decorticans			**M**				8
Agapetes incurvata			**C**				10
Agapetes serpens			**P C**				10
Alangium chinense			**M L**				7
Aloysia citrodora			**S M**				10
Amelanchier alnifolia			**M L**				4
Amelanchier laevis cultivars			**L**				4
Amelanchier lamarckii			**L**				4
Amelanchier 'La Paloma'			**M**				4
Amelanchier ovalis 'Edelweiss'			**L**				4
Amomyrtus luma			**L**				7
Amomyrtus mali ICE 127			**M L**				8
Amorpha fruticosa			**M**				5
Andrachne colchica			**C**				6
Andromeda polifolia cultivars			**C**				4
Anopterus glandulosus			**M**				8
Aralia elata			**M L**				5
Arbutus andrachne			**M L**				7
Arbutus ×*andrachnoides*			**M L**				7
Arbutus menziesii			**L**				7
Arbutus unedo			**M L**				7
Arctostaphylos manzanita			**M**				8
Arctostaphylos pajaroensis			**M**				8
Arctostaphylos uva-ursi 'Vancouver Jade'			**P**				4
Ardisia japonica			**C**				9
Aristotelia chilensis			**L**				9
Aronia arbutifolia			**M**				4

NAME OF SHRUB	FOLIAGE	FLOWER COLOUR	SIZE	LIGHT	FLOWERING SEASON	SOIL	ZONE
Aronia melanocarpa			S M	sun			5
Artemisia arborescens			S	sun			8
Asimina triloba			L	sun			5
Astelia chathamica 'Silver Spear'			S	sun			10
Atherosperma moschatum			L	sun; partial shade			8
Aucuba japonica cultivars			M L	partial shade; shade			7
Aucuba omeiensis			L	partial shade; shade			8
Azara integrifolia			L	sun; partial shade			8
Azara lanceolata			L	sun; partial shade			7
Azara microphylla			L	sun; partial shade			7
Azara serrata			M L	sun; partial shade			8
Baccharis patagonica			S M	sun			8
Ballota acetabulosa			S	sun			8
Ballota pseudodictamnus			C	sun			8
Banksia integrifolia			M L	sun			9
Berberis amurensis var. *latifolia*			M L	sun; partial shade			5
Berberis ×antoniana			S	sun; partial shade			6
Berberis buxifolia			S M	sun; partial shade			5
Berberis calliantha			C	sun			4
Berberis darwinii			M	sun; partial shade			7
Berberis empetrifolia			C S	sun; partial shade			7
Berberis 'Georgei'			M L	sun; partial shade			4
Berberis 'Goldilocks'			L	sun; partial shade			7
Berberis linearifolia 'Jewel'			M	sun			6
Berberis ×lologensis cultivars			M	sun; partial shade			7
Berberis manipurana			M	sun; partial shade			7
Berberis montana			M	sun			6
Berberis pruinosa			M	sun; partial shade			6
Berberis sieboldii			S	sun			5
Berberis ×stenophylla 'Pink Pearl'			M	sun; partial shade			5
Berberis temolaica			M	sun; partial shade			5
Berberis thunbergii cultivars			C S	sun			5
Berberis valdiviana			M L	sun; partial shade			8
Berberis wilsoniae			C S	sun			5
Beschorneria yuccoides			M	sun			9
Boronia heterophylla			S M	sun			10
Bouvardia ternifolia			C	partial shade			10
Brachyglottis grayi			S	sun			8
Brachyglottis hectoris			M L	sun; partial shade			8
Brachyglottis 'Otari Cloud'			C S	sun			8
Brachyglottis repanda			L	sun; partial shade			10
Brachyglottis rotundifolia			M L	sun; partial shade			9
Brachyglottis 'Sunshine'			C S	sun			8
Buddleja alternifolia			M L	sun			5
Buddleja colvilei 'Kewensis'			M L	sun; partial shade			7
Buddleja crispa			M L	sun			7
Buddleja davidii cultivars			M	sun			6
Buddleja fallowiana 'Alba'			M L	sun			8

FOLIAGE: = evergreen; = semievergreen; = deciduous; = variagated

FLOWER COLOUR: = yellow; = orange; = pink; = red; = purple; = blue; = green; = white; = black

SIZE: **P** = prostrate; **C** = compact; **S** = small; **M** = medium; **L** = large

LIGHT: = sun; = partial shade; = shade

FLOWERING SEASON: = winter; = spring; = summer; = autumn

SOIL: = acid; = alkaline; = fertile; = fertile, well drained; = well drained

NAME OF SHRUB	FOLIAGE	FLOWER COLOUR	SIZE	LIGHT	FLOWERING SEASON	SOIL	ZONE
Buddleja globosa			M L				7
Buddleja lindleyana			M				7
Buddleja 'Lochinch'			M				8
Buddleja madagascariensis			M L				10
Buddleja officinalis			M				10
Buddleja 'Pink Delight'			M				7
Buddleja salviifolia			M L				8
Buddleja ×*weyeriana* 'Sungold'			M L				6
Bupleurum fruticosum			S M				7
Buxus balearica			M L				8
Buxus microphylla var. *japonica* 'Morris Dwarf'			C				6
Buxus sempervirens			S M				6
Caesalpinia decapetala var. *japonica*			L				9
Caesalpinia gilliesii			L				8
Calceolaria integrifolia			S				9
Callicarpa bodinieri			M				6
Callicarpa dichotoma			C S				6
Callistemon citrinus 'Splendens'			S M				8
Callistemon pallidus			M				8
Calluna vulgaris cultivars			C				4
Calycanthus floridus cultivars			C M				5
Calycanthus occidentalis			M				7
Camellia 'Bravo'			L				9
Camellia 'Doctor Clifford Parks'			L				8
Camellia 'Freedom Bell'			L				8
Camellia hiemalis 'Sparkling Burgundy'			M L				8
Camellia 'Inspiration'			L				8
Camellia japonica cultivars			M L				7
Camellia 'Knight Rider'			M L				7
Camellia 'Leonard Messel'			L				7
Camellia oleifera			M L				8
Camellia 'Purple Gown'			L				7
Camellia reticulata cultivars			L				9
Camellia saluenensis			M L				8
Camellia sasanqua cultivars			M L				8
Camellia transarisanensis			M				8
Camellia ×*williamsii* cultivars			L				7
Camellia yuhsienensis			M				8
Campylotropis macrocarpa			S				7
Cantua bicolor			S M				9
Cantua buxifolia			S M				9
Caragana microphylla			M				3
Caragana sinica			M				6
Carmichaelia australis			M				8
Carmichaelia stevensonii			M				8
Carpenteria californica			M				8
Caryopteris ×*clandonensis* cultivars			C				7
Cassiope 'George Taylor'			P				4
Cassiope lycopodioides			P				3
Cassiope 'Randle Cooke'			P				3
Cassiope wardii			P				4
Ceanothus arboreus 'Trewithen Blue'			L				8
Ceanothus 'Blue Buttons'			M				8
Ceanothus 'Blue Cushion'			S				8
Ceanothus 'Blue Jeans'			S				8

NAME OF SHRUB	FOLIAGE	FLOWER COLOUR	SIZE	LIGHT	FLOWERING SEASON	SOIL	ZONE
Ceanothus 'Burkwoodii'			M				8
Ceanothus 'Concha'			M				8
Ceanothus 'Cynthia Postan'			M				8
Ceanothus 'Dark Star'			M				8
Ceanothus ×*delileanus* cultivars			M				8
Ceanothus impressus			S M				7
Ceanothus 'Italian Skies'			S M				8
Ceanothus ×*pallidus* cultivars			S M				7
Ceanothus 'Puget Blue'			M				8
Ceanothus thyrsiflorus cultivars			M				8
Cephalanthus occidentalis			M				6
Ceratostigma willmottianum			C				7
Cercis canadensis cultivars			L				4
Cercis chinensis			L				6
Cercis racemosa			L				7
Cercocarpus montanus			M				4
Cestrum ×*cultum* 'Orange Essence'			S M				9
Cestrum fasciculatum			S M				9
Cestrum parqui			S M				9
Chaenomeles cathayensis			L				6
Chaenomeles speciosa cultivars			M				5
Chaenomeles ×*superba* cultivars			S M				5
Chamaecytisus ×*versicolor*			C				6
Chiliotrichum diffusum			S				8
Chimonanthus praecox cultivars			M				6
Chionanthus retusus			L				6
Chionanthus virginicus			L				4
Choisya ×*dewitteana* 'Aztec Pearl'			S M				7
Choisya dumosa var. *arizonica*			S				8
Choisya ternata SUNDANCE 'Lich'			M				8
Cistus ×*aguilarii*			M				8
Cistus ×*argenteus* cultivars			S M				8
Cistus ×*canescens*			S				8
Cistus ×*cyprius*			M				7
Cistus ×*dansereaui*			S				7
Cistus ladanifer			M				8
Cistus ×*pulverulentus* 'Sunset'			C				8
Cistus 'Snow Fire'			S				7
Clerodendrum bungei			M				7
Clerodendrum trichotomum var. *fargesii*			L				7
Clethra alnifolia			M				4
Clethra barbinervis			M				5
Cleyera japonica			M				8
Clianthus puniceus			M				8
Coleonema album			S				9
Colletia hystrix			M				8
Colletia ulicina			M				8
Colquhounia coccinea			M				8

FOLIAGE: = evergreen; = semievergreen; = deciduous; = variagated

FLOWER COLOUR: = yellow; = orange; = pink; = red; = purple; = blue; = green; = white; = black

SIZE: **P** = prostrate; **C** = compact; **S** = small; **M** = medium; **L** = large

LIGHT: = sun; = partial shade; = shade

FLOWERING SEASON: = winter; = spring; = summer; = autumn

SOIL: = acid; = alkaline; = fertile; = fertile, well drained; = well drained

NAME OF SHRUB	FOLIAGE	FLOWER COLOUR	SIZE	LIGHT	FLOWERING SEASON	SOIL	ZONE
Colutea arborescens			L				5
Colutea ×media 'Copper Beauty'			M				6
Convolvulus cneorum			C				8
Cordyline australis			L				8
Cordyline indivisa			M L				10
Coriaria pteridoides			C S				8
Coriaria terminalis var. *xanthocarpa*			C				8
Cornus alba cultivars			S M				4
Cornus alternifolia cultivars			M L				3
Cornus angustata			L				8
Cornus 'Ascona'			L				7
Cornus bretschneideri			L				5
Cornus capitata			L				8
Cornus chinensis			L				8
Cornus controversa 'Variegata'			L				5
Cornus 'Eddie's White Wonder'			L				5
Cornus florida			L				5
Cornus kousa			L				5
Cornus mas			L				5
Cornus 'Norman Hadden'			L				7
Cornus nuttallii			L				7
Cornus officinalis			L				6
Cornus 'Ormonde'			L				7
Cornus 'Porlock'			L				7
Cornus RUTH ELLEN 'Rutlan'			L				5
Cornus sanguinea cultivars			S				5
Cornus sericea cultivars			M				2
Corokia buddlejoides			M				8
Corokia cotoneaster			S M				8
Coronilla valentina subsp. *glauca*			S				8
Correa 'Mannii'			S				8
Correa 'Marian's Marvel'			S				8
Correa pulchella			S				8
Corylopsis coreana			M L				6
Corylopsis glabrescens			M L				6
Corylopsis pauciflora			S M				7
Corylopsis sinensis			L				6
Corylus avellana 'Contorta'			L				4
Corylus tibetica			L				7
Cotinus coggygria			M L				5
Cotinus 'Flame'			L				7
Cotinus 'Grace'			L				7
Cotinus obovatus			L				5
Cotoneaster conspicuus 'Decorus'			C S				6
Cotoneaster 'Coral Burst'			M L				5
Cotoneaster 'Cornubia'			L				6
Cotoneaster 'Exburiensis'			L				6
Cotoneaster frigidus			L				7
Cotoneaster horizontalis			P C				4
Cotoneaster induratus			S M				6
Cotoneaster lacteus			M L				6
Cotoneaster pluriflorus			S				7
Cotoneaster poluninii			P				7
Cotoneaster rehderi			M L				5
Cotoneaster 'Rothschildianus'			L				6

NAME OF SHRUB	FOLIAGE	FLOWER COLOUR	SIZE	LIGHT	FLOWERING SEASON	SOIL	ZONE
Cotoneaster salicifolius cultivars			P L				6
Cotoneaster shannanensis			M				6
Cotoneaster shansiensis			M				7
Cotoneaster 'Streib's Findling'			P				5
Cotoneaster ×*suecicus* 'Juliette'			C				5
Cotoneaster veitchii			M L				5
Cotoneaster ×*watereri* cultivars			L				6
Crinodendron hookerianum			L				8
Crinodendron patagua			L				8
Croton alabamense			S M				7
Cyathodes colensoi			P				7
Cyrilla racemiflora			S M				5
Cytisus battandieri			L				8
Cytisus ×*beanii*			C				6
Cytisus 'Golden Carpet'			P				5
Cytisus 'Jessica'			S M				6
Cytisus ×*kewensis*			C				6
Cytisus nigricans			S				5
Cytisus 'Palette'			M				6
Cytisus ×*praecox* cultivars			S				6
Daboecia cantabrica cultivars			C				6
Danae racemosa			S				7
Daphne albowiana			S				6
Daphne arbuscula			C				6
Daphne bholua forms			M				7
Daphne blagayana			C				5
Daphne ×*burkwoodii* cultivars			S				5
Daphne calcicola 'Sichuan Gold'			C				6
Daphne cneorum			C				4
Daphne genkwa			S				5
Daphne glomerata			P				6
Daphne ×*hendersonii* 'Jeanette Brickell'			C				5
Daphne ×*houtteana*			S				6
Daphne laureola			S				7
Daphne mezereum			S				5
Daphne odora			S				7
Daphne petraea 'Grandiflora'			P				6
Daphne pontica			S				6
Daphne ×*rollsdorfii* 'Arnold Chlorz'			C				5
Daphne ×*susannae* 'Cheriton'			C				6
Daphne tangutica			S				6
Daphniphyllum macropodum			L				6
Decaisnea fargesii			M L				5
Dendromecon rigidum			L				9
Desfontainia spinosa			M				8
Desmodium callianthum			S M				8
Desmodium elegans			S M				8
Desmodium sinuatum			S M				9

FOLIAGE: = evergreen; = semievergreen; = deciduous; = variagated

FLOWER COLOUR: = yellow; = orange; = pink; = red; = purple; = blue; = green; = white; = black

SIZE: **P** = prostrate; **C** = compact; **S** = small; **M** = medium; **L** = large

LIGHT: = sun; = partial shade; = shade

FLOWERING SEASON: = winter; = spring; = summer; = autumn

SOIL: = acid; = alkaline; = fertile; = fertile, well drained; = well drained

NAME OF SHRUB	FOLIAGE	FLOWER COLOUR	SIZE	LIGHT	FLOWERING SEASON	SOIL	ZONE
Desmodium yunnanense			L				9
Deutzia calycosa			M				6
Deutzia compacta SBEC 604			S M				6
Deutzia coreana			M				6
Deutzia discolor			S M				5
Deutzia ×elegantissima 'Rosealind'			S				6
Deutzia glomeruliflora			S M				5
Deutzia gracilis			M				4
Deutzia ×hybrida 'Strawberry Fields'			M				6
Deutzia longifolia			M				6
Deutzia ×magnifica cultivars			M				5
Deutzia monbeigii			S				6
Deutzia ningpoensis			M				5
Deutzia pulchra			M L				6
Deutzia purpurascens			S M				6
Deutzia ×rosea			C				5
Deutzia scabra cultivars			M				5
Deutzia setchuenensis var. *corymbiflora*			S M				7
Dichroa febrifuga			M				9
Diervilla sessilifolia			S M				4
Dipelta floribunda			L				6
Dipelta ventricosa			M L				6
Dipelta yunnanensis			L				6
Disanthus cercidifolius			M L				8
Discaria chacaye			M				8
Distylium racemosum			M L				8
Dodonaea viscosa 'Purpurea'			M				9
Dracophyllum latifolium			M L				9
Drimys lanceolata			M				8
Drimys latifolia			L				8
Drimys winteri			L				8
Dryas octopetala			P				2
Echium candicans			S M				9
Edgeworthia chrysantha			S M				8
Elaeagnus ×ebbingei			L				6
Elaeagnus macrophylla			L				8
Elaeagnus multiflora			M				6
Elaeagnus pungens cultivars			M				7
Elaeagnus 'Quicksilver'			L				3
Elaeagnus ×reflexa			L				7
Elaeagnus thunbergii ETOT 193			M L				7
Eleutherococcus divaricatus			L				6
Eleutherococcus lasiogyne			L				6
Eleutherococcus sieboldianus 'Variegatus'			M				4
Elliottia racemosa			M				8
Embothrium coccineum			L				8
Enkianthus campanulatus			M				5
Enkianthus perulatus			M				6
Epacris impressa var. *ovata*			C				9
Epacris paludosa			S				9
Ephedra andina			P				6
Ephedra gerrardiana var. *sikkimensis*			P C				7
Epigaea gaultherioides			P				4
Erica arborea cultivars			M				8
Erica australis			S M				9

NAME OF SHRUB	FOLIAGE	FLOWER COLOUR	SIZE	LIGHT	FLOWERING SEASON	SOIL	ZONE
Erica canaliculata			M				8
Erica carnea			C				5
Erica ciliaris			C				7
Erica cinerea			C				5
Erica ×darleyensis cultivars			C				6
Erica erigena cultivars			C				9
Erica ×griffithsii 'Valerie Griffiths'			C				6
Erica lusitanica			M				8
Erica mackayana f. *eburnea* 'Doctor Ronald Gray'			C				3
Erica ×oldenburgensis 'Ammerland'			S				6
Erica scoparia			M				9
Erica spiculifolia			C				9
Erica ×stuartii 'Connemara'			C				9
Erica tetralix f. *alba*			C				3
Erica vagans cultivars			C				5
Erica ×veitchii 'Exeter'			M				8
Erica ×watsonii			C				5
Erinacea anthylis			C				8
Eriobotrya japonica			L				7
Erythrina crista-galli			L				9
Escallonia 'Apple Blossom'			S M				8
Escallonia 'C. F. Ball'			M				8
Escallonia 'Donard Radiance'			M				8
Escallonia 'Donard Seedling'			M				8
Escallonia 'Iveyi'			M L				8
Escallonia laevis 'Gold Brian'			S M				8
Escallonia 'Saint Keverne'			M				8
Escallonia 'Slieve Donard'			M				8
Eucryphia cordifolia			L				9
Eucryphia glutinosa			L				8
Eucryphia ×intermedia			L				7
Eucryphia lucida 'Pink Cloud'			L				8
Eucryphia milliganii			S				8
Eucryphia moorei			M L				10
Eucryphia ×nymansensis 'Nymansay'			L				8
Euonymus alatus			M				3
Euonymus carnosus			M L				8
Euonymus cornutus var. *quinquecornutus*			S M				9
Euonymus europaeus cultivars			L				3
Euonymus fortunei cultivars			S M				5
Euonymus grandiflorus			L				9
Euonymus hamiltonianus var. *maackii*			L				4
Euonymus japonicus			L				7
Euonymus myrianthus			L				9
Euonymus nanus var. *turkestanicus*			C				2
Euonymus oxyphyllus			M L				5
Euonymus phellomanus			L				5
Euonymus planipes			L				4

FOLIAGE: = evergreen; = semievergreen; = deciduous; = variagated

FLOWER COLOUR: = yellow; = orange; = pink; = red; = purple; = blue; = green; = white; = black

SIZE: **P** = prostrate; **C** = compact; **S** = small; **M** = medium; **L** = large

LIGHT: = sun; = partial shade; = shade

FLOWERING SEASON: = winter; = spring; = summer; = autumn

SOIL: = acid; = alkaline; = fertile; = fertile, well drained; = well drained

NAME OF SHRUB	FOLIAGE	FLOWER COLOUR	SIZE	LIGHT	FLOWERING SEASON	SOIL	ZONE
Euonymus vagans Lancaster 551			P				6
Euphorbia amygdaloides cultivars			C				7
Euphorbia characias cultivars			C S				8
Euphorbia ×*martinii*			C				7
Euphorbia mellifera			S M				9
Euphorbia rigida			C				8
Euphorbia stygiana			C S				9
Euryops acraeus			C				8
Euryops candollei			C				8
Euryops pectinatus			S				9
Euscaphis japonica			L				7
Exochorda giraldii var. *wilsonii*			M L				5
Exochorda ×*macrantha* 'The Bride'			M L				5
Fabiana imbricata f. *violacea*			S				8
Fallugia paradoxa			M				8
Fascicularia bicolor			C				8
Fatsia japonica			M				7
Ficus pumila			P				9
Fontanesia phillyreoides subsp. *fortunei*			M				6
Forsythia 'Beatrix Farrand'			M L				5
Forsythia 'Golden Nugget'			M L				5
Forsythia ×*intermedia* cultivars			M L				5
Forsythia mandschurica			M				5
Forsythia ovata			S				5
Forsythia suspensa			M L				5
Forsythia viridissima cultivars			M				5
Fothergilla gardenii			S				5
Fothergilla major			M				5
Franklinia alatamaha			M L				5
Fremontodendron 'California Glory'			L				9
Fuchsia 'Baby Blue Eyes'			S				8
Fuchsia 'Blue Bush'			S				8
Fuchsia 'Charming'			S				9
Fuchsia 'Flocon de Neige'			S				9
Fuchsia 'Globosa'			S				9
Fuchsia 'Lady Boothby'			S M				9
Fuchsia magellanica			M				7
Fuchsia regia subsp. *reitzii*			L				10
Fuchsia 'Saturnus'			S				8
Fuchsia 'Wharfedale'			S				9
Garrya elliptica			L				7
Garrya ×*issaquahensis* cultivars			M L				8
Gaultheria depressa var. *nova-zealandii*			P				9
Gaultheria forrestii			S				6
Gaultheria fragrantissima HWJCM 149			M				8
Gaultheria hookeri			C S				6
Gaultheria itoana			P				6
Gaultheria miqueliana			C				6
Gaultheria mucronata 'Cherry Ripe'			C				6
Gaultheria semi-infera			S				8
Gaultheria shallon			S				5
Gaultheria trichophylla			P C				8
Gaultheria ×*wisleyensis*			S				6
Gaylussacia brachysera			C				5
Genista aetnensis			L				8

NAME OF SHRUB	FOLIAGE	FLOWER COLOUR	SIZE	LIGHT	FLOWERING SEASON	SOIL	ZONE
Genista canariensis			M	sun			9
Genista hispanica			C	sun			6
Genista lydia			P C	sun			7
Genista 'Porlock'			L	sun			9
Gevuina avellana			L	partial shade, shade			8
Grevillea 'Canberra Gem'			M	sun			8
Grevillea juniperina 'Sulphurea'			M	sun			9
Grindelia chiloensis			S	sun			6
Griselinia littoralis			L	sun, partial shade			8
Hakea lissosperma			L	sun			8
Halesia diptera Magniflora Group			L	sun, partial shade			6
Halesia monticola			L	sun, partial shade			6
×*Halimiocistus* 'Ingwersenii'			C	sun			8
×*Halimiocistus sahucii*			C	sun			8
×*Halimiocistus wintonensis* & cultivar			C	sun			8
Halimium atriplicifolium			M	sun			8
Halimium calycinum			C	sun			8
Halimium lasianthium 'Concolor'			C	sun			8
Halimium ocymoides			C	sun			8
Halimium ×*pauanum*			S M	sun			8
Halimium 'Sarah'			C	sun			8
Halimium umbellatum			C	sun			8
Hamamelis 'Brevipetala'			M L	sun, partial shade			5
Hamamelis ×*intermedia* cultivars			L	sun, partial shade			5
Hamamelis japonica cultivars			L	sun, partial shade			5
Hamamelis mollis			L	sun, partial shade			6
Hamamelis vernalis cultivars			L	sun, partial shade			5
Hamamelis virginiana			L	sun, partial shade			5
Hebe 'Autumn Glory'			S	sun			9
Hebe cupressoides 'Boughton Dome'			C	sun			7
Hebe 'Great Orme'			S	sun			9
Hebe 'Headfortii'			S	sun			9
Hebe 'Heartbreaker'			C	sun			9
Hebe macrantha			C	sun			8
Hebe 'Midsummer Beauty'			S M	sun			7
Hebe ochracea 'James Stirling'			C	sun			7
Hebe 'Pewter Dome'			C	sun			7
Hebe 'Pink Elephant'			C	sun			7
Hebe recurva 'Aoira'			S	sun			7
Hebe 'Red Edge'			C	sun			7
Hebe salicifolia			M	sun			7
Hebe speciosa			S M	sun			9
Hebe venustula			C S	sun			7
Hebe 'Winter Glow'			C	sun			8
Hebe 'Youngii'			C	sun			8
Heimia salicifolia			S M	sun			7
Helianthemum 'Ben Ledi'			P	sun			7
Helianthemum 'Golden Queen'			P	sun			7

FOLIAGE: = evergreen; = semievergreen; = deciduous; = variagated

FLOWER COLOUR: = yellow; = orange; = pink; = red; = purple; = blue; = green; = white; = black

SIZE: **P** = prostrate; **C** = compact; **S** = small; **M** = medium; **L** = large

LIGHT: = sun; = partial shade; = shade

FLOWERING SEASON: = winter; = spring; = summer; = autumn

SOIL: = acid; = alkaline; = fertile; = fertile, well drained; = well drained

NAME OF SHRUB	FOLIAGE	FLOWER COLOUR	SIZE	LIGHT	FLOWERING SEASON	SOIL	ZONE
Helianthemum 'Henfield Brilliant'			P				7
Helianthemum nummularium			P				5
Helianthemum 'Rhodanthe Carneum'			P				7
Helianthemum 'Ruth'			P				7
Helianthemum 'Wisley White'			P				7
Helichrysum splendidum			S				8
Helwingia japonica			M				8
Heptacodium miconioides			L				6
Heteromeles salicifolia			L				8
Hibiscus sinosyriacus cultivars			M				8
Hibiscus syriacus cultivars			M				5
Hippocrepis balearica			C				9
Hippocrepis emerus			M				7
Hoheria 'Glory of Amlwch'			L				8
Hoheria angustifolia			L				8
Hoheria lyallii			L				8
Hoheria populnea			L				9
Hoheria sexstylosa 'Stardust'			L				8
Holodiscus discolor			M L				5
Hydrangea arborescens 'Annabelle'			M				3
Hydrangea aspera cultivars			M				7
Hydrangea heteromalla 'Jermyns Lace'			M L				7
Hydrangea involucrata 'Hortensis'			S				7
Hydrangea macrophylla cultivars			S				6
Hydrangea paniculata cultivars			M				4
Hydrangea quercifolia cultivars			S				6
Hydrangea serrata cultivars			S				6
Hypericum androsaemum cultivars			C				6
Hypericum ×*dummeri* 'Peter Dummer'			C				7
Hypericum forrestii			S				5
Hypericum frondosum 'Sunburst'			S				5
Hypericum 'Hidcote'			S M				7
Hypericum hircanum subsp. *albimontanum*			S				7
Hypericum ×*inodorum* 'Elstead'			S				7
Hypericum olympicum			C				6
Hypericum reptans			P				7
Hypericum 'Rowallane'			S M				8
Iberis sempervirens			C				8
Ilex ×*altaclerensis* cultivars			L				7
Ilex aquifolium cultivars			L				6
Ilex ×*attenuata* cultivars			M L				7
Ilex 'Bonfire'			M				4
Ilex cornuta			M				7
Ilex crenata cultivars			S M				6
Ilex fargesii			L				7
Ilex ×*koehneana* 'Adonis'			L				7
Ilex ×*meserveae* Blue Princess 'Conapry'			S M				6
Ilex 'Nellie R. Stevens'			L				6
Ilex opaca 'Maryland Dwarf'			S				5
Ilex pedunculosa			L				6
Ilex perado subsp. *platyphylla*			L				8
Ilex verticillata			M				3
Illicium anisatum			M L				8
Illicium floridanum			M				8
Illicium simonsii			S M				8

NAME OF SHRUB	FOLIAGE	FLOWER COLOUR	SIZE	LIGHT	FLOWERING SEASON	SOIL	ZONE
Illicium 'Woodland Ruby'			M				8
Indigofera amblyantha			S M				5
Indigofera hebepetala			S				8
Indigofera pendula			S M				9
Indigofera potaninii			S				5
Indigofera setchuenensis SICH1038			M				7
Iochroma australe			M				10
Itea ilicifolia			M L				7
Itea virginica 'Henry's Garnet'			M				5
Jamesia americana			M				5
Jasminum fruticans			S M				8
Jasminum humile			S M				8
Jasminium nudiflorum			M L				6
Jasminum parkeri			P				8
Jovellana punctata			S				10
Jovellana violacea			S				9
Kalmia angustifolia			C S				2
Kalmia latifolia			M				2
Kalmia polifolia			C				2
Kalmiopsis leachiana			C				7
Kerria japonica cultivars			S M				5
Kolkwitzia amabilis			M				4
Kunzea ericoides			M L				9
Lagerstroemia fauriei cultivars			L				7
Lagerstroemia 'Sioux'			L				7
Lagerstroemia 'Tuscarora'			M L				7
Laurus azorica			L				9
Laurus nobilis			L				8
Lavandula angustifolia cultivars			C				7
Lavandula pedunculata subsp. *pedunculata*			C				8
Lavatera ×*clementii* cultivars			M				8
Lavatera maritima			S M				9
Lavatera oblongifolia			S M				10
Lavatera olbia			M				8
Lavatera thuringiaca			M				8
Leiophyllum buxifolium var. *prostratum*			P				5
Leptodactylon californicum			C				8
Leptodermis scabrida			S M				8
Leptospermum saparium cultivars			M				8
Lespedeza bicolor			M				5
Lespedeza thunbergii			S M				5
Leucadendron 'Safari Sunset'			M				9
Leucadendron 'Wilson's Wonder'			M				9
Leucophyllum frutescens var. *compactum*			M				9
Leucothoe fontanesiana			S M				5
Leycesteria crocothyrsos			M				9
Leycesteria formosa			M				7
Ligustrum delavayanum			M				7

FOLIAGE: = evergreen; = semievergreen; = deciduous; = variagated

FLOWER COLOUR: = yellow; = orange; = pink; = red; = purple; = blue; = green; = white; = black

SIZE: P = prostrate; C = compact; S = small; M = medium; L = large

LIGHT: = sun; = partial shade; = shade

FLOWERING SEASON: = winter; = spring; = summer; = autumn

SOIL: = acid; = alkaline; = fertile; = fertile, well drained; = well drained

NAME OF SHRUB	FOLIAGE	FLOWER COLOUR	SIZE	LIGHT	FLOWERING SEASON	SOIL	ZONE
Ligustrum lucidum			L				7
Ligustrum obtusifolium			M L				3
Ligustrum quihoui			M L				5
Ligustrum sinense			L				7
Lindera angustifolia			M				7
Lindera communis			M L				8
Lindera glauca			M				6
Lindera obtusiloba			M L				6
Lindera salicifolia			L				6
Linum 'Gemmell's Hybrid'			C				8
Lithodora diffusa 'Heavenly Blue'			P C				7
Lithodora oleifolia			P C				8
Lithodora zahnii			C				9
Loiseleuria procumbens			P				2
Lomatia ferruginea			L				9
Lomatia silaifolia			S M				8
Lomatia tinctoria			S M				8
Lonicera ×*amoena* 'Rosea'			M				5
Lonicera bracteolaris			L				5
Lonicera chaetocarpa			S M				5
Lonicera fragrantissima			M				5
Lonicera involucrata			M				4
Lonicera maackii			L				2
Lonicera mitis			M				6
Lonicera morrowii			M				3
Lonicera nitida 'Twiggy'			C				8
Lonicera pileata			C S				5
Lonicera ×*purpusii*			M				6
Lonicera quinquelocularis			L				5
Lonicera setifera			M				8
Lonicera tatarica 'Hack's Red'			L				3
Lonicera trichosantha			M				6
Lophomyrtus ×*ralphii* 'Kathryn'			M				9
Loropetalum chinense			M				9
Lotus hirsutus			P				8
Luma apiculata			L				8
Lupinus arboreus			M				8
Lycium chinense			M				6
Lyonia ligustrina			S M				7
Maesa bullata			M L				10
Magnolia 'Ann'			M L				5
Magnolia cylindrica			L				6
Magnolia 'David Clulow'			L				5
Magnolia denudata			L				6
Magnolia 'George Henry Kern'			S				5
Magnolia 'Gold Star'			M L				5
Magnolia 'Joe McDaniel'			L				5
Magnolia kobus			L				5
Magnolia laevifolia			M L				8
Magnolia 'Lileny'			M				5
Magnolia liliiflora			M				6
Magnolia ×*loebneri* cultivars			S M L				5
Magnolia maudiae			L				9
Magnolia 'Pickard's Stardust'			M L				5
Magnolia 'Pinkie'			M				5

NAME OF SHRUB	FOLIAGE	FLOWER COLOUR	SIZE	LIGHT	FLOWERING SEASON	SOIL	ZONE
Magnolia 'Randy'			M				5
Magnolia sieboldii			M				7
Magnolia sinensis			M L				7
Magnolia ×*soulangeana*			L				5
Magnolia stellata			M				5
Magnolia 'Susan'			M				5
Magnolia virginiana			M L				5
Magnolia ×*wieseneri*			L				6
Magnolia wilsonii			M				7
×*Mahoberberis aquisargentii*			M				6
Mahonia aquifolium cultivars			C				5
Mahonia 'Arthur Menzies'			M				7
Mahonia confusa			S				8
Mahonia fremontii			S M				8
Mahonia gracilipes			S				7
Mahonia japonica			M				6
Mahonia lomariifolia			L				7
Mahonia mairei			M				9
Mahonia ×*media* cultivars			M L				7
Mahonia nervosa			C				6
Mahonia nevinii			S				8
Mahonia nitens			S				8
Mahonia polyodonta			C S				7
Mahonia russellii JR 442			M				8
Mahonia ×*savilliana* 'Verderer'			M				7
Mahonia ×*wagneri* cultivars			S				7
Mallotus japonica			M				9
Matudaea trinervia			L				9
Medicago arborea			S				8
Melaleuca gibbosa			S M				9
Melaleuca squamea			S M				9
Melianthus major			S M				9
Melicytus angustifolius			S				9
Menziesia ciliicalyx var. *purpurea*			S				6
Meterosideros robusta			L				9
Mitraria coccinea			P C				9
Moltkia petraea			C				6
Myrsine africana			S				9
Myrtus communis			L				8
Nandina domestica			M				7
Neillia thibetica			M				6
Neolitsea sericea			M L				9
Nerium oleander			M L				8
Neviusia alabamensis			S M				5
Oemleria cerasiformis			M				6
Olearia arborescens			L				9
Olearia cheesmannii			M L				9
Olearia erubescens			S				9

FOLIAGE: = evergreen; = semievergreen; = deciduous; = variagated

FLOWER COLOUR: = yellow; = orange; = pink; = red; = purple; = blue; = green; = white; = black

SIZE: **P** = prostrate; **C** = compact; **S** = small; **M** = medium; **L** = large

LIGHT: = sun; = partial shade; = shade

FLOWERING SEASON: = winter; = spring; = summer; = autumn

SOIL: = acid; = alkaline; = fertile; = fertile, well drained; = well drained

NAME OF SHRUB	FOLIAGE	FLOWER COLOUR	SIZE	LIGHT	FLOWERING SEASON	SOIL	ZONE
Olearia ×haastii			S M				8
Olearia 'Henry Travers'			M				9
Olearia ilicifolia			M L				8
Olearia ×mollis			M				8
Olearia ×mollis 'Zennorensis'			S M				8
Olearia nummularifolia			M				8
Olearia paniculata			L				9
Olearia phlogopappa			M				9
Olearia ×scilloniensis			M				8
Olearia 'Waikariensis'			S M				8
Orixa japonica			M				6
Osmanthus ×burkwoodii			M				6
Osmanthus decorus			M				7
Osmanthus delavayi			M				7
Osmanthus fragrans f. *aurantiacus*			L				9
Osmanthus heterophllus			L				6
Osmanthus yunnanensis			L				7
Osteomeles schweriniae			M L				8
Ozothamnus coralloides			C				8
Ozothamnus ledifolius			S M				8
Ozothamnus leptophyllus Fulvidus Group			S				8
Ozothamnus rosmarinifolius			M				8
Ozothamnus selago			P				7
Pachysandra axillaris			P				6
Pachysandra procumbens			P				6
Pachysandra terminalis 'Variegata'			P				5
Pachystegia insignis			M				9
Paeonia 'Bartzella'			M				7
Paeonia delavayi			S M				6
Paeonia ×lemoinei 'Souvenir de Maxime Cornu'			S M				7
Paeonia ludlowii			S M				6
Paeonia ostii 'Feng Dan Bai'			S M				7
Paeonia rockii			S M				7
Paeonia suffruticosa			S M				7
Paliurus spina-christi			M L				8
Parahebe formosa			C				9
Parahebe hookeriana			P				9
Parahebe perfoliata			C				8
Parrotia persica			L				5
Parrotiopsis jacquemontiana			M L				7
Penstemon newberryi			C				8
Perovskia atriplicifolia			S				6
Philadelphus argyrocalyx			S M				7
Philadelphus 'Beauclerk'			M				5
Philadelphus 'Belle Etoile'			S M				5
Philadelphus 'Bialy Karzel'			S M				5
Philadelphus 'Bialy Sopel'			M				5
Philadelphus 'Bicolore'			S M				5
Philadelphus coronarius 'Variegatus'			M				5
Philadelphus delavayi f. *melanocalyx*			L				7
Philadelphus 'Frosty Morn'			S				5
Philadelphus 'Innocence'			M				5
Philadelphus 'Karolinka'			M L				5
Philadelphus madrensis			M				9
Philadelphus mexicanus			S M L				9

NAME OF SHRUB	FOLIAGE	FLOWER COLOUR	SIZE	LIGHT	FLOWERING SEASON	SOIL	ZONE
Philadelphus 'Mont Blanc'			M				5
Philadelphus 'Norma'			M				5
Philadelphus 'Oeil de Pourpre'			S				5
Philadelphus palmeri			M L				8
Philadelphus 'Sybille'			S				5
Philesia magellanica			C				9
Phillyrea angustifolia			M L				7
Phlomis 'Edward Bowles'			S M				7
Phlomis fruticosa			S				7
Phlomis grandiflora			M				8
Phlomis italica			C				8
Phlomis lanata			C				8
Phlomis longifolia var. *bailanica*			S				8
Phormium cookianum			M				8
Phormium tenax cultivars			C S M				8
Phormium 'Yellow Wave'			M				8
Photinia beauverdiana			L				6
Photinia davidiana			L				8
Photinia ×fraseri 'Red Robin'			M L				8
Photinia glabra			S M L				7
Photinia serratifolia			L				7
Photinia villosa			L				4
Phygelius aequalis 'Yellow Trumpet'			S				8
Phygelius capensis			S				8
Phygelius ×rectus cultivars			S				8
Phylliopsis hillieri 'Pinocchio'			C				6
Phyllodoce caerulea			P				2
Phyllodoce ×intermedia 'Fred Stoker'			P				3
×Phyllothamnus erectus			C				3
Physocarpus opulifolius cultivars			M				2
Pieris 'Bert Chandler'			S M				6
Pieris 'Brouwer's Beauty'			M				7
Pieris 'Firecrest'			M L				7
Pieris 'Flaming Silver'			S M				7
Pieris formosa			M L				7
Pieris japonica cultivars			S M				6
Pieris 'Tilford'			S M				5
Pittosporum eugenioides 'Variegatum'			M				9
Pittosporum tenuifolium			L				9
Plagianthus regius			M L				8
Platycrater arguta			C				8
Plumbago auriculata			M				9
Polygala chamaebuxus var. *grandiflora*			P C				6
Polygala ×dalmaisiana			S				10
Polylepis australis			M L				8
Pomaderris apetala			L				9
Poncirus trifoliata			L				5
Potentilla fruticosa cultivars			C				4

FOLIAGE: = evergreen; = semievergreen; = deciduous; = variagated

FLOWER COLOUR: = yellow; = orange; = pink; = red; = purple; = blue; = green; = white; = black

SIZE: **P** = prostrate; **C** = compact; **S** = small; **M** = medium; **L** = large

LIGHT: = sun; = partial shade; = shade

FLOWERING SEASON: = winter; = spring; = summer; = autumn

SOIL: = acid; = alkaline; = fertile; = fertile, well drained; = well drained

NAME OF SHRUB	FOLIAGE	FLOWER COLOUR	SIZE	LIGHT	FLOWERING SEASON	SOIL	ZONE
Potentilla 'Rhodocalyx'			S				4
Prinsepia sinensis			S M				4
Prinsepia utilis			S M				5
Prostanthera cuneata			C				8
Prostanthera incisa 'Rosea'			S				9
Prunus laurocerasus 'Latifolia'			L				7
Prunus laurocerasus 'Otto Luyken'			C S				7
Prunus lusitanica			L				7
Prunus tenella 'Fire Hill'			S				2
Prunus tomentosa			M				2
Pseudopanax (Adiantifolius Group) 'Cyril Watson'			L				9
Pseudopanax ferox			L				9
Pseudopanax laetus			L				10
Pseudowintera colorata			C S				8
Punica granatum cultivars			S M				9
Puya chilensis			S M				8
Pyracantha atalantioides 'Aurea'			L				7
Pyracantha coccinea			L				5
Pyracantha 'Golden Charmer'			L				5
Pyracantha 'Orange Charmer'			L				5
Pyracantha 'Rosedale'			L				7
Pyracantha SAPHYR ORANGE 'Cadange'			M				5
Pyracantha 'Watereri'			M				5
Raphiolepis ×*delacourii* 'Spring Song'			S M				8
Rhamnus alaternus 'Argenteovariegatus'			M				7
Rhaphithamnus spinosus			M L				9
Rhododendron albrechtii			S M				5
Rhododendron atlanticum Choptank River hybrids			S				6
Rhododendron augustinii			M				6
Rhododendron barbatum			L				7
Rhododendron campylocarpum Spring-Smyth 32A			M				7
Rhododendron canadense			S				3
Rhododendron dauricum 'Midwinter'			S M				5
Rhododendron davidsonianum			M				7
Rhododendron decorum			L				7
Rhododendron falconeri			L				8
Rhododendron forrestii var. *repens*			P C				6
Rhododendron fortunei			L				6
Rhododendron griersonianum			M				8
Rhododendron groenlandicum			C				2
Rhododendron hodgsonii			L				9
Rhododendron hybrids and cultivars			C S M L				7
Rhododendron indicum			S				10
Rhododendron keiskei 'Yaku Fairy'			P C				5
Rhododendron kiusianum			C				7
Rhododendron Kurume Hybrids			S				7
Rhododendron lepidostylum			C S				7
Rhododendron luteum			M				5
Rhododendron macabeanum			L				8
Rhododendron molle subsp. *japonicum*			M				7
Rhododendron mucronulatum 'Cornell Pink'			M				4
Rhododendron occidentale			S M				6
Rhododendron prinophyllum 'Marie Hoffman'			M				6
Rhododendron reticulatum			S M				6
Rhododendron sichotense			M				7

NAME OF SHRUB	FOLIAGE	FLOWER COLOUR	SIZE	LIGHT	FLOWERING SEASON	SOIL	ZONE
Rhododendron sinogrande			L				8
Rhododendron Solent Series		Various	S				5
Rhododendron trichostomum			S				6
Rhododendron vaseyi			M				6
Rhododendron wardii			M				7
Rhododendron williamsianum			C S				7
Rhododendron yakushimanum 'Koichiro Wada'			C				7
Rhododendron yunnanense			M				7
Rhodothamnus chamaecistus			C				6
Rhodotypos scandens			M				5
Rhus copallina			S M				5
Rhus glabra			M				2
Rhus ×pulvinata 'Red Autumn Lace'			M L				3
Rhus typhina 'Dissecta'			M L				3
Ribes ×gordonianum			M				6
Ribes himalayense			S				6
Ribes magellanicum			M L				6
Ribes odoratum			S M				5
Ribes sanguineum cultivars			M				6
Ribes speciosum			S M				7
Richea scoparia			C				8
Rosa 'Andersonii'			M				6
Rosa foetida			S				4
Rosa macrophylla			M L				7
Rosa moyesii			M				5
Rosa roxburghii f. *normalis*			M L				5
Rosa sericea subsp. *omeiensis*			M				6
Rosa soulieana			L				7
Rosa villosa			M				5
Rosa webbiana			M				6
Rosmarinus eriocalyx			P C				8
Rosmarinus officinalis cultivars			S				7
Rostrinucula dependens			S				8
Rubus 'Benenden'			M				5
Rubus biflorus			M				8
Rubus cockburnianus 'Goldenvale'			M				6
Rubus coreanus 'Dart's Mahogany'			M L				6
Rubus odoratus			M				3
Rubus spectabilis 'Olympic Double'			M				5
Rubus tricolor			P				7
Rubus 'Walberton'			M				6
Ruscus aculeatus 'Sparkler'			C				7
Ruscus colchicus			C				7
Ruscus hypoglossum			C				7
Ruscus ×microglossus			C				7
Ruta chalepensis			C				8
Ruta graveolens			C				5
Salix alba var. *vitellina*			L				2

FOLIAGE: = evergreen; = semievergreen; = deciduous; = variagated

FLOWER COLOUR: = yellow; = orange; = pink; = red; = purple; = blue; = green; = white; = black

SIZE: **P** = prostrate; **C** = compact; **S** = small; **M** = medium; **L** = large

LIGHT: = sun; = partial shade; = shade

FLOWERING SEASON: = winter; = spring; = summer; = autumn

SOIL: = acid; = alkaline; = fertile; = fertile, well drained; = well drained

NAME OF SHRUB	FOLIAGE	FLOWER COLOUR	SIZE	LIGHT	FLOWERING SEASON	SOIL	ZONE
Salix apoda			P				6
Salix caprea 'Curlilocks'			S M				3
Salix fargesii			M				6
Salix gracilistylla 'Melanostachys'			L				6
Salix hastata 'Wehrhahnii'			S				6
Salix helvetica			P C				6
Salix herbacea			P				2
Salix hookeriana			S M				6
Salix integra 'Hakuro-nishiki'			S M				6
Salix irrorata			M				5
Salix phylicifolia			S M				5
Salix reticulata			P				1
Salix udensis 'Sekka'			L				5
Salvia elegans			S				9
Salvia gesneriiflora			C				9
Salvia greggii			C				8
Salvia guaranitica 'Blue Enigma'			S M				9
Salvia ×jamensis cultivars			S				8
Salvia leucantha			C S				10
Salvia microphylla cultivars			S				9
Salvia 'Silke's Dream'			C				9
Salvia splendens 'Van-Houttei'			C S				10
Salvia uliginosa			S M				9
Sambucus nigra cultivars			L				5
Sambucus racemosa 'Plumosa Aurea'			L				4
Santolina chamaecyparissus			C				8
Santolina pinnata subsp. *neapolitana*			C				8
Santolina rosmarinifolia			C				8
Sapium japonicum			L				8
Sarcococca confusa			C S				6
Sarcococca hookeriana varieties			S				6
Sarcococca orientalis			S				6
Schefflera taiwaniana			L				9
Senecio petasitis			S				9
Sibiraea laevigata			S				7
Sinocalycanthus chinensis			M L				5
Sinojackia rehderiana			M L				8
Skimmia anquetilia			C				7
Skimmia ×confusa 'Kew Green'			S				7
Skimmia japonica			C S				7
Skimmia laureola subsp. *lancasteri*			S				7
Solanum valdiviense			M L				9
Sophora davidii			M				6
Sophora microphylla			L				8
Sophora tetraptera			L				8
Sorbaria sorbifolia			M				2
Sorbaria tomentosa var. *angustifolia*			L				6
Sorbus poteriifolia			P				7
Sorbus reducta			C				6
Sparmannia africana			L				9
Spartium junceum			M				8
Sphaeralcea 'Hyde Hall'			S				9
Spiraea betulifolia var. *aemiliana*			C				6
Spiraea cantoniensis			M				6
Spiraea ×fontenaysii 'Rosea'			M				6

NAME OF SHRUB	FOLIAGE	FLOWER COLOUR	SIZE	LIGHT	FLOWERING SEASON	SOIL	ZONE
Spiraea japonica cultivars			C S				5
Spiraea nipponica 'Snowmound'			M				4
Spiraea ×*pseudosalicifolia* 'Triumphans'			M				4
Spiraea sargentiana			M				6
Spiraea thunbergii			S				4
Spiraea veitchii			L				5
Stachyurus chinensis			M				7
Stachyurus himalaicus			M				9
Stachyurus 'Magpie'			M				7
Stachyurus praecox			M				7
Stachyurus 'Rubriflorus'			S M				8
Stachyurus salicifolius			M				9
Stachyurus sp. ETOT 72			M				8
Staphylea bolanderi			L				6
Staphylea colchica			L				6
Staphylea holocarpa			L				6
Staphylea pinnata			L				6
Stephanandra incisa 'Crispa'			C				5
Stephanandra tanakae			M				6
Sutherlandia montana			S				9
Sycopsis sinensis			L				8
Symphoricarpos ×*doorenbosii* 'White Hedge'			S M				4
Symplocos sawafutagi			L				5
Symplocos tinctoria			L				8
Syringa ×*chinensis* 'Saugeana'			M L				4
Syringa emodi 'Aureovariegata'			L				6
Syringa ×*hyacinthiflora* cultivars			L				4
Syringa komarowii subsp. *reflexa*			M L				5
Syringa ×*laciniata*			M				5
Syringa meyeri 'Palibin'			S				5
Syringa oblata			L				5
Syringa pinnatifolia Lancaster 1916			M				6
Syringa ×*prestoniae* 'Elinor'			M				4
Syringa pubescens subsp. *julianae* 'George Eastman'			M				6
Syringa reticulata subsp. *pekinensis* CHINA SNOW 'Morton'			L				6
Syringa vulgaris cultivars			L				5
Tamarix ramosissima			L				3
Tamarix tetrandra			L				6
Telopea oreades			M				9
Telopea truncata			M				9
Tetrapanax papyrifera			L				8
Teucrium fruticans			S				8
Thryptomene saxicola 'F. C. Payne'			C				8
Tripetaleia bracteata			S				6
Trochocarpa thymifolia			P				9
Trochodendron aralioides			L				8
Ugni molinae			M				9
Ulex europaeus			S				6

FOLIAGE: = evergreen; = semievergreen; = deciduous; = variagated

FLOWER COLOUR: = yellow; = orange; = pink; = red; = purple; = blue; = green; = white; = black

SIZE: **P** = prostrate; **C** = compact; **S** = small; **M** = medium; **L** = large

LIGHT: = sun; = partial shade; = shade

FLOWERING SEASON: = winter; = spring; = summer; = autumn

SOIL: = acid; = alkaline; = fertile; = fertile, well drained; = well drained

NAME OF SHRUB	FOLIAGE	FLOWER COLOUR	SIZE	LIGHT	FLOWERING SEASON	SOIL	ZONE
Vaccinium corymbosum			S M				3
Vaccinium cylindraceum			M				9
Vaccinium floribundum			S M				9
Vaccinium glaucoalbum			S				8
Vaccinium macrocarpon			P				2
Vaccinium ovatum			M				7
Vaccinium sikkimense			C				9
Vaccinium stamineum			M				5
Vestia foetida			S				9
Viburnum awabuki			L				9
Viburnum betulifolium			L				5
Viburnum ×bodnantense 'Charles Lamont'			M L				7
Viburnum ×burkwoodii 'Mohawk'			M				5
Viburnum carlesii			M				8
Viburnum cassinoides			M				2
Viburnum cylindricum			L				6
Viburnum davidii			C				7
Viburnum dilatatum			M				5
Viburnum erubescens			M L				6
Viburnum 'Eskimo'			S				7
Viburnum farreri			M				6
Viburnum foetidum			M L				8
Viburnum furcatum			L				6
Viburnum ×globosum 'Jermyn's Globe'			S M				7
Viburnum grandiflorum			M				7
Viburnum ×hillieri 'Winton'			M L				6
Viburnum ×juddii 'Arlene'			S M				5
Viburnum lantana 'Aureum'			M L				3
Viburnum lantanoides			M L				3
Viburnum lentago			L				2
Viburnum macrocephalum			M				7
Viburnum nudum 'Pink Beauty'			M				6
Viburnum opulus cultivars			S L				3
Viburnum parvifolium ETOT 71			M				7
Viburnum plicatum cultivars			S M L				4
Viburnum 'Pragense'			M L				6
Viburnum prunifolium			L				3
Viburnum ×rhytidophylloides Dart's Duke 'Interduke'			L				5
Viburnum rhytidophyllum			L				6
Viburnum sargentii			L				4
Viburnum setigerum			M				5
Viburnum sieboldii			M L				4
Viburnum tinus			M L				7
Viburnum trilobum 'Snowball'			M				2
Viburnum utile			S M				7
Viburnum wrightii 'Hessei'			C S				5
Vinca difformis			P C				8
Vinca major cultivars			P C				7
Vinca minor			P				4
Vitex agnus-castus			M				7
Weigela 'Abel Carrière'			S M				5
Weigela Briant Rubidor 'Olympiade'			M				5
Weigela Carnaval 'Courtalor'			M				5
Weigela coraeensis			S M				6
Weigela 'Eva Rathke'			S M				5

NAME OF SHRUB	FOLIAGE	FLOWER COLOUR	SIZE	LIGHT	FLOWERING SEASON	SOIL	ZONE
Weigela 'Féerie'			S				5
Weigela 'Florida Variegata'			S M				6
Weigela florida 'Versicolor'			S M				5
Weigela hortensis 'Nivea'			S M				5
Weigela 'Looymansii Aurea'			S M				5
Weigela middendorffiana WHHD 4950			S M				5
Weigela 'Praecox Variegata'			S M				5
Weigela 'Ruby Queen'			S M				5
Weigela 'Victoria'			S M				5
Weinmannia racemosa 'Harlequin'			M L				9
Weinmannia trichosperma			L				8
Westringia fruticosa			S				9
Wigandia caracasana			L				10
Wikstroemia gemmata			C				9
Xanthoceras sorbifolium			M L				6
Xanthorrhiza simplicissima			C				4
Yucca filamentosa 'Variegata'			M				7
Yucca flaccida 'Golden Sword'			M				8
Yucca glauca			M				4
Yucca gloriosa			M				8
Yucca recurvifolia			M				8
Yucca whipplei			M				8
Zanthoxylum ailanthoides			L				9
Zanthoxylum americanum			L				3
Zanthoxylum piperitum			L				6
Zanthoxylum schinifolium			L				6
Zauschneria californica			C				8
Zenobia pulverulenta 'Blue Sky'			S M				5

FOLIAGE: = evergreen; = semievergreen; = deciduous; = variagated

FLOWER COLOUR: = yellow; = orange; = pink; = red; = purple; = blue; = green; = white; = black

SIZE: **P** = prostrate; **C** = compact; **S** = small; **M** = medium; **L** = large

LIGHT: = sun; = partial shade; = shade

FLOWERING SEASON: = winter; = spring; = summer; = autumn

SOIL: = acid; = alkaline; = fertile; = fertile, well drained; = well drained

Glossary

Calyx, calyces The cluster of modified leaves (sepals) surrounding a flower.

Chlorotic Having yellow leaf tissue due to insufficient chlorophyll, primarily due to lack of essential nutrients or a physiological disorder caused by nutrient deficiency or immobility in an alkaline soil.

Coppice Cutting back trees or shrubs to ground level to encourage regrowth (for example, coloured dogwood stems).

Dead-head To remove dead flower heads from a plant to improve the appearance of the plant and to encourage further vegetative growth and/or flowering.

Epiphyte A plant that uses another as a host but does not feed on it, instead gathering moisture from the air and nutrients from dead bark or leaf litter.

Ericaceous (a) resembling *Erica* in habit (for example, *Fabiana*); (b) a member of the family Ericaceae; (c) growing in an acidic, free-draining soil, as needed by many Ericaceae.

Formative pruning Cutting back stems and branches on young trees or shrubs to establish a particular shape and to produce a strong, open framework of evenly spaced stems or branches.

Free flowering Blooming continually throughout the flowering period.

Fruit set The stage in a plant's growth process where flowers are fertilized (set) to become fruit.

Hard pruning Cutting a woody plant down to the ground or severely reducing branches to renew it.

Indumentum A feltlike coating of hairs, generally on the underside of a leaf.

Obovate Egg-shaped, with the widest part at the top end.

Palmate Having three or more parts radiating from a common point. Handlike.

Pinnate Having parts arranged in opposite pairs along an axis. Featherlike.

Pollard Shoots of a tree or shrub cut back to the main stem (for example, willows) at a predetermined height above the ground.

Rootstock Part of a budded or grafted plant which supplies the roots and often controls the vigour.

Scandent Climbing

Scree A sloping area adjacent to a rock garden where the soil is free draining and made up of rock fragments and gravels.

Self-fertile Able to pollinate itself.

Semievergreen A shrub that retains its leaves during mild winters or will lose many more during more severe winters.

Spur pruning Cutting back last season's growth to one or two buds per cane (spur).

Subshrub A low-growing plant with a woody stem that can be cut back each year in the spring to ground level to encourage regrowth.

Sucker A shoot arising from an underground root or stem.

Tepal Part of the flower which cannot be distinguished as a sepal or a petal (for example, magnolias).

Trifoliate Having three leaflets.

Collectors' References

Some plant names in this encyclopedia are followed by a name or abbreviation with a number. These refer to a specific plant collected by a specific person(s). The collectors referred to in this book are as follows:

ETOT = T. S. Kirkham & Mark Flanagan
Forrest = G. Forrest
H = Paul Huggins
HWJCM = Crûg Heronswood Expedition
ICE = Instituto de Investigaciónes Ecológicas Chiloé & RBGE
JR = J. Russell
Lancaster = C. Roy Lancaster
Rock = J. F. C. Rock
SBEC = Sino-British Expedition to Cangshan
Schilling = Anthony D. Schilling
SICH = Simmons, Erskine, Howick & McNamara
Spring-Smyth = T. L. M. Spring Smyth
Wilson = Ernest H. Wilson

Further Reading

Asian Plants

The Garden Plants of China, Peter Valder, 1999.
Garden Plants of Japan, Ran Levy-Yamamori and Gerard Taaffe, 2004.
The Himalayan Garden: Growing Plants from the Roof of the World, Jim Jermyn, 2001.
The Jade Garden: New and Notable Plants from Asia, Peter Wharton, Brent Hine, and Douglas Justice, 2005.
Plants from the Edge of the World: New Explorations in the Far East, Mark Flanagan and Tony Kirkham, 2005.

Buddlejas

Buddlejas, David D. Stuart, 2006.

Camellias

Camellias: A Practical Gardening Guide, Jim Rolfe and Yvonne Cave, 2003.
Camellias: The Gardener's Encyclopedia, Jennifer Trehane, 2007.

Ceanothus

Ceanothus, David Fross and Dieter Wilken, 2006.

Cotoneasters

Cotoneasters: A Comprehensive Guide to Shrubs for Flowers, Fruit, and Foliage, Jeanette Fryer and Bertil Hylmö, 2009.

Daphnes

Daphnes: A Practical Guide for Gardeners, Robin White, 2006.

Dogwoods

Dogwoods: The Genus Cornus, Paul Cappiello and Don Shadow, 2005.

Heathers

Gardening with Hardy Heathers, David Small and Ella May T. Wulff, 2008.

Hebes

Hebes: A Guide to Species, Hybrids, and Allied Genera, Lawrie Metcalf, 2006

Herbs

The Encyclopedia of Herbs: A Comprehensive Reference to Herbs of Flavor and Fragrance, Arthur O. Tucker and Thomas DeBaggio, 2009.

Hibiscus

Hibiscus: Hardy and Tropical Plants for the Garden, Barbara Perry Lawton, 2004.

Hollies

Hollies for Gardeners, Christopher Bailes, 2006.

Hydrangeas

Encyclopedia of Hydrangeas, C. J. van Gelderen and D. M. van Gelderen, 2004.
Hydrangeas for American Gardens, Michael A. Dirr, 2004.

Kalmias

Kalmia: Mountain Laurel and Related Species, 3rd edition, Richard A. Jaynes, 2009.

Lavender

Lavender: The Grower's Guide, Virginia McNaughton, 2010.

Lilacs

Lilacs: A Gardener's Encyclopedia, John L. Fiala and Freek Vrugtman, 2008.

Magnolias

Magnolias: A Gardener's Guide, Jim Gardiner, 2000.

Maples

Japanese Maples: The Complete Guide to Selection and Cultivation, 4th edition, J. D. Vertrees and Peter Gregory, 2010.
Maples of the World, D. M. van Gelderen, P. C. de Jong, and H. J. Oterdoom, 1994.

Peonies

The Gardener's Peony: Herbaceous and Tree Peonies, Martin Page, 2005.

Rhododendrons and Azaleas

Hardy Rhododendron Species: A Guide to Identification, James Cullen, 2005.
The Rhododendrom Series, 4 vols., H. H. Davidian, 1982–2003.
Success with Rhododendrons and Azaleas, revised edition, H. Edward Reilly, 2004.

Salvias

The New Book of Salvias: Sages for Every Garden, Betsy Clebsch, 2008

Shrubs

400 Trees and Shrubs for Small Spaces, Diana M. Miller, 2008.
Dirr's Hardy Trees and Shrubs: An Illustrated Encyclopedia, Michael A. Dirr, 1997.

The Explorer's Garden: Shrubs and Vines from the Four Corners of the World, Daniel J. Hinkley, 2009.
The Gossler Guide to the Best Hardy Shrubs, Roger, Eric, and Marjory Gossler, 2009.
Plant Exploration for Longwood Gardens, Tomasz Aniśko, 2006.
The Plant Hunter's Garden: The New Explorers and Their Discoveries, Bobby J. Ward, 2004.
Plants That Merit Attention, vol. 2, *Shrubs*, Janet Meakin Poor and Nancy Peterson Brewster, 1996.
Variegated Trees and Shrubs: The Illustrated Encyclopedia, Ronald Houtman, 2004.
Winter-flowering Shrubs, Michael W. Buffin, 2005.

Vacciniums

Blueberries, Cranberries, and Other Vacciniums, Jennifer Trehane, 2004.

Viburnums

Viburnums: Flowering Shrubs for Every Season, Michael A. Dirr, 2007.

Witch Hazels

Witch Hazels, Chris Lane, 2005.

Yuccas

Agaves, Yuccas, and Related Plants: A Gardener's Guide, Mary Irish and Gary Irish, 2000.

Index of Common Names and Synonyms

Abelia tyaihyoni var. *mosanensis*. See *A. mosanensis*
Acanthopanax gracistyla. See *Eleutherococcus lasiogyne*
Acanthopanax ×*henryi*. See *Eleutherococcus divaricatus*
African hemp. See *Sparmannia africana*
Alabama snow wreath. See *Neviusia alabemensis*
alder-leaved serviceberry. See *Amelanchier alnifolia*
Alexandrian laurel. See *Danae racemosa*
Allegheny sand myrtle. See *Leiophyllum buxifolium*
Allegheny serviceberry. See *Amelanchier laevis*
Aloysia triphylla. See *A. citrodora*
alpine azalea. See *Loiseleuria procumbens*
alpine heath. See *Epacris paludosa*
alpine mint bush. See *Prostanthera cuneata*
American blueberry. See *Vaccinium corymbosum*
American cranberry. See *Vaccinium macrocarpon*
American cranberry bush. See *Viburnum trilobum*
American dogwood. See *Cornus sericea*
American holly. See *Ilex opaca*
American smokewood. See *Cotinus obovatus*
angelica tree. See *Aralia elata*
Apache plume. See *Fallugia paradoxa*
apple rose. See *Rosa villosa*
arrayan. See *Luma apiculata*
Australian fuchsia. See *Correa*
Australian copperbriar. See *Rosa foetida*
autumn sage. See *Salvia greggii*
Azores laurelcherry. See *Prunus lusitanica*

Balearic boxwood. See *Buxus balearica*
bay tree. See *Laurus nobilis*
beauty bush. See *Kolkwitzia amabilis*
bell heather. See *Erica cinerea*
Bentham's cornel. See *Cornus capitata*
bergkanker bossie. See *Sutherlandia montana*
besom heath. See *Erica scoparia*
bird of paradise. See *Caesalpinia gillesii*
black alder. See *Ilex verticillata*
black chokeberry. See *Aronia melanocarpa*
black haw. See *Viburnum prunifolium*
black pussy willow. See *Salix gracilistylla* 'Melanostachys'
black titi. See *Cyrilla racemiflora*
bladder senna. See *Colutea arborescens*
bladdernut. See *Staphylea pinnata*
blood-twig. See *Cornus sanguinea*
blue brush. See *Ceanothus thyrsiflorus*
blueberry. See *Vaccinium corymbosum*
bog laurel. See *Kalmia polifolia*
bog rosemary. See *Andromeda polifolia*
bog sage. See *Salvia uliginosa*
bourtree. See *Sambucus nigra*
box holly. See *Ilex crenata, Ruscus aculeatus*
box huckleberry. See *Gaylussacia brachysera*
branch thorns. See *Erinacea anthyllis*
broadleaf lilac. See *Syringa oblata* var. *oblata*
Bruckenthalia spiculifolia. See *Erica spiculifolia*
buffalo currant. See *Ribes odoratum*
bush honeysuckle. See *Diervilla*
bush jasmine. See *Jasminum fruticans*
bush pepper. See *Clethra alnifolia*
butcher's broom. See *Ruscus aculeatus*
buttercup witch-hazel. See *Corylopsis pauciflora*
butterfly bush. See *Buddleja davidii*
button bush. See *Cephalanthus occidentalis*

cabbage tree. See *Cordyline australis*
cabrera. See *Grindelia chiloensis*
calico bush. See *Kalmia latifolia*
California allspice. See *Calycanthus occidentalis*
California fuchsia. See *Zauschneria californica*
California holly. See *Heteromeles salicifolia*
Californian huckleberry. See *Vaccinium ovatum*
Camellia sasanqua 'Sparkling Burgundy'. See *C. hiemalis* 'Sparkling Burgundy'
Camellia 'Zipao'. See *C.* 'Purple Gown'
Canary Island holly. See *Ilex perado* subsp. *platyphylla*
Canary Island laurel. See *Laurus azorica*
Cape figwort. See *Phygelius capensis*
Cape fuchsia. See *Phygelius capensis*
Cape leadwort. See *Plumbago auriculata*
Cape myrtle. See *Myrsine africana*
Carolina allspice. See *Calycanthus floridus*
Cassinia leptophylla subsp. *fulvida*. See *Ozothamnus leptophyllus* Fulvidus Group
catkin bush. See *Garrya elliptica*
cauchao. See *Amomyrtus luma*
chaste tree. See *Vitex agnus-castus*
cherry laurel. See *Prunus laurocerasus* 'Latifolia'
cherry sage. See *Salvia microphylla* 'Cerro Potosi'
chestnut rose. See *Rosa roxburghii*
Chile lantern tree. See *Crinodendron hookerianum*
Chilean fire bush. See *Embothrium coccineum*
Chilean hazelnut. See *Gevuina avellana*
Chilean myrtle. See *Luma apiculata*
Chinese fringe flower. See *Lorapetalum chinense*
Chinese fringe tree. See *Chionanthus retusus*
Chinese holly. See *Ilex cornuta*
Chinese kousa dogwood. See *Cornus kousa* var. *chinensis*
Chinese plumbago. See *Ceratostigma willmottianum*

Chinese privet. See *Ligustrum sinense*
Chinese redbud. See *Cercis chinensis*
Chinese witch hazel. See *Hamamelis mollis*
chinquapin rose. See *Rosa roxburghii*
Chordospartium. See *Carmichaelia*
Christmas box. See *Sarcococca confusa*
Christ's thorn. See *Paliurus spina-christi*
cliffbush. See *Jamesia americana*
coast banksia. See *Banksia integrifolia*
coastal rosemary. See *Westringia fruticosa*
coastal willow. See *Salix hookeriana*
collimamol. See *Luma apiculata*
common box. See *Buxus sempervirens*
common dogwood. See *Cornus sanguinea*
common elder. See *Sambucus nigra*
common holly. See *Ilex aquifolium*
common lilac. See *Syringa vulgaris*
common myrtle. See *Myrtus communis*
confetti bush. See *Coleonema album*
connemara heath. See *Daboecia cantabrica*
coral tree. See *Erythrina crista-galli*
cornelian cherry. See *Cornus mas*
Cornish heath. See *Erica vagans*
cotton lavender. See *Santolina chamaecyparissus*
cranberry. See *Vaccinium macrocarpon*
crape myrtle. See *Lagerstroemia*
creambush. See *Holodiscus discolor*
creeping fig. See *Ficus pumila*
crinkle bush. See *Lomatia silaifolia*
cross-leaved heath. See *Erica tetralix*
cut-leaf lilac. See *Syringa ×laciniata*
cut-leafed mint bush. See *Prostanthera incisa* 'Rosea'
cut-leaved stag horn sumach. See *Rhus typhina* 'Dissecta'

daphne lilac. See *Syringa pubescens* subsp. *microphylla*
David viburnum. See *Viburnum davidii*
deerberry. See *Vaccinium stamineum*
Delavay privet. See *Ligustrum delavayanum*
desert mountain mock orange. See *Philadelphus madrensis*
dogwood. See *Cornus*
drooping laurel. See *Leucothoe fontanesiana*
dusty daisy bush. See *Olearia phlogopappa*
dwarf Korean lilac. See *Syringa meyeri* 'Palibin'
dwarf sumac See *Rhus copallina*

early lilac. See *Syringa oblata* var. *oblata*
eastern flowering dogwood. See *Cornus florida*
eastern redbud. See *Cercis canadensis*
English holly. See *Ilex aquifolium*
English lavender. See *Lavandula angustifolia*
evergreen candytuft. See *Iberis sempervirens*
ezo-yama-hagi. See *Lespedeza bicolor*

flannel bush. See *Fremontodendron*
Florida anise. See *Illicium floridanum*
flowering currant. See *Ribes sanguineum*
flowering dogwood. See *Cornus florida*
flowering quince. See *Chaenomeles speciosa*
fragrant olive. See *Osmanthus fragrans*
Franklin tree. See *Franklinia alatamaha*
French hybrid ceanothus. See *Ceanothus ×delilianus*
French lavender. See *Lavandula pedunculata*
fringe tree. See *Chionanthus virginicus*
fuchsia-flowered currant. See *Ribes speciosum*
fuchsia-flowered gooseberry. See *Ribes speciosum*
furin-tsutsuji. See *Enkianthus campanulatus*
furze. See *Ulex europaeus*

Georgia plume. See *Elliottia racemosa*
Gippsland waratah. See *Telopea oreades*
glory flower. See *Clerodendrum bungei*
glory pea. See *Clianthus puniceus*
goji berry. See *Lycium chinense*
golden bells. See *Forsythia suspensa*
golden heather. See *Ozothamnus leptophyllus*
golden willow. See *Salix alba*
gorse. See *Ulex europaeus*
green osier. See *Cornus alternifolia*
guelder rose. See *Viburnum opulus*
gum cistus. See *Cistus ladanifer*
gum weed. See *Grindelia chiloensis*

hairy canary clover. See *Lotus hirsutus*
hako-tsutsuji. See *Tripetaleia bracteata*
Harry Lauder's walking stick hazel. See *Corylus avellana* 'Contorta'
heather. See *Calluna vulgaris*
heavenly bamboo. See *Nandina domestica*
hedgehog broom. See *Erinacea anthylis*
herb-of-grace. See *Ruta graveolens*
Himalayan honeysuckle. See *Leycesteria formosa*
Himalayan lilac. See *Syringa emodi*
holly. See *Ilex*
holly-leaved sweetspire. See *Itea ilicifolia*
honey flower. See *Melianthus major*
hopbush. See *Dodonaea viscosa*
horseshoe vetch. See *Hippocrepis balearica*
huckleberry. See *Lyonia ligustrina*
Hydrangea macrophylla 'White Wave'. See *H. macrophylla* 'Mariesii Grandiflora'

Indian evergreen azalea. See *Rhododendron indicum*
Indian plum. See *Oemleria cerasiformis*
Irish heath. See *Erica erigena*
ironwood. See *Parrotia persica*
isu tree. See *Distylium racemosum*

Japanese angelica tree. See *Aralia elata*
Japanese bitter orange. See *Poncirus trifoliata*
Japanese box. See *Buxus microphylla* var. *japonica*
Japanese cornelian cherry. See *Cornus officinalis*
Japanese fatsia. See *Fatsia japonica*
Japanese lilac tree. See *Syringa reticulata* subsp. *pekinensis*
Japanese rose. See *Kerria*

Japanese spicebush. See *Lindera obtusiloba*
Japanese witch hazel. See *Hamamelis japonica*
Jerusalem sage. See *Phlomis fruticosa*

kamahi. See *Weinmannia racemosa*
kapuka. See *Griselinia littoralis*
kerosene bush. See *Ozothamnus ledifolius, Richea scoparia*
kobus magnolia. See *Magnolia kobus*
kobushi magnolia. See *Magnolia kobus*
kohuhu. See *Pittosporum tenuifolium*
Korean forsythia. See *Forsythia ovata*
korokio. See *Corokia buddlejoides*
koromiko. See *Hebe salicifolia*
kousa dogwood. See *Cornus kousa*
kowhai. See *Sophora tetraptera*

Labrador tea. See *Rhododendron groenlandicum*
lacebark. See *Hoheria populnea*
large-flowered silverbell. See *Halesia diptera* Magniflora Group
large-leaf privet. See *Ligustrum lucidum*
laurustinus. See *Viburnum tinus*
lavender-cotton. See *Santolina chamaecyparissus*
leatherwood. See *Cyrilla racemiflora, Eucryphia lucida*
lemon bottlebrush. See *Callistemon pallidus*
lesser periwinkle. See *Vinca minor*
lilac. See *Syringa*
ling. See *Calluna vulgaris*
lobster claw. See *Clianthus puniceus*
longstalk holly. See *Ilex pedunculosa*
loquat. See *Eriobotrya japonica*

maden. See *Weinmannia trichosperma*
manuka. See *Leptospermum saparium*
Marlborough rock daisy. See *Olearia ilicifolia, Pachystegia insignis*
Mexican orange blossom. See *Choisya ternata*
Mexican sage bush. See *Salvia leucantha*
mezereon. See *Daphne mezereum*
mini angel's trumpet. See *Iochroma australe*
miyagino-hagi. See *Lespedeza thunbergii*
Mount Etna broom. See *Genista aetnensis*
mountain avens. See *Dryas octopetala*
mountain azalea. See *Loiseleuria procumbens*
mountain cabbage tree. See *Cordyline indivisa*
mountain dogwood. See *Cornus nuttallii*
mountain flax. See *Phormium cookianum*
mountain mahogany. See *Cercocarpus montanus*
mountain laurel. See *Kalmia latifolia*
mountain riverwood. See *Hoheria lyallii*
mountain sumach. See *Rhus copallina*
Moutan peony. See *Paeonia suffruticosa*
mulan. See *Magnolia liliiflora*
myrtle. See *Myrtus communis*

nana. See *Clethra alnifolia*
narrow-leaved lacebark. See *Hoheria angustifolia*
needlebush. See *Hakea lissosperma*
needlepoint holly. See *Ilex cornuta* 'Anicet Delcambre'
neinei. See *Dracophyllum latifolium*
New Zealand flax. See *Phormium tenax*
New Zealand myrtle. See *Lophomyrtus* ×*ralphii*
nirrhe. See *Encryphia glutinosa*
northern rata. See *Meterosideros robusta*

oak-leafed hydrangea. See *Hydrangea quercifolia*
Olearia insignis. See *Pachystegia insignis*
orange ball tree. See *Buddleja globosa*
Oregon grape. See *Mahonia aquifolium*
Oregon plum. See *Oemleria*
osoberry. See *Oemleria*
Ozark witch hazel. See *Hamamelis vernalis*
Ozothamnus leptophyllus Fulvidus Group. See *Cassinia leptophylla* subsp. *fulvida*

paper bush. See *Edgeworthia chrysantha*
parrot's beak *Clianthus puniceus*
pepper tree. See *Drimys lanceolata*
periwinkle. See *Vinca major*
pichi. See *Fabiana imbricata*
pineapple guava. See *Acca selloana*
pineapple sage. See *Salvia elegans*
pink dogwood. See *Cornus florida* f. *rubra*
pinkwood. See *Eucryphia moorei*
pomegranate. See *Punica granatum*
Portugal laurel. See *Prunus lusitanica*
Portuguese heath. See *Erica lusitanica*
prickly phlox. See *Leptodactylon californicum*
pride of Madeira. See *Echium candicans*

red boronia. See *Boronia heterophylla*
red chokeberry. See *Aronia arbutifolia*
ribbonwood. See *Plagianthus regius*
rice-paper plant. See *Tetrapanax papyrifera*
roble de Chile. See *Eucryphia cordifolia*
rock rose. See *Helianthemum*
rosemary. See *Rosmarinus officinalis*
rose of Sharon. See *Hibiscus syriacus*
rough-leaf hydrangea. See *Hydrangea aspera*
rue. See *Ruta graveolens*
Russian almond. See *Prunus tenella*
Russian sage. See *Perovskia atriplicifolia*

sacred flower of the Incas. See *Cantua buxifolia*
sakaki. See *Cleyera japonica*
Santa Barbara ceanothus. See *Ceanothus impressus*
sapphire berry. See *Symplocos sawafutagi*
scarlet sage. See *Salvia splendens* 'Van-Houttei'
scorpion senna. See *Hippocrepis emerus*
sea mallow. See *Lavatera maritima*
Senecio reinholdii. See *Brachyglottis rotundifolia*
seven son flower of Zhejiang. See *Heptacodium miconioides*
shallon. See *Gaultheria shallon*
shrubby germander. See *Teucrium fruticans*

silverbush. See *Convolvulus cneorum*
silvercup mock orange. See *Philadelphus argyrocalyx*
slender honey myrtle. See *Melaleuca gibbosa*
smoke tree. See *Cotinus coggygria*
smooth hydrangea. See *Hydrangea arborescens*
smooth sumach. See *Rhus glabra*
snowy mespilus. See *Amelanchier* species
South African sage wood. See *Buddleja salviifolia*
southern bush honeysuckle. See *Diervilla sessilifolia*
Spanish broom. See *Spartium junceum*
Spanish gorse. See *Genista hispanica*
Spanish heath. See *Erica australis*
spindle tree. See *Euonymus europaeus*
spiderwood. See *Dracophyllum latifolium*
spike heath. See *Erica spiculifolia*
spurge laurel. See *Daphne laureola*
St. Dabeoc's heath. See *Daboecia cantabrica*
star anise. See *Illicium anisatum*
strawberry tree. See *Arbutus unedo*
sun rose. See *Helianthemum*
sweet bay magnolia. See *Magnolia virginiana*
sweet box. See *Sarcococca*
sweet olive. See *Osmanthus*
sweet pepper bush. See *Clethra alnifolia*
sweetspire. See *Itea virginica*
Swiss willow. See *Salix helvetica*

Tasmanian laurel. See *Anopterus glandulosus*
Tasmanian waratah. See *Telopea truncata*
tea-leaved willow. See *Salix phylicifolia*
Texas redbud. See *Cercis canadensis* var. *texensis*
Tibetan hazel. See *Corylus tibetica*
tineo. See *Weinmannia trichosperma*
toothed lancewood. See *Pseudopanax ferox*
topal holly. See *Ilex* ×*attenuata*
tortosa. See *Discaria chacaye*
toyon. See *Heteromeles*
tree anemone. See *Carpenteria californica*
tree heath. See *Erica arborea*
tree lavatera. See *Lavatera thuringiaca*
tree lupin. See *Lupinus arboreus*
tree poppy. See *Dendromecon rigidum*
tutsan. See *Hypericum androsaemum*
twinberry. See *Lonicera involucrata*

velvet groundsel. See *Senecio petasitis*
Venetian sumac. See *Cotinus coggygria*
Virginia sweetspire. See *Itea virginica* 'Henry's Garnet'
Virginia witch hazel. See *Hamamelis virginiana*

warminster broom. See *Cytisus* ×*praecox*
wayfaring tree. See *Viburnum lantana*
weeping forsythia. See *Forsythia suspensa*
whin. See *Ulex europaeus*
whipcord hebe. See *Hebe cupressoides*
white dogwood. See *Cornus florida*
white tea-tree. See *Kunzea ericoides*
willow-leaf bay. See *Laurus nobilis* 'Angustifolia'
willow-leaf spicebush. See *Lindera salicifolia*
Wilson's magnolia. See *Magnolia wilsonii*
winged spindle tree. See *Euonymus alatus*
winterberry. See *Ilex verticillata*
wintersweet. See *Chimonanthus praecox*
wire-netting bush. See *Corokia cotoneaster*
witch alder. See *Fothergilla gardenii*
witch hazel. See *Hamamelis*
wolfberry. See *Lycium chinense*
woody orchid. See *Magnolia liliiflora*

yellow jasmine. See *Jasminum humile*, *Jasminum nudiflorum*
yulan. See *Magnolia denudata*